The Mixed Multitude

The Mixed Multitude

Jacob Frank and the Frankist Movement, 1755–1816

PAWEŁ MACIEJKO

PENN

UNIVERSITY OF PENNSYLVANIA PRESS

PHILADELPHIA

Publication of this volume was assisted by a grant
from the Herbert D. Katz Publications Fund
of the Center for Avanced Judaic Studies.

Published by
University of Pennsylvania Press
Philadelphia, Pennsylvania 19104-4112
www.upenn.edu/pennpress

Printed in the United States of America on acid-free paper
2 4 6 8 10 9 7 5 3 1

Library of Congress Cataloging-in-Publication Data

Maciejko, Paweł, 1971–
    The mixed multitude : Jacob Frank and the Frankist movement, 1755–
1816 / Paweł Maciejko. — 1st ed.
        p. cm. — (Jewish culture and contexts)
    Includes bibliographical references and index.
    ISBN 978-0-8122-4315-4 (hardcover : alk. paper)
1. Frank, Jacob, ca. 1726–1791. 2. Jewish Messianic movements—Europe,
Eastern— History. 3. Judaism—Europe, Eastern—History—18th century.
4. Judaism—Europe, Eastern—History—19th century. I. Title. II. Series:
Jewish culture and contexts.
BM755.F68M33 2011
296.8'3—dc22   2010036520

*To my mother and the
memory of my father*

And the People of Israel journeyed from Rameses to Succoth, about six hundred thousand on foot, who were men, beside children. And a mixed multitude went up also with them; and flocks, and herds, and very many cattle.

—Exod. 12:37-38

It is them [the mixed multitude] who cause the world to revert to the state of waste and void. The mystery of this matter is that because of them the Temple was destroyed, "and the earth was waste and void" [Gen. 1:2], for [the Temple] is the center and foundation of the world. Yet as soon as the light, which is the Holy One, blessed be He, comes, they will be wiped off the face of the earth and will perish.

—Zohar 1:25b

Contents

Preface

The linguistic and political complexity of the region where Frankism developed means that several variants of place and personal names exist. Where there is an accepted English spelling, I have used it (therefore Warsaw, Prague, Vienna). Otherwise, I have preferred the official forms as they were during the time that the events described in this book took place (thus the Lwów—not Lemberg, Lviv, or Lvov—disputation of 1759). For the names of people, I have employed either the existing English equivalents (thus Jacob Frank, not Ya'akov or Jakub Frank or Frenk) or the forms most frequently used in the documents discussed in the body of the present work (Elyakim ben Asher Zelig and not Jankiel Selek).

An attempt has been made to achieve consistency in the transliteration of words written in scripts other than Latin. For Hebrew and Aramaic, I have employed the slightly modified system of *Encyclopaedia Judaica*. *Tsadi* is written *ts*; *khaf* is written *kh*; no distinction is made between *he* and *het* and between *alef* and *ayin*; *dagesh hazak* is represented by doubling the consonant; *sheva nah*—by *e*. In very few instances, in which eighteenth-century sources written in Latin characters contain transliterated Hebrew words or expressions, I have retained the original spelling reflecting either local (usually Ashkenazic) pronunciation of Hebrew or idiosyncrasies of the scribes. For Yiddish, the transliteration adopted follows the YIVO system; for Cyrillic, the British Standard scheme is followed.

Quotations from the Hebrew Bible follow the Jewish Publication Society's *Tanakh: A New Translation of the Holy Scriptures According to the Traditional Hebrew Text* (Philadelphia, 1988); from the Talmud, the Soncino edition: *Hebrew-English Edition of the Babylonian Talmud* (London, 1960–). Citations from the Zohar present special difficulties. The superb translation of Daniel Matt (the Pritzker edition) has not yet been published in its entirety (to date, the first five volumes of a projected twelve-volume edition have appeared). Other English translations are selective and not always reliable. Moreover, Frankist and sometimes rabbinic documents often treat Zoharic passages very freely. In most cases, I have translated quotations from the Zohar directly from Aramaic (I have used the Żółkiew 1756 edition). In a few cases, I have translated fragments of the Zohar quoted in other sources directly from these sources.

This work makes extensive use of archive and manuscript material housed in libraries and archives in Poland, Germany, the Czech Republic, the U.K., the Vatican, and Israel. I shall discuss the majority of the relevant sources directly in the main body of the book. Two preliminary remarks, however, are in order.

The most important internal Frankist documents are two Polish manuscripts: the chronicle of the sect, *Rozmaite adnotacyie, przypadki, czynności, i anektody Pańskie* (Various notes, occurrences, activities, and anecdotes of the Lord), hereafter *RA* in the notes and "the Frankist chronicle" in the main body of the text; and the collection of Frank's dicta, *Zbiór Słów Pańskich* (The collection of the words of the Lord), hereafter *ZSP* or "the dicta."[1] In 1984, Hillel Levine published a transcription of the Polish manuscript of the Frankist chronicle accompanied by a Hebrew translation and commentary.[2] This was followed by a publication of the Polish original of the same text by Jan Doktór in 1996.[3] A year later, the same scholar published an edition of Frank's dicta titled *Księga Słów Pańskich: Ezoteryczne wykłady Jakuba Franka* (The book of the words of the Lord: Esoteric teachings of Jacob Frank).[4]

Unfortunately, Levine's and Doktór's editions are flawed in some respects. Levine's reading of the manuscript of the chronicle is erroneous in numerous instances, which consequently led to misunderstandings and inaccuracies in the Hebrew translation and commentary. Most of the misreadings of the text of *RA* have been corrected by the publication of the Polish original by Jan Doktór. Yet Doktór's reading of the manuscripts in the larger work, *ZSP*, is often also debatable. Moreover, his editorial policy was to make the texts available to a broad readership. The archaic spelling and punctuation have been modernized. Three different recensions of the manuscript have been compiled into one, which resulted not only in effacing differences between diverse versions but also in a confusion regarding the numbering of the fragments. In consequence, Doktór's edition of *ZSP* greatly facilitates access to Frankist documents but does not allow for a more in-depth analysis.

Accordingly, when quoting *RA*, I rely on Doktór's edition, occasionally correcting minor errors of transcription. When discussing *ZSP*, I decided to quote directly from the manuscripts (Jagiellonian Library, Kraków, Mss. 6968 and 6869; Łopaciński Library, Lublin, Ms. 2118). After much hesitation, I decided not to use the yet unpublished English translations of Harris Lenowitz (*The Collection of the Words of the Lord*, available online).

One of the most important anti-Frankist sources is the account of the beginnings of Frank's sect composed by Dov Ber Birkenthal of Bolechów (1723-1805). A respected wine merchant with numerous connections at the *wojewoda* court in Lwów, as well as links to foreign trade centers, he is sometimes considered the first Jew to master the Polish literary language. During the 1759 Lwów disputation between the Frankists and the rabbis of Podolia, Ber served as a secretary and an interpreter of the speaker of the rabbis, Rabbi Hayyim Cohen Rapaport, and was largely responsible for the composition of the anti-Frankist case. His account of the Frankist affair, titled *Divre binah*, was composed in 1800.

The autograph was discovered in Tarnopol during World War I by Abraham Brawer, who published sections of it first as "Makor Ivri hadash le-toledot Frank ve-si'ato," *Ha-Shilo'ah* 33 (1918) to 38 (1929) and later incorporated them into his book *Galitsiah vi-Yehudehah* (Jerusalem, 1956). As Birkenthal's autograph has mysteriously disappeared shortly thereafter, Brawer's publications have been widely used by scholars of Frankism. It was only a few years ago that the manuscript was found again in the Jewish National Library in Jerusalem (Ms. Heb 8° 7507). A comparison of the rediscovered manuscript with Brawer's publications reveals that the latter bowdlerized the text, omitting entire fragments without notice, inserting his own interpolations, and switching the order of paragraphs to fit his argument. Consequently, in my discussion of *Divre binah*, I decided to rely solely on Ber Birkenthal's original manuscript.

North Sea

Baltic Sea

KINGDOM OF PRUSSIA

COMMONWEALTH OF POLAND AND LITHUANIA

EMPIRE

OF

Berlin

KINGDOM OF PRUSSIA

Warsaw

Korolowka

Leipzig

SAXONY

Częstochowa

Lublin

RUSSIA

Dresden

GERMAN

Offenbach am Main

Prague

Lanckoroń

Żółkiew   Busk

Lwów   Gliniany

Rohatyn   Podhajce

LANDS

Prossnitz

Brünn   Holleschau

Buczacz   Uścieczko

Nadwórna   Kamieniec Podolski

BAVARIA

Vienna

Iwanie/Harmackie   Chocim
Czernowitz

SWISS CONFEDERATION

SALZBURG

HABSBURG MONARCHY

MOLDAVIA

WALLACHIA

Bucharest

Nikopol

Giurgiu
Rousse

Black Sea

OTTOMAN

Sofia

EMPIRE

Salonika

Constantinople

Smyrna

Mediterranean Sea

East and Central Europe ca. 1770

Introduction

Conversions to Christianity were among the most traumatic events in the history of medieval and early modern Jewish communities. Jews regarded baptism as a "betrayal of communal values, a rejection of Jewish destiny, a submission to the illusory verdict of history."[1] Willing apostates were seen as the worst traitors and renegades, forced conversions were considered the ultimate form of persecution of Israel by the Gentiles, and, according to the common ideal, it was better to choose a martyr's death than to submit to the power of the Church.[2] Each soul that Judaism lost was mourned. The dominant narrative did not even entertain the possibility that a Jew might embrace Christianity without any threat or ulterior motive. Christians themselves, while officially praising the apostates and expressing hope for "the blind synagogue's" future recognition of the "obvious" truth of Christianity, privately voiced doubts concerning the sincerity of the converts and the very ability of the Jews to truly accept Christ.

In the Polish-Lithuanian Commonwealth, the largest Catholic country in Europe and, at the same time, the home of the largest Jewish community in premodern times, baptisms of Jews were rare.[3] Neither the local church nor the state conducted systematic missionary campaigns targeting the Jews. Forced conversions of individuals were forbidden by law and were few. Mass apostasies, like those known in Western Europe, did not occur—with one significant exception. In late summer and early autumn 1759, a sizable group of Jews—thousands, by most accounts—led by one Jacob Frank embraced Roman Catholicism in the city of Lwów. The conversion was unique not only in its sheer size. It was also—or at least appeared to be—voluntary: whatever caused Frank and his followers to approach the baptismal font, they were not facing a choice between baptism and expulsion or violent death like their brethren in medieval German lands or Portugal. What was most unusual, however, was the reaction of most Jewish contemporaries. In contrast to typical reactions of sadness, anger, or despair, many Jews saw the conversion of

Frank and his group as a God-given miracle and a great victory for Judaism. Entire communities celebrated.

Among early Jewish accounts of the 1759 conversion, only one departed from the prevailing triumphant mood and expressed radically different sentiments. Israel Ba'al Shem Tov, known as the BeSh"T (1698–1760), who was the founder of Hasidism, the most important spiritual movement in Judaism of the period, was said to have bemoaned the Lwów mass apostasy or even to have died of pain caused by it.[4] According to the story recorded in the hagiographic collection *Shivhe ha-BeSh"T*, the Ba'al Shem Tov laid the blame for the eruption of the entire affair on the Jewish establishment; he was "very angry with the rabbis and said that it was because of them, since they invented lies of their own."[5] The leader of Hasidism saw Frank and his group as part of the mystical body of Israel and presented their baptism as the amputation of a limb from the *Shekhinah*, the Divine Presence on earth: "I heard from the rabbi of our community that concerning those who converted [in Lwów], the Besht said: As long as the member is connected, there is some hope that it will recover, but when the member is cut off, there is no repair possible. Each person of Israel is a member of the *Shekhinah*."[6]

The Ba'al Shem Tov died in 1760, a year after the Lwów apostasy. Some 150 years later, in Berlin, Shmuel Yosef Agnon, an aspiring writer who was later to become the State of Israel's most celebrated author and a winner of the Nobel Prize in Literature, wrote a short essay on Frank. He juxtaposed various Jewish accounts of the 1759 conversion, ending his piece with the testimony concerning the BeSh"T's words. He concluded:

> We are only dust under the feet of this holy man, yet we dare to be
> of another opinion. Frank and his gang were not a limb of the body
> of Israel; rather, they were a [pathological] excrescence. Praise and
> thanks to our doctors, who cut it off in time, before it took root
> in the body! . . . Undoubtedly, Frank and his group were descen-
> dants of the foreign rabble, which tacked itself onto Israel during
> the Exodus from Egypt, and followed it thereafter. In the desert, in
> the Land of Israel, and later in the Exile, this multitude defiled the
> purity of Israel and defiled its holiness. May we be freed from them
> forever![7]

In recounting the BeSh"T's reaction to Frank's conversion, Agnon alluded to the symbolism of the "mixed rabble" or "mixed multitude," the *erev rav*. The concept appears in the Hebrew Bible in the narrative account of the Exodus (Exod. 12:37–38): "And the People of Israel journeyed from Rameses to Succoth, about six hundred thousand on foot, who were men, beside children. And a mixed multitude [*erev rav*] went up also with them; and flocks, and herds, and very many cattle." Jewish tradition interpreted the phrase *erev rav* as denoting a group of foreigners who joined the Israelites following Moses from Egypt. While some midrashim understood it as a reference to the "righteous among the Egyptians, who celebrated Passover together with Israel,"[8] a prototype for future converts to Judaism, the majority of rabbinic exegetes saw in the mixed multitude the source of corruption, sin, and discord: accustomed to idolatry, the *erev rav* enticed Israelites to make the Golden Calf[9] and angered God by demanding the abolition of the prohibition of incest.[10] Thus, the emblem of the *erev rav* came to evoke the image of unwelcome strangers present in the very midst of the Holy People; the mixed multitude were not true "children of Abraham"[11] but Egyptian rabble who mingled with Israelites, contaminated their purity, incited them to sin, and caused them to stray from the right path in the wilderness. It was because of them that the generation of the Exodus lost the right path on the desert and Moses did not enter the Land of Israel.

In the Middle Ages, the symbolism established by the ancient midrash was taken up and developed by kabbalah, particularly the book of the Zohar. The Zohar universalized the midrashic image by removing it from its original place in the sequence of biblical narrative: the presence and activity of the mixed multitude were not restricted to the generation of the Exodus but extended over the entire history of humanity. The *erev rav* were the impurity that the serpent injected into Eve;[12] they were the descendants of Cain;[13] the *nefilim*, "sons of God" who procreated with the daughters of men (Gen. 6:2–4);[14] the wicked ones who survived the deluge.[15] They were progeny of the demonic rulers, Samael and Lilith.[16] They contributed to the building of the Tower of Babel[17] and caused the destruction of the Jerusalem Temple.[18] They practiced incest, idolatry, and witchcraft.[19] They were the cause of the imprisonment of the Divine Presence in the demonic realm of the "husks" (*kelippot*) and, likewise, the exile of Israel among the nations.[20]

In the Zohar's narrative, the activity of the mixed multitude was by no means restricted to the past. Rather, the *erev rav* represented the ever-present force of destruction, whose aim was to bring the world back to the state of biblical "waste and void," the primordial chaos (*tohu va-vohu*).[21] And, it should be noted, this force was located within the Jewish people. As the mixed multitude mingled with Israelites in the desert, their descendants became outwardly undistinguishable from other Jews and existed in every generation: in accordance with its wider mythology of metempsychosis, the Zohar depicted present-day Jewish sinners as Jews the "roots of whose souls" originated among the *erev rav*.

The topos of the mixed multitude thus became the figure of the ultimate enemy within, as opposed to Gentile haters of Israel. As Yitzhak Baer has demonstrated, in its original Zoharic setting, this motif had already been employed as a vehicle of a powerful social critique directed against the contemporary Jewish establishment, which was said to oppress scholars and abuse the poor. The rabbis and *parnassim* (lay leaders), who "studied Torah not for its own sake," "erected synagogues not for the glory of God but rather to make a name for themselves," and turned into "false shepherds of Israel," were surely not "true children of Israel" but the descendants of the Egyptian hangers-on who had joined Moses in the wilderness.[22] Thus, the rich, powerful, materialistic rabbinic and secular powers were contrasted with holy spiritualists lacking riches or high social position and extolling poverty for the sake of God. In the eyes of kabbalists, only the latter formed the true congregation of Israel.[23]

The Jews who converted in Lwów in 1759 were Sabbatians—followers of a religious movement triggered by messianic claims of the Ottoman Jew Sabbatai Tsevi (1626–76). Sabbatai first voiced his pretensions to the messiahship in 1648, but the movement that formed around him began to gain momentum only in 1665, when a young kabbalist, Nathan of Gaza (1643–80), "recognized" the truth of his mandate in an ecstatic vision.[24] Shortly after proclaiming Sabbatai as the messiah, Nathan—who was soon to become "at once the John the Baptist and the Paul of the new messiah"[25]—composed a commentary on an ancient apocalyptic text that he had supposedly discovered in an old synagogue's storage room. In order to counter rabbinic opposition to the budding messianic upheaval, he invoked the symbolism of the mixed multitude: the messiah's contemporaries "shall rise against him with reproaches and blasphemies—they are the 'mixed multitude,' the sons of Lilith, the 'caul above the liver' [Lev. 3:4], the leaders and rabbis of the generation."[26]

In his subsequent writings, Nathan developed a doctrine of salvation attainable by messianic belief alone (as opposed to the observance of commandments) and extended his use of the motif of the *erev rav* claiming that all Jews who fully observed the Law but denied Sabbatai's mandate had souls of the mixed multitude.[27] As Gershom Scholem observed, by linking the symbolism of the mixed multitude with eschatology and messianic mysteries, Nathan combined two distinct motifs that function separately in the Zohar. For the Sabbatians, the litmus test of what was the root of one's soul became not, as in the Zohar, spiritual piety and "observance of the Torah for its own sake" but faith in the messiah Sabbatai Tsevi (or lack thereof): the sectarians "increasingly felt themselves to be the true Israel, harassed by the 'mixed multitude' because of their faith."[28]

The radical dichotomy between the messianic believers and the rabbinic skeptics was further elaborated in the *Commentary on the Midnight-Vigil Liturgy*,[29] composed by Nathan's disciple Rabbi Israel Hazzan of Kastoria. Hazzan argued that the true messiah would be recognized not by the Jewish leaders, whom he defined as the progeny of the mixed multitude, but by simpletons.[30] The denial of Sabbatai Tsevi as the messiah and the failure to understand hints about him in the Jewish canon came to be attributed to a kind of metaphysical blindness stemming from the very roots of the nonbelievers' souls. According to the Sabbatians, the "pretended rabbis"[31] could no longer assert any rights to leadership over the Jewish people or lay claims to the authoritative interpretation of Jewish tradition. Their learning was false, their worldly position based on abuses of power, their ostensible piety worthless and lacking deeper sense.

As Nathan of Gaza and Israel Hazzan composed their polemics against the rabbis, detractors of the new messiah attempted to turn the tables on the Sabbatians. Rabbi Jacob Sasportas, the preeminent adversary of early Sabbatianism, heard about Nathan's statements.[32] Angered by the preposterous claims that the very cream of the cream of the rabbinic elite consisted of descendants of the mixed multitude, Sasportas proclaimed that it was not the leaders of the generation but the Sabbatians themselves whose souls originated among the *erev rav*. In a short time, the symbolic opposition of the "mixed multitude" and the "true Israelites" permanently entered the lexicon of the debate between the Sabbatians and their opponents. This became especially pronounced in the eighteenth century and in the documents directly concerning Frank. In one of the first accounts of the Lwów conversion, Ber Birkenthal of Bolechów reported that "they call us [the anti-Sabbatians] the *erev rav*, and their faction they call the *mahaneh* [company, fellowship]."[33] Frank's most important competitor for leadership over all the Eastern and Central European Sabbatians, Wolf Eibeschütz, also defined the conflict between the sectarians and the rabbinate as a struggle between *bne mehimenuta* (children of the faith) and the children of the *erev rav*.[34] On the other side of the barricade, Rabbi Jacob Emden, the most zealous anti-Sabbatian of the period, interpreted Frank's baptism as the final severance of the *erev rav* from the chosen people, so that the purified Israel might taste from the Tree of Life and achieve redemption.[35] Shortly after the conversion of the Frankists, Emden composed a laudatory poem praising God for "separating between the unclean and the pure . . . between us and the mixed multitude, who tried to bring the world back to its antediluvian state."[36]

The issue was not merely terminological and went far beyond the mutual mudslinging. The dichotomy between the true Israel and the mixed multitude constituted the major conceptual axis of the theological controversies that tore apart eighteenth-century Judaism. Approximately a century after the advent of Sabbatai Tsevi, most debates concerning Sabbatianism (and, more broadly, Jewish heterodoxy) did not revolve around messianism, let alone Sabbatai's specific messianic claims. Rather, the disputes concentrated on the limits of religion and conditions for belonging to the Jewish people.[37] Each side considered only its own version of Judaism legitimate and claimed to be the one true Israel. Each party branded the other as "progeny of the mixed multitude," implicitly denying its Jewishness. Thus the discourse of the mixed multitude endeavored to establish the boundaries of Judaism and of the Jewish people independently of the traditional halakhic criteria of who is a Jew: within the framework of this discourse, certain groups of people might have been "externally" Jewish for generations but were said to remain alien in the depths of their souls. By drawing a line between those whose souls originated from "children of Abraham" and those who came from the *erev rav*, the Sabbatian debate aimed to distinguish between the "real" Jews and pseudo-Jews, "true" Judaism and false faith. Frankism, the movement that crystallized around Jacob Frank in the 1750s, was the last—and, in many ways, most dramatic—word in this debate.

Sabbatianism in the Eighteenth Century

The beginning of Sabbatianism was Sabbatai Tsevi's messianic self-revelation and the prophecies of Nathan of Gaza. The news of the messiah's advent spread like wildfire through Jewish communities in the Ottoman Empire and Europe and, for a brief period, the majority of the Jewish people seem to have been inclined to accept his claims. Sabbatianism became "the most important messianic movement in Judaism since the destruction of the Second Temple."[38] Yet Sabbatai was an odd messiah. The concept of true Israel's simplicity, as expressed in the commentaries of Rabbi Israel Hazzan, had two fundamental aspects: belief in the superiority of non-mediated religious experience over any learned knowledge and the established religious canon; and the conviction that this experience by its very nature articulates itself in a totally paradoxical, incomprehensible way, one that may even be scandalous for nonbelievers. During the early stages of Sabbatai's career, the second aspect quickly found its expression and theological elaboration in the concept of *ma'asim zarim*, "strange deeds"—odd or absurd acts that the messiah "had to commit under the spell of a mysterious impulse."[39] Some of these acts were merely bizarre. For instance, one day Sabbatai bought a large fish, dressed it up like a baby, and put it into a cradle.[40] Others displayed a clearly antinomian character and were typified by evident transgressions of Jewish religious law, such as contravening the Sabbath and dietary laws, shifting the dates of religious festivals,[41] abolishing fasts,[42] and pronouncing aloud the ineffable Name of God.[43]

Worried by the rise of religious enthusiasm among the Jews, the Ottoman authorities had Sabbatai arrested. In September 1666, he faced Sultan Mehmed IV, and—in a move completely unexpected and profoundly shocking even to his most faithful followers—he performed the most bizarre of his bizarre acts: he cast off his Jewish garb and donned a turban, thereby signaling that he had embraced Islam. Most of his followers parted ways with Sabbatai and proclaimed him yet another false messiah. They undertook penitence and returned to their daily lives. But some did not. Sabbatianism did not die with Sabbatai's conversion to Islam, but that act radically altered its social profile. After the conversion, Sabbatianism as a public messianic movement gave way to sectarian crypto-Sabbatianism: a secret creed observed by clandestine believers who pretended to be perfectly orthodox Jews but continued to regard Sabbatai Tsevi as the true messiah, redeemer of Israel. Confronted with rabbinic opposition, crypto-Sabbatians protested their innocence, vociferously rejected heresy, and, in some cases, even signed anti-Sabbatian bans of excommunication. Never did they intend to separate themselves openly from Judaism, and, for the most part, they practiced Sabbatian rituals in addition to normative Jewish observances rather than instead of them.

The two largest Jewish religious controversies that erupted in the eighteenth century were connected with crypto-Sabbatianism. The first scandal broke out in 1713 in Amsterdam, when the kabbalist Nehemiah Hayon (ca. 1650–ca. 1730) succeeded in publishing a tract titled *Oz le-Elohim*. Even though the book was printed with the approbations of several prominent rabbis and its text did not mention Sabbatai Tsevi by name, the Sabbatian character of the work was recognized almost immediately. This led to a bitter and protracted quarrel between Hayon's supporters and his opponents, the latter led by Rabbi Moses Hagiz (ca. 1671–1750), who managed to rally other rabbis against heretics and, in the words of Elisheva Carlebach, transfigured "the rabbinate to a vigorous, aggressive force in the pursuit of Sabbatianism."[44]

Twelve years later, another scandal emerged. In 1725, Moses Meir Kamenker, a Sabbatian emissary traveling from Poland to Germany, was detained by rabbinic authorities in Mannheim. A search of his luggage revealed a manuscript of the heretical treatise *Va-avo ha-yom el ha-ayyin*. The subsequent investigation disclosed that Kamenker had been disseminating copies of this work among sectarians all over Europe, and a clandestine network linking Sabbatian groups in different European countries came to light.[45]

The treatise itself, although distributed anonymously, was widely attributed to Rabbi Jonathan Eibeschütz of Prague (1690–1764), one of the most illustrious rabbinic scholars of the time. Along the lines of the crypto-Sabbatian paradigm, Eibeschütz promptly distanced himself from the heretics and signed a ban publicly condemning Sabbatai Tsevi and his followers.[46] For a time, the matter was closed. But the accusations refused to go away. In 1751, Eibeschütz, by then having attained the position of chief rabbi of the triple community of Altona-Hamburg-Wandsbeck, was again charged with Sabbatianism, this time by another well-respected Jewish scholar, Rabbi Jacob Emden (1697–1776).

The Emden-Eibeschütz controversy turned into the most contentious rabbinic dispute of the early modern period: every major European community as well as virtually all the prominent rabbis became embroiled in the debate on one side or another. The European Jewish establishment split into two hostile factions. Excommunications and counter-excommunications were issued. Pamphlets and brochures supporting and denouncing the parties were printed and widely disseminated (especially by Emden, whose private printing press played a crucial role in the controversy).[47] In some places, there were outbreaks of physical violence. Both sides sought justice in Gentile courts and sponsored press coverage promoting their respective positions. Non-Jewish authorities became involved in the quarrel, and Christian scholars took a keen interest in the debate.

Finally, in 1753, the Council of Four Lands of Poland, the most important organ of Jewish autonomous governance, stepped in. While some of the council's rabbis were undoubtedly convinced that there was truth to Emden's charges (the pro-Emden party among the council was led by its *shtadlan* (intercessor), Baruch me-Erets Yavan),[48] the assembly as a whole resolved to do everything possible to quell the public dispute and restore the shattered image of the homogeneity of Jewish leadership: in October of that year, it issued a ban on printing and distributing publications supporting either side. Crypto-Sabbatianism might have been a theological threat for normative Judaism; a public quarrel that engulfed entire communities, compromised the reputation of the rabbinate, and exposed Jews to the interventions of Christian authorities and the prying of strangers was far worse. It cannot be emphasized too strongly that in the eyes of most rabbis, the man who had gone too far was not the (alleged or real) crypto-Sabbatian Eibeschütz but the anti-Sabbatian Emden: by incessantly trumpeting the charges of heresy, he turned an otherwise marginal matter into a central issue in Jewish life. In addition, he placed before the Gentiles' eyes a dispute that most Jews would rather have preserved as an internal affair.

Crypto-Sabbatianism was the form that the Sabbatian movement took in eighteenth-century Western Europe. In the Polish-Lithuanian Commonwealth, developments followed a different route. In Poland, the Sabbatian movement spread particularly in the southeastern part of the country, in Podolia. "Podolia" is a name of a geographical area (the Podolian Upland) and of an administrative division of the Crown of Poland (the Podolian Voivodeship or Palatinate of Podolia). To add to the confusion, early modern Jewish sources speak of "the Province of Podolia" (*mahoz* or *galil Podoly'ah*), usually meaning something in between: an area larger than the Palatinate of Podolia but smaller than the entire Podolian Upland and roughly encompassing the Podolian, the Bracław, and the eastern part of the Ruthenian Palatinates of the Commonwealth. This usage entered Jewish historiography, and I shall continue to use the term in this "Jewish" sense, although some locations most commonly associated with Podolia in works on Eastern European Jewry (such as Żółkiew and Podhajce) never belonged to the Podolian Palatinate.

From the perspective of the Jewish autonomous system of government, the territory of the Crown of Poland was divided into four large regions called "Lands" (Hebr., *aratsot* or *medinot*; Pol., *ziemstwa*), jointly administered by the umbrella organization of Jewish communities in the kingdom, the Council of Four Lands. The Land authorities collected poll tax paid to the Crown from all communities belonging to it, and the rabbi of the Land served as head of a court hearing appeals from verdicts of local *bate din*.[49] The Province of Podolia belonged to the Land of Ruthenia with the seat of the Land rabbi in Lwów; the remaining three Lands were Greater Poland, Little Poland, and Volhynia.

In the late seventeenth century, the situation of Podolian Jewry went through a significant change. Following the disastrous war with the Porte and the Crimean Khanate, the Commonwealth signed a humiliating peace treaty in Buczacz in 1672, ceding the Palatinates of Podolia and Bracław to the Ottoman Empire. Poland-Lithuania had regained part of its territories by the following year, and all of them after the treaty of Karlowitz (1699); yet the impact upon the province's Jewish communities of twenty-seven years of practical independence from the central administrative bodies of Polish Jewry was profound.[50] Podolian Jews developed close ties with their brethren in Turkey, and for over twenty years, Turkish, Wallachian, and Moldavian Jews settled in the region. Even after the province was returned to Poland in 1699, the Council of Four Lands did not regain full control: local Jews often voiced their dissent from the decisions of the council or the rabbi of the Ruthenian Land in Lwów, and many disgruntled individuals moved to Podolia to seek a measure of freedom from the scrutiny imposed by the rabbinate in other parts of the Commonwealth.

After their return to Poland, the Podolian communities refused to pay their poll tax to the Land of Ruthenia, and the tax evasion in Podolia severely increased the fiscal burden placed on other regions.[51] On 1 June 1713, King Augustus II ordered the creation of a separate, fifth Land, with the seat of the presiding rabbi in Satanów.[52] Initially, the Council of Four Lands ignored the ruling. After several years, the new division of Polish Jewry into five Lands in fiscal matters became a fait accompli; in 1719, Jerzy Przebendowski, secretary of the royal treasury, confirmed that the Jews of Podolia were to pay the poll tax through their own Land, independently from the Lwów rabbinate.[53] However, the central Jewish authorities still considered the split of Podolia from the Land of Ruthenia a source of danger to their power over the region, and, on several occasions, they sought to reintegrate the province into the previous structures. The spread of Sabbatianism among the Podolian Jews was both the reason for the rabbinate's worries and an ever present pretext for its interventions.

In the mid-eighteenth century, Podolia became for Judaism what twelfth-century Languedoc was for Christianity: a seditious province where dissenters gathered and heterodoxy was practiced openly and publicly. Podolia was the only place in the world where—almost a hundred years after Sabbatai Tsevi's conversion to Islam—many Jews openly adhered to Sabbatianism. A number of communal rabbis belonged to the sect and drew in their entire communities. Many Podolian Sabbatians were scholars: among some twenty sectarians

identified by name in Ber Birkenthal's *Divre binah*, the names of eight of them
are preceded by the title *morenu* ("our teacher"), a rabbinic equivalent of the
title of doctor conferred by Christian universities.[54]

In the early 1700s, the main channel of transmission of esoteric doctrines from the Ottoman territories to Poland was Hayyim Malakh, the open
Sabbatian and acknowledged rabbinic scholar[55] who had studied with several
famous kabbalists in Italy and Turkey and become acquainted with all the
major Sabbatian schools of the period.[56] In 1700, Malakh had taken part in
the abortive attempt to resettle the Land of Israel led by Rabbi Yehudah Hasid
(1650–1700).[57] Expelled from Jerusalem, he made his way to Podolia, where
he established vibrant Sabbatian groups in Buczacz, Nadworna, Rohatyn, and
other places. He is said to have transformed the prestigious center of rabbinic learning, the *bet midrash* (house of study) of Żółkiew, into a hotbed of
radical Sabbatianism.[58] In the end, he was excommunicated and expelled by
the rabbinate. Yet others followed in his footsteps. Fishel of Złoczów, also a
noted Torah scholar, reputed to know the entire Talmud by heart and greatly
honored for his extreme piety, suddenly "revealed that he belonged to the sect
of Sabbatai Tsevi" and confessed that he had been committing numerous offenses for many years.[59]

Another well-known ascetic (and another ex-member of the group of
Rabbi Yehudah Hasid), Moses of Wodzisław, who used to fast every day of the
week except for the Shabbat and who refrained from eating meat at all, "publicly announced that none other than Sabbatai Tsevi is the messiah." When
reproached by some members of the community, he stated that he "would be
prepared to stand upon the tallest tower of the city and loudly proclaim his
belief, and was not afraid even to die for it."[60] Rabbi Moses David, an eminent
kabbalist to whom I shall return in Chapter 5, overtly preached Sabbatianism
in Podhajce;[61] the same is true of Rabbi Mordechai Ashkenazi in Żółkiew.[62]
Messianic beliefs were upheld in public by the communal rabbi and rabbinic
judge of Rozdół.[63] Documents from 1759 state as a known fact that the towns
of Busk and Gliniany were "under the control" of Sabbatians.[64] The anti-Sabbatians also confirmed that the sectarians had completely taken over some
communities: Rabbi Jacob Emden lamented that "in a town called Nadworna,
the entire community turned to heresy, following Sabbatai Tsevi."[65]

Indeed, Nadworna seemed to be particularly notorious for the open practice of Sabbatianism. Ber Birkenthal of Bolechów reported that in 1742, a
known Sabbatian from Nadworna stayed at his father's inn. Those present
were told a story about how, on the fast day of the Ninth of Av (the fast

commemorating the destruction of the Jerusalem Temple by the Romans, abolished and turned into a feast day by Sabbatai Tsevi),[66] the people of Nadworna went to the surrounding fields and stole a sheep. They slaughtered it without observing the requirements regarding ritual slaughter, cooked it in milk (thereby breaking another dietary prohibition), and celebrated merrily, hoping for Sabbatai's second coming and expecting imminent liberation from exile.[67] In the years directly preceding Frank's appearance in Podolia, the most prominent Sabbatian from Nadworna was Leyb son of Nata, called Leyb Krysa. Ber Birkenthal, who met him in Lwów in 1752, recounts that Krysa was known as a kabbalist and came to Ber's house to study the Zohar from the Amsterdam edition, which Birkenthal owned. He used to "wander through all the towns of Podolia in order to deceive and incite the people of Israel . . . to accept the faith of Sabbatai Tsevi,"[68] and he established a Sabbatian house of study in Lwów.[69] Insofar as we can judge from the few existing sources, in the year or so preceding Frank's appearance, Krysa gained a substantial following and was singularly successful in uniting Podolian Sabbatian groups under his leadership; it seems that many of the later "Frankists" were initially the "Krysists." But suddenly, Frank showed up and stole the show.

Frank's Beginnings

According to the Frankist chronicle, *Pan* ("the Lord"), Ya'akov ben Leyb, later known as Jacob Frank, was born in 1726 in Berczanie, a small village in Podolia.[70] Other sources give other Podolian locations, Korolowka[71] or Buczacz,[72] as the place of his birth. The family had strong Sabbatian connections: his father, Leyb Buchbinder, was a brother of Moses Meir Kamenker, the Sabbatian emissary detained in Mannheim while distributing *Va-avo ha-yom el ha-ayyin* (Kamenker was a brother-in-law of Fishel of Złoczów);[73] Jacob Frank's mother, Rachel Hirschl of Rzeszów, was a sister of Löbl, father of Schöndl Dobruschka, the *spiritus movens* of Sabbatianism in Moravia.[74] When Frank was only a few months old, his family left Poland and moved to the Ottoman Empire; it is likely that the move was connected to the affair that erupted after the detention of his uncle Moses Meir Kamenker a year earlier.

Young Jacob grew up in the Danubian principalities of Moldavia and Wallachia, spending extended periods in the Ottoman territories proper; he lived in Czernowitz, Smyrna, Bucharest, Sofia, and Constantinople. At some point during his stay in Turkey, he acquired the nickname "Frank" or "Frenk."

The word is a Turkish equivalent of the Arabic *ifrandj* or *firandj*, referring initially to the Franks, inhabitants of the empire of Charlemagne and then, by extension, to the Crusaders. By the sixteenth century, in many oriental languages (for example, Persian, *farangi*; Armenian, *frank*), the term had become a common appellation for Europeans in general as well as for "various things believed to have been introduced by the Franks, such as syphilis, cannon, European dress, and modern civilization."[75] In Jacob Frank's milieu, his nickname betrayed his foreign European origins, identifying him as a Polish Ashkenazic Jew, a native Yiddish speaker who found himself among the Ladino-speaking Turkish Sephardim.

The Frankist chronicle informs us that in 1752, in Nikopol (present-day Bulgaria), Frank married Hana, the daughter of a certain Rabbi Tova; the rite was conducted according to the "Jewish-Turkish religion," and his groomsmen were Rabbi Mordechai and Rabbi Nahman.[76] Another source adds that on the night of his wedding, the groomsmen disclosed "the mystery of faith" to him, and one of them told the bridegroom that "there was a messiah in Salonika."[77] The practice of initiating new members of the sect on their wedding nights is known from Sabbatian rituals, and the "mystery of faith" was the final revelation of Sabbatai Tsevi, which he divulged only to those of his disciples who converted to Islam; its content was transferred orally among the sectarian elite.[78] It is a matter of conjecture, but there is reason to believe that Frank's father-in-law, called by the chronicle "Rabbi Tova," was one of the most important Turkish Sabbatian leaders, Yehudah Levi Tova (Frank's first biographer, the Jesuit Father Awedyk, confirms that Tova, father of Frank's wife, was a Levite).[79] The "Jewish-Turkish" religion was nothing other than the faith of the Muslim-Sabbatian group known as the Dönmeh.

After the death of Sabbatai Tsevi (1676), his last wife, Jocheved, proclaimed that the soul of the messiah had not left the earthly world but had reincarnated in her brother, Jacob Querido. Shortly thereafter, Querido received a series of revelations urging him to continue upon the path of Sabbatai and apostatize. Following these revelations, a group of some three hundred Jewish families converted to Islam in 1683 in the city of Salonika, thus founding the Sabbatian-Muslim sect of the Dönmeh.[80] The Turkish word *dönmeh* signifies a recent convert, a neophyte, and has strong negative connotations; in modern Turkish, it might also be used as a slur against a male-to-female transsexual. It was intended as a term of abuse heaped upon the Salonika apostates by their enemies; the group's own term was *ma'aminim* ("believers"; the standard Sabbatian self-designation) or *sazanikos*. *Sazan* is Turkish for carp, a fish that lives both in fresh- and in seawater. Thus the converts conducted their double lives under Judaism and under Islam; and just as the carp seems to change color, so they changed external appearances in accordance with changing needs and circumstances.[81]

The Dönmeh formed a close-knit group shunning exogamous marriage with either Jews or Muslims, and they developed their own version of Sabbatian theology, focusing on the radical duality between the Torah of the Created World (*torah de-beri'ah*) and the new spiritual Torah known as the Torah of Emanation (*torah de-atsilut*). With the coming of the messiah, the former— identified with the commandments of Judaism—was replaced with the latter, and Sabbatai Tsevi's "strange deeds" provided a pattern for normative behavior. Accordingly, the Dönmeh's brand of Sabbatianism acquired a very pronounced antinomian tendency, whereby ritual violations of the principles and rites of Jewish religion became a significant part of religious practice. Since the advent of redemption signified liberation from the yoke of the commandments, their further observance would be not only senseless, but blasphemous. Conversely, almost the only way to demonstrate that the redemption had arrived was to break the laws and statutes of the unredeemed world. In the words of Rabbi Moses Hagiz: "It is their custom to argue that with the arrival of Sabbatai Zevi, the sin of Adam has already been corrected and the good selected out of the evil and the 'dross.' Since that time, according to them, a new Torah has become law under which all manner of things formerly prohibited are now permitted, not least the categories of sexual intercourse hitherto prohibited. For since everything is pure, there is no sin or harm in these things."[82]

Jacob Querido died during a pilgrimage to Mecca in 1690. As the principle of leadership among the Dönmeh was based on the idea of reincarnation of Sabbatai Tsevi's soul into a new leader, several pretenders appeared, each claiming to be the new abode of the soul of the messiah. The Salonika group splintered into three principal branches—the Kavalieros, the Jakubis, and the Koniosos; the most important one for the present discussion is the last, led by Berukhiah Russo (in Islam: Osman Baba; 1677–1720).[83] Berukhiah's group was the most radical among the Dönmeh subsects: not only did he believe that the traditional laws of Judaism had been abrogated, but he claimed that, with the arrival of the messianic era, the thirty-six most serious transgressions punishable by the ultimate punishment of *karet*[84] had turned into positive commandments (the category includes all sexual prohibitions, mainly various forms of incest). In 1716, Berukhiah's followers declared him the incarnation not merely of the soul of the human messiah Sabbatai, but also of the God of Israel (the idea of the divinity of the messiah or some form of the doctrine of divine incarnation had appeared in earlier Sabbatian theology but was eschewed by most Sabbatians). His group promulgated this claim among other Sabbatian groups, and until his death in 1720, Berukhiah was worshiped by some Sabbatians of Salonika as a divine being, Signor Santo, Holy Lord.

At first, Frank was skeptical about the revelation of the "mystery of faith" that he had received during his wedding. He told his mystagogues that he would not believe their words until he saw that they possessed "the wisdom of making gold."[85] He also questioned Berukhiah's divinity, asking: "If he really belonged to the Godhead, why did he die?" When told in response that the divine Berukhiah had to experience everything in the world, including the bitterness of death, Frank continued: "If he came to experience everything, why, then, did he not taste how it would be to be pasha, vizier, or sultan? Why did he not experience power? I don't believe it."[86] Yet, notwithstanding his initial incredulity, Frank's interest in the messiah of Salonika was aroused. Perhaps his ambitions were also awakened at this critical juncture: Frank decided to go to Salonika and take up where Berukhiah had left off, that is, to experience the only thing missing from the messiah's catalog of accomplished experiences: power.

According to the Frankist chronicle, a year or so after his wedding, in November 1753, Frank arrived in Salonika accompanied by Rabbi Mordechai, his groomsman. Rabbi Mordechai ben Elias Margalit was a known Sabbatian from Prague; accused of adultery and other antinomian conduct, he also left Bohemia and moved to the Ottoman Empire after Moses Meir Kamenker was caught smuggling Sabbatian literature into Germany in 1725.[87] According to Rabbi Jacob Emden, Frank arrived in Salonika as Rabbi Mordechai's servant. The leaders of the Dönmeh told Rabbi Mordechai that secrets of the Torah could be revealed only through a young and unlearned man and asked him to let his servant act as a medium. Indeed, on the very first night that he stood before the Dönmeh, Frank entered a trance, fell to the ground, and revealed many secrets and mysteries.[88] The Frankist chronicle, skimpier in details and—rather predictably—contrary to Emden in its appraisal of the protagonists of the story, described the same event as follows: "It was the first night on which the Lord had the *Ru'ah hakodesh*—sending of the Holy Spirit. . . . He said: '*Mostro Signor abascharo*, Our Lord descends.'"[89] On the very first night that he spent among the Dönmeh, the soul of Signor Santo, Berukhiah, entered Frank's body.

Following this dramatic event, Frank's star rose quickly in Salonika. He established his own house of study, where he expounded the Zohar, and came to be known as Hakham Jacob (*hakham*, lit., "sage," is a Sephardic equivalent to the title "rabbi" as employed by Ashkenazic Jews). His former teachers, Rabbi Mordechai and Rabbi Nahman, became his first pupils.[90] He debated the secrets of Torah with Jewish scholars in Salonika[91] and tried to bolster his Sabbatian credentials by mimicking some of the actions of Sabbatai Tsevi: he threw himself into the sea, which did not want to take him and resuscitated him alive,[92] and performed "strange deeds," publicly violating the Shabbat[93] or—during a service in a synagogue—taking the Torah scroll, lowering his trousers, and sitting on it with his naked buttocks.[94] He also made a pilgrimage to the grave of Sabbatai's prophet, Nathan of Gaza, in Skoplje.[95] At the grave of Nathan, he formulated his program for the first time: "The Ran [Rabbi Nathan of Gaza] ordered that after he died, a bag of earth should be placed in his coffin, thus giving a sign that he wished to convert the spiritual world into the world of flesh. But I tell you that already in this world, everything that is in spirit must be made into flesh like our flesh. Then everyone will see, as any visible thing is seen."[96]

Frank's meteoric rise did not go down well with some of the Dönmeh. Hints scattered in the Frankist dicta suggest that, in pretending to be the incarnation of Berukhiah, Frank became embroiled in a ferocious power struggle with other leaders of the Salonika Sabbatians.[97] "The messiah of Salonika," about whom Frank had been told by Rabbi Mordechai on his nuptial night, was most likely Berukhiah's son and designated successor.[98] Frank was told that he would not even be able to speak to him (he finally managed to do so, only once, after singing a song in Ladino in front of his window).[99] Many years later, during the investigation at the Warsaw consistory after his conversion to Christianity, Frank testified that he had demanded a miracle from the alleged messiah of Salonika, but the "messiah" could not deliver; in a conversation with his disciples, Frank pronounced him the Antichrist.[100]

Clearly, the sect of Berukhiah, the Koniosos, were loyal to the accepted line of succession and refused to recognize Frank—a foreigner and an upstart among the Turkish Sabbatian elites—as the vessel of their messiah's soul. It seems that another faction of the Dönmeh, the Kavalieros, were more forthcoming: according to a Frankist source, they offered Frank fifty purses of gold if he would agree to lead them. Initially, Frank was inclined to agree; but during the night, he had a dream telling him that it was not his destiny to become a leader of the Dönmeh. He declined and remained steadfast in his refusal even after the Kavalieros raised the offer to a hundred purses of gold and a maiden from their group.[101] Frank might really have had a vision advising him not to tie his future to the Kavalieros. He might also have realized that no matter how well he played his hand in Salonika, he would always remain a maverick among the Turkish Sabbatians. And perhaps, precisely at this time, he might have understood that another option had opened up.

According to Dov Ber Birkenthal, sometime in the early 1750s, two emissaries from Podolia, the *dayyan* (rabbinic judge) of Strzyże Rabbi Mordechai Baharab and Morenu Ze'ev Wolf Benditsch of Nadworna, were sent by all the Podolian Sabbatians to welcome the messiah Berukhiah. They arrived in Salonika and found Berukhiah severely ill, lying on his deathbed. They witnessed how "Berukhiah passed away while revealing secrets of the Torah, but, before his holy soul departed, he anointed Hakham Morenu Rabbi Jacob Frank of Korolowka by placing two hands on his head. . . . And [Frank] stood up and left for Poland."[102]

As it stands, Birkenthal's story is inaccurate, at best. Berukhiah died in 1720, before Frank was even born; it is also highly unlikely that the Podolian Sabbatians did not know about his death some thirty years after it happened. However, Rabbi Jacob Emden confirms that a certain Wolf of Nadworna (accompanied by Frank's uncle Moses Meir Kamenker!) indeed went to Salonika on a mission sometime before the eruption of the 1725 scandal concerning Eibeschütz.[103] Sabbatian sources, in turn, attest that throughout the first half of the eighteenth century, European sectarian Jewish groups often sent emissaries to the Ottoman Empire seeking to access the authentic esoteric traditions transmitted orally among the Turkish Sabbatians. I conjecture that Ber Birkenthal conflated the mission of the early 1720s, during which the Podolian Sabbatians learned about the death of Berukhiah, with another, which took place in the early 1750s, when emissaries from Podolia heard about the incarnation of Berukhiah's soul in Jacob Frank (indeed, it is even possible that Ze'ev Wolf of Nadworna took part in both missions). Be that as it may, the news that Frank was a reincarnation of Berukhiah certainly began to spread in Podolia around 1753–54. The scene was thus prepared, and the return to Poland suddenly began to look like an attractive possibility.

In May 1754, Jacob Frank, accompanied by two disciples, left Salonika. He spent some months in the Moldavian town of Romani, than in Czernowitz.[104] On 3 December 1755, he crossed the Dniester River and entered the territory of the Polish-Lithuanian Commonwealth. After arriving in Poland, Frank took a kind of tour through the principal centers of Sabbatianism in Podolia, retracing the steps of Hayyim Malakh.[105] He went first to Korolowka, and then to

Jezierzany, Podhajce, and Busk, where his disciple Nahman was a rabbi. From Busk, Frank journeyed to Lwów. After a short stay in Lwów, Frank came to Rohatyn, where he established contacts with the Shorrs, probably the most important Sabbatian family in Podolia. The family descended from Rabbi Zalman Naftali Shorr, whose book *Tevu'at Shorr* was held in high esteem among rabbinic scholars,[106] and the Shorrs enjoyed a high status among all Jews. Elisha Shorr, the doyen of the family, was known as a principal leader of the Sabbatian movement in the region; his daughter Hayah was considered a prophetess.[107] Through marriages, the Shorrs were tied to Sabbatians in all the major towns of the province.[108] If Frank managed to win them over, his success in Podolia would be assured. Indeed, before long, Elisha's three sons, Salomon, Nathan, and Leyb, accepted Frank as their leader. As Frank's following was growing, Yehudah Leyb Krysa also joined his group. However, tension between the two never abated, and Krysa challenged Frank's leadership on several occasions.

Frank's authority among the Podolian Sabbatians was based on the claim that he had inherited the mantle of Berukhiah and his transmission and dissemination of Turkish Sabbatian teachings and rites in Poland. Baruch me-Erets Yavan, the chief opponent of the Frankists during the early phase of the development of the movement, recorded a prayer introduced by Frank in Podolia; the prayer addressed Berukhiah as God of Israel incarnate and mentioned the abolishment of the *torah de-beri'ah* and its replacement by the *torah de-atsilut*.[109] In a letter to Emden accompanying the text of the prayer, Yavan claimed that Frank had spread Berukhiah's teachings in Podolia, advocating abolition of the prohibition of incest and introducing idolatry in the proper sense of the term: worship of a deified human being.[110]

Indeed, Frankist sources also confirm that during his first months in Poland, Frank recited the Ladino prayer *Mi dio barach io* (Berukhiah my God),[111] and his followers responded with a verse from the "credo" of the Dönmeh: "I believe with perfect faith in the faith of the God of truth . . . the three knots of faith that are one."[112] On the basis of such accounts, Gershom Scholem argued that Frankism was "for generations nothing other than a particularly radical [off]shoot of the Dönmeh, only with a Catholic façade."[113] Scholem's claim is only partly true: if Frank's followers were, in some sense, "nothing other than a particularly radical offshoot of the Dönmeh," this was not for generations but only before they acquired their "Catholic façade": during the first two months of Frank's activity in Podolia. Afterward, Frankism became something entirely different.

Sabbatianism, particularly the Turkish variety, is the indispensable context for the study of Frankism. However, I believe that Frank consciously—and, to a large extent, successfully—attempted to discard his Sabbatian legacy and to separate himself from other Sabbatian groups, including (and perhaps particularly) the Dönmeh. Most scholars have tended to treat Frankism as an extension, branch, or late phase of Sabbatianism. Thus Simon Dubnow stated that "Jacob Frank was for the Polish-Russian Jews of the eighteenth century what Sabbatai Tsevi was for entire Jewry of the seventeenth."[114] Scholem argued that "there is no basic difference between the terms Sabbatianism and Frankism."[115] Such an approach oversimplifies the issue. Not all Polish (or even not all Podolian), Czech, or German Sabbatians accepted Frank's leadership, and some of Frank's followers did not come from Sabbatian backgrounds. Essential theological differences, as well as dissimilarities between the Frankists and other Sabbatian subsects in their social makeup and political aspirations, will be presented in the following chapters.

Most important, in his later activity Frank did not see himself as a continuator or an incarnation of Sabbatai Tsevi or Berukhiah. As he put it, Sabbatai Tsevi "did not accomplish anything."[116] It was only himself, Frank, who "came to this world to bring forth into the world a new thing of which neither your forefathers nor their forefathers heard."[117]

Jacob Frank's very name indicated his foreignness and showed that he remained an outsider in his milieu: in Salonika, despite his family ties to Tova and his success among local Sabbatians, he was a Pole among the Turks. Upon his arrival in Poland, this perspective was reversed: the term *frenk* in the Orient denoted a European custom or object or a visitor from Europe; in Yiddish, by a peculiar linguistic inversion, it came to signify a Sephardic, that is, an Oriental, Jew. When two preachers from Podolia, Yiddish speakers, told a story "about how a certain *Frenk* had come to Poland, and caused there a great uproar,"[118] they meant to say that, in the Commonwealth, Jacob Frank was a stranger coming from the East. To my mind, nothing better illustrates Frank's personality and his fate than this inversion: wherever he went, he remained an outsider, escaping qualifications and provoking contradictory reactions.

Two depictions of Frank were written by eyewitnesses in 1759, the year of his conversion. One, composed by the Jesuit Konstanty Awedyk, described Frank as a man "beautiful, of imposing posture and resounding voice."[119] The other one, Jewish, preserved in Rabbi Jacob Emden's *Sefer shimush*, claimed that he was a small man, "incredibly ugly, not resembling a human being, with the face of a demon."[120] Awedyk further marveled at his linguistic capabilities, claiming that Frank fully mastered "Hebrew, Turkish, Wallachian, Italian,

German, and Ladino [*Frencki*]";[121] the Jewish account stated that "Frank had no command at all of any language or speech whatsoever but stammered, whistled, and cried like a rooster so that anyone who was not well accustomed to him could not understand anything."[122]

Such contrasting accounts of Frank are many. He was an Ashkenazi among the Sephardim, a Sephardi among the Ashkenazim, a Pole among the Turks, a Turk among the Poles, an unlearned boor among the sages, a sage among the simpletons, a believer among skeptics, a libertine among the pious. Following his conversion in 1759, he continued to be seen as a Jew among the Christians and yet was considered a Christian among the Jews. Heinrich Graetz, the first monographer of Frankism, characterized the founder of the movement as "one of the worst, slyest, and most deceitful villains of the eighteenth century."[123] A Polish Catholic encyclopedia defined him as "the greatest reformer of Polish Jewry."[124] Aleksander Kraushar called Frank's dicta a "theosophical system arisen in a head of a boor, a teaching lacking any theological background, in which shreds of Christian dogmas are associated in a disorderly manner with concepts from the Zohar, with traces of occultist tenets, and with chaos of incomprehensible tones."[125] Gershom Scholem claimed that they "contained a genuine creed of life."[126] In short, Frank was the most mercurial of all Jewish leaders. In this work, I seek to penetrate his merculiality and uncover the facts of his astonishing career.

Chapter 1

In the Shadow of the *Herem*

The Lanckoronie Affair

Toward the end of January 1756, Jacob Frank and a group of other Sabbatians were discovered conducting a secret ritual in the little town of Lanckoronie, near the Moldavian border. The discovery set a process in motion, which led to the emergence of Frankism as a phenomenon distinct from other branches of the wider Sabbatian movement. The ensuing sequence of events included the arrest of the participants in the ritual, a series of unusually harsh punitive measures by the Jewish authorities, public clashes between Sabbatian and non-Sabbatian Jews in Podolia, the involvement of Christians in what would seem an internal Jewish affair, public disputations between the representatives of the Frankists and of the rabbinate, and, ultimately, the conversion of Frank and his followers to Roman Catholicism.

The Lanckoronie incident is one of the most widely known events from the history of Frankism. The sect's reputation for orgiastic rites and antinomian ideology is based mainly on the descriptions of the Lanckoronie ritual and the testimony gathered by the authorities in its wake. Indeed, the key concept of *mitsvah ha-ba'ah ba-averah* (lit., a commandment fulfilled by breaking another commandment), which gave the title to Gershom Scholem's seminal essay on what he termed "radical Sabbatianism,"[1] derives from one item of this testimony and does not appear in any other source. Scholem's essay—especially after its title's mistranslation into English as "Redemption through Sin"—became the best-known scholarly account of eighteenth-century Sabbatianism and shaped the perception of the movement among scholars and the wider public alike.

Given the impact of the Lanckoronie affair on the later history of the

Frankist movement, surprisingly little is known about the incident itself. The
extant sources disagree about almost everything: the exact date and character
of the ritual, the manner and circumstances of its discovery, the number and
names of the participants, and the nature of the subsequent developments.
Scholarly accounts based on these sources contradict one another.[2] In order to
clarify some ingrained misunderstandings (and to avoid exacerbating the existing confusion), I shall first lay out the available primary evidence, juxtapose
the contradictory statements in it, and then try to establish the basic outline
of what happened. On that basis, I shall offer suggestions as to the nature and
the theological significance of the ritual.

Frankist sources (written twenty to thirty years after the incident) give
only brief accounts of the Lanckoronie affair. Thus, the Frankist chronicle
states: "[Frank] traveled from Lwów to Kopyczyńce. On 21 January, after having stayed there for only one night, the Lord traveled on the 25th [sic] to
Lanckoronie with Jakubowski and Jacob Lwowski. In Lanckoronie, all the
True Believers sang, danced, and then they were jailed together with the Lord.
On the third day, Turks came from no one knows where and why and ordered
to set the Lord alone free."[3]

The muddled chronology of the account does not allow us to date the
ritual with precision, though it evidently took place during the last week of
January 1756, and Frank arrived in Lanckoronie only a day or a few days before its commencement. "Jakubowski" was the Christian name taken later by
Frank's groomsman and teacher-turned-disciple, Nahman ben Samuel, then
rabbi of Busk; Jacob Lwowski, otherwise hardly mentioned in Frankist documents, was the stepson of Frank's other teacher and patron Mordechai ben
Elias of Prague. The identities and number of other Sabbatians are not known;
also unclear is the character of the ceremony, except that it involved singing
and dancing.

The only mention of the Lanckoronie affair in *The Words of the Lord*
is even more cursory: "When I came to Lanckoronie and you were singing
songs, having covered the windows during the night, I went out and opened
the window so that everything would inevitably be heard."[4] Again, the only
thing we know about the character of the ceremony is that the participants
sang songs. However, the text does present an interesting and important piece
of information: the disclosure of the secret ritual was an intentional provoca-
tion on Frank's part, and the Sabbatians were revealed because he opened the
windows to let the town's inhabitants hear them singing during the night.

Jewish sources contain more detailed accounts of the Lanckoronie ritual. The earliest of these comes from Rabbi Jacob Emden's *Sefer shimush* (1760):

> And they took the wife of the local rabbi (who also belonged to the sect), a woman beautiful but lacking discretion,[5] they undressed her naked and placed the Crown of the Torah on her head, sat her under the canopy like a bride, and danced a dance around her. They celebrated with bread and wine of the condemned,[6] and they pleased their hearts with music like King David . . . and in dance they fell upon her kissing her, and called her 'mezuzah,' as if they were kissing a mezuzah.[7]

Emden supplemented this report by telling how a few local Jews wanted to purchase a drink in a house adjacent to the place where the rite took place. They heard the sounds of singing, burst into the house, and severely beat up those present; only after calling for help from Gentile neighbors were the Frankists left alone. The following day, a message was sent to the nearby communities. Rabbinic courts gathered testimony from witnesses and pronounced a *herem* (ban of excommunication) against the participants in the ritual. Emden named Frank as leader of the group and stated that he had come to Lanckoronie "for he knew that the sect of Sabbatai Tsevi would gather there."[8] Aside from Frank, the only participants in the ritual identified by Emden were the rabbi of Lanckoronie and his wife. No information was given about the other participants, the date of the event, or the exact character of the non-Jewish neighbors' intervention.

Another Jewish account appeared in Abraham of Szarogród's "Ma'aseh nora be-Podolia", first published in 1769.[9] According to the author (who claimed to be an eyewitness of the affair), the incident took place not in Lanckoronie but in his hometown of Szarogród. A group of visitors led by Frank came to this town a few days before the festival of Shavuot (in early June) and stayed in the house of a certain Rabbi Hayyim Maggid. The community offered the visitors bread and meat; Frank, however, refused to have any dealings with local Jews, whom he claimed to be "descendants of the mixed multitude."[10]

On the Shabbat before the commencement of the festival, the congregation awaited Frank's group in the synagogue in order to begin the evening service. As the strangers were late, the rabbi sent a beadle to bring them over. The beadle went to Rabbi Hayyim's house, where he saw a young woman naked to the waist with her head uncovered and hair loose; Frank and his company were dancing around her, hugging and kissing her. They had crosses (*tselamim*) hung on their necks.[11] Alerted by the beadle, the entire community ran to see the abomination. The following day, the rabbi of Szarogród pronounced a *herem* on the delinquents and sent information about the ban into other communities of Podolia. The sectarians ignored the ban and started a countercampaign against the rabbinate, which ultimately led to the staging of a public disputation between the parties.[12]

The most extensive Jewish account of the Lanckoronie affair can be found in Dov Ber Birkenthal's *Divre binah* (1800).[13] According to Birkenthal, Frank called upon the Lwów Sabbatians, followers of Krysa, to go with him to Salonika, where they would prostrate themselves on the grave of Berukhiah and would see him perform wonders. Some fifteen people, including a son of one of the leaders of the community and a young woman dressed as a man, heeded his call and left Lwów. On the way to Salonika, they reached the small town of Lanckoronie, where they took lodgings in the house of one Leyb. They were joined by several people from Lanckoronie and nearby communities and organized celebrations with singing and dancing that lasted several days.

One night, a peasant came to Lanckoronie to sell wood; having seen the celebrations, he asked the local rabbi, Gershon Katz, why they were being held. The rabbi knew nothing about the festivities and sent a boy to spy on Leyb's house. On his return, the boy reported that the windows were covered with heavy carpets, so that he could not see much; but through a hole in the wall, he had seen men and women dancing together. The following night, Rabbi Gershon, officials of the Jewish community, Romanowski (the Polish governor of the town), and the local magistrate went to Leyb's house; peeping through holes in the wall, they all saw naked men and women dancing and heard them singing rhymed chants in praise of Sabbatai Tsevi and Berukhiah. The governor immediately ordered the arrest of eight of those present (including Frank); they were jailed in the Lanckoronie military encampment and were set to work hewing heavy stones. The rest were set free.

A search carried out in the house revealed many subversive and heretical writings. The writings were confiscated by the rabbi, who also wrote to the district rabbi, Menahem Mendel of Satanów, asking him to come to Lanckoronie in person and investigate the incident. However, Rabbi Menahem Mendel was ill and sent his brother-in-law, Eleazar Lippman, accompanied by several community functionaries. An impromptu *bet din* was set up in Lanckoronie, and those arrested were brought before it in fetters, one by one. Some of them confessed to various misdeeds and sought repentance; they also reported the names and crimes of other Sabbatians. The delinquents were placed under a ban, and the property of the Jews who left Lwów with Frank was confiscated by the rabbinate.

Ber Birkenthal's account was composed more than half a century after the events described. In recounting what had happened in Lanckoronie, its author relied on oral sources, as well as on the official protocol of a Christian investigation of the affair (I shall discuss the details of this investigation below). This protocol was written in 1757 by the canon of the Kamieniec consistory, Franciszek Kazimierz Kleyn, and published a year later under the title *Coram iudicio recolendae memoriae Nicolai de stemmate Jelitarum a Dembowa Góra Dembowski, Dei & Apostolicae Sedis Gratia Episcopi Camenecenis . . . Pars III: De decisoriis Processus inter infideles Iudaeos Dioecesis Camenecensis, in materia iudaicae eorum perfidiae, aliorumque muto obiectorum* A.D. *1757 expedita ac in executis pendens.* It is the most important Christian account of the Lanckoronie incident.

Kleyn's protocol placed the Lanckoronie ritual on the night of 27–28 January 1756 in the house of Leyb Aaron.[14] Those who had gathered there closed the door and covered the windows with carpets to avoid being disturbed by people coming to the market the following day. Long into the night, they devoted themselves to the "reading of the Scriptures and singing of the Psalms."[15] A local arendator, one Gershon, summoned a few Jews, who, accompanied by the magistrate's attendants, broke into the house, arrested the participants in the ritual, beat them, and confiscated their property, including books and manuscripts. A boy (in Kleyn's account, he is one of the participants in the ritual, not the rabbi's servant) was brought before the town governor, Romanowski, flogged, and compelled to describe the ritual and repeat the chants. Those arrested were forced to do menial labor. Romanowski feared that Gershon was trying to implicate him in a scandalous legal case and tried to restrain the arendator, stating that "he found no cause in these Jews."[16]

Yet Gershon paid no heed to Romanowski and sued the arrested Jews in the municipal court of Lanckoronie. Parallel to the proceedings of the magistrates, the Jews initiated their own case before the gathering of the elders of the Lanckoronie, Satanów, and Smotrycz communities. The arrested parties were shackled by their necks and interrogated under coercion; one of them was beaten "almost to death" by the beadle of the Lanckoronie synagogue.[17] Their houses were broken into, their property looted, and their books and manuscripts confiscated. The participants in the ritual whom Kleyn mentioned by name were Frank, Woł (the rabbi of Krzywcze), and Leyb Aaron of Lanckoronie (owner of the house).

On the basis of the extant sources, a few basic facts can be established. Following Kleyn's protocol, we can date the Lanckoronie incident to the night of 27–28 January 1756. The Frankist chronicle (often inaccurate in matters of chronology) shifted it by a few days; Abraham of Szarogród, who dated it to May or June of the same year, confused the timing of the event itself with that of the conclusion of the rabbinic investigation and the issuing of the excommunications. (Abraham's moving the event from Lanckoronie to Szarogród, an attempt to give himself extra credibility as an eyewitness, can be discounted.) About a dozen men and women participated in the ritual; the list certainly includes Frank and the owner of the house, Leyb of Lanckoronie. Most reports also attest to the participation of one or more communal rabbis: the Frankist chronicle mentions Nahman of Busk (Jakubowski); Kleyn Woł of Krzywcze, and Emden the unnamed rabbi of Lanckoronie.[18] A few participants were arrested by local Polish authorities. Frank, a Turkish subject, was released almost immediately; the Polish Jews were jailed for a longer period of time.

Following the discovery and the arrest, there was some physical violence, and books were confiscated. The exact character of the Frankists' actions is more difficult to determine: the only element on which all sources agree is that the Lanckoronie celebrations involved singing and dancing. Information about the particulars of the ritual can be found only in Jewish anti-Frankist accounts. Whereas it is impossible to verify the accuracy of every detail, I am inclined to accept the basic veracity of Emden's description: while extremely tendentious in his judgments and interpretations, on many occasions Emden has been proved to be careful and trustworthy with regard to facts,[19] and there is no reason to assume that he invented an entire ritual in this particular instance; his account therefore will provide a point of departure for an interpretation of the theological meaning of the ceremony.

Emden's description of the Lanckoronie incident suggests that Frank and his followers performed a rite based on Jewish rituals of the adulation of or the mystical marriage with the Torah. For instance, the festival of Simhat Torah, which concludes the annual cycle of the public reading of the Law, includes carrying the Torah scrolls around the synagogue accompanied by singing and dancing. When the scrolls are carried through the congregation, it is customary for men to touch the edge of their prayer shawl to them and then kiss the prayer shawl as a sign of respect and veneration. The Simhat Torah rite also includes a great deal of marriage symbolism: the person who completes the reading of the Torah is called *hatan Torah*—bridegroom of the Torah—and in some communities, he is placed, together with the scroll, under the bridal canopy.[20] Also, kabbalistic tradition interpreted the festival as a marriage between Israel and the Torah.[21]

While these customs and interpretations belong to the perfectly normative Jewish practice, in Sabbatianism the mystical marriage with the Torah acquired a special significance: in 1648, Sabbatai Tsevi, having invited the most prominent rabbis to a banquet, erected a bridal canopy, had a Torah scroll brought in, and performed the marriage ceremony between himself and the Torah.[22] He signed his letters "the bridegroom coming out from under the canopy, the husband of the dearly beloved Torah, who is the most beauteous and lovely lady" and was fond of singing his favorite song, the Spanish *romanza* "Meliselda," while hugging a Torah scroll in his arms.[23]

Sabbatai was severely censured by the rabbis for his performances; still, the concept of the mystical marriage of a Jew and the Torah was deeply rooted in the Jewish tradition, and his action only stretched the boundaries of mainstream Judaism. The Lanckoronie rite, however, seemed to go far beyond Sabbatai's stretching the boundaries of the acceptable: it turned the acceptable upside down. Sabbatai replaced the human bride with the Torah; participants in the Lanckoronie ritual replaced the Torah with a naked woman. In imitation of Simhat Torah observances, the wife of the Lanckoronie rabbi was adorned with typical ornaments of the Torah scroll (the Crown of the Law), seated under the canopy like a bride, and kissed and hugged in veneration. This first account of a Frankist rite encapsulated the relationship between Frankism and Sabbatianism *sensu largo*. While Sabbatai Tsevi—the "true" messiah—ascended to the status of the bridegroom of the true word of God, in Frankism the true word of God descended into palpably material female flesh.

The idea of systematically turning everything spiritual into material, voiced by Frank for the first time at the grave of Nathan of Gaza, was put into practice. Aside from its heavily transgressive nature, this trope also encompassed the seeds of Frankism's romance with Christianity and anticipated its later acceptance of the concept of incarnation (as opposed to the deification expounded by the sect of Berukhiah) and the eventual appropriation of elements of Catholic Mariology. This sheds special light on Emden's otherwise obscure remark that the ritual involved celebrations with the "bread and wine of the condemned."

The phrase "wine of the condemned" (*yein anushim*) appears in the Hebrew Bible only once, in the prophet Amos's description of Israel's transgressions and its backsliding into idol worship (Amos 2:9). Taken in itself, Emden's statement could have been understood as a merely formulaic emphasis on the transgressive and idolatrous character of the Frankist rite. Yet juxtaposed with other accounts, it might hint that the Lanckoronie ritual entailed some form of imitation (or parody) of the Christian Eucharist. This impression is strengthened by Abraham of Szarogród's mention that participants in the ritual wore crosses on their necks. Whereas, as we have seen, Abraham's account is unreliable when it comes to the date and the place of the event (and many other things as well), I am prepared to take his word on this particular detail: Kleyn's *Coram iudicio* mentions that, after the discovery of the ritual, one of the anti-Sabbatian Jews "burned the cross"[24]—an act otherwise inexplicable—and Frankist sources confirm that Frank and his followers used crucifixes in other ceremonies.[25]

The Investigations

All the sources agree that non-Jews were involved in the Lanckoronie case from the very outset: on the request of their Jewish opponents, participants in the ritual were apprehended by magistrates and brought before the town's governor. By the standards of eighteenth-century Poland, there was nothing unusual about this request: both the official Jewish leadership and individual Jews often called upon Polish authorities in internal Jewish matters, and sometimes they even had recourse to non-Jewish courts as an arbiter in conflicts among Jews.[26] What happened next, however, was highly unusual: the case became a matter of interest for not only the town governor and the magistrates but for the Catholic ecclesiastical authorities.

Only four days after the Lanckoronie incident, on 1 February 1756, the bishop's consistory court of the Kamieniec Podolski diocese demanded that the books confiscated in Lanckoronie be submitted to it for inspection; three days later, the court ordered the arrested participants in the ceremony to be brought to Kamieniec for interrogation. The directives of the court touched upon a moot legal issue: following Sigmundus III's privilege of 1592, the Jews of the Polish-Lithuanian Commonwealth were granted full legal autonomy and were not subject to the jurisdiction of the Church unless they lived on Church-owned estates. While individual members of the clergy sometimes violated this privilege and encroached on the rights of the Jews, Church tribunals normally did not hear cases in which none of the parties was a Christian. Ostensibly, the intervention of the Kamieniec episcopal court in the Lanckoronie affair constituted an open—and unprecedented—breach of jurisdiction.

At the time of the Lanckoronie incident, the Kamieniec diocese was headed by Bishop Mikołaj of Dębowa Góra Dembowski (1680–1757). Jew-ish historiography has routinely regarded Dembowski as a rabid anti-Semite (as exemplified, for instance, by his 1750 edict expelling the Jews from the city of Kamieniec) and maintained that the bishop "heard" about the events in Lanckoronie, overstepped his prerogatives, violated the laws granting Jews legal autonomy, and forced them to appear before his court. What is certainly true about this scenario is that the bishop indeed *was* a rabid anti-Semite. However, the scholars who have propounded this line of argument never bothered to explain how exactly Dembowski—head of a diocese the size of half of France—could have "heard" about an incident involving a few Jews in a remote townlet only three days after it took place.

The official protocol of the consistory court's investigation was published in Franciszek Kleyn's *Coram iudicio* and was already known to the first scholars of Frankism. While Kleyn's tortuous Latin is not free of ambiguities, the pro-tocol is clear and unequivocal in this particular case: the episcopal court took up the case because it was explicitly and directly asked to do so by the Jewish authorities. Immediately after the arrest of the participants in the ritual by the Lanckoronie magistrates, the "elders of the Satanów and Lanckoronie syna-gogues" brought suit against them at the Kamieniec consistory for "deviating from the Mosaic Law and the ancient [Jewish] traditions."[27] This formulation of the accusation was fraught with consequences.

The canon law principle that the Catholic Church has supreme authority in the internal religious affairs of not only Christians but all peoples and all confessions has a long history. The popes claimed power to punish the Jews for deviations from Mosaic Law, exactly as they were empowered to punish pagans for transgressing natural law.[28] Innocent IV (1243–54) already stated that "the pope can judge the Jews . . . if they invent heresies against their own law."[29] As Jeremy Cohen has noted, "Innocent's line of thought quickly be-came the common opinion of thirteenth- and fourteenth-century canonists. It apparently guided the friars of the papal Inquisition. By the second half of the fourteenth century, the Dominican Inquisitor Nicholas Eymeric consid-ered it a direct mandate to the Inquisition to defend genuine Judaism against internal heresy."[30] The functionaries of Bishop Dembowski's court followed Eymeric's position. They invoked the bull of Gregory XIII *Antiqua Iudaeo-rum improbitas*,[31] giving the Inquisition jurisdiction over the Jews of Rome in cases of blasphemy, protection of heretics, and possession of forbidden works, and stated that since the papal Inquisition did not operate in Poland, local consistories had the right and obligation to conduct proceedings in its place. Upon the request of the Jewish authorities, the consistory court of the Kamieniec diocese claimed general jurisdiction in cases concerning heresy (*nobis quoque, . . . potestats inquisitionis contra haereticam pravitatem . . . de iure competat*)[32] and undertook to investigate specific allegations of heresy against the Sabbatians.

To the best of my knowledge, the Kamieniec investigation was the first case in early modern Poland in which a Christian ecclesiastical court looked into allegations of a Jewish heresy. It is not clear whether the *bet din* of Satanów knew what they were doing when they denounced the arrested Sabbatians to Dembowski and approached the bishop's court. The explicit formulation of the nature of the crime as "deviation from the true teachings of Mosaic Law" would suggest that the accusers knew that the Church had prima facie jurisdiction in such cases, and it seems to be no coincidence that they approached precisely this court.

Very quickly, however, the rabbis realized that the voluntary renunciation of the Jewish judicial autonomy was not a good idea. A week after the commencement of the investigation in Kamieniec, they tried to backtrack; the consistory protocol noted that "on 9 February, the accusers withdrew their case and refused to continue the proceedings."[33] But it was too late: the Catholic clergy had already gained the opportunity to meddle in what until then had been an internal Jewish affair. The consistory "decided to continue the proceedings for its own information," demanded that the arrested parties be transferred from Lanckoronie to Kamieniec, and ordered that the inspection of books and manuscripts confiscated by the *bet din* be carried out by qualified priests.[34]

The Kamieniec consistory also demanded more information. Detentions and interrogations of suspected Sabbatian heretics by local Polish authorities occurred in other locations in Podolia: on 1 March, four suspects were apprehended in Jezierzany, and three weeks later, a large group was arrested in Wielchowiec. The detainees were brought to Kamieniec for questioning and faced Bishop Dembowski.[35] Further incidents attesting to the antinomian behavior of the Sabbatians took place. One Shabbat, the Sabbatian Samuel of Busk "out of spite" rode a horse and smoked tobacco in front of the house of the chief rabbi of Lwów and the Land rabbi of Ruthenia, Hayyim Cohen Rapaport. He also publicly reviled the rabbi.[36] Rapaport's response was similar to that of the elders of Satanów and Lanckoronie: he brought Samuel to the court of the archbishop of Lwów, Mikołaj Wyżycki.

The protocols of the Lwów consistory for 1756 are no longer extant, so we do not know the legal basis of the case; all that is left is an index to the protocols that attests that the bishop's court indeed heard the case against Samuel *in causa intuitu certarum cathegoriarum*.[37] The Lwów trial was apparently similar to the one from Kamieniec and invoked the Church's jurisdiction in cases of heresy against the Mosaic Law and natural law. Some information can be culled from a Latin letter sent in 1757 to the papal nuncio in Warsaw by the *shtadlan* of the Council of Four Lands, Baruch me-Erets Yavan. When describing the case to the nuncio, Yavan stated that Samuel "professed and disseminated new religious tenets contrary to the Ten Commandments, the Old [Testament] Law as well as the natural law."[38]

The *shtadlan* also mentioned that the delinquent was deemed a heretic by Bishop Wyżycki's court and was delivered to the secular authorities for punishment (*pro quibus criminibus fuit haereticus adinventus, et pro paenis ad forum saeculare remissus*).[39] According to Emden's anonymous informant, Samuel was condemned to death and hanged. Neither the Jews nor the Christians wanted to bury him, so the body lay under the gallows for days.[40] Emden's informant seemed to have exaggerated: execution for heresy was extremely rare in Poland, and when it did occur (as in the 1689 case of the nobleman Kazimierz Łyszczyński, author of the tractate *De non existentia Dei*),[41] it was widely publicized and discussed. The complete absence of any mention of Samuel's case in Polish sources suggests that it did not end in any spectacular way. Ber Birkenthal (who mentioned a trial in Bishop Wyżycki's court without giving Samuel's name) reported that the defendant was accused of "inventing a new faith and new religion" (*al hamtsa'ah emunah ve-dat hadashah*) and that he was pronounced guilty but that bribery had saved him from any punishment.[42]

Regardless of what the true outcome of Samuel of Busk's case was, it is clear that a new paradigm of the struggle between the Sabbatians and their opponents was being established in Podolia. Provocative public violations of normative Judaism and challenges to rabbinic authority became a daily matter. The standard response of the rabbinate became denunciation to Christian ecclesiastical authorities and the accusation of heresy. The involvement of episcopal courts and of such prominent and powerful clergymen as Dembowski and Wyżycki constituted a mortal danger for the Sabbatians (even if the testimony about Samuel's hanging is probably untrue), but it also gave them a chance to argue their case before the state and the Church authorities. In mid-March, during the Fast of Esther, Frank gathered the Sabbatians in Kopczyńce and announced: "'If we have the True God and you believe in him, why should we hide? Let us go in the open and do public damage. Whoever wants to give his body and cling to the love of the Faith, let him walk with me.' And they went. . . . The Lord himself had jam and vodka in his hand and gave everyone in public in the streets something to eat."[43]

Open violation of the Fast of Esther must have been part of Frank's wider strategy of instigating public confrontation with the rabbis. The account fits nicely with the claim that he deliberately opened the windows in Lanckoronie; Frank apparently sought to provoke the Jewish authorities in hopes that he would be given access to the bishop and thus gain the support of the Christians. He succeeded: two days after the Kopczyńce incident, he was arrested, together with several other participants, and brought to face Dembowski. Those arrested were released after a week and granted *salvus conductus* for the duration of the consistory's proceedings.[44] The Sabbatians dispersed to their homes; Frank left the Commonwealth and headed for Salonika.[45]

While the cases were being tried before the consistories of Kamieniec and Lwów, Jewish authorities conducted their own investigation. The rabbinic council of the Land of Ruthenia gathered in Lwów on 10 May[46] and obliged the rabbi of Satanów to collect testimony concerning Sabbatianism in the area of his jurisdiction. The Satanów *bet din* sat between 31 May and 13 June; the testimony that it collected (along with the testimony from the Lwów case of Samuel of Busk sent to the nuncio by Baruch me-Erets Yavan) is the fullest extant account of Sabbatian antinomianism.

The Satanów rabbinic court collected twenty-seven short depositions and one long confession from a repentant Sabbatian. The vast majority of the short depositions were given not by the Sabbatians themselves but by people who saw their misdeeds (on one occasion, spying through a keyhole)[47] or even by those who had only heard about them. Most deponents took great pains to emphasize that they themselves did not participate in the crimes ascribed to others; some claimed that they had been given the opportunity to participate but had declined to do so or escaped at the last minute.[48] The offenses attributed to the Sabbatians pertained to three main spheres of activity. First, they involved violations of Shabbat and dietary laws. Thus Joseph of Rohatyn, who did admit to having taken part in prohibited rites, described in detail how during Passover he had eaten a slice of bread with "the other thing" (pork) and butter and had drunk nonkosher wine; he also stated that it was customary among the Sabbatians to include a piece of pork and a piece of cheese in a Shabbat meal.[49]

Second, they touched upon theological issues. For instance, Samuel of Busk professed his belief that "there is One God in the Trinity, and the Fourth Person is the Holy Mother";[50] others mentioned the belief in the annulment of the Torah of Moses and its replacement by the new Torah of Sabbatai Tsevi[51] and admitted possessing and copying heretical books and manuscripts.[52] Third, they constituted sexual transgressions. Samuel of Busk stated that "it is permissible to have children and to have sexual intercourse with someone else's wife or one's own sister, or even—though only in secret—with one's own mother. As I am old now, I no longer do it, but twenty years ago (and I have professed this faith for twenty-four years), I had carnal relations with the wife of my son. . . . And I believe that all this is permitted because God commanded us to do thus."[53]

Other testimonies described the breaking of the prohibition of incest,[54] having sexual relations with menstruating women,[55] masturbation (also in public),[56] as well as the practice of "sexual hospitality," whereby a host offered his wife or daughter to a stranger coming as a guest to his house. This custom was known to the Hebrew Bible, as attested by the episodes with Lot's daughters (Gen. 19) and the Levite and his concubine (Judg. 19:22–30); it had been widespread in the ancient Middle East and Central Asia and was known to survive in tribal societies until modern times.[57] The Dönmeh branch led by Frank's putative father-in-law, Yehudah Levi Tova, also was rumored to practice sexual hospitality,[58] and it seems that the custom filtered down to the Podolian Sabbatians as well. Thus, the women interrogated by the Satanów *bet din* reported that they slept with strangers "upon the wish of the[ir] husband[s],"[59] who "told [them] it was a positive commandment."[60] One deposition dealt with a woman who had had intercourse with a stranger without her husband's permission and thereby provoked his ire, "for such a deed is not considered by them a commandment."[61] Another mentioned a complaint voiced by a Sabbatian who came to a house of a fellow believer: "Why did we come here? He would not honor us with his wife."[62]

After completing the proceedings, the Satanów *bet din* imposed penalties. Joseph of Rohatyn made a public confession of sins and described his deeds in front of the entire congregation (a matter uncommon in Jewish tradition, which normally forbade public description of one's sin). Then he received thirty-nine lashes and prostrated himself on the threshold of the synagogue so that those coming and going would tread upon his body. He divorced his wife (because she had had sexual relations with others)[63] and declared his children bastards. He was banished from the Rohatyn community and was prohibited ever to make any contacts with other Jews. He was supposed to wander alone for the rest of his days.[64]

Herem

The humiliating ceremony undergone by Joseph of Rohatyn in his hometown synagogue—public confession followed by thirty-nine lashes with the congregation treading upon the penitent—is not unknown in early modern Judaism: Uriel da Costa underwent exactly the same ordeal in Amsterdam in 1639.[65] In da Costa's case, the ceremony was expiation preceding the annulment of a ban of excommunication previously imposed upon him. In the case of Joseph, the Satanów documents make no explicit reference to such a ban, but the banishment and prohibition of *communicatio civilis* were typical sanctions associated with excommunication.

Jewish sources describing the Lanckoronie incident mention that the participants in the rite were placed under a ban; we also know that on 26 May 1756, a week or so before the launching of the proceedings of the Satanów *bet din*, the rabbinic assembly of Brody pronounced a *herem* on the Sabbatians. "The wicked men" belonging to the sect of Sabbatai Tsevi were to be "excluded and repudiated by the community of Israel; their wives and daughters were to be regarded as harlots, their offspring as bastards." Other Jews were forbidden to have any dealings with them or to assist them in any way. The ban restricted the study of printed kabbalistic works, which had an official rabbinic approval, to those over the age of thirty, and manuscript works (including Lurianic writings) to the age of forty.[66] It is highly interesting that on the very same day, the very same assembly also issued a pro-Eibeschütz proclamation.[67] The "Sabbatian" and "anti-Sabbatian" camps, often depicted as monolithic, had much more fluid boundaries: the same rabbis simultaneously exonerated the alleged Sabbatian Eibeschütz and vigorously condemned the Frankists, thereby drawing a clear line between the two cases.[68]

Herem (the Jewish ban of excommunication) developed from the biblical anathema and became one of the chief means of social control and coercion available to the leadership of medieval and early modern Jewry. Technically, the *herem* could have been imposed by an individual Jew (especially in matters relating to debt settlement), but it was normally used by rabbinic tribunals as a judicial measure for certain prescribed offenses. The Talmud lists twenty-four such offenses (the list ranges from speaking ill of a learned man to failure on the part of a ritual slaughterer to show his knife to the rabbi for examination), but common practice substantially extended the applicability of the *herem*. The scope of its authority also increased over time: initially, the ban was applicable only in the area under the direct jurisdiction of a given *bet din*; but later times increasingly saw instances of pronouncing a *herem* on foreigners. As with Christian excommunication, a procedure developed for informing other communities that a *herem* had been imposed so that it could be repeated and enforced in other localities.[69]

There were several levels of severity of the ban (with some forms specifying the duration of the punishment from the outset and limiting the harshness of the sanctions imposed) as well as different levels of formality in its imposition. The most rigorous form, called "the great *herem*," "the solemn *herem*," or "the *herem* of Joshua son of Nun," encompassed an elaborate ritual that demanded the presence of the entire congregation and included sounding the ram's horn, extinguishing black candles, and blowing hoses made of animal intestines until they burst with a bang; such a *herem* was imposed for an indefinite period. The sanctions of the great *herem* amounted to the civil death of the excommunicated: other Jews were prohibited to associate with him or to benefit him or benefit from him in any way; he was not be counted among the ten men necessary for the performance of a public religious function; his sons were not to be circumcised; his bread and wine were to be considered nonkosher; and after his death, he was not to be accorded any honor due to the dead.

In the words of the most comprehensive study of the *herem* in premodern Poland, "from the historical point of view, excommunication formed the very basis of communal organization of Old Poland's Jewry."[70] In addition to its function as a punitive measure in cases concerning both religious and secular matters, *herem* (or the threat of a *herem*) was invoked in guaranteeing contracts and in the execution of judicial verdicts, and it was tantamount to an oath in legal proceedings.

From the sixteenth century onward, the kings of Poland recognized in the *herem* the prime means for implementing the tax regime among the Jews and therefore granted the rabbinic authorities an unparalleled measure of *bracchium saeculare*: only one month after the pronouncement of the ban, the delinquent who failed to repent was to be delivered to secular authorities and executed, and all his property was to be confiscated (in the case of Christian excommunication, similar measures were to be implemented only after a year).[71] This ultimate step was virtually never applied; however, rabbinic courts often called on Polish secular authorities to enforce their bans, and excommunication remained the most powerful tool of social control accessible to the Jewish establishment. Writing in 1797, the maskil Jacob Calmanson still described the use of the *herem* as "the most efficacious measure used by the rabbis [*doktorowie żydowscy*] to keep the people in slavish subjection and to reinforce the command they had usurped over the people's minds."[72]

Most rabbinic bans of excommunication did not target religious dissenters, but instead targeted those who violated community ordinances, those considered disruptive to communal discipline, or even common criminals. The first *herem* against the Sabbatians in Poland was issued in 1670. In September of the following year, the Council of Four Lands announced that "a great *herem* with sounding of the ram's horn and extinguishing the candles" was pronounced upon the "criminals and reckless people belonging to the sect of Sabbatai Tsevi." The council ordered—on pain of a heavy fine—the reading of the text of the ban in all the synagogues of Podolia and gave the leaders of the provinces and individual communities the authority to persecute the Sabbatians and to punish them with "infamy, fines, jail, and even to deliver them to the justice of the Gentiles [*afilu ba-dine amim*]." The delinquents should be expelled from every community and every province for all their days, they should not be assisted in danger, and all the curses of the Torah should fall upon them.[73]

In 1671, the council forbade the dissemination of manuscripts said to contain Sabbatian secret lore;[74] in 1687 or slightly earlier, it placed restrictions on the printing of homiletic works that might have contributed to spreading the heresy.[75] In 1705, on the request of Jerusalem rabbis, the body pronounced a ban on Hayyim Malakh. The 1670 *herem* was renewed by the council in 1722.[76] In October 1753, the rabbis ordered the burning of the writings generated by the Emden-Eibeschütz controversy, including the latter's allegedly Sabbatian writings.[77] In the same year, "the sages of Brody" banned the "secret writings" of the Sabbatian Leibele Prossnitz[78] as well as manuscripts ascribed to Rabbi Jonathan Eibeschütz: *Va-avo ha-yom el ha-ayyin*, commentaries on the Song of Songs and the Book of Esther, and the *kavvanot* accompanying the blowing of the shofar.[79]

Both contemporary sources and modern academic scholarship disagree on the true meaning and real effect of the bans of excommunications. Gershom Scholem has emphasized that the text of the 1670 ban was the first instance of the appearance of the term "sect of Sabbatai Tsevi" (which, in his view, proved that four years after Sabbatai's conversion to Islam, the Polish rabbis already saw the Sabbatians as an organized group) and that it was unusually harsh in tone (which demonstrated that the Sabbatians were recognized as a strong and dangerous force). On the other hand, Scholem noted that the pronouncement of the *herem* had little practical consequence: a few weeks after drafting the text of the ban in another document, the same scribe referred to Sabbatai Tsevi as the messiah.[80]

According to Scholem, the first excommunications "did not work for the simple reason that the Sabbatians did not recognize the authority of the rabbis." From the Sabbatians' perspective, the rabbinic bans were invalid, since their authors, rather than those targeted, were the "mixed multitude," "heretics," and "enemies of the faith of Israel."[81] Later excommunications were said to have more impact, and a few contemporary testimonies claimed that in consequence of the series of bans, "the wicked sect was uprooted in the entire country of Poland."[82] Some scholars have accepted this uplifting conclusion; others have argued that the very frequency with which the excommunications were repeated proves the contrary and only demonstrates the strength of the Sabbatians. It has also been pointed out that the repeated and indiscriminate use of the bans led to the weakening of their authority: "the force of the herem diminished with frequent use, and the image of rabbinic contentiousness was heightened. . . . By the late eighteenth century their use—by any authority—was a formality with very little real impact."[83]

While agreeing with the analyses noting the inflation of the power of the *herem*, I wish to emphasize another aspect of the issue. I believe that prior to the eruption of the Frankist affair, there was no organized effort to eradicate Sabbatianism in Poland. Scholars who have described the systematic rabbinic "persecution" of the heretics took rhetoric for reality: the harshness of the language of the bans should not overshadow the fact that there is no evidence of any attempt to put them into force (and, while we are on the subject, even the harshness of language so emphasized by Scholem should not be overestimated and might be largely attributed to the formulaic character of the *herem*; the 1671 ban against the Sabbatians is in no way "harsher" than a ban against common thieves coming from the same period).[84]

I would suggest further that this failure to enforce was not due only to the "crisis of authority" and the limits of the rabbinic power but also stemmed from the very nature of the anti-Sabbatian excommunications: with the sole exception of the 1705 ban against Hayyim Malakh, no *herem* issued in Poland mentioned any Sabbatian by name. Essentially, the Polish rabbis' anti-Sabbatian excommunications fell into two broad categories: those imposed on books and other writings; and those against the unspecified "people of the sect of Sabbatai Tsevi." The first might have signified attempts to stop the spread of Sabbatian propaganda but might equally well have been intended to appease the general Jewish opinion: we have ample evidence that despite the excommunications, forbidden writings were in the possession of many rabbis, including some of the signatories of the bans.[85]

As for the latter, as long as "the people of the sect of Sabbatai Tsevi" remained unnamed and did not purposefully provoke the rabbinate, they could go untroubled by the authorities. Within the framework of crypto-Sabbatianism, this amounted to a "don't ask don't tell" policy; in the case of the more overt Sabbatianism of Podolia, it signified a shaky balance of power where some localities were effectively outside the control of the rabbinic bodies (and, in some cases, under the control of Sabbatian rabbis). The Satanów testimonies and the confession of Samuel of Busk might sound shocking, yet it is clear that they depict a state of affairs that had existed in Podolia for a long time (Samuel of Busk goes back twenty years for his account, while Joseph of Rohatyn, author of the longest testimony, described events that took place nine years before the Satanów investigation). The famed Frankist "orgies" were, in fact, the custom of sexual hospitality, which was not a singular ritual but a daily practice; according to the testimonies, it was upheld by the Sabbatians for years before Frank's appearance in Poland and was in no way connected to his activity. It is highly unlikely that none of this had come to the attention of the rabbis prior to the Lanckoronie incident; even less likely is that it would not have came to their attention had they really wanted to pursue the matter.

As for the specific practices involved, stories about a Sabbatian who wanted to "copulate with a married woman while she was menstruant" and another one, who publicly masturbated in the study hall, had already emerged in 1725; the concerned congregants went to their rabbi who "replied that he knew of many worse acts" and did nothing.[86] None of the earlier cases gave rise to a public investigation like the one in Satanów; in none of them were the Sabbatians forced to describe their misdeeds in public.

Before the Lanckoronie incident, the Polish rabbinate's standing policy toward Sabbatianism was to let sleeping dogs lie. There seems to have been a tacit agreement between the Sabbatian and anti-Sabbatian factions within Polish Jewry, and even the anti-Sabbatian rabbis clearly thought that open scandal was not a price worth paying for the eradication of heresy. This agreement was broken only if one side failed to keep to the bargain. Until the eruption of the Frankist affair, the so-called anti-Sabbatian campaigns were, in fact, individual campaigns of zealots such as rabbis Moses Hagiz or Jacob Emden. During Hagiz's campaign against Hayon, the Council of Four Lands refused to get involved and did not answer his pleas for Hayon's condemnation.[87] During Emden's controversy with Rabbi Jonathan Eibeschütz, the council put much more effort into silencing Emden than into censuring Eibeschütz: the October 1753 *herem* of the council targeted not so much Sabbatian manuscripts as it targeted Emden's anti-Eibeschütz pamphlets. The council's explicit intention was to hush up the quarrel and to avoid spreading public discord among the Jews; silence, not loud condemnation, was seen as the most appropriate response to heresy.

The very first known event involving Frank, the Lanckoronie incident, shattered the status quo between the Sabbatians and the rabbinate and caused the abandonment of the "don't ask, don't tell" policy, preferred up to that point by most Polish rabbis. The question remains as to why, in this particular instance, the Polish rabbinate discarded its standard (and largely successful) policy of appeasement, embarked upon a public investigation in Satanów, and reported the Sabbatians to the Catholic Church. I suggest that at least some of the rabbis recognized that the Lanckoronie rite had transgressed the boundaries not only of normative Judaism but also of earlier Sabbatian antinomianism. This, I believe, was not due to the sexual element of the rite: as noted, the sexual misdeeds of the Sabbatians had been known before and never caused such an upheaval.

What really troubled the rabbinate was the use of Christian symbols in the ritual: regardless of the Frankists' intention (be it antinomian or syncretistic), the use of a cross in a Jewish rite put all the Jews in danger and exposed them to Christian charges of desecration and blasphemy. The participation of several communal rabbis in the rite further complicated the situation. While rabbis (and even prominent rabbis) had previously been accused of Sabbatianism, the illusion of the unity of the Jewish religious establishment in opposition to heresy remained. Both halakhah and widespread practice were reluctant to excommunicate rabbinic scholars: the accused rabbis loudly denied any involvement in heresy and quickly made appropriate anti-Sabbatian gestures. Yet, in contrast to the earlier cases of banning the unspecified "people of the sect of Sabbatai Tsevi," the post-Lanckoronie rabbinic reaction targeted five specific communities: Lanckoronie, Busk, Jezierzany, Opoczna, and Krzywcze;[88] one cannot fail to notice that the rabbis of three of these communities (Lanckoronie, Busk, and Krzywcze) figured in testimonies as alleged participants of the Lanckoronie ritual.

While the text of the May 1756 *herem* of Brody did not depart from standard texts of earlier anti-Sabbatian bans, the form of its imposition significantly differed from the established pattern: according to the testimony of Isaac of Biała, before imposing the *herem* the chief rabbi of Lwów, Hayyim

Cohen Rapaport, "stood before bishop [Wyżycki] . . . and obtained permission to excommunicate them and put them in prison."[89] Rapaport did not
need permission from the bishop to pronounce a ban of excommunication on
Jews, and such a practice had never been employed by Polish rabbis: he was
apparently trying to hedge his bets by ensuring that he had Church backing
for his *herem*. Yet Christian involvement was a double-edged sword. Initially,
it might have given the author of the *herem* unprecedented power. But before
long, the Sabbatians bribed the bishop to pressure the rabbi to cancel the ban,
and Rapaport was forced to have a beadle pronounce in the synagogue that
"people of the sect of Sabbatai Tsevi are no longer excommunicated."[90] Like
the elders of the Satanów synagogue who approached Bishop Dembowski, the
rabbi of Lwów overplayed his hand.

Chapter 2

The Peril of Heresy,
the Birth of a New Faith

Prehistory of Eighteenth-Century
Anti-Sabbatianism: Rabbi Jacob Sasportas

From the very outset, the Frankist case deviated from the established pattern of the rabbinic struggle against Sabbatianism in the first part of the eighteenth century. Frankism was unique in its extraordinary public profile, in the level of involvement of Gentile authorities in an ostensibly internal Jewish affair, and in the brutality of the rabbinic campaign against it. In order to understand these developments, we must extend our inquiry beyond eighteenth-century anti-Sabbatianism and retrace the strategies of opposition to Sabbatai Tsevi during his lifetime. Rabbi Jacob Sasportas (1610–98) was the principal opponent of the messianic movement that arose around the figure of Sabbatai in the 1660s. Sasportas was born in North Africa and served as rabbi in a number of Sephardic communities in Western Europe. During the outbreak of Sabbatian enthusiasm, he was living as a private individual in Hamburg. *Tsitsat novel Tsevi*, his collection of letters and accounts pertaining to the period directly preceding and following Sabbatai's conversion to Islam, remains the indispensable source for any analysis of the early stages of Sabbatianism.

Rabbi Jacob Sasportas's activities were first reconstructed in Gershom Scholem's monumental monograph on Sabbatai Tsevi. Scholem had little sympathy for his subject: on just one page of his book, he managed to attribute to Sasportas harshness, irascibility, arrogance, fanaticism, hunger for the power and status of rabbinic offices, bitterness and frustration, arrogance and unsteadiness in human relations, egotism and excessive self-confidence.

On the adjacent page, he called the rabbi "a Jewish Grand Inquisitor."[1] If
Scholem's discussion of Rabbi Jacob's character is, to put it mildly, somewhat
biased,[2] his reconstruction of Sasportas's polemical activities is masterful.
What Scholem did not analyze, however, was the content of Sasportas's ideas
about Sabbatianism. *Tsitsat novel Tsevi* was presented by Scholem not as a text
expounding a consistent theological position but as an expression of its author's twisted character. Since Sasportas's book described otherwise unknown
events from the early phase of the Sabbatian movement, it had paramount
significance for historical research, but it has not been subjected to a more in-
depth conceptual analysis. In my opinion, Sasportas's ideas should be treated
with the utmost seriousness: in addition to his being the first prominent anti-
Sabbatian strategist, the rabbi was the first to try to understand what the Sabbatian movement was all about.

Scholars have emphasized that Sasportas attacked Sabbatai well before
his apostasy, and the target of his ire was not the messianic enthusiasm per
se: the rabbi explicitly stated that he would be prepared to accept Tsevi as the
messiah if the latter fulfilled the traditional criteria of the messiahship.[3] Isaiah Tishby and Rivka Shatz-Uffenheimer have argued that Sabbatianism was
for Sasportas first and foremost a halakhic issue: the polemic was motivated
mainly by Sabbatai's systematic violations of the principles of religious law.[4]
Matt Goldish posited that Sasportas took issue with the rise of the "unauthorized" prophecy as a source of religious legitimacy independent of or even
hostile to the rabbinic establishment.[5] Thus, according to Goldish, Sabbatianism was for Sasportas "simply another chapter in the continuing onslaught
against the Talmudic tradition and rabbinic authority," and the rabbi largely
lost interest in the movement after Sabbatai's conversion: as the aspiring messiah was no longer Jewish, his purported claims had no significance for Jews
and Judaism.[6]

Sasportas was certainly taken aback by Sabbatai's antinomianism and worried about the subversion of the position of the rabbis brought on by popular
prophets. Yet it seems to me that his true fears lay elsewhere. In the opening
pages of *Tsitsat novel Tsevi*, Sasportas favorably quoted the young Sabbatai
Tsevi's teacher, Rabbi Joseph Eskapa, who stated, some twenty years before
his pupil's conversion to Islam, that "whoever forestalls him first deserves well,
for he will lead many into sin and make a new religion."[7] In a letter to one
of the believers, Rabbi Isaac Nahar (also written before Sabbatai's apostasy),
Sasportas remarked that whoever accepts Sabbatai's messianic claim takes "a
new Torah" upon himself and abandons his old faith.[8] In July 1666, Sasportas

described his dread that because of the upheaval surrounding Sabbatai, "before long, our religion will become two religions."[9] Around the same time, he wrote to the rabbi of Vienna: "our faith might become like two faiths and our people like two peoples. . . . So began the faith of Jesus and his followers."[10] In September 1666, upon hearing the news that Sabbatai Tsevi had instituted new festivals and abolished traditional fasts, Sasportas again expressed his fear that the "faith of the Lord would collapse and would be entirely uprooted and replaced by a new faith, unlike our Torah, for they accepted [as the messiah] a strange man . . . who will give a new Torah, like Jesus the Nazarene."[11] Following the apostasy, he claimed that Nathan's latest pronouncements finally made it clear to the sages that "from the outset, his intention was to deceive Israel and to create a new Torah" for them.[12] Sasportas's understanding of Sabbatianism has been recapitulated as follows: "It seems to me that this is the beginning of irreligion [apikorsut] among the Jews and that it constitutes the foundation of a new faith and a different religion, as happened in the days of that man [Jesus]. And it is incumbent upon all the sages in every city to come together and gird themselves and hound those who follow this irreligion."[13]

It is significant that Sasportas called Sabbatianism "irreligion" (apikorsut) and not "heresy" (minut). While rabbinic literature often used both terms imprecisely or even interchangeably, their strict technical senses were different. The term apikorsut—etymologically deriving from Epicureanism—denoted not so much a deviation from specific theological principles of Judaism as it did the absolute rejection of revealed religion combined with disrespect for religious authority: the Talmud defines the apikoros as "one who despises the word of the Lord" and "one who insults a scholar."[14] I believe that the author of Tsitsat novel Tsevi used the term in its precise meaning; he considered Sabbatianism a rebellion against the very fundaments of religiosity rather than a particular transgression against an existing religion.

Matt Goldish has noted that what first "tripped the sensors" of Sasportas was Nathan of Gaza's claim that the messiah had the right and power to judge all men and to make "a new Torah." Goldish has interpreted this assertion as a rebellion against the official institutions of the rabbinate and an attempt at a radical overturn of the authority of rabbinic tradition.[15] This might have been the way that the Sabbatians themselves saw it: for all its rhetorical flourish, the Sabbatian talk about the "new Torah" and the new prophecies being "like the Torah of Moses"[16] were meant simply to emphasize Nathan's higher status as one possessing direct revelation unmediated by the rabbis. His followers saw in Sabbatai the fulfillment of the traditional redemptive promises; they regarded themselves not as founders of a completely new religion but as faithful Jews seeking to renew Judaism from within.

Sasportas, however, took the ideas about the "new Torah" in a deliberately literal fashion. Sabbatianism was for him not a narrow halakhic problem, which could be settled by legalistic decision, or a theological deviation, which could be countered by speculative argument. It was not a heresy challenging particular tenets of Jewish belief but a schism threatening the unity of Judaism as a whole; it might have led to the split of the Jewish people and the establishment of a completely new faith. In this context, Sasportas's scattered remarks about Jesus and Christianity assume a special significance. The rabbi was not worried about Christian "influences" on Judaism introduced by Sabbatian theosophy or about messianic "enthusiasm" that might play into the hands of the Catholic priests.[17] He displayed little or no interest in contemporary Christendom: in fact, all mentions of Christianity in *Tsitsat novel Tsevi* refer not to the seventeenth-century Church and her clergy but to the ancient Jewish sect that led some Jews astray.[18] Before Sabbatai's conversion to Islam, Rabbi Jacob Sasportas foresaw the danger that Sabbatianism would become a new religion, separate from Judaism, like early Christianity. He expressed hope that the Jewish sages would manage to do what they had failed to do in the case of Jesus: nip the new faith in the bud.[19]

It is in this context that Sasportas invoked the symbolism of the mixed multitude. As discussed in the Introduction, Nathan of Gaza's idea that those denying Sabbatai's messiahship were descendants of the mixed multitude was gaining currency among his followers. Sasportas knew Nathan's statements about disbelievers coming from the *erev rav* and "laughed at them."[20] Inspired by the writings of Nathan, Hosea Nantava, a Sabbatian serving as a rabbi of Alexandria, claimed that rejecting Sabbatai Tsevi was like rejecting the Law of Moses as well as the doctrine of the resurrection of the dead. He, too, linked the rejection of the messiah with the symbol of the mixed multitude.[21] Sasportas responded to the rabbi as follows:

> And you destroyed your place in the land of the living [i.e., the afterlife] by saying: "Anyone who does not believe in [Sabbatai's messianic mandate] is like one who rejects the Torah of Moses our teacher and the resurrection of the dead, and he is from the mixed multitude." This was expressed in the letter of your prophet. May boiling liquid and molten lead be poured down the throat of the one who says such things! . . . How can he who denies your mes-

siah . . . be like the one who denies the entire Torah?! . . . But you
said that those who deny your messiah are not the [true] leaders
and sages of the generation, but they are from the mixed multitude,
the seed of Lilith, and the "caul upon the liver."[22] You opened your
mouth to do evil and spoke about things you do not comprehend.
He who *does* believe in him . . . is one of the mixed multitude! The
truth is not what his prophet wrote but what was written by the
holy Rabbi Simeon bar Yohai [purported author of the Zohar]:
"The evil handmaid [Lilith] is a grave, and in it she imprisons her
mistress, the *Shekhinah*, and she is cold and dry [as] Saturn [*Sabbatai*]. . . . "Her mistress" is a garden; "the handmaid" is a dunghill,
and she is soiled from the side of the mixed multitude, a dunghill
mingled with a garden in order to grow seeds from the side of the
Tree of Knowledge of Good and Evil, and from the side of idolatry
she is called Saturn [*Sabbatai*], Lilith, soiled dunghill. It consists of
all kinds of filth and vermin and dead dogs and donkeys are thrown
upon it."[23] And so you see that he who comes from the side of
Saturn [*Sabbatai*] really comes from the mixed multitude and the
seed of Lilith.[24]

"Sabbatai" is the Hebrew name of the planet Saturn, and the Jewish tradition often linked "the reign of Sabbatai" (the astrologically elevated position
of the planet Saturn) with the advent of the messiah. In a fascinating paper,
Moshe Idel has argued that the outburst of messianism in the seventeenth
century owed much of its potency to such speculations. Young Sabbatai Tsevi's
messianic convictions were shaped by the deep awareness of the astrological
meaning of his name, and the nexus between Saturn and the coming of the
messiah was of prime importance to Tsevi himself, his followers, and to many
contemporary observers.[25]

Sasportas was clearly well acquainted with astrological interpretations of
the advent of Sabbatianism: in a letter to Rabbi Raphael Supino, he noted
that "it is not enough, as you said, for the Gentile sages and astronomers to
claim that the ascension of the planet Saturn hints [at the coming of the mes-
siah] and is a sign of Redemption,"[26] and he linked the renewal of messianic
claims among the Jews with the ascent of the "bloody star," Sabbatai-Saturn.[27]
In this context, Sasportas's invocation of the quotation from the Zohar tying
the symbolism of Saturn with that of the mixed multitude was an exegetical masterstroke: it drew upon previous separate Sabbatian interpretations of

both motifs and, by connecting them, inverted their meanings: the ascension of Saturn was indeed linked with the advent of Sabbatai Tsevi, but it signified the beginning of the reign of the *erev rav,* not the coming of the messiah. The mixed multitude were not, as Nathan of Gaza would have it, the rabbis who opposed Sabbatai but the Sabbatians themselves. What is even more interesting is what Sasportas left out of the passage he quoted: in printed editions of the Zohar, the dead dogs and donkeys that are thrown onto the dunghill are equated with "sons of Esau and Ishmael," the Christians and the Muslims, respectively. Some manuscript versions explicitly identified the dead dog with Jesus and the dead donkey with Muhammad.[28]

The astrological notion that the advent of Sabbatianism paralleled the birth of Christianity was strengthened by the concept of the so-called *coniunctio maxima,* the conjunction between Saturn and Jupiter. Astrology—both Jewish and Christian—often interpreted the great conjunction as the moment of emergence of a new religion.[29] The Star of Bethlehem was taken to be a great conjunction,[30] and some astrologers linked the messianic pronouncements of Sabbatai Tsevi with the great conjunction that took place in November 1648. While Sasportas made no explicit mention of the 1648 conjunction, he linked the ascension of the planet Saturn with the rise of a threat of a profound rift within the Jewish people that "would turn the hearts of sons from their fathers and set husband against wife."[31]

Intellectually fascinating as it must have been, this interpretation was far too radical for other rabbis; the subsequent rabbinic anti-Sabbatian works used the literary form of *Tsitsat novel Tsevi* (a collection of letters, firsthand testimonies, and polemical commentary) as a blueprint for polemics and borrowed many specific motifs from Sasportas's writings, but they largely refrained from accepting his conclusions. Sasportas's conceptualization of Sabbatianism as a new religion had no direct continuation: the most important anti-Sabbatian work of the early eighteenth century, Moses Hagiz's *Shever poshe'im* (1714), contained only one reference each to the *erev rav* and the establishment of a new faith, and both terms were used loosely to suit the argument.[32] It also lacked any mention of Sasportas.[33]

During his lifetime, Sasportas was a lone fighter against Sabbatianism: his open opposition to Sabbatai during the height of the movement earned him little sympathy among the Jews of Hamburg and might even have endangered his life.[34] *Tsitsat novel Tsevi* had been prepared for publication but remained in manuscript.[35] In 1737, Sasportas's son produced an abridged edition of his father's magnum opus. However, leaders of the community, who were eager to suppress the memory of the involvement of their families in Sabbatian enthusiasm sixty years earlier, ordered that the entire print run be confiscated and destroyed.[36]

The book would have disappeared completely, if not for the fact that a copy (allegedly the only remaining one) of this suppressed edition was found in Amsterdam by Rabbi Jacob Emden. In 1757, at the height of the polemics against the Frankists, Emden published this abridged version of *Tsitsat novel Tsevi*.[37] The publisher felt a deep affinity between himself and Sasportas: he emphasized that his namesake Rabbi Jacob shared the same anti-Sabbatian zeal and had been required to pay a similarly high price for his relentless campaign against the heretics. Like Sasportas—and in contrast to other rabbis of the period—he also believed that heresy should not be swept under the carpet but engaged in an open polemics, without regard for communal feelings, family ties, reputation, or the high social status of his opponents. Since the pattern of rabbinic apologetics established in the first half of the eighteenth century failed to eradicate Sabbatianism, and the conceptual tools employed in the battle against crypto-Sabbatians in Western Europe were not apt to engage their more outspoken brethren in Podolia, Emden abandoned the line of polemics exemplified by Hagiz and returned to the first major opponent of Sabbatai Tsevi, Rabbi Jacob Sasportas. He became the most important figure in the rabbinic campaign against the Frankists. Before analyzing his understanding of Sabbatianism, I shall discuss the practical side of his involvement in the Frankist affair.

The Contacts between the Council
of Four Lands and Rabbi Jacob Emden

Shortly after the Lanckoronie affair, Rabbi Jacob Emden was contacted by one of the most prominent members of the Jewish establishment in eighteenth-century Poland, Abraham ha-Kohen of Zamość, a district rabbi in Brześć and a rabbinic judge in Tarle. The extant sources first mention him in 1751; despite his relative youth, he already belonged to the inner circle of trustees (*ne'emanim*) of the Council of Four Lands and signed the council's approbation for the Amsterdam edition of the Talmud.[38] A year later, he became embroiled in the Emden-Eibeschütz controversy and denounced "the writer of the amulets,"[39] stating, nevertheless, that it could not be conclusively determined who this writer was.[40] In October 1753, when the council condemned the printing

and distribution of pamphlets related to the controversy and ordered the existing writings to be burned (which, in practice, meant burning mainly of the
writings of Emden), he signed the writ of condemnation together with other
Polish rabbis.[41] Nevertheless, Abraham of Zamość was apparently not actually
convinced of Eibeschütz's innocence. Two months later, he wrote a letter calling for the public condemnation of Sabbatians and qualified some writings
attributed to Eibeschütz as clearly heretical.[42]

In 1755, the victory of the Eibeschütz supporters seemed to be complete: Rabbi Jonathan collected letters of prominent scholars in his favor and
published them in Altona under the title *Luhot edut*. Within a few months,
Emden responded with his refutation, *Shevirat luhot ha-even*. The Council
of Four Lands' 1753 ban on publications pertaining to the Eibeschütz controversy was still in force; however, in contrast to earlier polemical works by
Emden, which all came from his private printing press in Altona, *Shevirat
luhot* was first printed in Żółkiew. The edition featured an approbation from
Abraham ha-Kohen of Zamość:[43] the open violation of the council's ban and
his endorsement of the publication of the book in Poland constituted an unequivocal signal of support for Emden. Abraham became a leader of the anti-
Eibeschütz faction among the rabbinic establishment in Poland.

The July–September 1756 sessions of the Council of Four Lands had two
main items on the agenda. The first one was the wave of blood libels—in
particular, the Jampol ritual murder trial, which had commenced in April of
the same year.[44] The second was the rise of Sabbatianism, culminating in its
repeated overt challenges to the authority of the rabbinate and in the involvement of the Catholic consistory of Kamieniec in the Lanckoronie affair. The
blood accusations will be discussed in detail in Chapter 4; for now, suffice it
to say that the council obviously spoke in one voice on this issue: in order to
counter the accusations, the delegates decided to send an emissary to Rome,
Elyakim ben Asher Zelig, and to seek an official papal condemnation of the
libel.

The matter of Sabbatianism was more complicated. As noted, during the
first part of the eighteenth century, the council avoided direct involvement
in the campaigns initiated by anti-Sabbatian activists. Throughout the early
1750s, the *parnas* (president) of the council, Abraham ben Hayyim of Lublin,
was a staunch Eibeschütz supporter and the major force behind the attempts
to quash the accusations against Rabbi Jonathan, which led to the burning of
Emden's pamphlets in 1753. However, during the 1756 sessions, Abraham
ha-Kohen of Zamość, Baruch me-Erets Yavan, and Isaac ben Meir of Biała[45]

managed to convince the *parnas* that Emden's writings did contain some true information (it is not clear if this referred to Eibeschütz himself or only to the cases of less prominent Sabbatians in Poland).[46] The former president of the council and a staunch rival of Abraham of Lublin, Abraham Yoski of Lissa, also threw his weight in favor of unequivocal and forceful action against the Sabbatians in Podolia: he agreed to disseminate anti-Sabbatian pamphlets among the rabbis and requested to be sent ten copies of each of Emden's polemical works, "for we cannot prevail if we do not have a weapon" against the heretics.[47]

In the summer of 1756, the competing factions of the Jewish establishment in Poland, which had so far been at odds over the matter of crypto-Sabbatianism and Rabbi Jonathan Eibeschütz, agreed upon a common policy against the open Sabbatians in Podolia. In late September, the Council of Four Lands confirmed the *herem* previously imposed in Brody and extended its validity to other communities.[48] Bans of excommunications were pronounced in the major Jewish centers of the region, including Lwów, Łuck, and Dubno.[49] While the wording of the bans repeated the more or less standardized texts of earlier excommunications, this time there seems to have been a concerted effort to put them into practice and to publicize the general condemnation of the Sabbatians. Toward the end of September, Abraham ha-Kohen of Zamość informed Emden that the president of the Council of Four Lands had ordered the bans to be printed and disseminated among all the Jewish communities of Poland.[50]

Concurrent with the July–September sessions of the Council of Four Lands, the investigation at the bishop of Kamieniec's consistory was gaining momentum. At the end of July, since the rabbis ignored the calls to appear at the gatherings of the tribunal, the body dispatched priests who were supposed to interview the Jews and gather evidence locally.[51] On 2 August, the Sabbatians submitted a Latin manifesto to the consistory detailing their position and attacking the Talmud and the "Talmudists." This manifesto contained an early version of the motions that were later put forward during the public disputation, which I shall discuss in the following chapter. The legal battle at the episcopal court raised the public profile of the Sabbatian controversy and embroiled the Jewish authorities in an unwanted—and potentially damaging—conflict with the bishop. Yet the involvement of the Catholic authorities was seen by some rabbis as the opportunity to eradicate Sabbatianism once and for all. On 28 September, the *shtadlan* Baruch me-Erets Yavan wrote to Emden: "The lords, bishops, and leaders of the righteous among the Gentiles already heard of the matter: the issue became of great significance and already reached the highest lord of their faith, the pope in the city of Rome. And also we will go ready armed before them[52] and will stand before the lords bishops here [in Poland] and will bring them to be burned [at the stake]."[53]

The idea that Christians should be asked to burn Sabbatians at the stake for inventing a new faith had previously appeared in a letter that Emden wrote to the Council of Four Lands in 1751:[54] Yavan was quoting Emden's own ideas to their author. Yavan's proposed solution was to pursue Christian involvement to the hilt and obtain a condemnation of the Sabbatians for heresy. The remark that the pope had been already informed seems to be an allusion to the hopes concerning Elyakim's trip to Rome. On 26 December 1756, Abraham ha-Kohen of Zamość wrote to Emden:

> And they wrote a manifesto against the Talmud. . . . There is certainly no way they can be brought back into the fold. Especially now, when they offered to the bishop to uproot [the faith of] Mount Sinai, the Temple, and God of Jacob . . . and we already gave money to the bishop and we pronounced upon them a *herem* . . . so the rest of Israel will not do as they do and will keep apart from them. And now we seek your advice, for we have no refuge except to obtain from the pope the writ of excommunication against this evil faith [*ha-emunah ha-ra-ah*]. So we here [Poland] and you there [Germany] should write to the [Jewish] leaders in Italy to make efforts toward this end.[55]

Since the priests of Kamieniec were already involved in the investigation concerning Sabbatianism, Abraham ha-Kohen of Zamość suggested that the rabbis should go straight to the highest authorities of the Catholic Church over the head of the local bishop. The fact that the Council of Four Lands was sending an emissary to Rome greatly helped to facilitate the matter in any case; indeed, in another section of the letter to Emden, Abraham explicitly confirmed that he had contacted Elyakim ben Asher Zelig on the issue of the Frankists.[56] Elyakim's primary mission was to acquire a writ against blood libels from the Holy See; his secondary objective was to obtain a papal condemnation of Sabbatianism.

Abraham ha-Kohen was an official of the Council of Four Lands, and Emden interpreted the remark "now we seek your advice" as a formal request on behalf of the council. In his autobiography, he later described how, in response to the request for assistance from the leaders of the Polish Jewry, he "advised that the abominations [of the Sabbatians] should be publicly exposed in print, and their evil be proved on the basis of Christian writings, for 'from the very forest itself comes the [handle of the] ax [that fells it].'"[57] He also mentioned that he had written an open letter to the council with the aim of "bridling the deceivers' tongues."

Such a letter was indeed written. It was composed sometime in the early months of 1757 and published for the first time as an appendix to Emden's edition of the midrash *Seder olam rabbah ve-zuta* (before July 1757). An expanded version appeared in *Sefer shimush* (1758–60). This expanded version was given the title *Resen mateh* (Bridle for the deceiver). The title is an allusion to the Hebrew translation of the New Testament's Epistle of James 1:26: "If anyone thinks himself to be religious and yet does not bridle his tongue but deceives his own heart, this man's religion is worthless." It is one of the most extraordinary documents spurred by the Frankist affair.

Emden's Letter to the Council of Four Lands

Even before Sabbatai's conversion to Islam, some rabbis expressed concern that the messianic enthusiasm that he had aroused would provide grist for the mills of Christian missionaries. Indeed, the Jews' naïveté in pinning their hopes on the "new impostor" immediately became a target of ridicule for anti-Jewish writers.[58] The fact that shortly thereafter "the messiah became a Turk" made things much worse: the story of Sabbatai's conversion was told and retold by Christians convinced that the obvious failure of yet another pseudo-messiah would finally pave the way for the Jewish acceptance of Jesus.

Sabbatian doctrines themselves offered Christian parallels as well. Many prominent Sabbatians, including the most important theologian of early Sabbatianism, Abraham Miguel Cardoso, were former Marranos who had been brought up as Christians and returned to Judaism only later in their lives. Cardoso's opponents promptly pointed out that many of his ideas were, in fact, elaborations of Christian concepts that he had acquired in his youth, garbed in Jewish terminology and ornamented with references to Jewish sources. Although Cardoso vehemently attacked Christianity, his Jewish adversaries argued that he never truly freed himself from his Christian upbringing and that his tracts supplied ammunition for the missionaries. The task of purging Judaism of heretical elements thus became closely intertwined with anti-Christian polemics, as rabbinic attacks on Sabbatianism routinely targeted the alleged and real links and parallels between Sabbatianism and Christianity.

Sasportas was the only one to pursue this issue to its ultimate theological conclusions; others worried mainly about the practical influences of Christians and Christian ideas upon Jews and Judaism. Emden accepted many of Sasportas's[59] theses and often employed the characteristic rhetoric of earlier anti-Sabbatians. Nevertheless, he departed from the previous anti-Sabbatian apologetics (of Sasportas and of other rabbis) in one crucial regard: he went to great lengths to break the link between anti-Sabbatian polemics and resistance to Christianity. The crux of the argument of his letter to Council of Four Lands was that, with regard to Sabbatianism, Jews and Christians were in the same boat.

Emden's letter to the leaders of the Council of Four Lands opened with praise for the rabbis of Poland, who had been divided on the issue of crypto-Sabbatianism, but after the Lanckoronie affair, they had finally taken a united and uncompromised stance against the heretics: they "excommunicated and cut off the mixed [multitude] from Israel, and gave their heretical writings to burning."[60]

The Podolian Sabbatians countered the excommunication, however, by telling the bishop and the Kamieniec clergy that the real reason for their persecution by the Jews was the similarity of the tenets of their belief to those of the Christianity: they portrayed themselves as representatives of a pristine version of Judaism who rejected the Talmud and accepted the Trinity and incarnation. By doing so, they immediately won the hearts of the Catholic clergy. Restoring the astrological symbolism of Saturn/Sabbatai (already discussed above in the context of Sasportas), Emden attributed the temporary advantage won by the Sabbatians and the support they had gained from Bishop Dembowski to the fact that the September 1756 consistory investigation took place at a time particularly propitious for the followers of Sabbatai: the autumnal equinox of that year fell on the hour ruled by the planet Saturn. However, continued Emden, astrology could not guarantee the victory of Sabbatians: even if Saturn stood like the sun in the middle of the sky, true Jews would reject the false prophets and triumph over heretics.[61]

The link between Sabbatianism and Christianity, seen so far in rabbinic attacks on Sabbatianism intended for an internal Jewish audience, immediately became a pressing theme of Jewish-Christian debate. The outer layer of Emden's writing provided Polish rabbis with handy arguments for confronting

Catholic theologians. If the priests challenged the council about the Frankists' claim that their belief was similar to Christianity or about their accusations against the Talmud, the rabbis would be able to argue on the basis of Christian writings that rabbinic Judaism had long been recognized by the Christians, while Sabbatianism—despite its apparent similarities with Christianity—actually contradicted the fundamentals of the Christian faith. Large parts of Emden's letter were thus written in the second person, directly addressing a Christian straw man and providing the potential Jewish disputant with useful quotations and lines of argument. As some priests might have been tempted to regard Sabbatianism as a "more progressive" version of Judaism entailing the abolishment of the "ceremonial law," Emden argued that Christianity's own principles demanded something very different:

> And it is known that also the Nazarene and his disciples, especially Paul, warned that all those circumcised are bound to keep the entire Torah of the Israelites. And you, the Christians, should accept this teaching and not the teachings of the new false messiah Sabbatai Tsevi. For truly, the Gospels do not permit the Jew to forsake the Torah. As Paul said in the Epistle to Galatians 5:3, "I testify again to every man who accepts circumcision that he is obligated to keep the whole law" and in the First Epistle to Corinthians 7:18, "Was anyone at the time of his call already circumcised? Let him not seek to remove the marks of circumcision. Was anyone at the time of his call uncircumcised? Let him not seek circumcision." And the Acts of Apostles 16:1 also mentioned that he circumcised his disciple Timothy. And they [Christian theologians] did not know how to interpret it, because this act contradicted his own statement that circumcision is a temporary commandment that will be abolished in the times of the messiah, and this happened in the times of the Nazarene. But from this, we know that the Nazarene and his apostles did not come to abolish the Torah of Israel. It is written in Matthew 10:17–18,[62] "Do not think that I have come to abolish the Law or the Prophets; I have not come to abolish them but to fulfill them. For truly, I say to you, until heaven and earth pass away, not an iota, not a dot, will pass from the Law until all is accomplished." And the episode with Timothy proves that, as he was the son of a Jewish woman and a Greek man, and Paul, who was a learned man and a disciple of Rabban Gamaliel the Elder, knew that the son of

a Jewish woman and a non-Jew is a Jew and therefore he should be circumcised and observe all the commandments.[63]

In Emden's view, the involvement of the Catholic authorities in the Lanckoronie affair was almost providential. Publicizing the deeds of the Sabbatians forced the hand of the rabbis and provided an incentive for using the Gentiles to quash the movement. While it put the Jewish community in temporary danger stemming from the Christian interference in an internal Jewish matter, it also opened an avenue for the ultimate eradication of Sabbatianism. What was needed was to demonstrate that, whereas rabbinic Judaism was legitimate according to Christian categories, Sabbatianism constituted a dangerous and heretical religious novelty: it not only contradicted strict Jewish precepts, but the teachings of the Church as well. Sabbatians were heretics, and Jewish heretics should be treated exactly the same way that the Church treated their Christian counterparts.

According to Emden, if the Christians became convinced that the self-proclaimed pro-Christian Jews deviated from the accepted forms of normative religiosity, "they would condemn them to burning, for they created a new faith that should not be allowed to be professed openly anywhere, even in the free countries where all old faiths are allowed, as it is the case in Muslim countries, or in Holland, or in England: nowhere is it allowed to invent a new faith."[64] As I mentioned in the previous section, Emden floated the idea of having the Christians burn the Sabbatians at the stake as early as 1751; at that time, however, no one took him seriously. This time, leaders of the Polish Jewry were more receptive to his suggestions. Emden argued that the rabbis were not only permitted, but obliged, to demand that the authorities burn the Sabbatians as heretics; it was hoped that, he remarked, "they soon will be burned on the order of the pope of Rome."[65]

Emden's argument had a deeper stratum, however. Besides providing the council with quotations from the Gospels and lines of reasoning for possible debate with priests, or even in addition to suggesting the general opportunistic strategy of having Sabbatianism eradicated by Christians, Emden wanted to convince the rabbis that the Christians should and could be their true allies in the fight against the Sabbatians. Whereas some fragments of the letter purported to defend Judaism from Christian charges and to demonstrate the legitimacy of the Jewish religion on the basis of Christian writings, others amounted to an apology for Christianity addressed to the Jews. For Emden, the advent of Sabbatianism fundamentally changed the relationship between

Judaism and Christianity: the Sabbatian movement constituted a common enemy, in the face of which erstwhile quarrels between Jews and Christians should immediately be set aside. The Christian should accept the validity of Judaism within the theological framework of his religion, while the Jew should understand that there was no real contradiction between Judaism and Christianity and that the mutual animosities stemmed from a series of misunderstandings: some Christian theologians misinterpreted the Gospels, claiming that Jesus called for abolishing the Torah of Moses, whereas "crazy people among the Jews who do not know left from right nor do they understand the Written or Oral Torah"[66] came to believe that Christianity was a bastardized, idolatrous faith.

The eradication of Sabbatianism required breaking the connection that the rabbis made between Sabbatianism and Christianity and concomitantly changing the stereotype of Christianity among the Jewish elite. Many arguments ostensibly aimed at Christians who disparaged Judaism were, in fact, aimed at the Jews, who mistook the existing Christian disparagement of Judaism for the true essence of Christianity:

> And the writers of the Gospels did not claim that the Nazarene
> came to abolish the Jewish faith. Rather, he came to establish a faith
> for the Gentiles from that day onward. And even this faith was not
> new, but old: it was [based on] the Seven Noahide Commandments
> that had been forgotten and reinstated by the apostles. . . . And so
> Paul wrote in Chapter 5 of his Epistle to the Corinthians that every-
> one should remain in his own faith.[67] . . . And so the Nazarene did
> double kindness to the world: on the one hand he sustained with
> all his powers the Torah of Moses . . . and on the other he reminded
> the Gentiles about the Seven Commandments.[68]

In rabbinic tradition, the Seven Commandments of the covenant between God and Noah (the prohibitions against idolatry, blasphemy, bloodshed, incest, theft, eating of flesh torn from a living animal, as well as the injunction to establish a legal system)[69] were considered the minimal moral standards enjoined by the Bible upon all mankind. In the Middle Ages, Jewish thinkers universally maintained that the strictly monotheistic religion of Islam was in accord with the Noahide laws, while the status of Christianity was subject to debate; some rabbis argued that it violated the prohibition of idolatry. From the sixteenth century onward, it became more and more common to exclude

Christians from the category of idolaters and therefore to consider the Christian religion, too, as compatible with the Seven Commandments.[70]

Yet Emden went much further than his predecessors. Not only did he claim that Christian doctrines were congruent with the Noahide Commandments; he also argued that the very essence of Jesus and the apostles' mission was to establish a faith based on Noahidism for pagans. In his commentary on *Pirke avot* (published in 1751), Emden had already stated that the "assembly" (a pun on the Hebrew word *knesi'ah*, which means "assembly" but also "the Church") of the contemporary peoples could be adequately termed an "assembly for the sake of heaven" (*knesi'ah le-shem shamayyim*): its aim was to spread monotheism among "those who otherwise worshiped wood and stone, did not believe in the reward in afterlife, and had no idea of good and evil."[71] In the letter to the Council of Four Lands, he advanced the same argument. The main line of division did not lie here between Jews and Christians (or, more broadly, non-Jews) but between members of legitimate religious groups on the one hand and heretics on the other. From this perspective, Sabbatianism was a kind of universal heresy, denying general human moral principles and embodying the idea of reversion to paganism or even—along the lines of the mythology of the mixed multitude—the primeval "waste and void" and immorality that preceded God's covenant with Noah: "O generation![72] Jews, Christians, and Muslims! The chief peoples, who uphold the fundamentals of the Torah of Moses and facilitate their proliferation in the world! Open your eyes and see . . . that there is no worse sect than the sect of Sabbatai Tsevi. . . . They are worse than all the ancient idolaters . . ., worse even than the generation of the Flood . . ., for they want to turn the world back to the state of waste and void [*tohu va-vohu*] . . . and they call good evil and evil they call good, they call light darkness and the sweet they call bitter. And such things are called heresy [*minut*]."[73]

To the Jews, Rabbi Jacob Sasportas had argued that for their faith, the nascent Sabbatian movement constituted a danger akin to that of early Christianity rising around Jesus and the apostles: he had viewed both Sabbatianism and Christianity as new, cancerous growths on the body of Judaism. Emden accepted Sasportas's idea that Sabbatianism was a new (and hence illegitimate and dangerous) faith but claimed that, from the Jewish perspective, Christianity had *never* been a new religion: early Christianity was not an illicit sectarian offshoot of Judaism; rather, Judaism and Christianity stemmed from the same roots and were equally legitimate, since they were intended for different people. Thus, in Emden's view, Christianity and Islam were elaborations of the fundamental Mosaic revelation, parallel to Judaism and sharing Judaism's moral principles and its redemptive goal.

Rabbi Jacob Emden's letter to the Council of Four Lands elicited substantial scholarly discussion. Jewish as well as Christian scholars were amazed by the rabbi's great familiarity with Christian texts, for in his account of Christianity, he did not use Jewish sources but went directly to the text of the New Testament.[74] The extensive citations from the Gospels and the Epistles of Paul drew special attention. While there existed several Hebrew translations of Christian Scriptures, Emden's renderings seemed original, and his consistent usage of Latinized personal names and titles of the books of the New Testament would suggest that he relied on a Latin or German text.

Some argued that the quotations might have been translated into Hebrew by Emden himself.[75] Such a possibility cannot be dismissed out of hand: there is no doubt that Emden knew some German, Dutch, and Latin and read numerous books in these languages in order—as he put it—to "know the views of different peoples in matters concerning their religions and customs and to understand their ideas about us and our holy faith."[76] It is entirely feasible that he had some firsthand knowledge of the New Testament. Nevertheless, it is clear that his command of foreign languages was superficial,[77] and it is unlikely that he would have been able to undertake a sophisticated exegesis of the Gospels solely on the basis of his own study.

I submit that Emden's ostensibly unmediated account of the New Testament's theology was based on an earlier Jewish source, a little-known manuscript titled *Hoda'at ba'al din*.[78] The work was supposedly written in 1430 by David Nasi of Candia, brother of the duke of Naxos, Joseph Nasi, and a factor in the service of Cardinal Francisco Bentivoglio. According to David, the cardinal became convinced of the falsity of his Christian belief through independent philosophical investigations and undertook to ponder the truth of Judaism. He therefore asked, in great secrecy, to be supplied with Jewish anti-Christian works. David Nasi lent the cardinal several polemical books and composed a short tract, *Hoda'at ba'al din*, for him. The title ("admission of the litigant") alludes to the talmudic principle according to which the admission of guilt by a person charged with crime takes precedence over witnesses' testimonies.[79] In this case, the principle metaphorically referred to the writers of the New Testament: the tract aimed to demonstrate that the authors of the Gospels and the Epistles unwittingly affirmed the principles of Judaism and contradicted the dogmas of Christianity.

The impact and reception of *Hoda'at ba'al din* have not been studied. It is certain that in the mid-eighteenth century, a copy existed in Amsterdam. It belonged to the treasurer of the Sephardic community, David Franco Mendes; Mendes had numerous contacts with Emden's father, Hakham Tsevi Ashkenazi, and might have had contacts with Emden as well.[80] Another manuscript might even have belonged to Emden himself.[81] In his letter to the Council of Four Lands, Emden drew heavily upon *Hoda'at ba'al din*: the titles of the books of the New Testament and personal names have the same or very similar Hebrew forms in *Hoda'at ba'al din* and in Emden's letter;[82] the Hebrew translations of excerpts from the Gospels and the Epistles quoted in the latter exactly reproduce or closely paraphrase those in the former;[83] and Emden's entire argument that baptism did not seek to replace circumcision is structured along the lines of *Hoda'at ba'al din*.[84] Moreover, the central thesis that Jesus and the Apostles never intended to abolish the Torah of Moses but wanted to perpetuate the fulfillment of the commandments of Judaism derives from the same source.[85]

The strategy of demonstrating the internal contradictions and incoherency of Christianity on the basis of the New Testament had antecedents in Jewish apologetics.[86] Nevertheless, using the Gospel as a prooftext for the truth of Judaism was highly original, and possibly entirely unprecedented. In his forthcoming study, Hayyim Hames argues that *Hoda'at ba'al din* might be an eighteenth-century pseudepigraphic composition: neither of the names "David Nasi" or "Cardinal Bentivoglio" appear in any other source, and neither personality ever existed; the earliest extant manuscripts date from the eighteenth century; and there is no mention of the work in other medieval Jewish polemical tracts.[87]

If Hames's conjectures are correct, *Hoda'at ba'al din* was composed not in the context of medieval Jewish-Christian polemics, but against the backdrop of the internal Jewish debate on Christianity spurred by Sabbatianism. The rise of Sabbatianism highlighted the need to make a clear distinction between the two religions, and this was the main aim of *Hoda'at ba'al din*. The work's central argument is that, since all major Jewish articles of faith are already present in the New Testament, conversion is an act of folly, and this, too, might be anti-Sabbatian in nature.

Despite its anti-Christian thrust, *Hoda'at ba'al din* legitimized Christian Scriptures in a way absent in earlier Jewish sources.[88] The same is true of Emden's letter to the Council of Four Lands: Jewish and Christian academics have marveled at the rabbi's "open-minded" or even "ecumenical" views of Christianity and other monotheistic religions. Emden has been portrayed as an "orthodox champion of religious tolerance," "enlightened traditionalist" interested in comparative religion, or "rabbinic zealot" preaching openness to outsiders and their beliefs. However, this scholarly praise mostly missed the polemical context in which the letter was written (indeed, the existing translations of the excerpts from the letter into English and German conveniently left out most of the fragments devoted to Sabbatianism).[89] Emden's aim was not to eulogize Jesus and the Christians but to combat Jewish sectarianism.

To be sure, the rabbi himself emphasized that his sympathetic views of Christianity were not empty flattery but a consistent theological position, which he developed and expressed also in other—non-polemical—works.[90] Nonetheless, it must be pointed out that his pro-Christian ideas took their shape in the context of a ferocious battle against internal Jewish heresy. To my mind, the real (if implicit) theme of Emden's letter was not a tribute to the common Jewish and Christian values but the issue of religious legitimacy versus religious deviance. Legitimate religions such as Judaism and Christianity (and Islam) were juxtaposed with and set against sectarian and heretical religious formations. In Emden, the concept of heresy acquired a trans-confessional character and became the epitome of opposition to any legitimate religiosity, be it Jewish or not. Indeed, the author of the letter to the council did praise the Christian religion. Yet he praised Christianity not qua Christianity, but Christianity as opposed to Sabbatianism.

For Emden, Christianity was a legitimate, true, and even noble religion, which—on the basis of its own theological tenets—should recognize Judaism's legitimacy, truth, and nobility. What this meant in practice was the acknowledgment of Judaism's total separateness. Judaism and Christianity were *parallel* paths to redemption: they did not intersect and should not attempt to do so. Jews and Christians should respect each other, but they had nothing substantial to offer each other. According to Emden, Jesus' intention was to reinstate the Noahide Commandments, thereby creating a sustainable moral creed for Gentiles; the founder of Christianity had no message for his contemporary Jews, and Emden's contemporary Jews had nothing to look for in their contemporary Christian religion.

It is no coincidence that Emden's account of Christianity drew so deeply on the Scriptures rather than on the works of later theologians or his own firsthand experience. Tolerant and open-minded as it was, this vision of Christianity was that of its early canonical texts, not of what he saw through his window: Emden had little to say about the Christianity of his own day but referred solely to the rather abstract and idealized vision of Christianity at the time of its inception. Despite the enlightened phraseology, the argument aimed at maintaining or even increasing the distance between the two religions; Emden wanted to preserve a utopian status quo, in which Jews and Christians deeply respected each other, but never met.

The letter to the Council of Four Lands depicted the ideal scheme of things, in which the two legitimate religious establishments—the rabbis and the priests—recognized each other's legitimacy without making attempts to interfere with each other's business or to proselytize in any way. Jew and Christian were to join in condemnation of Jewish and Christian heretics. What is really striking in Emden's letter is not his explicitly tolerant view of Christianity but his implicit understanding of Judaism. The true novelty of Emden's position did not lie in the view that Christianity was based on the Noahide Commandments (which, by the mid-eighteenth century, had been generally accepted among the rabbis, though most of them based their argumentation on the Talmud rather than the Gospels).

The true novelty was the idea that the theological and practical boundaries of Judaism could and should be unequivocally demarcated once and for all. What Emden proposed was a hard ontology of Judaism: the Jewish religion was eternal and immutable, like a Platonic idea; it had clearly defined boundaries, centralized structure, and well-defined dogmas. I believe that Emden imagined his ideal Judaism in clear—though probably unconscious—analogy to the Catholic theologians' ideal vision of Christianity. In the rabbis, he saw a professional clerical caste, hierarchically organized, uniformly trained and disciplined, and controlling the minds and bodies of the wider Jewish community. In the *herem*, he saw not a localized and limited tool of social control employed within a specific community but a kind of universal ban of excommunication, condemning the excommunicated to eternal punishment and having validity everywhere and for everyone. In religious dissenters, he saw "heretics" who should be burned at the stake. He saw the Jewish religion as a set of systematic and systematized doctrines incumbent upon every Jew and believed that one could abandon Judaism not only by a formal conversion to another religion but through lack of correct understanding of theological tenets: a Jew who deviated from the right path was no longer a Jew in the proper sense of the term. He belonged to another religion entirely.

As Judaism had always been a religion without clearly defined dogmas and lacking centralized religious authority, earlier rabbinic attacks on heresy were proscriptive rather than analytical. No attempt had been made to establish a contrastive taxonomy of different heretical positions or to demarcate unequivocally what distinguished one "sect" from another. Names of ancient groups, such as Sadducees or Boethusians, were routinely used to designate modern-day heretics; terms such as Karaism were utilized as a generic synonym for sectarianism. Pre-Emden rabbinic polemics against the followers of Sabbatai Tsevi habitually conflated Sabbatianism with other Jewish sects of the past and systematically obfuscated differences among various heretical groups.[91]

Emden deeply internalized the Christian understanding of heresy as theological error and became a kind of Jewish Irenaeus or Hippolytus: a chief heresiologist. Such an understanding of heresy has no meaning if it is not relativized to some orthodoxy: a clear definition of deviance demands an equally clear definition of the normative. Following the studies of Jacob Katz, Jewish historians have been reluctant to use the word "orthodox" in discussions of phenomena preceding the advent of Orthodox Judaism in nineteenth-century Germany. However, it should be noted that the term "orthodoxy" was already used in the 1750s by the Lutheran scholar Friedrich David Megerlin specifically to describe Emden's position in his controversy with Eibeschütz.[92] Emden was orthodox in the sense that he saw his version of Judaism as the only natural and true point of reference for all other versions of Judaism, which he considered inherently inferior, heretical, and deviant. This, in turn, made sense only within the framework of an organized church: it is little surprise that Emden's vision of Judaism so resembled that of the Church and that his rabbis were so like the priests.

Emden brought into play the half-forgotten anti-Sabbatian apologetics of Sasportas and neglected anti-Christian works such as *Hoda'at ba'al din*. He then turned both on their heads. He accepted Sasportas's idea of Sabbatianism being a new religion but used it as an argument for establishing a common front with Christianity. He employed *Hoda'at ba'al din*'s notion that Jewish principles were expounded in the Gospels but argued that this only proved the legitimacy of the Church in Jewish eyes. Like Sasportas, Emden believed that Sabbatianism was not Judaism and argued that the Sabbatians were descendants of the *erev rav*: they were ostensibly Jewish but, in fact, did not belong to the people of Israel.[93]

After Sasportas in the mid-seventeenth century, no other opponent of Sabbatianism took up this line of argumentation; as Sid Leiman has noted, during the first stages of polemics against Eibeschütz in the early 1750s, Emden "was a loose cannon, if not worse."[94] Yet, thanks to the mediation of Abraham of Zamość and others, Emden's highly radical (and highly original) perspective on Sabbatianism was accepted by the Council of Four Lands in their dealings with case of the Frankists. At the end of 1756 Emden became what he had dreamed of becoming but had never managed to achieve in his campaign against Eibeschütz: the mind behind the anti-heretical policy of the most powerful body in world Jewry.

Chapter 3

Where Does Frankism Fit In?

The Contra-Talmudists

Emden's strategy of involving the Christians in the campaign against the Sabbatians was designed to appeal to the sentiments of the priests. The mid-eighteenth-century Polish Church, determined to wage an intense battle against the religious dissent among the country's Christian population, could be expected to be sympathetic to an anti-heretical case. In approaching Bishop Dembowski, the rabbis counted on his concern for established religious authority. For the Sabbatians, a natural response to this strategy was to resort to the prevalent Christian stereotype of "rabbinism" as an empty shell of legalistic casuistry and present their version of Judaism as more spiritual and based on direct divine inspiration of a mystical type. The battle lines were thus drawn: in their contacts with the Catholic clergy, the Sabbatians would play on the Church's view of Jewish religion as "letter" without "spirit," "law" without "grace" (and would even use this latter notion), while the rabbis would appeal to the priests' distrust of "enthusiasm" and of private revelations *extra ecclesiam*. Various understandings of the fundamental nature of what was gradually becoming a mass religious movement forming around Frank were formulated, put forward, and tested against one another during the ongoing debate. Podolian Sabbatians, the Jewish authorities, and the bishop and his aides all tried to fit the developing events into their respective visions of history, redemption, and society; what we know today as Frankism emerged as a product of the clash of ideas, contradictory strategies, interests, and commitments of these groups.

As discussed in Chapter 1, after the public violation of the Fast of Esther in Kopczyńce and the hearing in Dembowski's court in late March 1756,

Frank left the Commonwealth and headed home to Salonika (according to a Polish source, those arrested in Kopczyńce were set free on condition that they would disperse to their homes).[1] He was not directly involved in the developments that took place in the Kamieniec diocese in 1756–57, and it is unclear what influence he did have on the course of events. Later Frankist sources imply that he did not authorize actions of the Sabbatian party in Kamieniec. He seems to have lost some authority: during Frank's sojourn in Turkey, Yehudah Leyb Krysa assumed the leadership of the group in Podolia and was probably responsible for the strategy developed in the contacts with the bishop.[2] However, the Jesuit Konstanty Awedyk claimed that Frank was constantly pulling strings behind the scenes and that upon leaving Poland, he told his followers to present themselves as adherents to two main tenets: a belief "in the Holy Trinity, that is, in One God in three persons" and the rejection of "the Talmud as full of errors and blasphemies."[3] While Awedyk's description of Frank's role is probably an *ex post* embellishment (his book was published in 1760, when Frank had firmly established his leadership over those Podolian Sabbatians, who were Christians by then), the description of the subject of debate is accurate.

On 2 August 1756, a manifesto was submitted to the Kamieniec consistory. Twenty-one named Sabbatians from Jezierzany, Kopczyńce, Nadworna, Busk, Zbrzezie, Rohatyn, Satanów, and Lanckoronie claimed to speak on behalf of Jews in other countries who held similar beliefs. They asserted that, upon lengthy consideration, they had concluded that the Talmud was blasphemous and contrary to reason and God's commandments. The signatories complained to the authorities that because of their anti-talmudic position, they had been persecuted, excommunicated, expelled, and falsely accused by their enemies, the "teachers and advocates of the Talmud." They demanded that the Talmud should be rejected and consigned to the flames and stated their intention to "declare to the entire world" the principles of their faith, which they proclaimed themselves to prove true in a public disputation. Their principles were:

1. We believe in everything that was taught and commanded by God in the Old Testament.
2. The Holy Scriptures cannot be comprehended by human reason without the assistance of Divine Grace.
3. The Talmud is full of scandalous blasphemies against God and should be rejected.

4. There is One God who created everything.
5. This God is in Three Persons, indivisible as to their nature.
6. God can take a human body upon Himself and be subject to all passions except for sin.
7. In accordance with the prophecies, the city of Jerusalem will not be rebuilt until the end of time.
8. The messiah promised in the Old Testament will not come again.
9. God Himself will remove the sin of the First Parents. This God is the true messiah, incarnate.[4]

The manifesto was presented in Latin and signed with the full Hebrew names of its proponents. The Latin translation from Hebrew was executed by one of the most interesting characters in the early phase of Frankism, the Polish nobleman Antoni Kossakowski, called Moliwda (1718–86).[5] Antoni grew up in the house of Dominik Kossakowski, father of the future bishop of Livonia and a member of the Targowica Confederation, Józef Kossakowski. Having secretly married "a peasant, daughter of a local mill man,"[6] he fled his family's wrath to Russia, where he became an "elder" of the Greek Orthodox sect of Philipovtsy (a radical branch of the schismatic Old Believers). Later, he claimed that "under the name Moliwda, he ruled one of the Greek islands"[7] and reportedly spent time in one of the monasteries on Mount Athos.[8] Contemporaries marveled at his mastery of oriental languages including Turkish, Tatar, Hebrew, and Aramaic, as well as his "profound knowledge of the Scriptures and Holy Fathers."[9]

The Philipovtsy had numerous contacts with the Jews; in Poland, their faith was considered so close to Judaism that some members of the Polish nobility wanted them to pay the Jewish poll tax.[10] Moliwda met Frank somewhere in the Balkans and saw in him a chance for a return to Poland. His exact role in the formulation of the Frankist manifestos and points for the disputations is a matter of conjecture, but it is certain that he was one of the most important sources of information on the selected Christian concepts that helped construct the Frankist teachings.[11]

Awedyk would have us believe that Frank was himself responsible for the formulation of the main points of the August 1756 manifesto. This seems unlikely: the anti-talmudic intent of the document had not appeared in earlier Sabbatian polemics, and it did not stem organically from any Sabbatian doctrines. The account of Ber of Bolechów, according to which this anti-talmudic element was the personal contribution of Bishop Dembowski, is more convincing. According to Ber, the Sabbatians told the bishop how they had been pursued by the rabbinate; they requested a formal edict granting them rights to establish an autonomous community, to engage in the same trades that other Jews engage in, and to be exempt from the jurisdiction of the rabbinate. The bishop responded: "We cannot set you apart and distinct from the whole community of Israel until you demonstrate that the statements of the Talmud are false and contain lies. Then you will be released from the [obligations] of the Talmud according to a verdict we will issue. And if you demonstrate the Talmud's hostility toward the Christian faith, it will be possible to condemn it for burning, and you will easily obtain a royal writ of privileges."[12]

Since the Jewish religion had in Poland the status of a recognized faith, *religio licta*, Dembowski (or the Frankists) could not launch a frontal attack on Judaism as such. They could, however, invert the strategy employed by the *bet din* of Satanów and condemn a particular form of Judaism for its alleged deviation from its own principles. Defining the target of polemics as "Talmudism" was a clever move: although formally the Sabbatians undermined only one text of a broader canon, for most Jews such a challenge would be tantamount to an attack on the very substance of their religion. Accordingly, Sabbatian tenets were presented as based solely on the text of the Pentateuch. Ber Birkenthal stated that at that critical juncture, "the Christians started to call [the Sabbatians] Contra-Talmudists."[13] Others maintain that the Frankists themselves "stopped calling themselves believers in Sabbatai Tsevi and started to call themselves Contra-Talmudists."[14] Whoever was behind the new denomination of the group, the intention was to adapt the Frankist case to the broader framework of the Catholic polemics against the Talmud.

The canon law principles giving the Church authority to defend Judaism against internal heresy, which I discussed in Chapter 1, were commonly employed by the priests in their polemics against the Talmud: in his argument that the pope may punish Jews for inventing heresies against their own religion, Innocent IV explicitly stated that this was the basis for his order to burn the Talmud.[15] The anti-talmudic thread appeared also in Christian documents concerning the Frankists: the initial justification of the Kamieniec consistory court's jurisdiction over the Jews arrested in Lanckoronie already contained a reference to Clement VIII's bull *Cum Hebraeorum malitia incipiente* (1569), forbidding the reading of the Talmud and condemning it to be burned.[16]

In February 1756, this reference might have been included without giving the matter deeper thought or intention. By August of the same year, it became a crucial element of a deliberate strategy: "anti-Talmudism" became the focal point of the Frankist case, and Sabbatianism came to be presented in Christian sources as a branch of Judaism closer to its original biblical form than was the Judaism of the rabbis. Suddenly, the tables were turned: Jewish leaders who had tried to denounce the heresy of Sabbatianism to the Christian authorities found themselves vulnerable to the Christian accusation of heresy because of their talmudic belief. The definition of Sabbatians as contra-talmudic Jews invited, of course, an analogy to the Karaites.

The Karaite schism emerged around the middle of the ninth century in Babylonia and Persia and defined itself as an opposition to the postbiblical rabbinic tradition. As a matter of principle, the Karaites held the Hebrew Bible as the one and only foundation of Judaism and maintained that all tenets of belief and conduct must derive directly from the literally interpreted Scriptures. The fundamental disagreement between the Karaites and other Jews (called the "Rabbanites" for the purpose of polemics) over the authority of the postbiblical oral tradition as embodied in the Talmud led to heated dispute and the development of a substantial apologetic and polemical literature on both sides. Karaism spread among the Jews in Egypt, North Africa, and the Land of Israel, as well as in the hotbed of the schism, Persia and Babylonia. By the thirteenth century, however, the movement had decayed and the intellectual debate had essentially been won by the anti-Karaite rabbis: while Karaite communities continued to exist in the Orient, they were no longer treated by the Rabbanites as a serious threat to their hegemony.

The Karaites never managed to establish a foothold in the Western world, and for medieval European rabbis, they remained a subject of a (quite limited) scholarly curiosity rather than actual polemics. However, despite the absence of actual Karaites in Christian Western Europe, from the early seventeenth century onward the appellation "Karaite" began to appear in rabbinic works attacking contemporary dissenters who sought to subvert the authority of the rabbinate and reject the rabbinic tradition. Shalom Rosenberg, the first scholar to discuss the issue, maintained that this new rabbinic anti-Karaism was a "purely literary" extension of the medieval polemic: when the seventeenth- and eighteenth-century rabbis spoke about the Karaites, "they refer[red] strictly to contemporaries who have arrived at conclusions which resemble those of the Karaites, but who owe[d] no actual intellectual debt to the Karaites."[17]

Other scholars have interpreted the phenomenon differently. In 1712, the Sephardic board of elders of Amsterdam excommunicated three local Jews for "following the sect of [the] Karaites and act[ing] as they do, entirely denying the Oral Law."[18] Yosef Kaplan, who analyzed the case in great detail, has argued that the "Karaism" of a few Amsterdam Jews was "nourished by growing interests [in the sect] among the Hebraists of Protestant Europe," among whom the idealized Karaites came to represent "the original, pure Judaism, before it was infected with the superstitions of the Talmud and the kabbalah."[19] According to Kaplan, the self-proclaimed Amsterdam Karaites did have a connection to actual Karaites, but this connection was indirect, mediated by Christian accounts of Karaism. In the context of the confessional cleavage between the Protestants and the Catholics, the very existence of a Jewish group that advocated the return to the uncorrupted text of the Bible naturally provoked interest.

Protestant scholars promptly interpreted Karaism as a Jewish embodiment of the *sola Scriptura* principle and thus an external confirmation of the Protestant rejection of papist distortions and corruptions of the original biblical message. Yet even Catholic scholars tended to view the Karaites with sympathy, emphasizing their rationalism and the rejection of rabbinic "fantasies and aberrations."[20] On the basis of such accounts, some dissenting members of the Amsterdam Sephardic community took upon themselves the garb of Karaites, viewing them as a "positive reference group"[21] and adopting the Christian ideal picture of Karaism.[22] According to Kaplan, while the image of Karaism expounded by the Amsterdam Sephardim was based on literary accounts, their "heresy" was a concrete "attempt to free themselves from the yoke of traditional Judaism and form a new kind of Judaism in keeping with their spiritual desires."[23]

The movement of the Amsterdam "Karaites" was an abortive one: the idealized Karaism never became an organized religious movement. In the Polish context, however, the Karaites were more than just a "positive reference group" for contemporary Jewish dissenters. The Polish-Lithuanian Commonwealth boasted the only sizable Karaite group in the Christian world. At the end of the fourteenth century, Grand Duke Witold of Lithuania granted right of residence in Troki (near Vilna) to a group of Karaite families arriving from Crimea; by the fifteenth century, Karaite settlements existed in Troki, Łuck, and Halicz. The Karaites were treated as Jews by the state authorities and paid their poll tax through existing Jewish institutions, such as the rabbinic council of the Duchy of Lithuania.[24] In places where they lived alongside the Rabbanites, the two communities often shared cemeteries and bathhouses,[25] and, in some cases, they also initiated litigation in common rabbinic courts.[26] Intermarriages between Rabbanites and Karaites were very infrequent, but a few cases are known to have occurred.[27] There were even cases of individuals moving from one community to the other.[28] Both groups were often embroiled in bitter economic competition, protected their boundaries against the other, and sometimes expressed mutual derision in proverbs and folktales. Nevertheless, they saw each other as two branches of a single Jewry.

For Polish rabbis, the Commonwealth's Karaites never became the subject of religious polemic. In addressing them in official writings, the Rabbanites of Poland-Lithuania used the expression *anshe britenu ha-yekarim*, "dear people of our covenant";[29] in internal documents, they usually spoke simply of "the Karaite congregation," *edat ha-karaim*,[30] without adding any positive epithets but also without dysphemisms habitually added by their Western counterparts. The Karaite leaders, in turn, addressed the rabbis as *ahenu* (our brethren).[31] The Christian authorities also acknowledged the legal equality of Rabbanites and Karaites, sometimes emphasizing that the Crown's grant of general privileges to the Jews included both communities.[32] The multiethnic, multireligious corporative structure of the Polish-Lithuanian Commonwealth provided a framework for treating the Karaites as another legitimate Jewish denomination. In contrast to other Christian countries, which officially acknowledged only one Jewish religion, the legal system of the Commonwealth explicitly allowed for the existence and free practice of Karaism as an alternative form of Judaism. The concept of rite, used in Poland to define the official status of Greek Catholics and Catholic Armenians (that is, recognized non-Roman denominations of Catholicism), was employed in delineating the status of the Karaites (that is, a recognized non-talmudic denomination of Judaism) as well: for instance, King Władysław IV guaranteed the freedom of confession to *Judaeorum Trociensum rithus Karaimici*.[33]

There is no evidence of any direct contact between the Frankists and the Karaites. However, defining the Sabbatians as anti-talmudic Jews who—on the basis of royal privileges—demanded equal rights with other Jews was clearly a strategy aimed at deploying the Karaite precedent as a legal framework to govern the case of the Frankists. The Karaites enjoyed the same rights as the Rabbanites and shared some communal institutions, but in matters of faith and ritual were practically autonomous. Since the legal system of the Commonwealth had already recognized two legitimate independent Jewish rites, there was no prima facie reason that it could not recognize Sabbatianism as a third, or, alternatively, simply subsume the Sabbatians and the Karaites under a wider rubric of "contra-talmudic Jews." Christian sources explicitly mentioned such a possibility; some later accounts even used the term "Karaite" when talking about Frank and his followers. Thus, the first dispatch of the papal nuncio in Warsaw concerning the Frankists defined the group as "the Jews of other religions, called Karaites [*gli ebrei di varie religioni, detti caraiti*],"[34] while Father Stanisław Mikulski, the administrator *sede vacante* of the Lwów archdiocese after the death of Bishop Wyżycki, described the Frankists as the "Karaites," whom he characterized as "the Contra-Talmudists confessing the Trinity, Incarnation, and other dogmas of the [Christian] faith [*Caraitarum nomine . . . non aliter interpretor, nisi Contratalmudistas profitentes Trinitatem, Incarnationem, et alia dogmata fidei*]."[35]

The Kamieniec Disputation[36]

The first hearing at the Kamieniec consistory in *materia perfidiae Iudaica* took place on 4 September 1756.[37] This time, it was the Frankists who acted as plaintiffs against the "synagogues of the Kamieniec diocese." They argued that the charges of immoral conduct in Lanckoronie constituted slander, and the subsequent excommunications were motivated by the desire to brand legitimate opponents of rabbinic Judaism as heretics: according to the Sabbatians, the real reason for the Council of Four Lands' campaign against them was their rejection of the Talmud and the proximity of their position to some of the tenets of Christianity. They also demanded a written response to their manifesto. On 17 October, Bishop Dembowski sent a pastoral letter to the Jewish leaders of his diocese, commanding that the rabbis come to Kamieniec in person and provide answers regarding the earlier bans of excommunication and the motions presented in the manifesto.

The rabbis failed to appear. Instead they sent a *shtadlan*, Simon Herszkowicz, who referred to the privileges of religious and judicial autonomy granted to the Jews by Polish kings, challenged the consistory court's authority to rule on a case involving Jews and Judaism, and demanded the postponement of the proceedings until the issue of jurisdiction was resolved.[38] He also argued that the rabbis needed time to prepare answers to a manifesto in Latin. Dembowski rejected Herszkowicz's arguments challenging his jurisdiction (stating that the Jews themselves had first approached his court) but agreed to give the rabbis time to translate documents and prepare answers. The cross-examination of both sides was postponed for four months, until 25 February 1757. Meanwhile, the consistory carried on with its interrogations of the Contra-Talmudists, who "continued to support their points and provided other interesting information."[39]

On 28 February, Herszkowicz presented the consistory with a written answer to the Frankist manifesto. This document is no longer extant; according to Ber of Bolechów, it "revealed to both Jews and Christians the abominations of the Sabbatians and exposed their misdeeds against the Torah and its commandments as well as against the natural law."[40] The rabbis tried to convince the Kamieniec clergy that the points of the Frankist manifesto were deliberately couched in terms designed to mislead the priests and make them believe that these resembled Christian doctrine; as it turned out, they argued, Sabbatianism was much closer to Islam than to Christianity.

However, the rabbinic response to the charges of the Contra-Talmudists was deemed unsatisfactory by the consistory. The court questioned Herszkowicz's right to represent the Jewish side and again demanded that the "elders of the synagogue" attend the hearing in person. It threatened to hold them in contempt should they fail to do so. Herszkowicz responded with pleas for clemency, to which the court responded by granting another postponement, until 23 March. When no representative of rabbinic Judaism showed up for the next hearing either, Dembowski issued an edict charging the rabbis with contumacy and obstruction of justice and imposed financial penalties on the Jewish communities in his diocese. He set the final deadline for the confrontation between the Contra-Talmudists and their adversaries for 20 June 1757.[41]

In early months of that year, the Contra-Talmudists composed an expanded version of their theses. As before, the original text was written in Hebrew and then translated into Polish and Latin by Moliwda.[42] This expanded version of the manifesto contained the following statements:

1. We believe in everything that was taught and commanded by God in the Old Testament.

2. The books of Moses and the other books of the Old Testament can be compared to a richly dressed Maiden, whose face is covered and whose beauty cannot be seen. These books are full of the hidden wisdom of God, they speak of things mysterious and of the future, and therefore, they cannot be comprehended by human reason without the assistance of Efficacious Divine Grace.

3. The rabbis of old times sought to expound the Old Testament. These explanations are known as the Talmud and contain many fables, lies, and much nonsense and hostility to God and His teachings.

4. On the basis of the Holy Bible of the Old Testament, we believe

that there is One God, without beginning or end, maker of Heaven and Earth and all things known and unknown.

5. On the basis of the same Scripture, we believe that there is one infinite God in three Persons, equal, indivisible, and [acting] in agreement.

6. We believe that God may take upon Himself mortal human flesh, be born, grow up, eat, drink, sense, sleep, and be subjected to all human passions save for sin.

7. In accord with Daniel's prophecy, we believe that the city of Jerusalem will not be rebuilt until the end of time.

8. We believe that the Jews have waited in vain for the messiah to come, bring them happiness, and grant them power over other nations.

9. We believe that God Himself cursed all of humankind for the sin of the First Parents. The same God would descend to earth and save the world from the curse. He is the true messiah, not for Jews alone, but for all peoples. All those who believe in Him and do good will be given Eternal Grace, and those who do not will be cast down to hell.[43]

As the consistory rejected the written rabbinic response to the first manifesto of the Contra-Talmudists, Bishop Dembowski demanded that the parties choose four representatives each and argue their respective positions in a public disputation. The representatives of the Contra-Talmudists were Leyb Krysa, Hayyim Moszkowicz, Leyb Rabinowicz, and Solomon Shorr; their opponents were represented by the rabbis Mendel of Satanów, Leyb of Międzybóż, Ber of Jazłowiec, and Joseph of Mohylew. The debate took place in the Kamieniec cathedral from 20 to 28 June 1757.[44] First, the Contra-Talmudists presented each motion orally and endorsed it with their signatures in the official protocol. Then the rabbis had a chance to put forward their response in a similar fashion. The live disputation was conducted in Hebrew with simultaneous Polish translation for the audience; the translation was provided by Moliwda.[45]

The rabbis unconditionally accepted points one, two, and four. They accepted the first part of point three, rejecting at the same time its second part. As for points five to nine, they refused to enter into the disputation, referring only to their written answer to the earlier manifesto submitted via Herszkowicz. The debate in Kamieniec provoked great interest in both the Jewish and Christian public: the crowd was so large that the bishop had guards posted to manage access to the cathedral.[46] *Kuryer Polski*, the most important Polish newspaper of the time, provided systematic coverage of the disputation. Some of the reports were also reprinted by foreign press.[47]

The paradigm of a public disputation between Christians and Jews was established in the thirteenth century with the great debates in Paris (1240) and Barcelona (1263). The Paris disputation centered on the status and the authority of the Talmud. Explicitly drawing upon the arguments of the Karaites, the apostate Nicolas Donin argued that the Talmud challenges the unique position of Scripture as the embodiment of the revelation given to Moses on Mount Sinai. He also maintained that it contains blasphemies against Jesus and Mary, as well as hostile remarks against Christians. The chief Christian protagonist of the Barcelona debate was also a convert from Judaism, Pablo Christiani. Christiani did not reject the Talmud outright; to the contrary, he claimed that the truth of Christianity can be proved on the basis of Jewish writings, including the Talmud. On the agenda of the debate were the thesis that the messiah had already come, the issue of his divinity, and the abolition of the "ceremonial law." However, the disputation also touched upon other issues, in particular on the doctrine of Original Sin. A Christian account of the Barcelona debate (but not Jewish accounts) also mentions the introduction of the subject of the Trinity.

The period of great public ceremonial disputations ended with the debate in Tortosa in 1413–14. However, eighteenth-century Poland saw an endeavor to revive the tradition. In the early 1740s, Franciszek Antoni Kobielski, bishop of Łuck and Brześć, attempted to institute the practice of presenting missionary sermons in the synagogues of Poland to "demonstrate to the Jews the truth of the Catholic faith."[48] The practice existed in Western Europe in the Middle Ages, but in the early modern period it was carried out only in the Papal States and in some parts of the Habsburg monarchy; although the Polish bishops were specifically reprimanded by Popes Gregory XIII (1584) and Clement XI (1705), no attempts to implement it in the Commonwealth ensued. Kobielski delivered a series of sermons in the synagogues of his diocese, and in January 1743 he challenged the Jews of Brody to a disputation about five points concerning the Trinity, the coming of the messiah, the virgin birth of Jesus, and the destitute state of Israel after the rejection of Christ.[49] The Jews of Brody prepared a written answer to Kobielski and complained to the owner of the town about the bishop's encroachment upon their religious autonomy. They do not appear to have been particularly upset by his missionary efforts or even to have taken them seriously. As for the sermons in the synagogues, a Protestant (and hence admittedly biased) source described what really happened: "Bishop [Kobielski] was taken by religious zeal, and he resolved to bring to the Roman faith not only the Jews, but also the Protestants. . . . Once he went to a synagogue in Węgrów and started to preach a sermon. Since he was completely drunk, he fell asleep while talking. A vicar had to finish the sermon in his stead and the bishop was carried out of the synagogue. . . . While he spoke, his eyes constantly kept closing and it took him a quarter of an hour to complete one sentence. The Jews could not stop laughing during the entire spectacle."[50]

Kobielski's sermonizing and his missionary ventures were more than a little pathetic and did not present a serious danger for the Jews. Still, they revived the memory of medieval public Jewish-Christian debates and set a precedent for such a disputation in Poland. The Brody precedent was almost certainly known to Bishop Mikołaj Dembowski of Kamieniec Podolski, especially since his brother (also a bishop) Antoni was also involved in Kobielski's campaign.[51]

The Brody debate of 1743 might be seen as a prelude to the disputation of Kamieniec in 1757 (much more sophisticated and much more dangerous from the Jewish perspective). During the ensuing fourteen years, Kobielski's rather primitive arguments became substantially refined. This process of refinement drew directly upon material from the medieval disputations. In 1681, the great Hebraist Johann Christian Wagenseil published a compilation of Jewish anti-Christian writings, *Tela Ignea Satanae*. Among other texts, the publication brought the Hebrew and Latin versions of the most important Jewish account of the Barcelona disputation, Nahmanides' *Sefer ha-viku'ah* (Wagenseil's Hebrew edition contained many interpolations, including some from the accounts of the earlier Paris debate).[52] There is direct evidence that Wagenseil's publication was known to some of the priests who became involved in the Frankist affair in 1759.[53] I suggest that in 1757, it was already known to Moliwda or some of the priests from the Kamieniec consistory. Five out of six controversial items on the Kamieniec agenda (the Trinity, the earlier coming of the messiah, the messiah's nature both divine and human, Original Sin, and the cessation of Jewish self-rule after the advent of the messiah) had also been raised in Barcelona. It is certain that Christians not only translated the manifestos of the Contra-Talmudists but also influenced their content. The Frankist theses reveal substantial knowledge of Christian Scriptures and employ very specific technical theological terminology, unlikely to be known to the Jews. For instance, thesis two uses the technical notion of *łaska Boska osobliwa* (the standard Polish rendering of *gratia efficax,* efficacious grace) and alludes to the Epistle to the Romans; thesis four is a loose paraphrase of the Nicene Creed.

The Barcelona disputation had marked the beginning of a completely new strategy of Christian anti-Jewish polemics, whereby the Jews were to be convinced that their own texts recognized fundamental truths of Christianity.[54] Kobielski's ventures show that five hundred years later, he was entirely unable to deploy this strategy: he merely repeated the pre-Barcelona apologetics, in which the arguments aimed at convincing the Jews of the truth of Christianity were drawn from typological exegesis of the Old Testament or based on scholastic logic. The few references to Jewish texts that appeared in his sermons had a clearly ornamental character: the bishop was not even able to get the names of the authors and the titles of the books right.[55]

However, Kobielski's primitive technique had one advantage over the more sophisticated counterpart first employed in Barcelona by Pablo Christiani. The apostate's strategy was laden with inner tension: Jewish canonical texts were condemned for their alleged absurdity and offensiveness to Christianity, yet they were to serve as the basis for the Christian anti-Jewish argument. Rhetoric, if not logic, demanded that some theory reconcile these two elements. Hyam Maccoby has argued that such a theory was provided by the "two-tier conception of the Talmud": the Christian position in Barcelona was based on the claim that the Talmud was "evil in its final redaction but the earliest strata, dating from the time of Jesus and before, contain material as yet undefiled by rabbinism."[56] This broad structure of medieval argumentation recurred during the Kamieniec disputation of 1757. The argument, however, underwent an important modification. The tension between attacking Jewish texts and simultaneously using them in a missionary effort was resolved not by reference to the "two-tier theory of the Talmud" but to the idea of a dichotomy of the Talmud and kabbalah: the former was entirely rejected for its supposed blasphemies and absurdities, while the latter was said to contain—albeit in a distorted form—the basic truths of Christianity.

The *Kabbalisshten*

Strong emphasis on kabbalah and its study characterized Sabbatianism from the very outset: Nathan of Gaza already called upon the believers "not to dabble any more in halakhah, but rather to study the Zohar, *tikkunim,* and midrashim."[57] He also stressed the prime role of kabbalah in determining halakhah, arguing that in matters not explicitly mentioned in the Talmud, the Zohar should be used as the basis for issuing binding legal rulings. Needless to say, the most important matters—from Nathan's perspective—were to be decided on this Zoharic foundation: the Talmud did not provide the foundation for judging the messianic mandate of Sabbatai Tsevi, yet his messiahship could be unequivocally established on the basis of the Zohar.[58]

Nathan's statements provoked angry reactions from some traditionally minded rabbis (including Jacob Sasportas)[59] but were enthusiastically received by Sabbatians themselves. Abraham Cardoso presented the entirety of the past thousand years of Jewish history as a conflict between the rival camps of kabbalists and "literalists" (*pashtanim*) and argued that the Judaism of the latter was in no way better than the idolatrous faiths of the Gentiles: it did not contain even the slightest speck of the knowledge of the True God.[60] Nehemiah Hayon boldly called for printing and distributing all kabbalistic works,[61] advocated open individual inquiry into esoteric matters, and demanded total abolition of any constraints imposed on the study of kabbalah.[62] In 1700, Hayyim Malakh wrote to Rabbi Abraham Broda of Prague "to send him learned people skilled in the matters of kabbalah in order to debate the faith of Sabbatai Tsevi together with him."[63] Two pupils of Broda went to Vienna to take up the challenge and suffered a miserable defeat in the disputation, in which Malakh argued that the Zohar unambiguously supported the truth of the faith in Sabbatai Tsevi. (Records of the Vienna disputation are not known to exist, but Emden—who did not witness them, either—mused that they might have formed a basis for the Kamieniec theses of the Frankists).[64]

The presentation of Sabbatian belief as a legitimate corollary of kabbalah in general, and the Zohar in particular, was a source of constant difficulty for its opponents. The Zohar had firmly established canonical status in Judaism, and many respectable halakhists engaged in kabbalistic speculation. Some maintained that the Zohar was more authoritative than any other source, insofar as it did not explicitly contradict the Babylonian Talmud. Over time, "the golden rule evolved that whenever halakhic rulings contradict the kabbalistic precepts, preference must be given to the former; otherwise, the kabbalistic precepts become mandatory."[65] Accordingly, Nathan's position on the role of the Zohar in making legal decisions might have posed special problems in the context of the debate about the current advent of the messiah, but it was, in itself, firmly grounded in accepted tradition. Unbridled kabbalistic speculation not directly linked to the mastery of halakhah also had precedents within normative Judaism and was by no means necessarily objectionable: in the sixteenth century, Rabbi Hayyim Vital argued for placing limitations on the study of the Mishnah and Talmud so that students could devote themselves more fully to esoteric lore. Not only was, in his view, a command of Jewish law unnecessary for dealing with the kabbalah; it also deprived the student of the time needed for exploring higher secrets.[66]

The polemics against Sabbatianism put an end to this relative laxity and the tolerance toward esoteric pursuits. Four out of six extant anti-Sabbatian bans pronounced in Poland between 1670 and 1753 forbade the dissemination of esoteric manuscripts (*megillot setarim*) and placed severe restrictions on printing kabbalistic works.[67] Mishaps such as the Vienna disputation made the matter urgent: in the eighteenth century, anti-Sabbatianism was increasingly taking the shape of a battle against all kabbalah. Following the arrest of the participants of the Lanckoronie ceremony, the rabbis of Satanów confiscated many subversive and heretical books and manuscripts.

In the course of its investigation of the case, the Kamieniec consistory issued an order to present the sequestered writings for inspection by the episcopal court. We do not know if this order was carried out by the rabbis, and we have no information concerning the titles or even the general character of the works in question. What we do know is that the consistory dispatched priests (sometimes accompanied by converted Jews who acted as interpreters)[68] to interview the suspected Sabbatians *in loco*. One of these priests was the Bernardine Gaudenty Pikulski, who later composed the most comprehensive Christian account of early Frankism. When recounting his meeting with Sabbatians in Lanckoronie in 1757, Father Pikulski wrote: "The tenets of [Sabbatai's] belief were described by his followers in their books. And the books are: first—*Or Izrael*, which means "the light of Israel." Second—*Hemdas Cwi*. Third—*Keyser Josef*. Fourth is the book published some seven years ago in Amsterdam by Emmanuel Chay Riky, and it is titled *Joser Leywawa*."[69]

Or Izrael (*Or Yisrael*) was a commentary on the Zohar and Lurianic dicta published in 1702 by Israel ben Aaron Jaffe. *Hemdas Cwi* (*Hemdat Tsevi*) was a work on *Tikkune ha-Zohar* by Rabbi Tsevi Hirsh Hotsh, published in Amsterdam in 1706. *Keyser Josef* (*Keter Yosef*) was a kabbalistic prayer book by Rabbi Joseph ben Moses of Przemyśl, first published in Berlin in 1700. Finally, *Joser Leywawa* (*Yosher Levav*), by Raphael Immanuel Ricchi Hai, appeared in Amsterdam in 1742 and dealt with the mystery of *tsimtsum* as well as Lurianic *kavvanot*. Two of the four books mentioned by Pikulski had already aroused suspicions in the first half of the eighteenth century. *Or Yisrael* was found to be "tainted by Sabbatianism and pervaded with confusion" by Moses Hagiz[70] and qualified as a "heretical book" by Jacob Emden.[71] *Keter Yosef* was similarly condemned by Hagiz,[72] while Emden claimed that without its author's knowledge, the printers had added Sabbatian elements based on the writings of Nathan of Gaza.[73] Yet Sabbatianism was alleged only with regard to these two of the four items and only by the most ardent heresy hunters such as Hagiz or Emden. None of the books in question was unreservedly condemned by the majority of the rabbis; all of them were printed with rabbinic approbations and were not generally regarded as contrary to accepted beliefs. What all four books had in common was not Sabbatianism (or at least not overt Sabbatianism) but their authors' pronounced tendency to disseminate and popularize kabbalah among the wider strata of Jewish society. This was especially true about Tsevi Hirsh Hotsh:[74] in addition to *Hemdat Tsevi*, he was the author of the first adaptation of the Zohar in Yiddish, *Nahalat Tsevi*; in the introduction to the latter work, he asserted that "everyone should study kabbalah according to his perception and comprehension."[75]

Three of the books mentioned by Father Pikulski appeared in the first decade of the eighteenth century and *Hemdat Tsevi* in 1711: during that period, the idea that every Jew should study kabbalah "according to his perception and comprehension" might have still slipped by rabbinic vigilance. By the 1750s, the situation had changed: regardless of whether all or some of the four books listed by Pikulski were indeed "tainted with" Sabbatian elements, in the minds of many rabbis the dissemination of kabbalah among the unlettered and statements about a plurality of readings had become unequivocally associated with heresy. This became immediately clear in the rabbinic responses to the discovery of the Lanckoronie ritual. For its participants, the ritual might or might not have had kabbalistic underpinnings; for the rabbinate, it was directly linked with the spread of kabbalah, the unauthorized and uncontrolled study of esoteric matters, and possible forgeries creeping into the accepted kabbalistic works. The letters of rabbis involved in formulating the bans against the Frankists placed special emphasis on the issue of heretical literature.[76] The fullest expression of this tendency can be found in the closing section of the May 1756 *herem* of Brody:

> We deem it necessary to place restrictions and create order with
> regard to those who . . . cast off the study of the Talmud and the
> codifiers and attempt to penetrate the deepest secrets of the Torah
> without learning first how to read its plain meaning and attain-
> ing the understanding of Gemarah. . . . And so we pronounce the

ruling that we prohibit anyone to study these writings, even the writings that are certainly of the ARI's [Isaac Luria's] authorship. It is strictly forbidden to study them until one has reached the age of forty. The Zohar, the books *Shomer emunim* [of Rabbi Joseph Ergas], and *Pardes rimonim*[77] of Rabbi Moses Cordovero alone may be studied by one who has attained the age of thirty, provided they are in printed form and not in manuscript.[78]

The idea of the prohibition of the study of kabbalah before the age of forty had a long history. However, never before did it receive the patronage and authority of a formal rabbinic assembly. Neither was it ever linked to the explicit demand that the mastery of halakhah must precede any kabbalistic inquiry.[79] The Brody pronouncement thus bore extraordinary weight and—in an unprecedented way—combined both conditions. The stipulations of the May 1756 *herem* were repeated four months later in the ban issued by the Council of Four Lands in Konstantynów; the endorsement of the council meant that the *herem* was to shape the official policy of Jewish authorities in Poland. For the first time, the restrictions were imposed on the entire Jewish population of the country and not only on the suspected or actual Sabbatians. In order to attack Sabbatianism, the rabbinate attempted to formulate a general rule about the study of kabbalah by all Jews.[80]

The position taken by the rabbis was ultraconservative: virtually none of the great kabbalists of the past had refrained from studying kabbalah before attaining the age of forty (the most famous of all kabbalists, Isaac Luria, died at the age of thirty-eight). The strict adherence to the letter of the Brody *herem* would excommunicate most (or perhaps all) of the kabbalists active in Poland at that time, including quite a few signatories to the ban, many of whom belonged to one of the most important centers of kabbalistic study in the Commonwealth, the *kloyz* (house of study) of Brody. Hence, the Brody ban was probably not intended to be taken literally. Rather, it should be seen as an attempt to formalize the limits of the permissible in dealing with kabbalah and ensuring the rabbinate's full supervision over esoteric pursuits.

More important than the exact age requirement demanded from would-be kabbalists was the fact that the rabbis officially restricted kabbalistic studies to the recognized institutional framework: after the ban, members of the established institutions such as the *kloyz* of Brody would undoubtedly pursue their kabbalistic interests (almost certainly even before the age of forty), while those learning outside the pale of rabbinic supervision would be automatically excommunicated. The prerequisite of gaining full mastery of the Talmud before engaging in the study of kabbalah was meant to limit the latter to members of the rabbinic elite and to eliminate kabbalistic autodidacts and independent students who lacked the establishment's formal seal of approval.

The polemics against Sabbatianism demanded the formalization of earlier unofficial restrictions on kabbalah study and the setting of clear limits to legitimate kabbalistic activity. While the rabbis stopped short of condemning kabbalah outright, they called for banning it from the sphere of public activity, confining its study to hermetically closed circles of authorized individuals. Not only did they downgrade the general importance of the Zohar; they denied its halakhic significance entirely[81] and demanded a sharp separation of halakhah and kabbalah. Kabbalah was to be relegated to the private field of pure speculation and was not to have any influence on religious *praxis* and legal decisions governing the daily life of the Jews. Its study was to be confined to the members of establishment.

The Brody and Konstantynów pronouncements raised the process of framing the battle against Sabbatianism as the condemnation of illicit kabbalah to its highest point. A hundred years of polemics had caused the radical polarization of both parties' positions vis-à-vis the nature and mutual relationship between exoteric and esoteric spheres of Jewish tradition. In the most extreme cases, the sides portrayed all of Judaism in terms of a battle between kabbalah and halakhah, between the Zohar and the Talmud. While this extreme dichotomization of opinion greatly facilitated the polemics by providing a clear target, it also oversimplified the respective positions of the sides almost *ad absurdum*.

The normative Judaism of even the most orthodox rabbis was never a Judaism of *just* the Talmud, and, in the opposing court, Sabbatianism also had sources other than kabbalah. Some of the known Sabbatians were acknowledged masters of Jewish law, while numerous anti-Sabbatians (including Emden) had a deep interest in kabbalah. Yet, as the Sabbatians were pigeonholed as "Contra-Talmudists" and "kabbalists," their opponents unavoidably became "Talmudists" and "anti-kabbalists." Both sides paid a high price for this mutual branding, yet the price paid by the anti-Sabbatians was higher by far: they placed themselves in constant danger of going one step too far and surrendering the entire esoteric stratum of Jewish religion to heretics.

This need to maintain the legitimacy of kabbalah within the framework of mainstream Judaism found its expression in the very language used in defining the Sabbatians by their opponents. According to Emden, the Frankists called themselves *zoharishten* (the "Zoharists").[82] His main supporter in Poland, Baruch Yavan, stated: "Ve-korim et atsman Kabbalisshten, she-omrim she-osim et ha-kol al-pi kabbalah min Sefer ha-Zohar (And they call themselves *kabbalisshten*, for they say they do everything according to a kabbalah of the book of the Zohar)."[83] Neither description used the Hebrew word for kabbalists (*mekkubbalim*). Instead, they both employed somewhat distorted transliterations of the vernacular terms, therefore suggesting that the Frankists were not "real" kabbalists but impostors lacking legitimate connection to the Jewish kabbalistic tradition.

The terms *zoharishten* or *kabbalisshten* are neologisms that have no precedent in earlier rabbinic writings, and their origins need to be examined. Neither term appeared in internal Frankists sources and—in contrast to what Emden and Yavan would have us believe—we have no evidence that the Frankists ever called themselves that. Frank's view on kabbalah is a perfect example of the inadequacy of the categorization of all Sabbatians as "kabbalists." To be sure, some of his followers saw Frank as a master of esoteric lore, and Frankist manuscripts contain numerous paraphrases of classical Zoharic stories and direct references to the Zohar. However, quantitatively (and, in my opinion, not only quantitatively), these references are overshadowed by references to the Pentateuch, the midrashim, Polish and Ukrainian folktales, and even—strangely for the alleged outright "Contra-Talmudist"—talmudic aggadot. More important, Frank himself repudiated the label of kabbalist. The following dictum from *The Words of the Lord* is the best illustration of Frank's attitude toward kabbalah: "When Rabbi Mordechai was telling me about the ten *sefirot,* drawing them on paper, I asked him what they were. He said: 'They are houses.' So I asked: 'But where is a privy?' Because when they build a house in Bucharest, they first dig a deep hole in the ground, then pour into it quicklime that burns the earth, then on top of it they construct a privy, and only finally they erect a house."[84]

The dictum recalls the exchange between Frank and his patron, teacher, and initiator into the Sabbatian mysteries, Rabbi Mordechai of Prague. Like many believers of the older generation, Mordechai presented Sabbatian theosophy as kabbalistic lore, mystical interpretation of the Zohar in the spirit of Nathan of Gaza, Cardoso, and Hayon. His disciple, however, held different views. According to *The Words of the Lord*, Frank explicitly repudiated the Zohar: "The whole Zohar is not satisfying for me, and we have no need for the books of kabbalah."[85] In contrast to some earlier Sabbatian texts, Frank's dicta did away with the traditional kabbalistic terminology. Very few of the kabbal-

istic concepts that still appear in the Frankist manuscripts have been subjected
to a radically demythologizing reading as in the fragment quoted above: if the
sefirot are "houses," they should also contain a privy!

Speaking of kabbalistic works, Frank always called them *your* books,
therefore emphasizing *his own* break with Jewish literary canon: "But I tell
you the truth that is not yet found in your books."[86] He demanded that his
followers "give away their old books for nothing" for "all books and laws will
be broken like a potsherd."[87] This demand was absolute: it referred not only to
the Talmud and halakhic literature of the anti-Sabbatian rabbis but also to the
Zohar and kabbalistic works of Frank's own Sabbatian teachers.

The Words of the Lord was not composed until the 1780s; it is, of course,
possible that Frank's anti-kabbalistic position, which was emphatically voiced
in this work, developed only at a later stage and had not yet been formulated
during the events of 1756–57. It is also possible (and even more likely) that the
positive evaluation of kabbalah and the title of a "kabbalist"—so insistently
rejected by Frank—were accepted by other leaders of the group during the
Kamieniec disputation, especially the chief disputant, Yehudah Leyb Krysa.
Yet even if Frank was still a "kabbalist" in 1757 and Krysa was quite pleased
with the label, this does not mean that the Frankists ever called themselves
kabbalisshten or *zoharishten*, nor does it explain the origins of the unusual terminology employed by Emden and Yavan. The real source of this terminology
is to be found elsewhere. The following fragment of Father Pikulski's book is
particularly illustrative:

> I have already said above that today's Contra-Talmudists existed in
> Israel even before the birth of Christ, Our Lord, though they were
> called by different names, according to their time. In the begin-
> ning they were called the "kabbalists" [*Kabalistami*] because they
> explained the Holy Scripture mystically, through the teachings
> of kabbalah; they were good and understood the mysteries of the
> Old Testament without any error. . . . Later, when the sages of the
> Jerusalem Synagogue started to favor their Talmuds, traditions, and
> laws above the Divine Law, which misled the Jewish masses, the
> kabbalists opposed them and they came to be called the Contra-Tal-
> mudists. . . . After a long period of time, the kabbalists or Contra-
> Talmudists started to hold [the Zohar] in high esteem, which led to
> a quarrel with the Talmudists; and some started to call the followers
> of the Zohar the Zoharites [*Zoharzystami*]. . . . Finally, from the

Contra-Talmudists, who followed the Zohar, arose Sabsy-Cewy [Sabbatai Tsevi], also known as Zebbathaj Zebbi, or Sabschacwii, famous in Greece; he clearly exposed the Zoharic teachings about the Holy Trinity and had a couple of thousand disciples in Wallachia and Podolia. The Talmudists called them "Sabsaćwinniki."[88]

As the quotation above indicates, while describing the Frankists, Pikulski (and other priests as well) employed such words as *kabalistowie* (the kabbalists), *sabsaćwinnikowie* (a distorted form of the Yiddish slur *shabsetsvinikes*), *zoharzystowie* (the Zoharists), and *kontratalmudystowie* (Contra-Talmudists) almost interchangeably. Emden's and Yavan's strange neologisms *zoharishten* and *kabbalisshten* do not appear to derive from any Frankist source; rather, they were attempts to render into Hebrew the Polish terminology used by the Catholic clergy. The borrowing reached deeper than just a verbal similarity. The understanding of the history of Judaism in terms of the perennial conflict between proponents of kabbalah and advocates of the Talmud, as well as the ensuing greatly reductive conceptualizations of rabbinic Judaism as pure "Talmudism" and Sabbatianism as "kabbalism," were historically untrue and alien to earlier Jewish tradition. They were, however, in full agreement with a paradigm advocated by the Christian kabbalah.

As Charles Mopsik has pointed out, kabbalah was the only element of postbiblical Judaism that aroused the constant interest and support of Christian elites.[89] In the early Renaissance, this support was translated into the creation of a mystical discipline in its own right—Christian kabbalah. This discipline, whose beginning can be traced to Giovanni Pico della Mirandola (1463–94) and Johannes Reuchlin (1455–1522), took two—sometimes parallel and sometimes conjoined—paths of development: the quest for the confirmation of the fundamental tenets of Christianity in esoteric Jewish sources; and the application of Jewish kabbalistic exegetical techniques to the reading of the Christians' own literary canon.[90] While initially the province of a small number of erudites, over the course of time "some knowledge of kabbalah was a part of the equipment of every [Christian] scholar in every part of Europe."[91] This incorporation of the kabbalah into the Christian context was the background against which the priests interpreted the dispute between the Sabbatians and their opponents: Christian accounts of Frankism abound in references to prominent Christian kabbalists such as Reuchlin and Pico.[92]

According to some Christian kabbalists, the alleged Christian tendency in Jewish texts existed not only in the Hebrew Bible but also in the kabbalistic literature as a whole: in the most developed form, Christian kabbalah assumed the form of a hostile takeover of this entire segment of Jewish tradition, whereby its practitioners appropriated canonical Jewish texts as their own and attempted to uncover a "progressive," pro-Christian wing of Judaism. In the context of the Frankist affair, this wing was, quite simply, equated with Sabbatianism.

First, Reuchlin: "The kabbalist, blessed with happiness, directs all his studies, all his efforts, all his judgment, all his diligent application away from the physical world, concentrating on bringing it into the world of the intellect. The Talmudist, on the other hand, remains in the world of the senses."[93]

And Pikulski: "Jewish traditions slowly split into two parties: the Talmudists and the kabbalists. The Talmudists elucidated traditions of their forefathers, that is, oral laws, rituals, and ceremonies of the Mosaic Law, with more and more false embellishments, while the kabbalists explained the tradition according to spiritual understanding and noble thought."[94]

Wittingly or not, the rabbis who defined the Sabbatian controversies in terms of a sharp conflict between kabbalah and the Talmud played into the hands of the priests, who understood the eighteenth-century debate as the continuation of a quarrel that harked back to the origins of the Jewish religion. Once the Podolian Sabbatians were identified as a modern incarnation of the ancient "kabbalists," the sympathy of many members of the Kamieniec clergy for their cause was assured, and their belief was immediately furnished with a respectable heritage: for many Christians, kabbalah was not only truly antique but truly divinely inspired.[95] This, in turn, added a particular twist to the notion that allusions to crucial tenets of Christianity were buried in ancient Jewish texts.

During the Barcelona disputation, Pablo Christiani argued that generations of rabbis from the compilers of the Talmud onward failed to understand the true meaning of their own Scriptures and were "blind" to the "obvious" Christian undertones of their own religious canon. Accordingly, in subsequent Christian apologetics, the Jews came to be presented as fools holding Christological views without understanding their implications: "[A]n already negative European image of the Jews was deepened; in yet one more way, the Jews were perceived as incapable of comprehending and assimilating obvious truths."[96]

Christian kabbalists, however, interpreted the Jews' "blindness" and lack of comprehension in a different fashion. The Franciscan Pietro Galatino (d. after 1539) claimed that the Jewish rabbinic establishment "knew" about the truth of Christianity concealed in Jewish sources but hid this knowledge from ordinary Jews. Galatino argued that "the Talmudists" deliberately falsified the Hebrew Bible and kabbalistic works, expunging from them fragments allegedly expounding the doctrines of the Trinity and Incarnation and confirming Jesus' claim to be the true messiah.[97] In the context of the Frankist debate, this idea of a deliberate forgery was applied to Sabbatianism: "It is a lie of the Talmudists that [Sabbatai Tsevi] is the founder of this sect: it was established a long time ago by Jews-kabbalists, such as Simeon ben Yohai who wrote the Zohar, a book praising the Holy Trinity. The books of Simeon were explicated by Sabbatai Tsevi and have been falsified by the Talmudists."[98]

The eruption of the Sabbatian movement in the 1660s triggered a vivid reaction among the Christian (both Catholic and Orthodox)[99] population in the Polish-Lithuanian Commonwealth. Public announcements of Sabbatai's messianic mandate and numerous processions with his portraits angered Christians, who saw them as an attack on their belief in the messiahship of Jesus. This led to anti-Jewish riots in several cities.[100] Secular and ecclesiastical authorities issued official proclamations,[101] and several pamphlets and polemical works were printed.[102] The priests involved in the Kamieniec disputation knew at least some of these documents.[103] However, in Christian accounts of the debate, Sabbatai was described as being only an expositor of the Zohar "more sensible than others"[104] or as a propagator of the doctrine of the Trinity among the Jews.[105]

The priests clearly identified Frankists as Sabbatians,[106] but the term "Sabbatians" did not denote for them the real movement inspired by Sabbatai Tsevi but the abovementioned kabbalistic, pro-Christian, tradition within Judaism. This conscious misrepresentation of Sabbatianism has a clear purpose. Given the attitude toward Sabbatianism expressed in earlier Polish polemical literature, as well as rabbinic arguments emphasizing the connection between the Frankists and crypto-Muslim Sabbatians in the Ottoman Empire, the priests surely wanted to break the link between the Contra-Talmudists participating in the Kamieniec disputation and messianic sectarians accused by both Jews and Christians of heresy and immorality.

For the purpose of the debate, the Frankists were presented as "kabbalists"; this allowed them to capitalize upon the already existing Christian knowledge of kabbalah and sympathy for the esoteric stratum of Judaism. However, once the disputation ended, the Church had to make it evident that the truth of Christianity goes beyond any Jewish mysteries and is therefore not accessible without official ecclesiastical intermediaries. This element came to the fore immediately after the end of the Kamieniec disputation.

The Aftermath of the Kamieniec Disputation

On 17 October 1757, Bishop Dembowski issued a decision declaring the Sabbatians victorious in the Kamieniec disputation.[107] The consistory court dismissed the Satanów accusations as slander.[108] It imposed a number of financial penalties on the rabbis,[109] ordered the flogging of the Jews responsible for wreaking havoc in Lanckoronie, and condemned the Talmud as worthless and corrupt, ordering it to be consigned to the flames.[110] Jewish books were brought to the city square in Kamieniec and publicly burned by the executioner. Although the verdict of the bishop targeted the Talmud first, other Jewish books were also condemned. A contemporary letter attests to the fact that aside from the Talmud, the *Shulhan arukh* and the Zohar were also burned.[111] An account of Israel Harif of Satanów mentions the burning of the Talmud, the *Shulhan arukh* together with *Ture zahav*, and *Tikkune ha-Zohar*.[112] This inclusion of the Zohar is particularly interesting: it seems that the bishop wanted to break the link between kabbalah and Sabbatianism that had played such an important role during the disputation. Dembowski ruled: "Kabbalah, which is a certain kind of superstition, is criminal, because it teaches one to worship God in a way in which He should not be worshiped. It allegedly gives one the ability to predict the future, or rather it involves engaging in magic, through which a hidden truth or a profitable way of acting can be revealed; it comes not from God but from Satan."[113]

From the bishop's point of view, the understanding of Sabbatianism as kabbalistic lore was useful for the purpose of the debate, but in the longer run, it gave too much power to the Sabbatians, who might have argued that they possessed religious mysteries unknown and inaccessible to the Christians. It was much safer for the Church to return to the formula of "Contra-Talmudism" and portray Sabbatianism as a "sound," not to say rationalistic, version of Judaism, one that rejected rabbinic aberrations present in the Talmud and in the kabbalah, and advocated going back to the uncorrupted text of the Old Testament. Accordingly, the verdict defined Contra-Talmudism as an ancient and legitimate form of Judaism legally recognized by Christian authorities. As for the Talmudists, the bishop's court decided that although their beliefs offended faith and authority, it was up to the civil authorities to decide whether they should be further tolerated in the Commonwealth.[114]

The magistrates of Kamieniec ignored the bishop's verdict regarding the flogging of the Jews but upheld the decision concerning the burning of the Talmud.[115] Priests were dispatched to towns and villages in Podolia. Jews and

Christians "of all rank or social status" were forbidden to "store, possess, read, copy, publish, print, write, order, buy, sell, give as a present, or exchange" the Talmud or kabbalistic books;[116] homes and synagogues were searched for copies of the Talmud, and many cartloads of books were burned in Lwów, Brody, and Żółkiew, among other places. One, clearly exaggerated, account stated that "no [Jewish] book survived in Poland, and everyone who wanted to save their books sent them to Turkey."[117]

For Jewish authorities, the bishop's ruling was a total disaster. From the perspective of the rabbinate, the real danger did not derive from isolated groups of Sabbatians conducting their (strongly antinomian, as they might have been) rituals in remote villages or secretly studying forbidden manuscripts. It lay in the legal recognition of "heresy" as a legitimate form of Jewish religion. In one stroke of the pen, Dembowski challenged the monopolistic position of the rabbinate and allowed Sabbatianism to be freely professed and practiced. Although his verdict was valid only within the Kamieniec diocese, its potential implications were much wider. The archbishop of Lwów, Wyżycki, died in April 1757, and Dembowski was nominated his successor. He explicitly expressed his intention to extend the Kamieniec verdict onto the entire Lwów archdiocese, and eventually the entire Commonwealth. Compounded with the fear of the further spreading of the bishop's policies was the trauma of the burning of the Talmud, an event unprecedented in Poland. Major Jewish communities in Podolia held public prayers to avert the evil decree and declared a special fast to mourn the "burning of the Torah."[118]

Everything changed on 9 November 1757: Bishop Dembowski suffered a sudden stroke and died after three days of hemiplegia.[119] Jewish sources portrayed Dembowski's unexpected and painful demise as a "miracle greater than the one that happened in the times of Haman and Ahasuerus,"[120] which was commemorated in the festival of Purim. One account stated that before his death, the bishop saw Hebrew letters from the burned books with the eyes of his soul and canceled his verdict.[121] Others described a plague that erupted in Kamieniec and its surroundings; the bishop's ghost started to haunt the priests, who dug out his corpse and cut off its head with the spade ("as their law says that the head of a sorcerer had to be cut off with an iron tool").[122] However, the plague continued to spread, and the bishop's ghost kept on appearing with his head under his arm. The terrible phenomena ceased only after Dembowski's corpse was burned in the place where the Talmud had been burned earlier.[123] According to Jewish sources, even the Kamieniec priests admitted that Dembowski's terrible death was a punishment for the burning of the Talmud and a clear sign of divine displeasure.

After Dembowski's death, Podolian Sabbatians unexpectedly found themselves in a sort of limbo between Judaism and Christianity, lacking support and protection from either side. The burning of the Talmud stopped, and the rabbinate initiated a campaign of persecution against the heretics. In the words of Rabbi Jacob Emden: "The pious Jews gathered and assailed the accursed sect that wanted to lead Israel astray, some of them they killed, others they hounded, yet others shaved their beards [converted to Christianity], and so [the sect] fell without a chance of rising again."[124] According to Frankist sources, eighteen sectarians were killed, and more than thirty wounded by other Jews in mob violence.[125] Podolian Sabbatians went into hiding; Ber Birkenthal relates that on arriving in the village of Czarnokozienice, Yehudah Leyb Krysa was recognized and beaten almost to death by Jewish youth (but "unfortunately did not die") and that the rabbis issued a ruling allowing the blood of the heretics to be shed and stating: "On the basis of the codifiers, we pronounce that it is a positive commandment to kill them."[126] The persecuted Podolian Sabbatians fled to Turkey; this gave Frank a chance to return to play.

Having left the Commonwealth in April 1756, Frank made a short trip to Salonika,[127] and then settled in the Danubian town of Giurgiu (the principality of Wallachia). He seemed to have little influence upon the course of events in Poland; the unquestioned leader of the Podolian Sabbatians at that point was Yehudah Leyb Krysa. During this period, Frank seems to have abandoned his hopes of gaining leadership of the Sabbatians in Poland. He converted to Islam; the conversion took place either in Giurgiu or in the Ottoman city of Rousse across the Danube, sometime between April 1756 and June 1757. The only extant description of this conversion can be found in a Latin source now housed in the Vatican:

> Having exchanged Jewish dress for the Turkish one, he similarly changed his old faith. As is common among the apostates, he entered a Turkish temple, raised his hands above his head and, saying the words "Allah is God and Mahomet is His prophet," he publicly renounced [his old faith]. Having become a Muslim, he went to Istanbul, where he obtained from the sultan a mandate commonly known as *firman*, which was addressed to the pasha of Chocim[128] and contained an order to give to Frank and his companions some

vacated lands. And it read as follows: "This is given in Istanbul,
in the name of the current sultan: Ahmed[129] addressed to us his
humble requests, saying that after accepting our faith he is lacking a
means of living and cannot support himself, so he asked us to provide him with support: if there is any free land in the area of your
jurisdiction, give it to him on account of the sultan's order."[130]

In June 1757, Ahmed Frank briefly returned to Poland "wearing a Turkish turban upon his head"; during the Kamieniec disputation, he stayed in
Rohatyn, but he returned to Giurgiu in September, before Bishop Dembowski's verdict was issued. After Dembowski's demise, some Podolian Sabbatians
found themselves under pressure to convert to Christianity (I shall return to
this issue in Chapter 5). They started to flock to Frank at Giurgiu. An account
of what happened at that time can be found in Ber Birkenthal's *Divre binah*:

> The evil congregation [*ha-edah ha-ra'ah*] . . . were thrown into
> panic, and their souls almost fled their bodies. And some of them
> started to doubt their faith. And Jacob Frank stood up and said to
> the company in these words: my beloved brothers, do not despair
> and do not fear, for "whatever the All-Merciful does is for good."[131]
> Why should we flatter the uncircumcised, who are more impure
> than any heathen [*AKU"M*]? It will be better for us to go to the
> Muslim countries. We will live in the town of Salonika and will
> prostate ourselves on the graves of our teachers, the pupils of our
> messiah, Sabbatai Tsevi: there, our choice will be to remain Jewish
> or—if the need arises and the Jews will not want to accept us back
> to their faith—to convert to the faith of the Muslims, circumcised
> as ourselves. And he showed them a fragment from the Zohar per-
> taining to this, and many of them believed him.[132]

During the run-up to the Kamieniec disputation, Frank was living in the
Ottoman territories as a Muslim; his trip to Rohatyn during the debate might
have been an attempt to regain some following in Poland, but his prompt
return to Giurgiu suggests that he was not successful. As long as Dembowski
was alive, Krysa's strategy of obtaining for Polish Sabbatians a special status
of religious autonomy within Judaism seemed to be working well. Dembowski's death changed everything. Instead of being recognized by the Church
and the Commonwealth authorities as an independent Jewish denomination

akin to the Karaites, the Sabbatians suddenly came under pressure to become Christians.

According to Dov Ber, they were adamantly hostile to the idea. Frank apparently saw in it a chance to gain an advantage over Krysa: he tried to take over some of Krysa's followers by advocating their conversion to Islam, clearly believing that since autonomy in Judaism was no longer an option, many Sabbatians would prefer to become Muslim rather than Christian. (Incidentally, Ber's account also explains why the Podolian clergy stopped supporting the Frankists after Dembowski's death, making possible the renewal of rabbinic persecution: since the Sabbatians refused to convert to Christianity, the Catholic authorities allowed the Jews to hound them at will).

At this time, Frank, who had been overshadowed by Krysa during the Kamieniec debate, regained prominence, and his followers again began to grow in numbers. Jan Doktór has argued that Frank's visit in Salonika was an attempt to win the leadership of the Dönmeh.[133] Even if Doktór's hypothesis cannot be categorically confirmed, it seems quite likely that at that time, Frank sought to establish himself as the leader of a nominally Muslim Sabbatian group in the borderlands between Poland and Turkey, competitive with the Dönmeh of Salonika and vying for the Polish Sabbatians persecuted by the rabbinate. In January 1758, four important Podolian Sabbatians and erstwhile participants in the Kamieniec disputation arrived in Giurgiu. Two months later, they rode across the Danube to Rousse: on the way, Frank "ordered [them] to sing songs aloud. They accepted the Mohammedan religion before the Grand Mufti and the Lord [Frank] gave everyone a Turkish name himself."[134] According to the Frankist chronicle, by May 1758, "all the true believers that were in Poland in the Jewish estate" had left the Commonwealth and moved to Turkey.[135]

Ber of Bolechów mentions that Polish rabbis tried to counteract Frank's initiatives. They wrote to the rabbis of Istanbul, who issued a *herem* against Jewish Sabbatians, and they also obtained a *firman* from the Turkish authorities prohibiting the acceptance of Jews to the Muslim faith for one year.[136] No other source mentions such a *firman*, and its existence seems unlikely, but the fact that Polish rabbis tried to intercede in Turkey in order to stop the flow of Sabbatians from Poland was independently corroborated by Frank.[137] If we are to believe *The Words of the Lord*, on four occasions Jews hired Turkish assassins, who made several attempts on Frank's life. Frank was unable to find a safe place to stay for the night and had to sleep in the canals of Salonika; even the Dönmeh were afraid to take him in.[138]

In Poland, the leader of the Contra-Talmudists during the disputation, Yehudah Leyb Krysa, did not fare much better. Following his beating, Krysa claimed that the hounding of the Sabbatians was a clear sign that the Zoharic prophecies were coming true: in messianic times, the faithful must be persecuted by the "mixed multitude."[139] Yet this theological consolation offered little practical help. In the autumn of 1757, Jewish sources pronounced triumphantly that "not a single Sabbatian remained in Poland, and Turkey, too, would not offer them refuge."[140] It seemed that the story of Podolian Sabbatianism was over for all time.

Chapter 4

The Politics of the Blood Libel

The Blood Accusations

In Jewish collective memory and, to some extent, in Jewish historiography, the blood accusation that was raised during the Lwów disputation in September 1759 is the best-known event associated with Frankism. The second volume of Majer Bałaban's two-volume book on Frankism is devoted almost solely to this issue;[1] extensive discussion can be also found in Dubnow.[2] The unique characteristics of this accusation can best be understood if it is placed against the backdrop of similar cases, in Poland and elsewhere.

Charges that the Jews used Christian blood for ritual purposes were first made in Western Europe in the twelfth and thirteenth centuries, and the first documented accusation is thought to be for the murder of William of Norwich in 1144.[3] In the early English and French cases, the Jews were accused of tormenting, flogging, and ultimately crucifying the victim, reenacting the passion of Jesus. At this stage, the magic use of blood did not seem to play any significant role in the accusations and the charges did not mention the observance of Passover. The Jews were accused of committing a cruel mockery of Christian rites rather than of using blood in their own rituals.

In the High Middle Ages, the blood libel spread to continental Europe, and an archetypal accusation took shape. The victim would be a prepubescent boy, who would disappear around Easter. The unburied body would be discovered dumped in a river or in forests. Autopsy would reveal numerous wounds inflicted with needles or daggers. Although the corpse would be completely drained of blood, it would start bleeding when approached by a Jew, thus miraculously revealing the identity of the murderer. Images of the crime itself came to be conflated with the Eucharist; the motive for the murder would be the Jews' ostensible need to obtain Christian blood, which was supposed to possess salvific and other magic powers.[4] The wave of accusations peaked toward the end of the fifteenth century, and the vast majority of cases followed a consistent and standardized pattern.

However, shortly after the consolidation of the ritual murder discourse, the coherent paradigm began to fall apart. In the sixteenth century, deviations from the archetype became more common: victims began to include people of all ages, both men and women; the identification of the murdered children with the Eucharistic offering gradually disappeared from the trials; and the belief in the magical potency of Christian blood was played down or completely abandoned. The disintegration of the magical and religious discourse of ritual murder was paralleled by the decline of the number of trials. Scholars have attributed these developments to the spread of the Reformation and the general "disenchantment of the world," including the rejection of the Catholic doctrine of transubstantiation.

Nevertheless, the decrease in the frequency of the trials did not mean that the blood libel had vanished completely: the belief that the Jews murdered Christian children persisted in popular discourse and in collective memory and "passed from the realm of the functional—where beliefs and actual accusations could lead to inquests, trials, sentencing, or dismissal—into th[e] nebulous region of myth . . . thus creating knowledge to be transmitted under the guise of history."[5] Whereas the trials gradually disappeared, the earlier accusations achieved the status of fact, attested by chronicles, stories, places of pilgrimage, paintings, and sculptures. By the time of the Enlightenment, the blood libel in Germany and in Western Europe had passed from the courtrooms to books.

The rumors about ritual murders committed by the Jews did not reach Poland until the late fifteenth century,[6] and the first documented trial took place in Rawa Mazowiecka in 1547.[7] However, what the historian Simon Dubnow termed "a frenzy of blood accusations" did not occur in the Polish-Lithuanian Commonwealth until the end of the seventeenth and the beginning of the eighteenth century.[8] Blood libels increased in frequency in Eastern while they decreased in Western Europe: very few cases occurred in Poland when the phenomenon reached its apogee in Germany, whereas in the eighteenth century, when the trials had virtually come to an end in the West, they rapidly increased in number in Poland-Lithuania, the lands of the Bohemian Crown and Hungary.[9]

The most important consequence of this phase difference between Eastern and Central Europe, on the one hand, and Western Europe, on the other, was that the blood libel discourse in Eastern Europe did not develop independently during the trials but was absorbed in the process of cultural transmission. Polish works that spread the blood libel treated medieval English, French, and German cases as historically established facts, often quoting earlier "scholarly" literature on the subject. Accordingly, the accusation in Poland was linked with the development of anti-Jewish literature more closely than in Western Europe. Although the German lands saw many more ritual murder court cases than Poland, the quantity of accusatory literature produced in Poland appears to have far surpassed anything ever published in Germany or, for that matter, anywhere else prior to the nineteenth and twentieth centuries.

Until 1800, no fewer than seventy-six works devoted solely to ritual murders appeared; newspaper reports, remarks scattered in works on other subjects, memoirs, and almanacs numbered in the hundreds.[10] The 1750s and 1760s saw a rapid increase of this publishing, surpassing by far the total of all material ever printed in Germany; some of the books and pamphlets that appeared then achieved the status of early modern best sellers and went through many editions. The Polish works propagating the accusation in the eighteenth century are arguably the most extensive and detailed examples of this sort of literature: their authors provided long descriptions of past cases, which had allegedly taken place in various countries, and they discussed the most arcane aspects of the blood rite attributed to the Jews.

Without risking too broad a generalization, we may say that in medieval and early modern Western Europe, blood libel discourse was associated mainly with folklore and concrete attacks on Jews and Judaism, and not with abstract theological polemics. Those who advocated for the blood libel seldom attacked the Talmud or the theological tenets of Judaism, and vice versa: Pope Gregory IX, who issued the ban on the Talmud after the Paris disputation of 1240, also issued a bull against the blood libel. For the most part, early modern anti-Jewish literature written by intellectual elites in Western Europe did not contain the blood accusation.

Many of the Christian theologians who attacked aspects of Jewish ritual and belief denied the truth of the libel.[11] Other anti-Jewish writers toyed with the idea that the Jews indeed used Christian blood for ritual purposes, but stopped short of taking an unequivocal position on the issue. For instance, Andreas Eisenmenger, author of the most learned work of early modern anti-Semitism, *Entdecktes Judenthums*, gave a list of ritual murder trials and concluded: "Not everything [I adduced here] is bound to be untrue, but I will leave the matter undecided."[12] To the best of my knowledge, none of the anti-Jewish writers of Western Europe claimed that the use of Christian blood was an intrinsic element of the Jewish religion as expounded by the Talmud and other sacred writings. In the words of Jonathan Frankel, "the perfect fit between the upper-level demonology and the folk belief in black magic, *maleficium*, which fueled the witch craze of the sixteenth and seventeenth centuries, was never fully achieved with regard to the ritual murder accusation."[13] I believe that this perfect fit *was* achieved in eighteenth-century Poland. Before discussing this point in greater detail, however, I want to concentrate on the parallel between ritual murder and witchcraft trials suggested by Frankel.

Ritual Murder and Witchcraft Trials in Poland

Similarities between the patterns of development of ritual murder and witchcraft accusations in Eastern and Central Europe have been noted, if not systematically discussed, by scholars.[14] Indeed, there is a striking chronological overlap between the two phenomena: the century time lag between the two regions of the continent applies equally to blood libel and to witchcraft trials. In Poland, the Czech lands, and Hungary, witchcraft accusations hardly occurred while they were rife in Germany, but became very common in the mid-eighteenth century, after the phenomenon had practically disappeared in the West.

A German scholar whose name should be left unmentioned explained the time lag by Eastern Europe's backwardness and especially by the delays encountered in the transmission of intellectual matters; the explanation is unconvincing not only because of the region's high achievements during the Renaissance and the vivid contacts with its Western counterpart, but also because the *lack* of persecution in the sixteenth and early seventeenth centuries is hardly a sign of cultural primitiveness. More compelling are explanations pointing to increased levels of fear and suspicion caused by wars, plague, and economic disaster that ravaged this part of the world between the 1650s and the 1750s. The effects of these catastrophes were further exacerbated by severe competition for resources. Scholars of witchcraft have noted that accusations against witches were more likely to surface in precisely these conditions,[15] and it might be argued that the same applies to the blood accusations against the Jews.[16]

The chronological convergence of the witchcraft trials and the ritual murder accusations in Poland should not obscure differences between the two phenomena. In fact, the parallel is useful precisely because it allows us to grasp the specificity of the ritual murder accusation by placing it against the background of a contemporary and seemingly very similar phenomenon. The number of the ritual murder accusations pales in comparison with the witchcraft trials during the same period. The statistics are not fully reliable, but they convey the respective proportions of both phenomena. The total number of ritual murder trials in the entire Polish-Lithuanian Commonwealth during the entire early modern period has been estimated at seventy to eighty cases, and Dubnow's "frenzy of blood accusations" refers to some twelve cases between the first trial in Sandomierz (1698) and the trial in Wojsławice (1761).

In contrast, in the province of Greater Poland alone, there were 246 witchcraft trials from 1501 to 1800, and ninety-three of these took place between 1700 and 1750.[17] Some scholars have estimated the number of executions in the witchcraft persecution in Poland at fifteen thousand;[18] even if this figure is exaggerated, it is certain that thousands of purported witches were condemned to death. Significantly, the high number of witchcraft cases did not translate into a significant increase in the volume of accusatory literature produced by or associated with the trials. As noted, the volume of Polish accusatorial literature related to the blood libel is immense and far exceeds the number of demonological works related to witchcraft cases. The latter consist mainly of reprints and translations of Western European publications. Moreover, as Wanda Wyporska has noted, in witchcraft cases there was no cyclical interaction between printed demonological works and judicial practice: demonology was hardly ever invoked in courts, and records of previous trials do not seem to have directly influenced subsequent cases.[19] The development of the blood libel in Poland attests to the opposite trend: printed and oral "expert testimonies" of Christian theologians or Jewish converts played a crucial role in prosecution, and earlier verdicts were used as case law in subsequent legal proceedings.

In Poland, as in the West, most of the ritual murder literature was produced by the Roman Catholic clergy. However, in Poland it was precisely the clergy who became the most vociferous critics of the witchcraft persecution. Different attitudes toward witchcraft and blood libel cannot be attributed to the difference between the "enlightened" and "backward" sectors of the clergy: in some cases, the very same bishop denounced the superstition and bias of the accusers in the witchcraft trials, condemned such practices as the swimming of witches, while he defended the truth of the blood libel or the application of torture during the trials of the Jews.[20] The papacy denied—if sometimes indecisively—that Jews used Christian blood for ritual purposes, and those involved in the accusations in the West were mainly local civil authorities or priests of lower rank. In contrast, in Poland, some of the eighteenth-century cases were orchestrated by the highest echelons of the clergy, and the proponents of the accusation produced imposing, if terrifying, literature. Local clergy at times openly rejected the papal pronouncements that denied the truth of the blood libel.

Witchcraft and ritual murder were different not only from the scholarly perspective but in the minds of contemporaries. From the legal point of view, the two were essentially different issues. In several cases, individual Jews were accused of witchcraft, without any explicit reference to their being Jewish or any other express religious overtones. A Christian account of the Sandomierz ritual murder trial (1711–13) mentioned that the accused Jews tried to defend themselves by soliciting help from a "Jewish sorcerer." The sorcerer was not charged with any crime during the trial, and the account discusses the Jews' attempts to employ magic in their defense in a completely matter-of-fact way.[21] The petition submitted by the Jews to the papal nuncio in connection with the Frankist blood libel of 1759 claimed that the Commonwealth's Christians routinely tried to defend themselves from "Polish witches" by employing the services of "Jewish exorcists."[22] The gender profile of the witchcraft and ritual murder trials also differed substantially: while the vast majority of those accused of witchcraft were women,[23] virtually all the accused in ritual murder trials were male, though Christian women were sometimes charged with selling their children to the Jews.

The parallel between the witch craze and the ritual murder accusations thus has clear limits. However, since research on early modern witchcraft is far more advanced than that on the blood libel, it might be useful to apply some of the concepts developed by the students of witchcraft to the analysis of the ritual murder accusations. The scholarship of witchcraft has developed two competing, if not entirely exclusive, broad modes of argument. According to the first line of thought, the persecution of witches was a direct extension of the persecution of the heretics. It entailed the active hunting down of the accused by the political and ecclesiastical elites, and its main function was political manipulation: the witchcraft trials were tools of social restraint used by the Church, state, and individual landholders.[24] The alternative explanation attributes witchcraft trials to competition within a community. In this interpretation, the trials were not initiated or consciously utilized by power brokers but were caused by the externalization of local quarrels and disputes, during which individuals abused the legal system to take revenge or seek reparations from their neighbors.[25]

Both these levels were present in the blood libel accusations, though in different ways. So far, most scholars working on ritual murder accusations have focused on the vertical aspect of the phenomenon and treated it as a tool of political and religious persecution of the Jews by Christian elites. From this perspective, the history of the libel can be seen as that of gradual politicization and internationalization. The majority of sixteenth- and early seventeenth-century accusers were Christian, mainly Roman Catholic, theologians, for whom the inferior status of Judaism derived from the Jews' rejection of Jesus as the messiah, and Jewish use of Christian blood for ritual or magic purposes was undeniable. The mid-seventeenth and eighteenth centuries saw an increase in the number of cases in which the blood libel was used as a political tool by people who were not motivated by religious reasons and who clearly knew that the accusations were untrue. Magical and theological discourse merged with—or, in some cases, was entirely replaced by—the language of politics and power struggle. Separate and localized cases turned into international affairs. This tendency reached its peak in the nineteenth and early twentieth centuries. Diplomats and journalists, not theologians, determined the course of events in the Damascus affair of 1840.[26] The Beilis trial of 1913 was probably the first blood libel sponsored by a national government.[27] Although the belief in the truth of the blood accusation gradually disappeared among Christian elites, the members of these elites often found it advantageous to use the superstition and prejudice in pursuing their political agendas.

The growing politicization of the accusation does not fully explain its development in eighteenth-century Poland. An analysis of vertical tensions between Jews and Christians has to be supplemented by a discussion of the horizontal frictions within the Jewish community. Converts from Judaism were involved in ritual murder accusations from the very outset; the apostate Theobald of Cambridge played a sinister role as early as the Norwich accusation of 1144.[28] However, most converts who composed tracts against their former religion and community attacked practical and theological aspects of Judaism while denying the truth of the blood accusation. This is true of such prominent authors as Johannes Pfefferkorn and Anthonius Margaritha.[29] The notorious *Jüdisches Ceremoniel* (1734), written by the convert Paul Christian Kirchner, does contain the accusation but mentions it in only one sentence, while discussing Jewish rites surrounding childbirth.[30] None of the West Eu-

ropean converts who propagated the libel placed it in the center of his narrative or devoted a whole work to the subject.

In some cases, the accusation was used in personal Jewish vendettas. In
1593, a certain Abraham came to Frankfurt, the most prosperous Jewish community in the Holy Roman Empire, and asked for charity on behalf of his
community in Lublin. Faced with scorn and ridicule by the Frankfurt Jews,
he bought a bottle of ox blood from a butcher, hid it in the synagogue, and reported to the authorities that the Jews had committed a ritual murder. In this
particular case, the truth was revealed during the investigation and the libel
came to naught.[31] In other cases, the accused were not so lucky.[32] However,
despite the involvement of Jewish converts to Christianity in many trials, the
accusation was too terrifying for common use as a weapon in internal Jewish
conflicts.

The Frankist affair can be understood only when we take into account
that this taboo was broken, and what was arguably the most malicious accusation against the Jewish people came to be used by Jews, who wanted to settle
scores with members of their own community or gain leverage in internal
power struggles. Indeed, one of the Frankists explicitly stated that their accusation was made in revenge for Rabbi Hayyim Rapaport's permission to
hound and even kill the Sabbatians: the rabbi allowed the heretics' blood to be
shed, so they accused him of shedding Christian blood.[33] Certainly, Christian
prejudice and ill will were still necessary conditions for the libel: the accusation would never have gotten anywhere if the Christian authorities and ordinary Christians had not been willing to encourage and attend to them.

The rapid increase in the number of accusations of ritual murder in eighteenth-century Poland, on the other hand, was directly related to the crisis of
leadership within the Jewish community. Jewish involvement directly affected
the development of the accusatory literature associated with the blood libel.
The sophistication and level of detail displayed by some Polish anti-Semitic
works would not have been possible unless Jews had supplied information
and quotations from Hebrew sources. This, in turn, raised the accusation to
an entirely new level: the blood ritual came to be presented not as a folk custom practiced by heretical sects or degenerate individuals but as an essential
theological principle of Judaism.

Although the number of blood libel cases in Poland was lower than, say,
in Germany, and much lower than the number of witchcraft cases, Dubnow's
phrase about the "frenzy of blood accusations" accurately reflects the atmosphere in the mid-eighteenth-century Polish-Lithuanian Commonwealth. Up

to that time, Poland was relatively untainted by the blood libel. Thus, the sudden appearance of the accusation must have shocked the Jews, especially since the charge was thought to be a thing of the past in the West. The simultaneous appearance of a large number of publications promulgating the libel must have given the impression of an orchestrated campaign, and—as attested by the efforts of Bishop Sołtyk, which will be discussed below—this impression was not far from the truth. The flow of books and pamphlets propagating the libel was not countered by the appearance of publications denying the truth of the charge. Certainly, as attested by numerous memoirs and letters, many members of the elites of the Commonwealth (including, for instance, King Stanislaus Augustus) did not believe the accusation and questioned the good faith and motives of the accusers. None of them, however, wrote a full-fledged account of his position. There is no single eighteenth-century Polish work devoted to dismantling the blood libel in a manner similar to the 1714 pronouncements of the Leipzig theologians[34] or Aloys Sonnenfels's *Jüdischer Blut-Eckel* (1753). This, again, demonstrates the limits of the parallel with witchcraft cases, for there is a substantial Polish literature defending alleged witches from deadly superstition and judicial abuse.[35]

All this overlapped with the unprecedented Jewish involvement in the charges. The "frenzy of blood accusations" occurred because of the deadly mixture: powerful Christian officials wanted to utilize the existing popular prejudice to promote their interests or pursue political projects, while renegade members of the Jewish community were willing to fabricate evidence supporting the accusation or, in some cases, were even ready to initiate the charges when seeking revenge or material gain. In consequence, the accusation as found in the medieval and early modern periods was gradually replaced by the highly politicized modern model. Before the eruption of the Frankist affair, the most important case illustrating this shift were "revelations" of a convert named Jan Serafinowicz.

The Accusation of Jan Serafinowicz

Elsewhere, I have discussed the case of Jan Serafinowicz in greater detail.[36] Here, I shall only summarize those elements of his charges that pertain to the Frankist accusation. Serafinowicz, allegedly a former rabbi, was baptized in Żółkiew on 10 April 1710. Following his conversion, he began to approach Christian officials with "revelations" regarding ritual murders of Christian children by the Jews and wrote a lengthy work describing Jewish rites involving the use of Christian blood. The original was written in Yiddish, but the manuscript was promptly translated into Polish as *Wyjawienie przed Bogiem i światem zdrad i obrządków żydowskich* (The exposure before God and the world of Jewish treacheries and ceremonies). The Polish version is said to have been printed, but the entire print run was supposedly purchased and destroyed by the Jews.[37] What is certain is that manuscript copies of *The Exposure* started to circulate among Polish clergy and laid the groundwork for the most important Polish works to promote the blood libel. Two priests involved in the Frankist accusation, Father Gaudenty Pikulski and Bishop Jan Andrzej Załuski, had copies of Serafinowicz's manuscript.

It was not unheard of for Jewish converts to Christianity to supply "evidence" in blood libel trials. But Serafinowicz went much further than his predecessors. To the best of my knowledge, no other Jewish convert devoted an entire work to the accusation, and none claimed that he himself had participated in such rituals before his conversion or had even witnessed them. Serafinowicz buttressed his accusation by confessing to four ritual murders, adding weight to his accusation. Moreover, he presented himself as a learned rabbi and based his argument on Jewish sources, making it possible to create a theological foundation for other ritual murder cases in Poland. Serafinowicz's aim was to demonstrate "from the Talmud" that holy books specifically commanded Jews to mutilate the host, to deface Christian images, especially that of Virgin Mary, and to use Christian blood in their rites. The Yiddish original and a copy of the Polish translation of the manuscript belonging to the National Library in Warsaw were burned in 1944.

However, it is possible to reconstruct substantial parts of Serafinowicz's manuscript on the basis of other works printed in the early and mid-eighteenth century. The work had the form of a kind of almanac, a calendar, describing what specific blasphemies and crimes the Jews were to commit in consecutive months of the Jewish year.[38] The section devoted to the month of Nisan presented the "history" of the ritual murder rite. According to Serafinowicz, when Christianity began to spread in the world and the Christians became apprehensive about the Jews, the rabbis held a council to decide what they could do to appease the Christians. Following the principles of Jewish sympathetic magic, and referring to the Talmud tractate Gittin 57b, which describes how Nabuzaradan stilled the bubbling blood of Zechariah by killing Jewish children, the rabbis decided to use the blood of Christian children to quiet the a blood of Christian rulers.[39]

Thereafter, it became common to employ Christian blood in Jewish magic. The specific uses of Christian blood were said to be as follows: there were two weeks every year during which the Jews marked the doorpost of Christian houses with blood to secure the goodwill of the inhabitants; newlyweds were given an egg spiced with Christian blood during the marriage ceremony; similarly prepared eggs were also given to the dying and were buried under houses; Christian blood was used for the preparation of matzot and in magical rites designed to discomfit business competitors.[40]

Given the unprecedented character of his accusations, the Jewish authorities had to produce a response of comparable impact. The officials of the Council of Four Lands wrote to Serafinowicz's godmother, Castelaness Elżbieta Sieniawska, requesting permission to hold a disputation during which they could refute his charges. This appears to have been the only instance in early modern Poland (and possibly anywhere else) in which the Jews demanded a public disputation on a sensitive religious issue with a Christian, not vice versa.[41] It was the Jewish side that wanted to publicize the issue, possibly believing that it was impossible to silence Serafinowicz. Permission was granted, and the arrangements for the disputation were made in Warsaw. However, Serafinowicz failed to show up. Sieniawska issued an edict exonerating the Jews and calling for a halt to the persecutions caused by the accusation.[42]

In contrast to earlier precedents, the Jewish side worked very hard to give the issue as prominent a public profile as possible. It was commonplace in anti-Jewish literature to claim that the Jews often managed to hush up ritual murder accusations and, through bribery and behind-the-scenes manipulations, to avoid bringing the matter to court. That this was not only an anti-Semitic stereotype is confirmed also by Jewish sources, which attest to expenses incurred by *shtadlanim* who employed this strategy. For the accusers, bribery and lobbying only confirmed their charges; for the Jews, they were nearly the only practical defense against the libel. However, the Serafinowicz case saw a significant shift of approach. The case set a precedent for public disputations concerning ritual murder in Poland, and, in the first round, the Jews were clearly victorious. The miscarried disputation between Serafinowicz and the rabbis in Warsaw had direct bearing on the very real disputation between the rabbis and the Frankists in Lwów some forty years later. However, before I turn to this disputation, I will discuss the ritual murder trials directly linked to the development of Frankism.

Ritual Murder Trials in Żytomierz and Jampol

The years following Serafinowicz's accusations saw the blood libel trials of Lwów (1728),[43] Poznań (1736),[44] Zasław (1747),[45] and Dunajogród (1748).[46] Although these accusations contributed to the general atmosphere of fear and persecution, they had no direct bearing on the development of Frankism. From the perspective of the current analysis, the most important trial was that of Żytomierz in 1753. On Easter Monday, the body of three-and-a-half-year-old Stefan Studzieński was found. Bishop Kajetan Sołtyk, at that time the coadjutor of the diocese in which the event took place, Kiev, ordered the imprisonment of thirty-one Jews, among whom were the richest leaseholders in the land. The district court subjected the accused to torture, found them guilty, and condemned six of them to be flayed alive and then quartered and six others to be quartered. The remaining Jews were acquitted. Some of those convicted decided to accept baptism; in their cases, the sentence was commuted to beheading rather than quartering. In the other cases, the verdict was carried out. After the executions, the bishop baptized thirteen other Jews.[47]

A similar trial took place three years later in Jampol, in the Łuck diocese. Prince Radziwiłł ordered an investigation, which determined that the body of a child found in the river showed no signs of a violent death. The court released the accused Jews. However, the bishop of Łuck, Antoni Wołłowicz, intervened: the accused were put on trial again, tortured, forced to give false testimonies, and condemned to death.[48]

The Jews initiated a vigorous campaign to counter the blood libels. They argued that the victims had died of illness and that Sołtyk was exploiting the incidents for personal gain. The bishop reportedly accepted five hundred red ducats and sable furs worth three hundred ducats in exchange for a promise to release the accused.[49] It was well known that Sołtyk was addicted to gambling, and his debts amounted to 200,000 ducats, while his annual income was only 45,000. It was widely rumored that Sołtyk had attempted to extort money from the Jews in order to pay his debts.[50]

In response to the ritual murder accusations, the Council of Four Lands dispatched an emissary, Elyakim ben Asher Zelig, to Rome.[51] Elyakim was admitted to an audience before Pope Benedict XIV, during which he presented a petition requesting defense against the ritual murder accusations.[52] The pope referred the matter to the Holy Office for investigation. The Inquisition, in turn, requested the opinion of Cardinal Lorenzo Ganganelli (later Pope Clement XIV). After demanding detailed reports from the papal nuncio in Warsaw,

Bishop Serra, and the bishops of Łuck (Wołłowicz) and Kiev (Sołtyk),[53] Gan-ganelli set about preparing a memorandum for the papacy.

In Poland, faced with the widespread condemnation of his greed and al-legations of orchestrating the trial and the illegal confiscation of Jewish prop-erty, Bishop Sołtyk found himself suddenly barred from appointment to a much higher Church office. Around that time, Sołtyk was playing for the highest stakes: Bishop Andrzej Załuski was terminally ill, so the bishopric of Kraków was about to become vacant. The diocese was one of the richest in Eu-rope, and the seat of the bishop of Kraków was by far the most lucrative eccle-siastical position in the Commonwealth; it was much more coveted than the largely titular job of the primate of Poland. Sołtyk intended to secure the post for himself. He managed to muster the support of the minister of Augustus III, Count Heinrich Brühl, and the Crown Court Marshal Jerzy Mniszech,[54] but he still needed to improve his public image, which had been tarnished by the Żytomierz affair. It was undoubtedly to his advantage to "prove" that the Żytomierz accusations were true and that Jews indeed used Christian blood for ritual purposes. If he could arrange to have the Jews confirm the accusa-tion of ritual murder independently, Sołtyk could silence his critics and thus be cleared of all charges.

The Propaganda Campaign of 1758

In early 1758, the anonymous pamphlet *Błędy talmudowe od samychże Żydów uznane y przez nową sektę Siapwscieciuchów, czyli Contratalmudystów wyiawione* (The errors of the Talmud acknowledged by the Jews themselves and revealed by the new sect of *Siapwscieciuchy* or the Contra-Talmudists) was published in Lwów.[55] This pamphlet was widely circulated, and within a year was reprinted at least twice. It stated that a sect of "Siapwscieciuchy" had arisen in distant countries and in 1757 had begun spreading among Polish Jews. The sectarians believed that the Talmud offended both human and divine laws and that the messiah had already arrived, and they professed the oneness of God in the Trinity.[56] Having arrived in Poland, the Siapwscieciuchy requested protection from Bishop Dembowski and demanded an opportunity to debate their faith with other Jews. Thereafter, they became known as "Contra-Talmudists." In addition to a short account of the events in Kamieniec, the pamphlet contains a kind of anti-Semitic almanac describing various Jewish anti-Christian cus-toms allegedly revealed by the Contra-Talmudists. The customs are arranged

according to the months of the Jewish and Christian calendars. The beginning
of the section devoted to April/Nisan reads:

> If there is any month in which it is appropriate to detest Jewish cus-
> toms, it is certainly this month. On the second day [of Nisan], the
> Jews are obliged to murder a Christian child in order to begin this
> month by shedding Christian blood. . . . They need the blood first
> and foremost to spellbind the Christians, so that they will be favor-
> ably inclined toward the Jews. Further, they need blood for newly-
> weds, who are given an egg spiced with blood during the ceremony
> of marriage. The rabbis also anoint dying Jews using the white of an
> egg mixed with blood. Finally, the Jews must use Christian blood
> for [the preparation] of the matzot.[57]

Jan Doktór, who has so far been the only scholar to discuss *Błędy talmudowe*, believed that the pamphlet was indeed written and printed by the Frankists.[58] His claim, however, seems completely unconvincing. To begin with,
although the term "siapwscieciuchy" is clearly a distorted form of the Polish
and Yiddish slur *szabsaćwinniki*, Sabbatians, this precise form of the word does
not appear in any other source and seems to be an ad hoc creation of someone
unfamiliar with the debates surrounding Sabbatianism in Poland. In 1758, the
Frankists were still in hiding in fear of the rabbinic persecution that followed
the death of Bishop Dembowski. At that time, members of the sect did not
know any Polish (the pamphlet is written in correct Polish, though not in a
very sophisticated style) and did not have access to printing facilities. Nor did
they have the funding to cover the costs of publication. The booklet was entirely based on Serafinowicz, both in detail and in its calendrical form. It seems
impossible that the Frankists knew or were able to utilize this material.

A few years later, in 1760, Sołtyk wrote his own account of the ritual
murder trials. The manuscript version of his work contains an account of
Frankism, which was not included in the printed edition.[59] The first printed
edition, titled *Złość żydowska w zamęczeniu dzieci katolickich* (Jewish wrath
and the torture of Catholic children), encompassed only the official documents pertaining to the Żytomierz trial.[60] In the second and subsequent editions of the book,[61] however, Sołtyk reproduced the entire brochure *Błędy
talmudowe*, claimed authorship, and said that his statements concerning the
ritual murder were based on evidence supplied by the Frankists. I propose
that the brochure ascribed to the Frankists was written in the circle of Bishop

Sołtyk in 1758 and constituted part of his campaign to deflect the allegations of evidence-forging, bribery, and the judicial murder of the Jews in the trial of Żytomierz in 1753.[62]

On 11 July 1758, King Augustus III issued a letter of *salvus conductus* for the Frankists who had fled to the Ottoman Empire after the death of Dembowski, and members of the sect gradually began to return to the Commonwealth.[63] To date, scholars have been unable to explain this sudden change of climate, attributing the issuance of the safe conduct to unspecified machinations at the royal court.[64] I believe that Augustus's order can be safely credited to Sołtyk's influence. The Frankists who returned from Turkey established themselves in Iwanie, Uścieczko, and Harmackie; all three villages belonged to Bishop Antoni Sebastian Dembowski, brother of Frank's late protector, Mikołaj Dembowski. Antoni Dembowski was a close friend of Sołtyk: both bishops belonged to the same political faction, close to King Augustus III and opposing the powerful Czartoryski family. As Sołtyk had a vital interest in using the Frankists for his own purposes, the scenario in which the bishop persuaded the king to bring the sect back to Poland is extremely likely.

While anti-Jewish propaganda was spreading in Poland, Elyakim ben Asher Zelig's mission to Rome began to achieve its first results. The reports of the papal nuncio, Serra, and Bishops Wołłowicz and Sołtyk finally reached the Holy Office. On the basis of these reports, and drawing upon papal pronouncements and judicial opinions in earlier ritual murder accusations, Ganganelli determined that there was no evidence that these practices actually took place. The account of the bishop of Łuck attested only that he was quick to "consign people to death for a crime supposed but never proved,"[65] while the report of the bishop of Kiev was, in fact, Sołtyk's defense against the "charge of cursed hunger for gold."[66] The accusations were often based on reports of "neophytes from Judaism, [who exhibit] a certain passion against their own nation, as a result of which they not infrequently go beyond the limits of truth."[67] Ganganelli concluded that the Holy See should "take some measure to protect the Jews of Poland" so that "the name of Christ may not be blasphemed by the Jews and their conversion not become more difficult."[68]

Favorable as it was for the Polish Jews, the memorandum was submitted to the Holy Office only toward the end of 1759 and read before Pope Clement XIII on 10 January 1760.[69] Meanwhile, events in Poland ran their course.

The Lwów Disputation

Frank returned to Poland in August 1758. The safe conduct granted by Augustus III was valid for only three months, and renewed persecution by the rabbinate against the sectarians who returned to Poland grew apace. Their bargaining position was very weak: they had already burned bridges with mainstream Judaism and could not receive support of the Christians without offering something in exchange. Accordingly, Frank changed his pro-Muslim, anti-Christian orientation expressed after the Kamieniec disputation; upon arrival in Lwów, he unequivocally declared himself a candidate for baptism and tried to conceal any information about his earlier conversion to Islam. This substantial change of position came to the fore in a petition titled *Suplika Żydów Wiarę Świętą Chrześcijańską przyjmujących i chrztu świętego rządzających* [*sic*] (Supplication of the Jews accepting the holy Catholic faith and requesting holy baptism), submitted on 20 February 1759 to the primate of Poland, Archbishop Łubieński. The supplication differs significantly from earlier Frankist petitions to secular and ecclesiastical authorities in Poland.

Previously, the Frankists always presented themselves as an autonomous group opposed to the power of the rabbis, but remaining a part of the Jewish people and willing to remain *within* Judaism. While they had presented some tenets of their belief as similar to Christian tenets, they had never unconditionally accepted Christianity or declared themselves as candidates for baptism. The supplication sent to Łubieński was the first Frankist document to express the idea that they might convert to Christianity explicitly. The signatories, Yehudah Leyb Krysa and Solomon Shorr of Rohatyn, claimed to speak in the name of "the Jews of Poland, Hungary, Turkey, Moldavia, Wallachia, and so on," who secretly professed the creed that had been put forward by the Contra-Talmudists during the Kamieniec disputation of 1757.

This time, however, their creed was not formulated in terms of the rejection of the Talmud and the belief in the triune character of the Godhead, but much more specifically: as a belief that "Jesus Christ, eternal Son of God, born of the Virgin Mary, true God and true Man, murdered by our fathers on the cross, was the true messiah promised by the prophets."[70] The supplication ended with a request for another disputation with the rabbis to demonstrate that "God came to the world in human flesh and was tormented for the sake of mankind." The avowed aims of the disputation were to facilitate the unity of all faiths and to prove that the Jews used Christian blood for ritual purposes.

The exact motions for the disputation were formulated for the first time in a manifesto submitted to the administrator of the Lwów diocese, Father Stanisław Mikulski, on 25 May 1759.[71] Yehudah Leyb Krysa and Solomon Shorr declared that they spoke on behalf of "the catechumens belonging to the formerly chosen" Jewish nation and declared that for the purification and trying of their faith, Divine Providence had ordained their persecution by the Talmudists. Referring to the letter of safe conduct issued by Augustus III, they again demanded protection. They stated that rabbinic persecution continued in clear violation of the king's order, and requested permission for a disputation after which they would undergo baptism. Finally, they presented the following seven points for the debate:

1. All prophecies about the coming of the messiah have already been fulfilled.
2. The messiah is the true God, whose name is Adonai. He took human form and suffered for our redemption.
3. Since the advent of the true messiah, sacrifices and ceremonies have been abolished.
4. Everyone should follow the teaching of the messiah, for salvation lies only within it.
5. The cross is the sign of the Holy Trinity and the seal of the messiah.
6. A person can achieve faith in the king messiah only through baptism.
7. The Talmud teaches that Jews need Christian blood, and whoever believes in the Talmud is bound to use it.

The disputations opened on 17 July 1759[72] and continued until 19 September.[73] The point concerning the Jews' "need" for Christian blood was first presented during the eleventh session, on 6 August. The rabbinate managed to postpone discussion of this point for almost a month, until 10 September. Finally, the debate took place. The Frankists stated that conclusive evidence confirming Jewish guilt in this matter had been adduced in many past trials in Poland and Lithuania. They confessed that they themselves had been taught "in their youth" to use Christian blood, but, enlightened by the teachings of the Church, they rejected their former ways and determined to reveal Jewish malice to the "entire world."[74]

Medieval and early modern defamatory writing presented the alleged use of Christian blood by the Jews as a barbaric folk custom or magical practice.

In addition to testimonies pertaining to a specific case, the general charges were supported by references to folklore (describing accounts of Jewish customs allegedly involving the use of blood) and by the authority of previous court rulings. Serafinowicz's writings introduced significant modifications to this tradition: his pamphlet had the wider aim of establishing that the blood rite is a theological principle of Judaism and merged magical discourse with theological argument based on quotations from Jewish sources. Furthermore, Serafinowicz was the first to buttress his accusation by claiming that he himself had participated in blood ceremonies and that his revelation should be understood as an act of expiation and atonement for his part in crimes. Not only did this lend additional weight to the accusation; it also helped to deflect the recurrent counterargument that the accuser was motivated by the desire for revenge or by malice.

All these elements were fully developed in the Frankist accusation, which differed substantially from earlier blood libels in Poland and elsewhere. Although previous accusations constituted a necessary background for the whole affair, earlier court cases played no direct role in the disputation. The Frankists did claim that these charges had already been proved in earlier trials, but only in their opening statement. Like Serafinowicz, the Frankists also admitted they had themselves committed ritual murders "in their youth." However, despite the references to Jewish sources, Serafinowicz's work was essentially based on folkloristic accounts and the underlying magical concept of the Jews' physical "need" for Christian blood: in Serafinowicz, the Jews were presented as vampires who were unable to live without consuming blood. This type of argumentation did not appear in the Frankist case. The explicit target of the attack here were not the mythologized "Jews" but "those who believe in the Talmud." The argument did not mention any folk customs but attempted to give a theological rationale for blood rituals from the Talmud and rabbinic literature.

As has been pointed out by scholars, medieval and early modern defenders of Jews and Judaism often accepted the basic premise of Jewish malice and hatred of Christians, seeking only to limit the damage by arguing that these characteristics were not congenital to the Jewish people or intrinsic to their customs but limited to single persons or isolated groups. In blood libel cases, the common line of defense was to cut the losses and state that the murders might indeed have happened but that they had been committed by corrupt individuals or depraved sectarians. The Jews as a group should not be blamed for the deeds of a few criminals any more than Christianity should be blamed for the actions of Christian lawbreakers or heretics. From this perspective, the Frankist accusation had the broadest possible aim: the accusers maintained that Judaism as such (and not only individual Jews or heretical sects) advocated human sacrifice and the shedding of Christian blood. The tactic employed by the accusers was to create a semblance of objectivity by dressing the argument as scholarly discourse, ornamented with technical terminology, references to rabbinic authorities, and phrases in Hebrew and Aramaic.

A full account of the case would exceed the scope of this chapter. I shall quote (with a few minor abridgments) the first motion of the debate and briefly summarize the remaining points.[75] The Frankists opened the disputation as follows:

> The book *Aurechaim Megine Erec*,[76] p. 242, chap. 412, states: *Micwe lachzeur acher jain udym* = It is a commandment to obtain red wine.[77] The reason [for this commandment] is given in the same book by Rabbi Abraham, who says *Zejcher lejdam*, the commemoration of blood. Could the Talmudists say, what blood? If they say: "This is for the commemoration of the blood that was among the Ten Plagues," why don't they commemorate all of the Plagues? They might say on the basis of the same book that Rabbi David wrote: *Od rejmez leudym zejher lejdam szochoju pare szojchet benaj Isruel*, another hint why [the wine] should be red is to commemorate the blood of the children of Israel slaughtered by Pharaoh.[78] [However,] the Bible . . . does not mention Pharaoh shedding the blood of Jewish children, so why do they commemorate something that did not happen? And why does the author write so secretively "another hint," that is, "I am giving you a sign," or "I am suggesting this to you so that no one understands"? Why didn't he write "another reason"? Why hint at something instead of saying it explicitly? It is written in the same book: *Wajhuidne nimneu milajikach jain Udym mipnej elilojs szejkurym* = Now we do not use red wine on account of the false accusations. The Jews should be asked: What are the accusations regarding the use of red wine for Easter? And if, as they themselves claim, the custom is no longer practiced on account of accusations, why do they still print [books that demand it to be practiced]? . . . We explain the teachings of the rabbis: . . . the rabbis, who guard the secret from the people, read [the fragment of *Shulhan arukh* as referring to] *yayin adom*, red wine, but in the

event, it refers to *yayin edom*, Christian blood, for, as Rambam p. 55 states, the term "Edom" denotes those who sanctify Sunday, the first day of the week.[79] For this reason, Rabbi David wrote *od rejmez*, another hint, which is a secret allusion that the rabbis should use not wine but blood, and that his statement does not refer to Jewish children killed by Pharaoh (which did not happen) but to the Jews being obliged to kill Christian children.[80]

The second motion drew upon the Passover Haggadah's abbreviation of the first letters of the Ten Plagues as *detsakh, adash, be'ahav*.[81] According to the Frankists, the acrostic did not refer to the Plagues, but to the sentence *dam tserikhim kulanu al derekh she-asu be-oto ish hakhamim bi-yerushalayim*, "We all need blood, just as the sages did to this man in Jerusalem."[82] Interestingly, the reference to Jesus ("this man") was not recognized as such by the Christian public and was not discussed during the disputation.

The third thesis again adduced a fragment of *Shulhan arukh*. The Frankists stated that the reason for the prohibition of kneading and baking of unleavened bread in the presence[83] of a heathen (which they interpreted as a reference to a Christian), a deaf person, an imbecile, or a minor on the first night of Passover is that the matzot contain blood.[84] They argued further that for the same reason, it was necessary to guard the matzot, and quoted the tractate Pesahim 41a, "R. Huna said: The dough of a heathen, a man may fill his stomach with them, providing that he eats as much as an olive of unleavened bread at the end" as proof that the Jews consume Christian blood.

The two following motions were also based on the talmudic tractate Pesahim.[85] The first quoted section 3b, describing a non-Jew who was killed for taking part in a Passover service in Jerusalem; the Frankists argued that the non-Jew, being uncircumcised, must have been a Christian and that the story alluded to the fact that the Jews killed Christians for Passover. The other motion summarized section 92a, about the proselyte to Judaism accepted on the eve of Passover. According to the Frankists, the statement "one who separates himself from the lack of circumcision is as though he separated from a grave" should be understood as meaning that a person who converts to Judaism before Passover thereby escapes death by Jewish hands during the festival.

The final motion was designed to forestall the obvious counterargument that since the Hebrew Bible prohibits the Jews even the blood of animals,[86] they cannot possibly be accused of the consumption of human blood.[87] To challenge this line of argumentation, the Frankist claimed that rabbinic writ-

ings present rules different from the Bible. They quoted the Talmud tractate Ketubbot[88] and Maimonides' *Mishneh Torah*,[89] and argued that human
blood is specifically excluded from the biblical prohibition and that the rabbis themselves deemed the blood of "two-legged creatures" permitted for
consumption.[90]

For the Jewish participants in the disputation, it was instantly clear that
the references to the Talmud and other Jewish sources had been misrepresented, quoted out of context, and, in some cases, mistranslated to suit the
point. For instance, the chief disputant on the rabbinic side, Rabbi Hayyim
Cohen Rapaport, immediately noted that the fragment of *Shulhan arukh* allegedly referring to the absolute commandment of using red wine for Passover
merely stated that red wine is preferred when it is better than white.[91] The
reading of Rabbi Yehudah's acrostic from the Haggadah was completely arbi-
trary, the quotation from tractate Pesahim referring to a Christian being present during the kneading of unleavened bread was deliberately mistranslated,
and the talmudic "permission to consume human blood" referred to the fact
that one may swallow blood that appears on one's gums.

Still, the Frankist argument, spiced with foreign words and exotic sources,
made a powerful impression on the Christian public. The accusation was much
more sophisticated than previous charges, even if from the Jewish perspective,
the Frankist "learning" was really a cruel mockery of Jewish tradition. Suddenly, some Jews were "proving" from their own most sacred writings that suspicions long voiced by Christian anti-Jewish writers were true. The quotations
adduced by the Frankists came from the Talmud, *Shulhan arukh*, *Ture zahav*,
the Code of Maimonides, and the Passover Haggadah. While this range of
references would not challenge an aspiring rabbinic student, it was beyond the
abilities of most Christian theologians even to verify whether the quotations
had been presented faithfully and if the arguments made sense at all. Indeed,
the most balanced account of the disputation, Ber Birkenthal's *Divre binah*,
confirms that even some fairly unprejudiced people among the audience could
not decide which side was right in the disputation.[92]

Most important, the Frankists managed to present the blood accusation
as an issue open to debate among experts in rabbinic literature. The charge was
presented not as an external accusation leveled against the Jews by their Gentile enemies but as something about which the Jews themselves disagree. Even
if the Frankists did not convince everyone present, they succeeded in placing
the polemics on an entirely new level.

Answers to the Blood Libel

The public disputation in Lwów was only the outer layer of the complex of issues that directed the course of events. Beneath it lay the behind-the-scenes machinations surrounding the debate. The papacy, represented in Poland by the nuncios Nicolai Serra (until January 1760) and Antonio Eugenio Visconti (from February 1760 until 1766), played a crucial role. The activities of the nuncios, as well as the development of the official position of the Church, can be reconstructed from regular dispatches sent from Warsaw to Rome, now housed in the Vatican Secret Archives. Normally, papal nuncios in European capitals dispatched reports to the Curia on specific days, usually twice a month. In addition to these "ordinary dispatches" (*dispacci ordinari*), nuncios also sent "extraordinary dispatches" (*dispacci straordinari*) when special circumstances arose. The importance of the Frankist affair for the papacy is indicated by the fact that from 1 August 1759 until 20 February 1760, all the ordinary and some 80 percent of the extraordinary dispatches of the Warsaw nuncios were devoted entirely or partly to this issue; Nuncio Serra explicitly stated that "the issue is so important that I do not fail to discuss it in any letter."[93]

Serra first learned about the blood accusation in Lwów not from members of the Polish clergy but from the representatives of the Jewish authorities. The *shtadlan* of the Council of Four Lands, Baruch me-Erets Yavan, had already been in touch with the nuncio in 1757, when Bishop Dembowski's edict was issued. Toward the end of July 1759, Yavan contacted Serra again and complained that the administrator of the Lwów diocese was forcing the Jews to participate in another disputation. In the dispatch dated 1 August, the nuncio expressed his displeasure regarding the idea of a public disputation and warned that "this kind of contentious debate leads more often to the escalation of the conflict than to its resolution."[94] Serra believed that the Jews did not know enough about Christianity to engage in a religious disputation touching upon, among other things, Christian dogmata. The Talmudists should be convinced by truth, virtue, and grace and not by coercion and penalties, which are contrary to the spirit of the Gospel.[95] Since the nuncio only learned about the disputation about a month after it had begun, he could not prevent it.

Following Yavan's second complaint, Serra contacted Mikulski, who told him that he had been approached by a group of Jews seeking baptism. However, these Jews insisted that they would not accept Christianity without a public declaration of their new faith and an opportunity to convince their coreligionists. They had also presented a manifesto to Mikulski. When it turned out that the manifesto contained ritual murder charges, Mikulski decided that the matter was too grave to forgo investigation and allowed for the debate. Although Serra considered the accusation "very improbable," he accepted this argument and agreed that a disputation should be conducted "in order to determine unequivocally, whether using Christian blood was indeed a precept of the Jewish religion, as it seems to follow from the Talmud. If this were the case, it would explain numerous murders of Christians, of which the Jews have often been accused in this kingdom. It would be worthwhile to clarify the matter to the Polish noblemen, who commonly use these people as leaseholders and mercantile agents, thereby causing great suffering of the common people."[96]

In his correspondence with the nuncio, Mikulski presented the matter as if the initial impulse for the disputation had come from the Frankists and the whole matter revolved around their willingness to convert to Christianity. In his account, the Frankists had approached him as prospective converts, and only during the investigation did it suddenly "turn out" that they were also accusing the Jews of using Christian blood for ritual purposes. In fact, it was exactly the other way around: initially, the Frankists did not want to convert, and the blood libel came first. The local clergy was in favor of proclaiming this point, and for Sołtyk and Wołłowicz the whole rationale for the debate consisted in proving the truth of the blood libel. There is some evidence that Mikulski lied to the nuncio and that it was he who pressed the Frankists to include the ritual murder accusation in the disputation.[97] Serra's own position was also ambiguous: he delayed forwarding reports from Lwów to Rome and dragged his feet under the pretext of waiting for clear instructions from the Curia and temporarily refraining from taking sides. For instance, on 5 December 1759, he stated:

> I cannot really say what would be the result of further disputation. It seems to me completely incredible that such a doctrine [commanding the use of Christian blood] is expounded in the books of the Talmud, but because of the deep and unclear character of the texts quoted during the last session in Lwów, it is impossible to pronounce a clear verdict, especially given that so few people mastered these dead languages [Hebrew and Aramaic] and that there are many controversies among the experts. Accordingly, I do not say anything about the last point concerning the doctrine, from which the practice of using Christian blood is said to follow.[98]

Whatever their personal beliefs might have been, both Serra and Mikulski clearly wanted to avoid raising their heads above the parapet. In the crucial months of 1759, Ganganelli's report was not yet ready, hence it was impossible to tell whether the Holy See would get involved in the affair at all and, if so, what the papacy's official position would be. Rejecting the accusation altogether would upset such powerful individuals as Sołtyk, while accepting it in whole or in part might contradict the eventual position of the papacy. Serra and Mikulski decided to play for time.

Meanwhile, doubts concerning the Frankists' true intentions began to accumulate. In early August, Serra remarked that "the whole affair might be the beginning of a new sect among the Jews."[99] In another dispatch, he stated that the Frankists "are probably a new sect that finds it advantageous to pretend they are half-Christians."[100] The nuncio distrusted Frank ("a swindler . . . possessed by the spirit of vanity and ambition . . ., who claims he has control over the fate of his followers in this world and the next")[101] and the Frankists' interpreter Moliwda ("a man of bad reputation who, acting for his own advantage and depending on changing circumstances, was selling his services to many different sects, whose beliefs he took for his own").[102] He also suspected that the authority of the Church was being abused in pursuit of the personal agendas of the local clergy. Mikulski, for his part, also began to backtrack: in a letter to Primate Łubieński, he emphasized that he had no clear impression regarding the purity of the Frankists' motives and expressed doubts concerning Moliwda's conduct.[103]

In the end, the ecclesiastical authorities in Poland decided not to render a decisive verdict. Mikulski announced that the Frankists had won the debate on all points except the crucial motion concerning the use of blood by the Jews. On this last point, the verdict was pending: the Jews were required to provide a written answer to the charges and to bring copies of the Talmud to the consistory for further examination by Catholic theologians. However, the authorities made no effort to enforce these requirements and let the matter rest. Serra described Mikulski's ruling as follows:

The intricacies of the Hebrew writings and the absence of people who knew the language made it impossible to decide the true meaning of the text and to determine [which interpretation is] supported by the [Jewish] tradition. The lack of clarity regarding this matter forced the administrator to request the support of two clergymen, one Franciscan and one Jesuit, both fluent in Hebrew.

Unfortunately, neither of them was in Lwów during the disputation. Accordingly, the Talmudists were told to deposit their books
[in the consistory] for further examination; it was well known, in
any event, that these books were full of godlessness, lies, slanders,
blasphemies against the Christian religion. That was the end of the
final session.[104]

The two clergymen mentioned in the dispatch were the Bernardine Gaudenty Pikulski and the Jesuit Konstanty Awedyk; in the event, neither of the two
was "fluent in Hebrew," and both were present in Lwów during the disputation.
It is unclear whether Serra was lying or misinformed. However, it is clear that
the highest echelon of the Polish clergy, aside from extremists such as Sołtyk,
wished to avoid an all-out condemnation of the Jews. Sołtyk's stance did not
prevail, and more moderate opinions gained a foothold. Primate Łubieński's
position, for instance, was much more nuanced than Sołtyk's. Łubieński's account of the Frankist case is no longer extant;[105] however, some of the conversations he had with his aides in 1759 were recorded by a visitor from Saxony,
Count Wackenbarth-Salmour. According to Wackenbarth, Łubieński had not
really wished for a total victory in the debate of the Frankists.[106]

Following the disputation, there were voices calling for the expulsion
of the Jews from Poland. Given the deep economic ties between the Polish
Church and the *kahal*, this was definitely not a result that the clergy—despite
its anti-Jewish rhetoric—wished to achieve. In the longer run, Łubieński's aim
was to preserve the status quo: keeping the Jews subjugated and exploiting
them for economic purposes. From the tactical point of view, the best outcome was failure to achieve a definitive solution: the accusation hung over
the heads of the Jews like the sword of Damocles, and the Frankists were not
granted a victory that would give them too much leverage. Łubieński and his
entourage supported the blood accusation not because they believed it to be
true but because they reckoned that it would create an unbridgeable gap between the Frankists and other Jews, thereby thwarting any suggestion of their
being granted autonomy within Judaism. After launching the accusation, the
Frankists could not possibly have justified any attempts to remain Jewish, nor
could they have hoped to be taken back by the rest of the Jewish community.
The passage from the accusation to conversion could not be avoided.

From the Jewish perspective, nothing could entirely undo the damage
caused by the Frankist accusation. The debate on the blood libel remained
formally unresolved: the Jews were obliged to provide a written answer to the

Frankists' charges and to deposit their books in the consistory for examination. The authorities did not implement these demands, but they could have begun enforcing them at any opportune moment. In order for the threat to remain palpable, the Frankists did not even have to win the live debate; it was enough to present the blood accusation as something about which experts in Judaism disagree. Given the lack of a competent arbiter, the rabbis' defense would be seen as, at best, one of two competing interpretations of arcane sources. Accordingly, about the only line of defense available to the Jews was to argue that the accusation had already been disproved by Christian scholars and that Christian rulers had rejected the libel in the past. Without waiting for the results of Elyakim's mission to Rome, the Jews approached prominent theologians to solicit their help in deflecting the accusation. The first positive result in this effort was obtained from the Halle Lutheran theologians, thanks to Rabbi Jonathan Eibeschütz.

As Sid Leiman has demonstrated, whether or not Eibeschütz himself was a Sabbatian, he never collaborated with the Frankists on the blood libel.[107] Quite the opposite: Eibeschütz used all his Christian contacts to obtain a condemnation of the ritual murder accusation. As early as 1736, he solicited a pronouncement against the libel from the censor of the Hebrew books in Prague, the Jesuit Franciscus Haselbauer.[108] A few months after the Lwów disputation, in December 1759, Eibeschütz wrote a refutation of the Frankist manifesto.[109] He sent it to the dean of the theological faculty at Halle, Johann Heinrich Callenberg, and requested support in combating the libel. Although Callenberg himself refused to get involved, the doyen of the Halle scholars, Benedict Michaelis, wrote a short statement concordant with Eibeschütz's position, while a younger member of the faculty, Johann Salomo Semler, prepared a lengthy dissertation on the subject.

Semler's report was the first printed defense of Jews and Judaism that responded directly to the specific charges of the Frankists. The text was titled "On the Renewed Accusation [*erneute Beschuldigung*] that Jews Need Christian Blood," and the whole argument was based on the premise that the accusation had been laid to rest a long time ago. Accordingly, Semler brought together a long list of condemnations of the accusation by Christian theologians and secular rulers. However, he did not restrict himself to quoting past authorities. He characterized his own position as based on the combination of common sense (*gesund Vernunft*) and Christian talmudic scholarship and argued that in the present age, Christian mastery of Jewish texts was "often superior to that of the Jews."[110] Therefore Christian scholars were not only perfectly capable of assessing the truth of the accusation, but they also could and should serve as arbiters in internal Jewish controversies. However, despite his ambitious aim, Semler failed to produce any talmudic references and quoted only one work written by a Jew, Manasseh ben Israel's *Vindicae Judaeorum* (1656).[111]

Semler's focus was whether the blood rite was a theological tenet of Judaism. He did not seek to examine specific ritual murder cases or verify past literary accounts. In fact, Semler did allow for the possibility that in "extreme situations," Jews had indeed killed Christian or other children. Even if these murders happened, however, they had no theological motive based on the Talmud but resulted merely from personal hatred and anger.[112] Since the Frankists argued "from the Talmud," Semler had to prove that not only were the past accusations untrue but also that the Talmud itself did not contain the ideas alleged by the accusers.[113]

What this meant for Semler was not an analysis of concrete customs or rituals of Judaism as expounded in the Talmud. The theologian's report was an early example of the emerging perception of Judaism as a system of ethics, which would later become widespread in Germany. For Semler, the Frankist accusation was "obviously" untrue, since the alleged act contradicted the moral teachings of the Jewish religion. The Jews, insofar as they followed their religion, rabbinic Judaism, were forbidden to commit murder, ritual or otherwise; if individual Jews committed murders, they did so in defiance of their religion. Consequently, Semler argued, the Frankist accusation might indeed have reflect existing practices, but these practices did not belong to a legitimate version of Judaism.[114] Hence, the rabbinic position versus the Frankists should be seen as mainstream Jewish opposition to heresy.

Semler's account was based on common sense and historical erudition, qualities clearly absent in the writings circulating in Poland of that time. While his report was at times superficial, it did touch upon the crux of the problem: from the theological perspective, the biggest difficulty of the Frankist affair in Poland was precisely to decide what constituted the mainstream of Judaism and what was heresy. However, neither Michaelis's nor Semler's writings appear to have had any impact on the developments in Poland. There is no evidence that they were known to the people behind the disputation in Lwów; even if they were, the writings of German Protestant theologians would not have exerted much influence upon the Catholic clergy.

A much more significant role was played by another document. While Ganganelli was working on his report, he realized that he could account for earlier Christian pronouncements on the blood libel but not verify Jewish sources adduced by the Frankists. Elyakim's attempts to prove that the Talmud did not contain the demand to use Christian blood could only appeal to the good faith of the papal officials: in Rome, there was no Christian theologian who could verify the talmudic references; moreover, in the city there was not a single copy of the Talmud, on which an argument could be based.[115] In addition to Ganganelli's report, the papal authorities requested further expert testimony, this time referring not to the general issue of the Christian position on the blood accusation but to the specific points raised by the Frankists during the disputation. As there was no one in Rome who could provide such testimony, the Holy Office requested the opinion of the chair of Hebrew at the Sorbonne, Jean-Baptiste de L'Advocat.

The chair of Hebrew in Paris was founded in 1751 by Louis Duke of Orléans "to provide an interpretation of the Holy Scripture according to the Hebrew text";[116] the polymath L'Advocat, who had served as a librarian at Sorbonne since 1742, was appointed its first holder. L'Advocat's primary interest was biblical criticism. He maintained that the Jews, motivated by their hatred of the Christian religion, intentionally "corrupted, altered, and falsified the Hebrew texts of the Bible."[117] Accordingly, all existing printed Hebrew Bibles were unreliable and the correct Christian exegesis of the Scripture required restoring the original text to its pristine state. The restoration of the original text would be an arduous philological task involving a collation of the extant Hebrew versions with the Hexapla, Septuagint, Targumim, and other ancient renderings, and L'Advocat took that task upon himself. However, his anti-Jewish exegetical position did not impede his critical accuracy. Philological sophistication and mastery of Jewish sources made L'Advocat uniquely qualified to answer the charges of the Frankists. His report was completed on 22 March 1760. It is currently housed in the Vatican Secret Archives and has never been discussed by scholars.

In accordance with the paradigm discussed in the previous chapter, in L'Advocat's testimony, the Frankists—the enemies of the Talmud—are referred to as "the Karaites." The argument opens with the statement that the very debate concerning the accusation was unnecessary and ridiculous: it was commonly known that the ritual murder accusations were a thing of the past, born in the ages of ignorance (*les siècles d'ignorance*) but dispelled by the progress of reason:

> It true that in the ages of ignorance, this terrible accusation was
> often leveled against the Jews, both the Rabbanites and the Kara-

ites, in Europe and that under this pretext, they were killed, [their property was] looted, and they were persecuted, often in the most barbaric and most unbelievable way, as one can gather from Jacques Basnages' *L'histoire des Juifs depuis Jésus Christ*, which details all these accusations and inhuman persecutions. However, we have finally left behind this heinousness, and for quite some time Jews live in peace, free from this accusation.[118]

L'Advocat observed that the blood accusation appeared only in Europe and was entirely unknown to the Muslim world and stated that whenever the matter was examined by honest and enlightened judges (*juges intègres et eclairés*), its slanderous character was immediately recognized.[119] The blood accusation had been proved false once and for all, and the Talmud was well known to Christian scholars, who had examined manuscript and printed versions. Indeed, according to L'Advocat, the best way to ensure that the libels against the Jews would no longer be repeated was the printing and popularization of the Talmud among the Christian public.

After these general statements, L'Advocat turned to specific issues raised during the Lwów disputation. Among these, he noted that the Frankists did not provide a precise reference for the claim that the Talmud teaches the shedding of Christian blood. The greater part of his account was devoted to philological criticism pointing to inaccuracies in the translations of the talmudic material and deliberate distortions in the quotations. Thus, for instance, L'Advocat noted that the third motion was based on a conscious misquotation of the text of *Shulhan arukh*, in which the Frankists replaced *al yade*, "by," with *al yad*, "near," thereby arguing that the text forbids the kneading and baking of matzot when Christians were present, while the text actually forbade the kneading and baking *by* the idolaters. The report concluded:

> Their accusations should not be listened to, and before admitting them to baptism they should be carefully and meticulously tested, for [after becoming Christians] they may defile our noble sacraments, they may increase the number of bad Christians, and it is likely that they intend to embrace Christianity for merely human and carnal reasons. What is most striking in their statement is the fact that they swear by God they do not lie, and were instructed from their childhood in this malice of the Talmudists. However, no one should trust an oath taken by men who are wicked enough to

forge quotations, invent fallacious explanations, and attribute to the Talmudists things that they themselves know perfectly to be false.[120]

L'Advocat's report was the strongest refutation of the Frankists' charges. By addressing specific issues raised during the disputation, L'Advocat dispelled any doubts that the Church officials might have had. By demonstrating that distortions in talmudic quotations and references must have been deliberate and conscious, he proved the bad will of the accusers. The document approached the disputation from the perspective of the Enlightenment, attacking the blood libel as a "superstition" that had already been refuted by the progress of reason: in the mid-eighteenth century, the atmosphere in Paris clearly differed from that in Lwów. However, the situation in Poland also began to change.

Cardinal Ganganelli's memorandum was accepted by the Holy See in January 1760 and shortly thereafter, its effects began to be felt in Warsaw. The acceptance of the memorandum coincided with the change of the nuncio in Warsaw: in early February, the conservative and cautious bishop Serra was replaced by a much more open-minded bishop, Visconti.[121] The new nuncio was instructed to notify Polish authorities of the content of Ganganelli's report and to press the Polish Church to distance itself from the libel unequivocally.[122] Elyakim ben Asher Zelig obtained not only an official pronouncement of the Holy See denying the truth of the accusation but also letters of recommendation to ecclesiastical authorities in Poland written by Cardinals Cavalchini and Corsini.[123] King Augustus III ratified the charters of his predecessors promising the Jews royal protection against any accusation of ritual murder. As opinion in Poland started to shift against the accusation, Bishop Sołtyk made another attempt to shore up support for the libel and enlisted another supporter.

After Sołtyk's acceptance of the Kraków diocese, his former position in Kiev was offered to Bishop Józef Andrzej Załuski. The Załuski family was related to the Sołtyks through the second wife of Józef Andrzej's father,[124] and the new bishop of Kiev was also a close friend of Bishop Antoni Dembowski, brother of the late protector of the Frankists, Mikołaj;[125] it is no surprise that the ceremony of his consecration was conducted by Sołtyk and assisted by Dembowski.[126] The ceremony took place on 4 November 1759. Two weeks later, the new bishop administered the sacrament of baptism to Frank in Warsaw; and in May 1760, he agreed to act as godfather to Frank's wife, Hana.[127] The Załuski family became deeply involved in the Frankists' case. A brother of the bishop, Jakub Załuski, allocated a generous fund for Frankists who converted to Catholicism; another brother, Marcin, founded a house for new converts in Warsaw.[128] The bishop's own project was of a more literary character. He intended to write an authoritative, "scientific," account of ritual murder, based on the available literature and primary sources and aimed mainly at an international audience.

Załuski was a personality full of contradictions. On the one hand, he belonged to the most conservative wing of the Polish clergy; on the other, he displayed many enlightened tendencies. He established the largest library in Poland and made it available to the general public; he protested against witchcraft trials and the use of judicial torture and exhibited broad ethnographic interests. Seeing himself as an amateur scholar, he tried to collect folkloristic curiosities from his diocese and planned to write a monograph on the Old Believers, the sect to which Moliwda belonged. He also expressed interest in the customs and rites of the Jews in Poland. His initial interest in the blood libel predated the Frankist case and seemed to be spurred by his ethnographic fascinations. Majer Bałaban has argued that Załuski was approached by the Jews, who sought the support of a Christian scholar in combating the accusation, for Załuski might have appeared to them both learned and not unsympathetic.[129]

The first attempt to write an account of the blood libel remains unfinished; the draft is titled *Information touchant les Juifs, leur Talmud et les infanticides par J[ózef] Z[ałuski] Ev[êque] de Kiovie*[130] and claims to have been written "on the occasion of a discovery of the body of a child found dead in the fields in this diocese and the accusations of new neophytes from Poland against the Talmudists." The text is indeed based on extensive sources and includes a discussion of Maimonides' articles of faith, a brief outline of the content of the orders of the Talmud and its existing Latin translations, and a list of 154 ritual murder accusations, one of the most comprehensive of its kind. Written in sloppy and ungrammatical French, full of repetitions and contradictions, the extant text is more a collection of notes that Załuski made for himself than a finished work. However, it seems clear that the intended conclusion was at least partly positive for the Jews. The myth of ritual murder arose, according to Załuski, out of misunderstandings regarding some Jewish rituals. Thus, for instance, he stated that the fact that the Hebrew word *dam* means both "blood" and "money" might have led to the interpretation of the Jewish greed of Christian money as their desire for blood. Similarly, he mentioned that a drink made of myrtle and wine is customarily given to newlyweds; the similarity of the letters in the name of the drink (*hadas*) and those of the word for blood (*ha-dam*) might have led to the suspicions that the Jews used blood during the wedding ceremony. In fact, Załuski claimed, the accusation was first spread by the Jews against the ancient Christians, and modern-day Jews pay the price for the foolishness of their ancestors.

All in all, in the first version of his brochure, Załuski argued that although the Jews indeed hated Christians and some ritual murders probably did happen in the past, there was no evidence that they constituted a precept of the Jewish religion, and the entire nation should not be blamed for the crimes of the few. However, blood was thicker than water. When approached by Sołtyk, Załuski changed his position. The second version of his work, written in the very month of November 1759 when Załuski baptized Frank, claimed that Judaism indeed required its practitioners to use Christian blood for rituals.[131] A more diluted conclusion appeared in the third, most extensive version, titled *La Pologne ditte* [sic] *Paradis des Juifs*.[132] This version was based mainly on Serafinowicz, whose manuscript Załuski had acquired for his library. Despite serious doubts about the reliability of Serafinowicz's account of Judaism in general and of the ritual murder in particular (he characterized Serafinowicz's account of the blood rite as "romanesque"), Załuski accepted as fact that ritual murders happened, especially in Poland, where the Jews "were most numerous and most superstitious."

After compiling a bibliography of the existing printed Polish literature on the accusation and the list of ritual murder cases that had taken place in Poland and abroad, Załuski proceeded to a systematic discussion of the works defending the Jews from the accusation written by Johann Christoph Wagenseil and Aloys Sonnenfels. After weighing all the pros and cons, he concluded that although infanticide was not explicitly propounded by the Talmud, there was sufficient evidence to claim that it was a magical custom widespread among the Polish Jewry. He ended the brochure with the proposal for a bill titled "A Decalogue of Anti-Jewish Laws" (*Dekalog przepisów antyżydowskich*). Załuski's initiative was to pass a law severely restricting Jewish autonomy and undermining Jewish life in Poland; aside from typical proposals such as a ban on Jewish trade on Christian holidays, the building of new synagogues, or money lending and usury, the Decalogue proposed such radical measures as forcing the Jews to participate in lessons on Christian religion and—most radically—prohibiting Jews from marrying before the age of thirty, since "the Jews multiply excessively."

Załuski's works on ritual murder were never published, and the idea of the anti-Jewish bill was never pursued. Evidently, the tide had begun to turn:

the radical stance advocated by Sołtyk and Załuski was not shared by other ecclesiastical and secular notables in Poland. Regardless of their anti-Jewish stereotypes and the official position of the papacy, the majority of the Polish clergy and nobility did not want to embark on an open war against the Jews and Judaism. Only Bishop Sołtyk continued to support the Frankists and made one more attempt to keep the matter alive. He intervened on behalf of Frank's wife, who was offered a small estate in Wojsławice.[133] Shortly thereafter, the town became the scene of another blood libel trial.

In April 1761, three people filed a complaint in the district court in Krasnystaw accusing the entire *kahal* of Wojsławice of kidnapping and murdering a Christian child. The court arrested the accused, including two rabbis and the secular leaders of the community, and subjected them to torture, during which the Jews confessed to numerous crimes, including several murders, robbing churches, and host desecration. They were condemned to death by quartering alive; at the request of the Jesuits, the sentence of those who agreed to convert to Christianity was changed to beheading. Four of the accused decided to convert; they were baptized, beheaded, and buried with honors in a ceremonious funeral led by the local bishop. One of the rabbis managed to hang himself in prison; his body was tied to a horse's tail, dragged to the city square, and burned at the stake, and the ashes were cast to the wind.[134]

One of the accusers was the local governor of Katarzyna Potocka, the protectress of Hana Frank and the owner of Wojsławice. The involvement of the Frankists in the Wojsławice affair is certain. Although the printed version of the official protocol from the trial does not mention it, a manuscript version housed at the Vatican Secret Archives and a letter of complaint sent to the nuncio by the *parnas* of the Council of Four Lands, Meir of Dubno, both refer to Frank's direct instigation.[135] A letter of Lippman of Danzig to Rabbi Jacob Emden recounts that a woman who belonged to the sect dressed up as the wife of the local rabbi, went to the priests, and informed them that her husband had killed several people. When the real wife sought to protest, she was raped by the Frankists, and a massacre of the Jewish community followed.[136]

The documents from the Wojsławice trial were included in Sołtyk's brochure *Złość żydowska*, which, like the pamphlets of 1758, was reprinted and widely distributed. To counteract this new ritual murder accusation, the Jews published a short pamphlet in Polish and Latin containing material obtained during Elyakim's missions to the Holy See. The pamphlet, *Documenta Judaeos in Polonia concernentia*,[137] reproduced three excerpts from the Book of Records of the Polish Crown (*Metryka Koronna*), including the text of a privilege of

Sigmundus III (1592) defending the Jews from the blood accusation and a letter of recommendation for Elyakim ben Asher Zelig written by the prefect of the Holy Office, Cardinal Corsini, to the new nuncio in Warsaw, Bishop Visconti. The letter stated that the Holy See had analyzed the accusation of ritual murder and, finding it baseless, had asked for protection and support for Elyakim.[138] The pamphlet also reproduced a letter from Visconti to Brühl, in which Visconti confirmed that the Jews had appealed to the pope and obtained an official refutation of the accusation. The brochure concluded: "The Holy See recently investigated all testimonies that the Jews use human blood in the preparation of their unleavened bread [called] matzot and for this reason kill children. It was determined that there is no evidence to substantiate this claim. If such accusation arises, the verdict should not be based on the said testimonies but on substantial criminal evidence."[139]

Sections of the Polish clergy in Lwów reacted to the publication of the pamphlet with shock and incredulity: one priest personally involved in the disputation, Father Stanisław Kleczewski, even tried to intervene in Rome, claiming that the Jews managed to deceive the Catholic authorities.[140] However, the pamphlet virtually closed the period of the "frenzy of blood accusations" in Poland.

The Frankist blood libel represented a crucial point in the transition between early modern and modern charges against the Jews. The Lwów libel did not directly originate from a specific trial. It did not refer to a concrete case, did not target particular suspects, and it did not deal with an actual victim. Instead, the Frankists endeavored to create a broad theological and political basis for anti-Jewish polemic and action by proving that the use of Christian blood for ritual purposes was an intrinsic part of the Jewish religion. The accusation was based not on Christian theological literature but on traditional Jewish sources. To be sure, these sources were misrepresented, mistranslated, and otherwise manipulated. However, the accusation provided ammunition for those who sought "proofs" for their charges. The affair was highly politicized, and both sides sought to have their respective voices heard by the public.

The disputation and its aftermath produced a vast body of literature, which provided a standard point of reference for later blood accusations. To give but one, perhaps the most prominent, example: during the Beilis trial, the Frankist arguments were quoted in court, printed, and disseminated as "expert testimonies."[141] The same holds for the other side of the affair. The most comprehensive official papal pronouncement on the blood libel was obtained in connection with the Frankist accusation, and the Jewish authorities had it printed and publicly circulated. As Bałaban has noticed, the brochure *Documenta Judaeos in Polonia Concerentia*, was probably the first publication in Latin and Polish brought about by Jewish efforts and funded by Jews.[142] Within a year, it went through four editions and was distributed by Jewish authorities to Jews as well as Christians. During the Damascus affair, when the papacy refused to publish anti–blood libel bulls,[143] the brochure was reprinted again, thanks to the efforts of Louis Loewe.[144] Abraham Berliner's German translation was spurred by the Tiszaeszlar accusation of 1882; and Cecil Roth's English rendering by the blood libels disseminated by the Nazis.

The Frankist accusation had a profound impact on later anti-Jewish writing and political action, and the Lwów disputation has been termed, more than once, "the most notorious" and "most terrifying" in Jewish history. Nevertheless, it is striking that the horror expressed by later historians did not seem to be shared by contemporaries and that the direct participants in the disputation did not see the blood libel as the most significant element of the Frankist affair. For the Catholic clergy, with the exception of Sołtyk and his cronies, the acceptance of Christianity by a large group of Jews was much more important than the blood charge. But even the Jews were, in principle, pleased with the disputation and its outcome. The aim of the rabbinate was the eradication of the Sabbatian heresy, and the temporary inflaming of anti-Jewish passions might have seemed like a price worth paying for the final separation of the Frankists from the rest of Jewry.

Chapter 5

How Rabbis and Priests Created the Frankist Movement

The Baptism of the Frankists

The conversion of the Frankists was not an outcome of the Lwów disputation, nor did it depend on that outcome; it was the condition under which the disputation was conducted in the first place. Even before the formal end of the debate, on 16 August 1759, the administrator *sede vacante* of the Lwów archdiocese, Father Stanisław Mikulski, issued an edict commanding the local clergy to begin instructing those who would convert in preparation for their baptisms.[1] Each of the larger churches or monasteries in Lwów and its surroundings took up a certain number of catechumens. The first baptisms took place on 20 August.[2] They were attended by a large public; many important noblemen served as godparents. On 17 September, Frank and Krysa were baptized in the Lwów cathedral.[3]

It is difficult to assess the exact number of those who converted. On the basis of the records of parish churches where the conversions took place, Kraushar listed 514 Contra-Talmudists who converted in Lwów (September 1759–November 1760),[4] twenty in Kamieniec (October 1759–July 1761),[5] and fourteen in Warsaw (January–April 1760).[6] It is clear, however, that Kraushar's inventory is incomplete. Some of the leading Frankists—including the future authors of the Red Letters, the brothers Nathan and Solomon Shorr (known after baptism as Michał and Franciszek Wołowscy) and Yerucham ben Lippman of Czarnokozienice (Jędrzej Dębowski)—were not listed.[7] Other converts were mentioned only in passing as the previously converted parents, spouses, or relatives of those on the list.[8] Ecclesiastical sources attest that baptisms that had been stimulated by the Lwów disputation continued at least until 1763; however, we have no data regarding the conversions that took place after July 1761. Finally, contemporary accounts show that among the converts was a large group of Jews who came to Poland from the Ottoman Empire and the Balkans especially for the purpose of converting to Roman Catholicism. The very same records on which Kraushar based his inventory contained a statement that Frank had arrived in Lwów "in assystentia multarum Judaeorum Antit[almudistarum] ex variis oppidis Turciae, Ungariae etc."[9] Ber of Bolechów mentioned Hungarian Jews coming to Lwów to receive baptism as well.[10] An anonymous Christian pamphlet printed in 1761 attested that about two hundred Jews from Hungary, Turkey, Moldavia, and Wallachia witnessed the disputation in Lwów and converted in its wake.[11] Alas, Kraushar's roster contains not a single name of a convert from outside the Polish-Lithuanian Commonwealth; indeed, with very few exceptions, his list covers only Jews from the communities within the Lwów archdiocese.

Since Kraushar's inventory is incomplete, we must turn to testimonies of participants and witnesses of the conversions. Some mention very large figures. Thus, Primate Łubieński stated that Frank had fifteen thousand followers ready to accept baptism.[12] David Kirchoff, a missionary of the Moravian Brethren from Herrnhut and an eyewitness to the Lwów disputation, gave the same figure.[13] Frank himself claimed to have collected the signatures of ten thousand Jews prepared to follow him into Christianity.[14] These figures are certainly inflated: Frank had a clear interest in exaggerating the size of his following, while his Christian patrons and supporters wanted to blow up the number of the converts to serve the missionary propaganda. The dispatches of the papal nuncio, which were intended only for the internal use of the Roman Curia, are much more reliable. The picture that emerges from these is that of a steady flow of converts and candidates for conversion.

Ten days after the first baptisms, on 29 August 1759, Bishop Serra reported that "some six hundred anti-Talmudist Jews just arrived in Lwów, and their number will probably soon reach a thousand. They are all determined to become Christians. . . . The number of the catechumens grows by the day."[15] On 6 September, he mentioned "hundreds" of prospective converts gathering in Lwów.[16] Two weeks later, he wrote: "Six hundred adults, mainly men but also some women, are undergoing instruction. There are also several hundred children here who are too young to undertake the study [of the Christian faith]. A few—though not many—people have withdrawn, but their loss is compensated by new candidates who arrive almost every day."[17]

On 28 September, the nuncio estimated the number of the catechumens at a thousand adult men and an unspecified number of women and children.[18] On 3 October, he informed the Curia that, in addition to those who had already converted, approximately seven hundred Jews still awaited the ceremony of baptism in Lwów and in Iwanie. He added that "recently, twenty Jewish families, together with their rabbi, declared in Śniatyń their wish to convert to Christianity."[19]

Unfortunately, the nuncio's dispatches for the period after 3 October 1759 contain only general remarks about conversions and make no attempt to estimate the number of the people involved. Still, if his assessments for August and September are accurate, it appears that during these crucial two months, more than a thousand adult Jews converted to Christianity in Lwów alone. This would confirm the accounts of the Catholic priests who took part in the disputation and reported that one to two thousand Jews converted shortly after the debate.[20] Similarly, the earliest Jewish source depicting the mass conversion of 1759, Abraham of Szarogród's *Ma'aseh nora be-Podolia*, gave the number of nine hundred apostates.[21] Ber Birkenthal, who wrote his account forty years later (but who, in contrast to Abraham of Szarogród, participated in the debate in person), also asserted that "more than a thousand people stayed in Lwów and converted."[22]

For the same period of August–October 1759, Kraushar listed for Lwów only 233 names (including children); thus his inventory seems to contain only some 25 percent of the converts. The total figure for 1759–63 should be calculated accordingly, taking into account, however, that after October 1759 the flow of the converts diminished gradually (Kraushar gave forty-one names for November 1759, twenty-four for January 1760, and eighteen for April of the same year. The list ends with three converts in October and only one in November 1760; 274 people converted in September–December 1759 and 240 in all of 1760). The incompleteness of Kraushar's data makes it impossible to extrapolate with precision. If, however, we accept the number of a thousand adult neophytes as the basic minimal figure for the period immediately after the disputation (August–October 1759) and we assume, as a rule of thumb, that the number of the converts diminished by 25 percent each year, we would arrive at the conclusion that more than three thousand adult Jews converted to Catholicism within five years after the Lwów disputation. To put this figure in a larger context, around 1764, the entire Jewish population of Lwów, the second-largest community in Poland (after Brody), approximated 7,400 people; only four communities had more than three thousand members.[23] In a word, the number of Frankist converts equaled the entire relatively large Polish community of the period.

This, of course, is a conservative assessment. Much higher numbers appeared in contemporary anecdotal accounts and have made their way into later scholarship. An anonymous pamphlet printed in Warsaw in 1791 estimated that two generations after the mass conversion of 1759–60, there were 24,000 baptized Frankists in all Poland.[24] The same figure appeared also in Tadeusz Czacki's account of Polish Jewry (1807).[25] In 1838, Jędrzej Słowaczyński claimed that following the disputation, seven thousand Frankists converted in one day in the Lwów cathedral.[26] Słowaczyński's claim was repeated—albeit somehow hesitantly—in the scholarly works of Skimborowicz and Graetz.[27] In turn, Czacki's statement was accepted—unreservedly—by Mateusz Mieses.[28]

These estimates have to be put into a broader framework. The first scholar to tackle the issue of the numerical profile of Jewish conversions in early modern Poland, Nahum Gelber, assessed the *total* number of converts in the eighteenth century (until the First Partition) at two thousand, 0.15–0.13 percent of what he estimated to be the Jewish population of the country (this included 514 Frankists listed in Kraushar, for Gelber accepted Kraushar's inventory as complete).[29] While more recent scholarship largely discounted Gelber's calculations both with regard to the number of the converts (as too low) and the general Jewish population (as too high),[30] scholars continue to agree that conversions of the Jews in the pre-partition Commonwealth were rare.[31] Against this backdrop, and even if we accept the most conservative assessments, the scale of the Frankist conversion is astounding. Never before did Poland-Lithuania experience a mass Jewish apostasy; normally, accepting Christianity was a matter of personal decision undertaken by individuals or—sometimes—nuclear families. Whereas the highly inflated numbers appearing in contemporary testimonies did not accurately reflect reality, they did express the feelings and perceptions of witnesses to the 1759–60 conversion: the Frankists' baptism was seen as a monumental event unique both in size and in its theological ramifications.

The amazement of the Christians and the shock of the Jews were amplified by the ostensibly voluntary nature of the Frankists' conversion. Even the most zealous priests were well aware that the vast majority of Jewish conversions throughout the ages did not stem from Jewish recognition of the truth of Christianity but rather from the desire for social advancement or to avoid persecution. From the outset, the Church presented the case of Frank and his followers as a positive counterexample: the fact that a large number of Jews approached the baptismal font of their own volition was portrayed as a signal that the "Jewish stubbornness" might be about to run its course.

For Jewish sensibilities, on the contrary, the idea that a few thousand Jews might have *willingly* abandoned Judaism for Christianity was profoundly shocking, not to say impossible to swallow. In a number of later Jewish accounts (including some scholarly ones), there appeared a pronounced tendency to diminish the scale of the conversion or to explain it away by claiming that, as it turned out, the sectarians were forced to apostatize. Some scholars have even claimed that—as had been the case in medieval Germany—the Catholic clergy presented the Frankists with the choice between conversion and death or expulsion. None of this appeared in contemporary accounts. However, the background of the Frankists' conversion and the positions of all parties involved in it must be carefully examined.

The Stance of the Rabbinate

The first Frankist document to mention baptism was the supplication submitted to Primate Łubieński on 20 February 1759, in which the petitioners requested permission to hold a public disputation with "the Talmudists" in Lwów. But the idea that the Frankists should convert to Christianity was first broached much earlier, shortly after the Kamieniec disputation of 1757. While official Christian documents connected to the Kamieniec debate expressed an abstract hope that rejection of the Talmud might be the first step on the path to Christianity, they made no specific reference to the idea of the Frankists' baptism: in these documents, the group was clearly defined as "contra-talmudic Jews" who remained and were to remain within the realm of the institutional Jewish religion. As noted in Chapter 3, after the end of the debate, on 17 October 1757, Bishop Dembowski issued a ruling that granted the Frankists autonomy within Judaism. The ruling was valid only in the Kamieniec diocese. In order to extend it to all of Poland, the bishop requested a special edict from the king, defining "Contra-Talmudism" as a legitimate form of Judaism recognized within the kingdom and equating the right and privileges of the Contra-Talmudists with those of other Jews of the Commonwealth.[32]

Such an edict was indeed issued in July 1758, some eight months after Dembowski's demise (9 November 1757). It was printed together with other documents pertaining to the Kamieniec debate and was never officially annulled; however, there were no attempts to put it into practice. The only testimony as to why and how the edict came to be disregarded is preserved in Ber Birkenthal of Bolechów's *Divre binah*. According to Ber's account, during a gathering of the Kamieniec consistory following Dembowski's death, it was decided not to deliver the writ to the Frankists. Instead, the consistory presented the Contra-Talmudists with the alternative: "And all the leaders of the priests told the people of the sect of Sabbatai Tsevi in one voice: 'We have hereby decided to give you a choice whether to stay Jewish and be faithful to the religion into which you were born and [to adhere] to the Torah and all [Jewish] customs, or to accept our Christian faith in its entirety and to be free men [*bne horin*] in every aspect, just as [other] Christians. And then you will not need edicts of tolerance [*kitve herut*] and privileges.'"[33]

The source of Ber's information is unknown, and its accuracy cannot be verified. *Divre binah* was written in 1800, some forty years after the eruption of Frankism, and Ber himself did not get involved in the affair until the Lwów debate of 1759: in describing the events of 1756–58, he relied on various testimonies and documents, written and oral, Jewish and non-Jewish. Nevertheless, when his account can be cross-checked with original sources from the early period, it is, save for minor inexactnesses, surprisingly accurate. In this particular case, we have another document suggesting that the Frankists might indeed have been given a sharp choice between adherence to traditional Judaism and conversion to Christianity already in 1757.

Shortly after Dembowski's death, the *shtadlan* of the Council of Four Lands, Baruch me-Erets Yavan, was admitted by the all-powerful minister of Augustus III, Count Heinrich Brühl. Brühl's contacts with Yavan, who also served as a factor of the royal treasury, was of many years' standing, and the minister was not unsympathetic to him and his case.[34] He advised Yavan to seek the support of the papal nuncio in Warsaw, Bishop Serra. Yavan prepared a supplication in Latin and delivered it to the nuncio. The supplication was meant as a formal appeal of the Jewish authorities in Poland against the verdict of the bishop of Kamieniec. Seeking to alarm the nuncio, Yavan stated—contrary to the facts and against his better knowledge—that the burgeoning Sabbatian heresy was gaining adherents not only among the Jews in Poland but also among Catholics. He claimed that the Sabbatians were spreading utterly immoral behavior involving incest, adultery, and other crimes; the movement constituted a heresy "contrary to the Ten Commandments, the Old [Testament] Law, and the natural law."

As the bishop of Kamieniec chose to support these "Jews, or rather new heresiarchs [*Iudaei seu novi heresiarchae*]," rabbinic authorities were forced to appeal to the nuncio—the representative of the pope in Poland. The document ended: "Therefore we appeal to the tribunal of Your Venerable Highness, we denounce the errors of these new heretics, and we demand that in order for them to be eradicated, they either fully embrace Roman Catholicism, or fully accept our Jewish religion, or [are recognized] as heretics even if they proclaim faith in the messiah and the Trinity [*ut aut cogantur omnio ad amplectendam fidem Catholico-Romanam aut Nostram Iudaicam, aut pro haereticis siquidem agnoscunt Messiam, et Trinitatem*]."[35]

Yavan's diagnosis of Sabbatianism did not differ substantially from Emden's position, analyzed above in Chapter 2: he portrayed the movement as pure idolatry and a kind of universal heresy hostile to the tenets and values of all monotheistic religions. Yet the tactics adopted by Yavan in fighting the Sabbatians differed from those advocated by Emden prior to the Kamieniec debate. Emden recommended seeking the support of ecclesiastical authorities; he believed that once the clergy learned of Sabbatianism's heretical character, they would "destroy the people of Sabbatai Tsevi's sect, both the clandestine ones and the revealed ones."[36] Accordingly, Emden called upon the priests not to offer the Sabbatians a safe haven in the Church: his strategy was to prevent Jewish heretics from escaping rabbinic persecution by converting to Christianity. Yavan's petition to the nuncio represented a radical departure from Emden's idea. Since the condemnation of the Sabbatians by the Christians failed to materialize and the bishop of Kamieniec chose to support them against the rabbis, Yavan decided to go to the nuncio over the heads of the local clergy and to force the Frankists to choose between Judaism and Christianity. It was the *shtadlan* of the Council of Four Lands who first suggested—as early as 1757—that the conversion of Jewish heretics was preferable to their remaining within Judaism.

Yavan's attitude was historically unprecedented. Since the time of the First Crusade, baptism of a Jew had become the most potent token of violent conflict between Judaism and Christianity. Hebrew chronicles of the Crusades and liturgical poems (*piyyutim*) composed in their wake eulogized those who had chosen death over conversion and presented martyrdom, suicide, or even taking the lives of one's own children as the ideal responses to forced conversion.[37] The very Hebrew terms denoting apostasy and apostate from Judaism, *shemmad*, *meshummad*, derive from the root *ShMD*, implying utter destruction; the words *lehashmid*, "to obliterate," and *hashmadah*, "extermination," come from the same root. Semantically, at least, *shemmad*, baptism, was tantamount to complete annihilation: conversion to Christianity was not seen as choosing one set of values and beliefs over another or transferring from the realm of one faith to another, but as, so to speak, turning into nothingness; indeed, within the families of apostates, it became customary to observe the mourning customs normally observed after a person's death. Becoming a Christian—whether voluntarily or under coercion—turned into one of the most powerful taboos in medieval and early modern Jewish society and came to be firmly associated with "physical violence, sexual degradation, and spiritual annihilation."[38] While post-Reformation Germany saw the gradual development of more nuanced narratives of Jewish conversions, in early modern Poland the medieval perspective continued to hold sway. In Poland, the established medieval paradigm was so strong that Jews sometimes tried to kidnap or even kill converts or prospective converts; the last recorded case of a father murdering his son who had expressed wish to become a Christian comes from 1869.[39]

Given the odium attached to the conversion to Christianity, it is not surprising that under normal circumstances, Jewish communities did everything to keep even the worst offenders within the fold and were known to temper their response to deviance from communal norms for fear that such measures could drive the deviant into apostasy.[40] The most important Polish medieval halakhist, Rabbi Moses Isserles, allowed in principle the excommunication of people who were known to be contemplating conversion to Christianity, but ruled that severe measures should be administered with care so that they would not drive those punished to baptism (Isserles explicitly emphasized the fear that the potential convert's children would be lost to Judaism).[41]

Typically, the rabbis warned dissenters, imposed bans of excommunication, and occasionally encouraged persecutions but shunned actions that might drive a Jew out of Judaism. Even the rabbinic polemics against the Sabbatians prior to the eruption of Frankism attested to the same attitude. Rabbi Jacob Sasportas invited back to the fold the Sabbatian prophet Sabbatai Raphael for fear that he might apostatize to Christianity.[42] In 1724–26, Nehemiah Hayon was pursued by his adversaries throughout Europe:

> He began to wander, spurned and rejected, from town to town,
> from state to state. He arrived at the capital city, Vienna, but the
> communal elders refused to admit him. He sat in the courtyard
> reserved for the Ottomans, claiming to be a Turk. . . . From there
> he went to Glogau, where he was recognized. . . . They expelled
> him. On that day, he arrived in Berlin, where he wrote to a former

adherent that if further antagonized, "great waters would surround him"[43] [he would be baptized]. Because of this, they gave him two marks and dispatched him from there, and he remained within the Jewish fold.[44]

In Western Europe, excommunicated Sabbatians were hounded, could not buy food, or find employment or a place to sleep, but the persecutions were normally alleviated when the threat of conversion arose. Baruch Yavan's petition to the papal nuncio represented a watershed in this attitude: it is the first anti-Sabbatian document explicitly affirming that heretics should be expelled from Judaism. Yavan's idea was put forward to the Catholic clergy after Dembowski's death, and echoes of this fact can be traced to the later account of Dov Ber of Bolechów. Ber was right that the Frankists were forced to choose between Judaism and Christianity; he was wrong in suggesting that the idea originated among the Kamieniec clergy. Bishop Dembowski did not exert any pressure upon the Frankists to convert, and there is no reason to assume that, immediately after his death, his aides, unprompted, radically altered this stance. Ber was not privy to the secret negotiations between the nuncio and the *shtadlan*. Indeed, his book does not mention Baruch Yavan at all. Following the meetings between Yavan and the nuncio, the local priests in Kamieniec were probably instructed by their superiors in Warsaw to present the Frankists with the choice between an unconditional return to mainstream Judaism and an equally unconditional acceptance of Christianity in its entirety.

However, as Yavan—and also the Kamieniec priests—knew very well, the alternative was a false one: given the attitude of the rabbinate, as analyzed in the previous chapters, it is extremely doubtful that the Frankists' repentance, had they taken that course, would have been accepted as sincere. In 1757, the sectarians who could not remain within normative Judaism and did not wish to convert to Christianity were driven out of Poland to the Ottoman Empire, and were allowed to return only two years later, after they had formally declared themselves candidates for baptism.

It is not surprising that the Catholic clergy wanted to press for the conversion of the Frankists. More astonishing is the attitude of the Jews. One might have expected that the tradition of doing everything possible to prevent fellow Jews from becoming Christians would predominate in this case as well. On the ground level, on some occasions, this seemed to be true. In June 1759, the newspaper *Kuryer Polski* reported that two Jews of Kamieniec Podolski, dressed as peasants and armed with spears, were caught trying to kidnap Libka, the wife of the Contra-Talmudist Leyba ben Abraham,[45] together with her child. Libka was preparing for baptism, and during the investigation the suspects testified they had acted with permission of the local rabbi and followed the wish of Libka's father, who sought to prevent her from turning Christian.[46] However, different attitudes prevailed among the leadership of Polish Jewry. Two years after it was initially put forward, Baruch Yavan's idea of driving the heretics out of Judaism was accepted by the leaders of the Council of Four Lands. On 22 October 1759, amid the wave of conversions after the Lwów disputation, Abraham ha-Kohen of Zamość wrote to Rabbi Jacob Emden:

> And the holy community of Lublin already spent a large sum, for the word is a medicine for all.[47] And the leaders [*roznim*] who gathered here at the council in the holy community of Konstantynów consulted secretly together [and arrived at the conclusion] that we have no other option than to employ a ruse and to force them to convert to Christianity, for it is written "the people shall live alone."[48] And [the council] already spent more than two thousand złotys. And thank God, some of them already converted, among them the son of Elisha the heretic [Elisha Shorr], may his name be obliterated. . . . And those who did not convert [still] wear Jewish clothes, and they still go to their prayer houses; we have already reported it to the [Christian] authorities. So we sent his honor the rabbi, *av bet din* of the holy community of Ciechanowiec,[49] to Warsaw to seek support, and with God's help he found favor with the bishop, the papal nuncio. And he was told to wait there until the arrival of the sect of the evildoers. And to obtain an announcement that they are cut off from the entire community of Israel.[50] . . . With God's help, we will publicize our court case in Warsaw. And the righteous will be given the opportunity to judge the wicked criminals, rebels, and dogs, destroyers [working] against the Lord, as was done to Moses David of Podhajce, who was ostracized and placed under ban in our country a few years ago.[51]

The harshness of the letter's formulation is striking: in 1757, Baruch Yavan intended to give the Frankists at least a theoretical choice between Judaism of Christianity; in 1759, the rabbinate decided to work actively toward forcing them to apostatize: "we have no other option than to employ a ruse and to force them to convert to Christianity" (*ein manos lanu, rak la'asot tahbulot lehakhrikhem lehitnatser*). The context of the letter needs to be explained. The meeting of the "leaders" mentioned in the letter was one of the sessions of the Council of Four Lands that took place on 21 August and 3 and 26 September 1759 in Konstantynów.[52] During these sessions, the author of the letter, Abraham ha-Kohen of Zamość, served as a trustee of the council, and the letter reflects the official position adopted by the delegates. Following the baptism in the Lwów cathedral, Frank, together with his six closest followers, departed for Warsaw at the end of September 1759. On the way, the group made a short stopover in Lublin, where they were attacked by local Jews; a swift court case granted the Frankists damages of two thousand złotys, and Abraham ha-Kohen's letter alluded to this verdict.[53] Frank's group arrived in Warsaw one day after the letter was dispatched to Emden, on 23 October. The Jewish authorities apparently tried to preempt Frank's possible influence among the clergy and nobility in the capital and to force those of his followers who were trying to remain within the Jewish fold to leave it and be baptized. The council allocated large sums of money for bribes for the nuncio and other priests to ensure and expedite the conversion of the Frankists.

Rather than mourn their conversion to Christianity in the customary manner, contemporary Jewish sources expressed happiness after the baptism of Frank and his followers. Some writers went so far as to proclaim that the baptism of the Frankists was "a great miracle": Sabbatians were compared to treacherous soldiers conspiring with the enemy at times of war, and their conversion was interpreted as a purifying act decreed by God himself, who prefers to have His people less numerous but entirely faithful.[54] Other rabbis claimed that Frank's conversion was a providential act preventing him from exerting corruptive influence upon other Jews: since he became a Christian, "he would no longer have depraved a single Jew."[55] Another official of the Council of Four Lands, Lippman of Danzig, stated: "And the rest of the depraved ones of the entire sect finally changed their faith and now they became as non-Jews [*ke-goyye aratsot*]. May the Lord be praised that they are distinguished from all the tribes of Israel. And as they were uprooted from the land of Poland, so they will certainly be uprooted from all other countries, and then our redemption will certainly come, so may the Lord help us."[56]

In the rabbinic narrative, the destructive sting of the *shemmad* was fully preserved, but as a therapeutic measure. The apostasy of a Jew was considered as a fate worse than death, in some regards; the council decided to facilitate the baptism of the Frankists not *despite* this, but precisely *for* that purpose. Emden explicitly stated that the Frankists were forced to convert by the rabbinate and that it was done "not for their good."[57] The rabbis exulted over the baptism of Jewish heretics because it implied their total destruction as human beings and Jews. The conversion was seen as the most conspicuous sign of the end of all affinity between Sabbatianism and Judaism. This line of thought was enabled by the former acceptance of Emden's radical conceptualization of Sabbatianism not as a Jewish sectarian movement but as an entirely separate religion, which contributed to the extreme stance taken by the Jewish authorities in Poland.

The unprecedented political strategy whereby Jews actively worked toward the conversion of other Jews to Christianity required a fundamental psychological and theological transformation. Rabbis could express delight over the conversion of the Frankists or even push them toward the baptism because they had ceased to see Sabbatians as fellow Jews. While technically the sectarians remained Jewish, something had changed in the way they were perceived by other Jews: they came to be considered not only outside the purview of normative Judaism but outside of the people of Israel as well. They belonged to the mixed multitude. From the rabbinic perspective, they had "converted" to Sabbatianism before they converted to Christianity. This feeling found its clearest expression in another letter of Baruch Yavan. The letter was written in 1768 during a mission to Moscow; the aim of the mission was to foil Frank's attempt to gain Russian support in exchange for the promise of a large Jewish conversion to Greek Orthodoxy (I shall discuss the mission and its circumstances in greater detail in Chapter 7). Not without justification, the *shtadlan* portrayed Frank as a serial convert: "Isn't it the fifth faith they intend to change?! First, [they professed] the Jewish [faith]. Second—in order to enter to the faith of Sabbatai Tsevi [*emunat Shabbatai Tsevi*]—they accepted the faith of Islam. Third, they became fully Sabbatians. Fourth, they were forced to convert to Christianity. . . . And now they intend to change into the fifth faith, the Greek Orthodoxy [*dat yevanit*]."[58]

In Yavan's letter, Sabbatianism was presented as a distinct denomination on par with Islam, Catholicism, and Greek Orthodoxy, and the adoption of the "faith of Sabbatai Tsevi" as a "conversion" from Judaism. Similarly, Ber of Bolechów described Leyb Krysa's early activity in Poland: "Thus Leyb Krysa wandered through all the towns of Podolia in order to deceive and to incite some of the people of Israel to change their faith and to [start] to profess the religion of Sabbatai Tsevi [*she-yamiru datam ve-she-yaminu be-dat Shabbatai Tsevi*]."[59]

As noted, Emden's conceptualization of Sabbatianism as a new religion was radical and novel. Until the Frankist affair, very few rabbis seemed to have taken such a radical position: militant anti-Sabbatianism was a campaign waged by a few professional heresy hunters. The vast majority of eighteenth-century rabbis tried to hush up rumors and to suppress the memory of seventeenth-century Sabbatianism—sometimes even forbidding the very mention of the name Sabbatai Tsevi.[60] Despite angry rhetoric, few serious efforts were made to eradicate crypto-Sabbatianism, and—as attested by the anti-Hayon campaign described above—the rabbinate was reluctant to lose even confirmed heretics to Christianity. The very same rabbis who were prepared to turn a blind eye to the heresies of other Sabbatians radicalized their stance in the case of the Frankists. In order to understand this shift of attitudes, we must now discuss the rabbinic perception of the dangers of Frankism for Judaism.

The Perceived Threat of Frankism

Two motifs from Abraham ha-Kohen's letter to Emden deserve special attention. First is the reference to Moses David of Podhajce, who "had been ostracized and placed under the ban" a few years before the eruption of the Frankist affair. Moses David was a Sabbatian kabbalist and itinerant *ba'al shem* (miracle worker) whose biography has been reconstructed by Chaim Wirszubski.[61] He was active in Poland in the early 1750s and was banished from a number of communities, including Leszno and Rogoźno, whence he was carried out on a cart full of dung. He moved to Germany, lived for some time in Fürth, was banished again, wandered through various communities of Bavaria, visited London, and, toward the end of the 1750s, finally arrived in Altona, where he joined the circle of Rabbi Jonathan Eibeschütz and his son Wolf. After the series of scandals surrounding Wolf Eibeschütz, Moses David was driven out of Altona as well and moved to Norden (Lower Saxony). Reportedly, he eventually ended up in Hungary, where he "died among the uncircumcised."[62]

For Emden and his supporters, Moses David of Podhajce was the test case for the success of their campaign of persecution against the sectarians: expelled from a dozen communities, he was pursued through half of Europe and managed not to settle anywhere for many years. The reference to his death among the uncircumcised—if true—might imply that he was eventually forced to apostatize. In light of the previous discussion, the question arises as to why the Jewish leadership was so severe in his particular case: while anti-Sabbatian rhetoric treated all "heretics" equally, in most cases the rabbis did not go to

such great lengths in persecuting them. The impression that his case was unusual is strengthened by the fact that in their battle against Moses David—as
in their battle against the Frankists—the rabbinate sought (or at least was willing to seek) the support of Christians.

In July 1758, the rabbi of Fürth wrote a letter to the rabbi of the province
of Grabfeld (on the border between Bavaria and Thuringia); the letter oddly
echoes what we know of Emden's initial appeal to the *parnassim* of the Council of Four Lands and Baruch Yavan's petition to the nuncio. Like Yavan, the
rabbi of Fürth believed that Sabbatianism subverts not only Judaism but also
natural law and universal human morality; like Emden, he thought that the
Jews should involve the authorities in the campaign against the heretics. He
concluded that the best course of action was to turn Moses David over to the
Christian ecclesiastical authorities and argued: "It is best to put [Moses David
of Podhajce] in everlasting ignominy, so that through his evil pursuits he will
not deceive any more Jewish souls. For these heretics came to destroy all ethical norms. And we—the sons of Israel—are not the only ones who would
persecute these criminals. All the peoples of the land will not bear among
themselves these evildoers, for they profess things contrary to reason and subvert the very foundation of the world by allowing the practice of incest."[63]

The similarity of the severe measures taken against Moses David and Jacob
Frank, as well as the tactic of involving outsiders in what would seem an internal Jewish religious affair were, I believe, grounded in the deeper resemblance
between the two cases. The first aspect of this similarity is obvious: in contrast
to the typical crypto-Sabbatians, who professed their heresy only within the
closed circle of fellow believers while outwardly remaining pious members of
the community, Moses David and Frank were, from the outset, clear and outspoken about their heterodoxy and unrepentant when confronted by the rabbis.[64] Their actions and heretical beliefs could not be ignored or swept under
the carpet: they constituted an open challenge to the authority of the rabbinate, a challenge that could not be disregarded without a total loss of face. Since
Frank and Moses David broke with the paradigm of crypto-Sabbatianism, the
rabbis had to break with the tactics of silence on the matter of internal Jewish
dissent or discord before non-Jews.

The second aspect of the similarity between Moses David and Frank is
more complicated. In his analysis, Wirszubski placed special emphasis on the
fact that the amulets written by Moses David often contained the symbol of
a cross and combinations of the names of Sabbatai Tsevi and Jesus; hence he
argued that the "general tendency" of the kabbalist was that of syncretization

of Sabbatianism and Christianity.[65] This leads us back to Abraham ha-Kohen of Zamość's letter to Emden and the Christian elements in the Lanckoronie ritual. It is highly significant that Abraham expressed so much indignation about the fact that some Frankists still wore Jewish clothes and attended a Jewish house of prayer. The same element also appeared in Christian accounts. When trying to learn more about the background of the Frankists, Father Pikulski spoke to the Jews in Lanckoronie and was told that "the whole problem with the Talmudists" was that they "did not wish the new Sabbatians to dress like the Jews." Pikulski commented on "the stupid apprehension of the Jews who put their entire faith in the beard and disgusting sidelocks [*peysach paskudnych*]" and treated his interlocutors to a sermon on the superiority of Christianity, which pays no attention to external appearances.[66] Not surprisingly, the Jews fell silent. Regarding the Frankists, the priest concluded: "As it seems, they would want to be simultaneously Jews and Catholics."[67]

While open challenges to the authority of the rabbis certainly played their role, I submit that precisely this syncretistic tendency more than anything else caused the Jewish leadership to act so harshly against both Moses David of Podhajce and the Frankists. Both theologically and politically, the stakes became extremely high, involving the very identity of Judaism as a distinct religion. The radical conceptualization of Sabbatianism as a new faith was grounded in the danger (real or perceived) of its blurring of the boundaries between the existing religions. The brutality of the rabbinic campaign against the Frankists can be understood as an attempt to delineate the confines of Judaism as clearly as possible. To return to the formulations of Yavan's petition to the nuncio, the heretics should not be allowed to seek middle positions between two separate religions: one should be either fully and unconditionally Jewish or equally fully and unconditionally Christian. In a nutshell, the aim of the rabbinic campaign of 1759 was to replace Pikulski's idea of the Sabbatians as "simultaneously Jews and Christians" with Emden's idea of their being "neither Jews nor Christians."[68]

Abraham ha-Kohen of Zamość's letter to Emden is not the only source that mentions the Frankists' attempts to retain elements of Jewish identity such as distinct dress or form of prayer after their conversion. In order to fully elucidate this element, we must again go back to Emden's letter to the *parnassim* of the Council of Four Lands discussed in Chapter 2. As I have argued, Emden's letter to the council should not be read as a Jewish praise of Christianity but as a call for the radical separation of Judaism and Christianity: the latter was to be considered a legitimate and even noble religion, which was intended for non-Jews alone, exactly as Judaism was intended only for the Jews.

Thus, in the same breath as he praised Christianity, Emden condemned *Christian* syncretism: Christianity ought to guard its boundaries exactly as Judaism guards its own. In the context of Sabbatian conversions, this point assumed a special importance: "And do not let them venerate the abominations of Sabbatai Tsevi, may the name of evil ones rot, among you, the worshipers of the Nazarene. As the well-known sect had done when they allowed the people of China to retain their cult of Confucius, and let them combine it with the faith of the Nazarene. And this worship of Sabbatai Tsevi [*avodat Sabbatai Tsevi*] is far worse than all pagan faiths [*avodot elilim*] that exist in the world."[69]

The "well-known sect" that allowed the Chinese to combine Confucianism with Christianity were, of course, the Jesuits. Father Matteo Ricci's adapted diaries, published by Nicolas Trigault under the name *De Christiana Expeditione apud Sinas suscepta ab Societate Jesu* (Augsburg, 1615), became a best seller in Europe; by 1648, it had gone through five editions in Latin, three in French, and one each in German, Spanish, and Italian.[70] Ricci's memoirs contained, among other things, an account of his visit in the synagogue of the Jewish community of Kaifeng in northern China. This account caused a considerable upheaval among the European literati (including, for instance, Leibniz), who speculated that the Kaifeng Jews might be remnants of the Lost Tribes and that their Torah scrolls might well be identical with the ancient scriptures that circulated in Judaea before the birth of Jesus.

Moreover, the accommodations made by the community of Kaifeng with regard to adopting Jewish practices and traditions to the Chinese context was used by Ricci and other Jesuit missionaries as a paradigm for creating the famous Chinese Rites,[71] which allowed Chinese converts to Catholicism to carry vestiges of Confucianism over into their adopted faith. Thus, for instance, the Chinese Catholics were to be allowed to refer to the Deity using traditional Confucian terms, to say the Mass in Chinese, and to practice some form of the traditional ancestor worship.

Before Emden, the only mention of the discovery of Kaifeng Jews and the Jesuit mission in China in Jewish sources appeared in Manasseh ben Israel's *Hope of Israel* (1652).[72] It is difficult to assess what exactly Emden knew about the Jesuits and the Chinese Rites. It seems, however, that he knew quite a bit. In his *Iggeret bikoret*, he related the story of Ignatius Loyola's wound during the siege of Pamplona and described the foundation of the Society of Jesus as "the foundation of the known sect of those who recluse themselves from motives of love."[73] In *Birat migdal oz*, he mentioned that he had read "a book from the land of China";[74] the most likely candidate is the German version of Ricci's memoirs.

On several occasions, Emden expressed apprehension about the contacts between Rabbi Jonathan Eibeschütz and the Prague Jesuits. The letter to the leaders of the Council of Four Lands was written in 1756; when reprinting it in 1760, he remarked: "I wrote [the letter to the council] a few years ago. And right now, the holy war erupted also among you [the Christians] against this sect [the Jesuits], for which Eibeschütz worked in Prague, watching daily at their gates,[75] and learning from them the art of forgery and fraud. And he and his cronies should be pursued as the Christians are pursuing this sect [the Jesuits]."[76]

The last section of this quotation seems to allude to the Távora affair and the suppression of the Society of Jesus in Portugal in 1759. Clearly, Emden, was highly apprehensive about the order's tactic of attracting non-Christians to the Church by accommodating Christian beliefs and concepts to their cultural and religious background. His aim was to preserve the traditional paradigm of conversion to Christianity, which was supposed to put an end to any affinity of the convert with Jews and Judaism. The reason that the Jewish authorities attacked the Frankists in the first place was the danger that Sabbatianism might be recognized by the Christians as a legitimate form of Judaism: the rabbinate could not afford to have the authorities of the Commonwealth treat the Sabbatians as an autonomous Jewish group akin to the Karaites. Following Dembowski's death and Yavan's successful intercession with the nuncio, this option was off the table. What was at stake, however, was the sect's autonomy within Christianity. During the negotiations preceding the Lwów disputation, the Frankists aimed at the creation of a special Jewish-Christian rite, analogous to the Confucian-Christian rite developed by the Jesuits in China. The fullest description of this element appears in Dov Ber's *Divre binah*.

According to Ber, the persecution of the Frankists by Turkish Jews when the former had escaped to the Ottoman Empire after Dembowski's death forced them to flee back to Poland. The sectarians went first to Kamieniec, where they were told that the seat of the bishop of Kamieniec was still vacant and that the former archbishop of Lwów, Mikołaj Wyżycki, had died recently. The current archbishop of Lwów, Łubieński, had just been nominated the primate of Poland; he was now residing in Warsaw, and the diocese was under the supervision of a temporary administrator. The Kamieniec priests advised the Frankists to write a supplication in Polish to the primate that should list the conditions under which they would accept baptism. If the supplication contained nothing contrary to the Christian faith, it was likely that Łubieński would accept the conditions.

Indeed, in Iyar 5519 (May 1759), the sectarians convened and composed a supplication in Hebrew. Drawing upon the symbolism of the mixed multitude, they stated that the true God, Lord Jesus, had heard their cries as He had heard the cries of the sons of Israel in Egypt. As God had sent Moses to lead the Israelites out of captivity in Egypt, He had sent Dembowski to lead the Frankists out of their plight among the Jews. As Moses had died before he managed to enter the Land of Israel, so Dembowski had died before he managed to lead the Frankists to the Holy Church. And as God again had shown His mercy and sent Joshua to lead the Israelites to the Land of Israel, He would again show His mercy and send the new Joshua in the person of Łubieński, who would lead the Frankists to the Holy (Christian) Faith.[77] The supplication contained the following conditions for baptism:[78]

1. The baptism would involve signing contracts (with the nobility) in Lwów and would not take place until the festival of the three kings (6 January 1760).
2. The converts would not have to shave their beards and sidelocks.
3. They would continue to wear Jewish clothes.
4. They would retain Jewish names in addition to the new Christian ones—for instance, Andrzej Whelwille.
5. They would not be forced to marry non-Jews and would be allowed to marry only between themselves.
6. They would not have to eat pork.
7. They would rest on Sabbath and also on Sunday, like the Christians.[79]
8. They would be allowed to continue to study the book of the Zohar and other books of kabbalah.[80]
9. They would argue from the Talmud in order to justify their acceptance of the Christian faith and to prove the greatness of the evil of the Talmud, which should be burned.[81]

As elsewhere, many details of Ber's account are confirmed by other sources: the bishopric of Kamieniec Podolski indeed remained vacant for some time after Dembowski's death, Wyżycki died in April 1757, Łubieński was nominated primate in April 1759,[82] and the Lwów archdiocese remained under the rule of the administrator *sede vacante*, Father Mikulski. Even the minor detail that the Frankists who returned from Turkey went first to Kamieniec finds corroboration in the Frankist chronicle.[83]

Still, the supplication summarized in *Divre binah* and the circumstances surrounding its composition require clarification. Ber mentioned that the petition was written in May 1759. Indeed, there is a supplication to Łubieński signed by Solomon Shorr and Yehudah Leyb Krysa and dated 16 May 1759. However, the content of the supplication differs completely from the summary in *Divre binah*. Rather, the first paragraphs of Ber's summary closely resemble the opening of another supplication, the one submitted by the Frankists to the consistory in February 1759. The preamble to this other supplication indeed compared Dembowski leading the Frankists out of Judaism to Moses leading the Israelites out of Egypt and Łubieński to Joshua saving them from their later quandaries (Ber also tied this preamble to the symbol of the mixed multitude).[84]

Birkenthal might have confused the supplications of February and of May 1759 or conflated them. However, the extant Polish versions of these two supplications contain no stipulations aiming at the preservation of Jewish identity after the baptism; the only condition mentioned in the Polish supplications is the request to hold a public disputation with the Talmudists. The nine conditions for baptism appear only in *Divre binah*: nevertheless, scholars have tended to take Dov Ber's word on their existence. Most details of Ber's story are corroborated by other sources, and, as noted, his account is generally very reliable. It is difficult to imagine that he would make up precisely these conditions; in contrast, it is not difficult to imagine that they were suppressed either by Moliwda, who translated the supplication from Hebrew into Polish, or by Łubieński, who had it printed.

The Background of the Jewish-Christian Rite: The Protestant Factor

Unusual as they were, the conditions listed in the Frankists' supplication were not unique. In 1730–31, two emissaries of the Pietistic Institutum Judaicum et Muhammedicum in Halle, Johann Georg Widmann and Johann Andreas Manitius, undertook a journey to Poland. The official purpose of the journey was to gather information on the "condition" of Polish Jewry; in the event, however, Manitius and Widmann sought to verify unconfirmed reports about the messianic "awakening" among the Jews and especially about the alleged pro-Christian sympathies or even conversionary inclinations of Rabbi Jacob Mordechai ha-Kohen of Płock.[85] In one of their conversations with Polish Jews, Manitius suggested that should they choose to convert to Lutheranism, the Halle Institute would be able to obtain written guarantees of far-reaching autonomy from the king of Prussia for the new Christians. He stated: "We could agree that you retain external ceremonies. You could keep wearing beards, not eat pork and eat only kosher meat, you could use your Hebrew language in liturgy and wear special clothes. In short, there are many rites that are neutral, [so you could keep them] if only you do not claim that they are necessary for redemption."[86]

The striking overlap between the conditions listed by Manitius and those demanded by the Frankists might be coincidental: Jewish converts or potential converts often sought to retain elements of their former identity after their baptism, and some of their concerns might have been similar. The wider context of Manitius's testimony is unknown: it is unclear whether he was authorized to offer any real guarantees of autonomy in the name of the king of Prussia and whether his suggestion was a part of serious negotiations or simply table talk.

For my discussion, the most important element is the justification of the proposal: since, from Manitius's perspective, such elements of Jewish identity as the observance dietary laws or prayer in Hebrew were purely conventional, "neutral," and "external," adhering to them after the conversion did not constitute any theological problem. Additional stimulus for the interchange was offered by both Christian and Jewish messianism: for the Pietists, the conversion of the Jews was a necessary part of a wider eschatological scheme according to which all of Israel would recognize of the truth of Christianity at the end of days. Some Jewish charismatics, in turn, saw the very interest in Judaism displayed by Christians within the framework of their own messianic expectations: the contacts between Halle Pietists and the rabbi of Płock were initiated as result of the latter's prediction that the messiah would come in 1740, and it seems that the rabbi saw a sign of approaching redemption in the recognition of the intrinsic value of Judaism by Christians.[87]

Missions of the Institutum Judaicum among Polish Jews ended ten years before Frank started his activity in Poland, in 1747, and there were no direct contacts between the Frankists and the Halle Pietists. This does not mean, however, that there was no indirect influence. In this context, it is important to dispel a common misconception concerning Protestant missions to the Jews in eighteenth-century Eastern Europe. Jewish scholars have often emphasized that the impact of missionary activity on the Polish communities was negligible. With respect to numbers, this is undoubtedly true: very few Jews converted as a result of the encounter with the emissaries of the Institutum. This uplifting conclusion, however, is based on a misunderstanding of the real aims of the Institutum: the journeys of the emissaries were not missions in the strict of the term.

On the face of it, the very idea of sending Protestant (and, in many cases, radical Protestant) missionaries to Roman Catholic Poland was utterly preposterous. A mass Jewish conversion to Lutheranism would have met with resistance not only from Jewish authorities but from the Roman Catholic clergy. Even if such a conversion were to occur, the project would have encountered insurmountable difficulties such as the employment and resettlements of the converts. Indeed, there are known instances of the emissaries turning down prospective converts, citing the practical difficulties of resettling them in Protestant countries.

Thus, the aim of the *Judenmission* of the Pietists was not to baptize individual Jews but to evangelize Jewry as a whole.[88] With this goal in mind, the emissaries attached much less importance to actual conversion than to distributing Christian books in Jewish languages and thereby acquainting Jews with selected Christian notions. During the 1730–31 mission alone, Widmann and Manitius distributed more than 650 books and pamphlets among the Jews.[89] While some of those books were burned or otherwise destroyed by rabbinic authorities (and, in some cases, by Catholics), others were read, passed from hand to hand, and sold and resold by the Jews. The exact scope of their impact is impossible to assess, but it is certain that they acquainted some Jews with key concepts of Christian theology as well as with Christian Scriptures.

While the missions of the Institutum Judaicum came to an end in 1747, other Protestant groups and churches continued to work for the evangelization of Eastern European Jewry. In the late 1750s, the Moravian Brethren of Herrnhut sent an emissary, the convert David Kirchoff, to Poland. In the course of his journey, Kirchoff encountered the Frankists. In his first dispatch to his superiors in Herrnhut, he related Bishop Dembowski's death and reported that he had met a large number of Jews "who believed that the messiah had already come but did not believe that Jesus was the messiah." He also mentioned that many Jews studied the Gospels.[90] The second report, written immediately after the Lwów disputation, shows a change: Kirchoff stated that more than fifteen thousand Jews (including fifty rabbis) had openly declared that "the true messiah already has come and Jesus of Nazareth is this messiah."

These believing Jews were ready to convert to Christianity officially but did not know in which Christian denomination they could find the pure evangelical truth. They had embarked upon the study of various Christian books but, because of unrest among the Jews, were forced to "take a shortcut and convert to Roman Catholicism."[91]

I have discussed Kirchoff and his reports elsewhere.[92] Although he was present in Lwów during the disputation, there is no evidence that he met Frank or any of his followers in person, and it is unlikely that he had any impact on the course of events. Yet the theological background of his reports is important here. The Moravians, like many other Protestant groups, envisaged the conversion of the Jews in eschatological terms, as a sign of the approach of the end of days. This direct link between the conversion of the Jewish people and eschatology led to the interpretation of the *absence* of this very conversion as a special act of divine grace: since such a conversion of the Jews would signify the end of the world, God Himself was postponing it in order to give more time for the Christianization of the pagans. Protestant missionary theology was marked by a peculiar duality: hope that the Jews would eventually convert to Christianity was counterbalanced by hope that it would not happen too soon. In this eschatological scheme, it was *necessary* for the Jews, for the time being, to remain Jews so that heathen peoples could be taught about Jesus.

During this interim period, the worst-case scenario would not be the Jews' continued adherence to their ancestral religion but their lapse into heresy, that is, conversion to the wrong kind of Christianity. The journeys of the Pietists and the Moravians to Poland might thus be seen as "anti-missions": the emissaries' aim was not to convert the Jews to Lutheranism but to acquaint them with "pure evangelical truth," thereby staving off their conversion to Roman Catholicism.

The missions of the Halle Pietists and the Moravian Brethren to the Polish Jewry were based on the fundamental theological principle of the agreement between pure Christianity freed of papal deformations and pure Judaism cleansed of rabbinic superstitions. In their exchanges with the Polish Jews, the Protestant emissaries presented themselves as the repository of the true Israelite religion and argued that, on a deep level, Jews and non-Jews shared the same faith and that the only difference between them was related to "external ceremonies." Accordingly, the emissaries asserted that "the Jews should remain Jews even after they become Christians"[93] and encouraged them to retain Jewish social identities while accepting Jesus as the messiah and redeemer. They believed that such a version of Christianity would be much more attractive to the Jews than unequivocal acceptance of the papist Church, with its "idolatrous" elements such as the cult of saints and the Virgin Mary.

Needless to say, the conversion of the Frankists in Lwów caused a real stir in Protestant circles in Western Europe. As early as June 1759, an anonymous correspondent of the well-known English periodical *Gentleman's Magazine* published a letter titled "Friendly Address to the Jews." He engaged in eschatological speculation concerning the restoration of the Jewish people to their own land before the final stage of redemption and promised that the Jews, after their conversion to Protestantism, would be transported to the Holy Land on English ships. Referring to the conversion of the Frankists, he stated:

> I was surprised to see an account that some thousands of Jews in
> Poland and Hungary had lately sent to the Polish bishop of Guesna
> [Łubieński; Gniezno was the seat of the primate of Poland] to
> inform him of their desire to embrace the Roman Catholic Reli-
> gion. . . . If indeed you begin to think that the Christian religion is
> true, if you believe the messiah is already come the first time, in his
> afflicted state, then embrace the Protestant religion, that true Chris-
> tianity which is delivered to us in the New Testament, or covenant,
> without the false traditions and wicked intentions and additions
> of the Popes, who have entirely perverted the truth, and corrupted
> primitive Christianity.[94]

The Protestant missions to Eastern European Jewry had a twofold impact on the development of Frankism. First, the emissaries' policy of distributing Christian texts in Jewish languages did seem to have borne fruit. Some Frankists had extensive—if not fully accurate—knowledge of Christian theology even before any encounters with Polish clergy, and one of the sources from which they gained their first ideas about Christianity was the missionary literature of the Pietists. Frankist sources attest to a thorough knowledge of the New Testament, and Frank himself claimed to have read the Gospel of Luke in Hebrew or Yiddish; the copy in his possession was most likely one of those printed and distributed by the Halle Institutum Judaicum.[95]

Second, the emissaries managed to acquaint many Jews with the idea of creating an independent Jewish-Christian community. The exact elements of Jewish identity that the prospective converts intended to retain after their baptism might have been subject to negotiations, but the idea that they were to form a community not only separate from other Jews but also from other Christians remained a pronounced part of the Frankist doctrine.

In one regard, however, the conversion of the Frankists dealt a serious blow to the hopes of the Protestants. The idea that the converting Jews would prefer to avoid the "idolatrous" elements of Roman Catholicism clearly did not appeal to Frank, who, as it were, was attracted precisely to these elements. To the Protestants' disappointment, Frank did not seek the "pure evangelical truth" of Lutheran confessions but rather, popish splendor and lavishness. His followers fancied flashy titles, ornate costumes, and elaborate rituals. Frank was also fascinated by the Catholic Mariology and the cult of the Virgin, which—as my subsequent discussion will show—were arguably the most important Christian influences upon his teachings. In fact, Frank's clear preference for the Roman Church went beyond his own choice of confession. The *Gentleman's Magazine* letter calling upon the Jews to "embrace the Protestant religion" instead of Catholicism found its ironic counterpart in the following statement of Frank: "All religions and all peoples, also the Philipovtsy [the Old Believers], the Ammonites [most likely the Mennonites], and the Herrnhuter [the Moravian Brethren], and other similar sects, will have to enter the Roman Catholic faith."[96]

The Background of the Jewish-Christian Rite:
The Catholic Factor

Following the 1570 consensus achieved by the principal Protestant denominations in Poland (Lutherans, Calvinists, and Bohemian Brethren) and the 1573 Constitution, which contained a clause guaranteeing freedom from persecution for "dissidents in matters of religion" (*dissidentes in religione*), religious toleration became one of the fundamentals of the legal system of the Polish-Lithuanian Commonwealth: before assuming power, each monarch had to swear not to impose one religion upon all and to protect the liberties of the nonconformists.

This measure of religious toleration was, of course, limited to the officially recognized denominations, thereby excluding from the outset all future sects as well as those who, like the anti-Trinitarian "Arians" (Polish Brethren), were considered heretics by both Protestants and Catholics. In the course of the seventeenth and the first half of the eighteenth century, the progress of the Counter-Reformation gradually encroached on the rights of the non-

Catholics, with the passage of discriminatory anti-Protestant legislation. Over time, numerous restrictions were imposed upon the Protestants, who were, for instance, precluded from making public shows of piety or from building new houses of worship and restoring old ones. The anti-Arian legislation of the 1660s established "apostasy"—understood as leaving Roman Catholicism for any other faith (including the recognized Christian denominations)—as a capital crime. By 1733, Protestants were prohibited from holding public office and banned from participating in the sessions of the national parliament of the Commonwealth, the Sejm.

As for Judaism, canon law as well as the law of the Commonwealth recognized it as *religio licta*, and the Jews were not the target of the Catholic campaign for religious unity in Poland. They were explicitly and specifically excluded from the prohibitions on constructing new places of worship by non-Catholics,[97] and, in several cases, erstwhile Protestant churches were turned into synagogues.[98] The state did not challenge their autonomous legal status, and the Polish Church never conducted a systematic missionary campaign directed toward the Jews. Such missionary efforts were sometimes undertaken by individual members of the clergy, such as Bishop Kobielski. However, their scope was extremely limited, and even the priests who were directly involved in these efforts admitted that they had met not only with resistance but with scorn, ridicule, and even violence on the part of the Jews (this includes a rather startling account of a Catholic who was slapped in his face by a rabbi for daring to try to preach to the Jews about Jesus; the rabbi did not seem to suffer any adverse consequences for his deed).[99]

The policy of the physical separation of Jews and Christians, similar to the one operating in Italy and some German states, was never implemented (and seldom even advocated) in Poland. Ecclesiastical legislation touching upon the Jews normally dealt not with the Jews as such, but with the Christians who violated canon law in their interactions with the Jews, and the Polish Church interfered in Jewish affairs only indirectly by regulating the sphere of Jewish-Christian interchange. Despite all this, anti-Jewish rhetoric constituted an integral and important part of the Catholic battle for primacy in Poland. As Magda Teter has demonstrated, references to Jews featured prominently in Catholic sermons and polemical literature "not as the actual focus but rather as a [general] symbol of the hostile forces."[100] The Church often used a "roundabout strategy" employing religious polemic against Judaism in defense of specifically Catholic tenets of belief and charging its Protestant adversaries with "Judaizing."[101]

The 1759 conversion of the Frankists provided the Church with a stimulus to expand this strategy. The *Gentleman's Magazine* letter attested to the panic of Protestants hearing about the conversion; its author explicitly referred to an account of "some thousands of Jews in Poland and Hungary" who petitioned the primate of Poland about their "desire to embrace the Roman Catholic Religion." This account was doubtless the February 1759 supplication of the Frankists to Łubieński (the supplication indeed opens with a preamble in which the Frankists claim to speak in the name of "the Jews of Poland, Hungary, Turkey, Moldavia, Wallachia, etc."). The primate had the supplication widely publicized.

According to Ber of Bolechów, before the end of the disputation, two thousand copies of the Polish texts of the petition were printed; a thousand were immediately disseminated among the clergy and nobility present in Lwów, and another thousand were expedited to Warsaw to be distributed as a broadside in the capital.[102] The newspaper *Kuryer Polski* reprinted the full text of the supplication in April 1759.[103] A Latin version was also published separately.[104] A French translation was executed around that time and dispatched, along with the Polish and the Latin, by the nuncio to Rome.[105] This French translation also appeared in print.[106] Several German newspapers published the supplication in spring 1759;[107] the author of the *Gentleman's Magazine* letter most likely learned about the document from one of these publications. Before the end of 1759, the supplication was also translated into Spanish and went through two separate imprints, one in Spain[108] and one in Mexico.[109] The Spanish version was subsequently translated into Portuguese by the Inquisition.[110]

The extraordinary dissemination of the Frankist supplication was part of a wider Catholic propaganda campaign. Primate Łubieński issued a pastoral letter urging Catholics to support the converts with alms and ordered that an abridged version of the minutes of the Lwów disputation be sent to parish churches and read instead of Sunday sermons.[111] A similar letter was also issued by Bishop Wołłowicz, who had been involved in the ritual murder trial in Jampol.[112] The Roman Catholic Church was planning to utilize the Lwów conversion in its preaching against Christian dissidents. The fact that a large group of Jews converted to Roman Catholicism and not to another Christian denomination was used as an argument for its truth; the impending conversion of all Jews was seen in millenarian terms, as an indication of the approaching triumph of the *Mater Ecclesia*. Thus, Łubieński sought to support the claim that there was only one true Christian Church by arguing that "in our times,

as the World seems to approach the end, the prophecy is beginning to be fulfilled and Jews strive to convert other Jews."[113] The author of the anonymous
pamphlet *Myśli z historii o kontratalmudystach* (Thoughts concerning the history of the Contra-Talmudists) stated: "The present-day heretics invented the
teaching—unknown to the ancient fathers—that the true Church of Jesus
Christ is invisible. If the Church is indeed invisible, I will ask the current dissidents: How did it happen that this flock [the Frankists] found their way to
this [Catholic] Church and not to any Lutheran or Calvinist temple?"[114]

The Church clearly saw the conversion of the Frankists as a golden opportunity to enliven and strengthen its propaganda against the non-Catholic
dissidents. It was prepared to disregard its doubts concerning the Contra-
Talmudists' purity of motive and the possibly sectarian or heretical character
of the group. Dispatches of the nuncio to the Curia are full of such doubts.
For instance, in June 1759, Bishop Serra expressed his misgivings, questioning
if "the true intention of the Contra-Talmudists was to accept the Christian religion";[115] the following month, he accused them of "coloring" their Christian
vocation.[116] In August, he wrote: "the secretive, strange, and unclear behavior
of Frank and his fellows does not correspond to their declared Christian faith.
One can surmise that this is the beginning of a new sect among the Jews; the
priests who work with them should proceed with utmost caution."[117]

Similarly, Łubieński inquired—in private correspondence with
Mikulski—about the genuineness of Frank's Christian belief and whether
his willingness to convert did not mask the search for personal gain (Mikulski diplomatically answered that he had not yet made up his mind on the
issue).[118] In another letter, he characterized the Frankists as "Jew-Puritans who
call themselves Anti-Talmudists."[119] To be sure, a contemporary Christian
observer could see an analogy between Frankism understood as an attempt
to purge Judaism from its talmudic (that is, nonbiblical) elements and the
Puritan struggle to eradicate the Catholic (also nonbiblical) remnants existing
in the English Church. But in the mouth of the head of the Roman Church
in Poland, the epithet had a clearly negative character. Whatever Łubieński
knew of Puritanism and whatever he meant by "Jew-Puritans," it is clear that
he saw the Frankists within the framework of a wider Christian dynamic and
that he understood the movement as analogous to spiritualistic—and, from
his perspective, heretical—trends within Christianity. Yet such doubts, suspicions, and reservations appear only in manuscript sources that were never
intended for wider circulation. Among the printed Christian accounts of the
Lwów disputation and the conversion of the Frankists, there is only one docu-

ment that related—in passing—to the fact that Sabbatianism was not exactly a mainstream current of Judaism, compared the quarrel between the rabbis and the Contra-Talmudists to disputes between Lutherans and Calvinists, and wondered if Frankism should not be considered a "schism" or a "heresy."[120] All other books, broadsides, and pamphlets written by the priests in the wake of the 1759 events hailed the conversion of the Frankists as the unconditional victory of the Catholic Church, proving the Church's superiority and foretelling its final triumph over "dissenters," "heretics," and "unbelievers."

The unconditional victory of the Catholic Church demanded, of course, that the conversion of the Frankists to Roman Catholicism be unconditional. On 19 June 1759, Łubieński responded to all the supplications of the Contra-Talmudists. He praised their intention to convert but urged them not to prolong their deliberations, so that they would not become a "devil's plaything" because of their foot-dragging. He also stressed that their acceptance of Catholicism must be without any restrictions and qualifications.[121] His emphasis on this point can be seen as additional evidence that the Frankists did indeed try to put forward some conditions for baptism and to retain elements of Jewish identity and belief even after their conversion to Christianity. The needs of the Catholic propaganda against Christian dissenters demanded that such conditions be suppressed.

The aim of the Council of Four Lands and other rabbis was to "eradicate and cut off" the heresy embodied by Frank and his group. At first, in 1757, they attempted to do so by trying to convince the priests that Jews and Christians should condemn the "heretics" equally. Having failed in this, they decided to rid the Jewish fold of the Frankists and to press for their conversion to Christianity. The Church, in turn, was prepared to take the suspected Jewish heretics under its wing, hoping to utilize their conversion for its own propaganda.

Paradoxically, the Catholic position reinforced the elements already present in the Jewish standpoint: Jews and Christians both attempted to separate Frankism from Judaism, efface its differences from Christianity, and eradicate its claims to independence. This overlapping of the interests of the clergy and the rabbinate went so far that it is not altogether clear from some contemporary reports that the priests—despite their anti-Jewish convictions and prejudices—really wished for a total victory of the Frankists during the disputations. An unconditional victory in the debate by the Frankists would not only have confounded the rabbis but would have immeasurably strengthened the bargaining position of Frank and his followers. In order to keep their leverage, the priests played the Frankists off against the rabbis *and* vice versa.

The alliance of the priests and the rabbis had a threefold impact on the development of the Frankist movement. First, during the Kamieniec debate, the Contra-Talmudists had tried to remain within Judaism, at the same time challenging the position of the rabbinate as the sole preserver of divine lore.[122] The persistence of their rabbinic opponents had forced them to sharpen their position and not only reject *rabbinic* Judaism as a possible form of Jewish religion but to reject Judaism as a religion of which they might be considered a denomination.

Second, the insistence of the rabbis that Sabbatianism was immoral, along with the emphasis placed on Frank's Sabbatian roots, forced the Frankists to disown Sabbatianism. Before the Kamieniec and the Lwów disputations, Frank and his disciples were merely a Podolian offshoot of the followers of Sabbatai Tsevi and Berukhiah. After the disputations, they had to reinvent themselves as a distinct religious group and thus sever the links to their origins. Accordingly, later Frankist documents manifest the gradual elimination of Sabbatian terminology and references to the major personalities of the Sabbatian movement. On a social level, this development reverses the trend characteristic of Jewish heresy in the seventeenth century. Sabbatianism started as a mass movement led by Sabbatai and Nathan of Gaza and ended up as a number of clandestine sectarian groups centered on different leaders. In 1755–57, the Contra-Talmudists were one such small sect lacking aspirations to attract a wider following; around 1759–60, a full-fledged mass movement coalesced around Frank. During that period, Frank called upon all Jews to convert to Christianity and embarked upon negotiations to obtain an autonomous territory for settlement. While these negotiations eventually failed to produce results, appeals to all Jews to convert remained an essential part of the Frankist doctrine throughout the existence of the movement.

Third, the combination of the rabbinic theological and moral praise of Christianity (as opposed to Sabbatianism) with behind-the-scenes machinations to force a group of Jews to convert to Roman Catholicism compelled the Frankists to define more precisely their own attitude toward the Christian religion. The Frankists were forced to define not only how they differed from other Jews but also what distinguished them from the Christians. This last element had a crucial impact on the development of Frank's teachings.

Politically and theologically, the Frankists were therefore under double pressure from Jewish as well as Christian authorities. This alliance of rabbis and priests has escaped the attention of Jewish and Christian scholars. The former have tended to emphasize (and exaggerate) the pressure put on Jews by

Catholic clergy, while the latter have liked to consider the conversion of the Frankists as fully voluntary. Some contemporaries were more perceptive. The maskil Jacob Calmanson described the Frankist affair as follows: "The entire class of learned Jews . . . unified against the dangerous innovator [Frank], in whom they saw—both individually and as a group—the most treacherous enemy. Yet the respect Frank had among the majority of simple Jews, as well as the massive size of his following, did not allow them to attack him openly. Accordingly, the rabbis went to the bishops. Our times are peculiar ones: for the first time, it could be seen that rabbis forged an alliance with bishops against their fellow Jews."[123]

Chapter 6

Ghosts of the Past, Heralds of the Future

Frank in Warsaw

After the conclusion of the Lwów disputation and the celebration of his baptism in the city's cathedral, Frank, accompanied by his six closest followers and the interpreter Moliwda, departed for Warsaw. The party reached the city on 23 October 1759. Upon their arrival, the group submitted a new petition to King Augustus III.[1] In contrast to earlier supplications, which had been signed by Yehudah Leyb Krysa and Solomon Shorr, this one was signed anonymously and collectively by "the faithful subjects of Your Majesty." It was the first official document to mention the name of Frank as leader of all the Jews who had accepted Catholicism. Krysa (after the baptism: Dominik Antoni Krysiński) had finally lost his struggle for power within the sect, and Frank's leadership was decisively established. A few months later, Krysiński, independently of Frank's group, quietly came to Warsaw. He settled in the capital, assimilated thoroughly into Polish society, and severed all links with the Frankists.[2] His son, Ludwik, was the first erstwhile member of the sect to marry a Catholic of non-Jewish descent, Maria Przyłuska.[3] Yehudah Leyb Krysa's name does not appear in any later Frankist documents.

The supplication to Augustus III of October 1757 was written in the name of the already baptized Contra-Talmudists, who had made pledges qualifying them to receive territory for settlement and royal protection from the rabbinate. The petitioners asked the king to intercede with regional magnates so that those believers still in hiding could reveal themselves without fear of persecution by the Jews. The document also demanded the establishment of special commissions in Kamieniec and Lwów, which would look into the matter of the forced divorces and the disinheritance of the sectarians' children by the rabbinate in 1756 and ensure the return of property confiscated by the rabbinic court of Satanów. Copies of the supplication were sent to Primate Łubieński and to Bishop Sołtyk in Kraków.

During the negotiations preceding his conversion in Lwów in September 1757, Frank managed to obtain permission for his initial baptism to be administered according to the simplified *ex fonto* rite (normally employed in cases of imminent danger of death), thereby prolonging his liminal suspension between Judaism and Christianity and leaving him some bargaining room preceding his final access to Catholicism. The formal reason for his trip to Warsaw was to complete the ritual. In late November[4] or early December,[5] Jakub Józef Frank and his wife, Hana (who assumed the names Józefa Scholastyka), were baptized for the second time in full ceremonials. The rites took place in the Royal Chapel; the very same Bishop Załuski, who had collaborated with Sołtyk in the ritual murder accusations, officiated. King Augustus III acted as godfather.[6] A few of those who had converted in Lwów also came to Warsaw at that time; other Frankists converted in the capital in the final months of 1759. The most prominent nobles and highest officials of the kingdom, including Lithuanian Hetman Michał Józef Massalski, Karl Christian the Duke of Courland, Crown Princes Albert and Clemens, and others were among the godparents.[7] The Frankist group in Warsaw grew to a few dozen members.[8]

After the baptism, Frank conducted himself with ostentatious splendor, attended theaters, and visited the homes of the most important magnates in Warsaw. He traveled in a chariot pulled by six horses, tossed handfuls of gold coins to the poor, "clothed himself like a king," and ate on gold and silver.[9] His followers shaved their beards, girded sabers, and "dressed like Christians."[10] Many of them were ennobled (I shall return to the issue of the ennoblements in Chapter 8). The Frankists were financed by generous donations and became local celebrities, greatly honored by Polish clergy as well as secular powers.

The elites of the Commonwealth decided to support Frank against contenders to power such as Krysa. The earlier idea of complete or even partial religious autonomy, associated with Krysa, was abandoned. However, in exchange for the promise of inducing a large number of Jews to accept Catholicism unconditionally, Frank demanded far-reaching political concessions. The Frankists would become fully and unconditionally Christian; they would, however, retain a distinct group identity, without mingling with other Christians, and a significant measure of self-government. Borne upon favorable winds, the leader of the Frankists embarked on negotiations regarding the settlement of the converts. Frank's aim was to establish a separate, semi-independent colony for Christian Sabbatians.

The demand of a special territory for settlement was not new: the May 1759 supplication to Łubieński had already requested a territory near the Turkish border, and claimed that the towns of Busk and Gliniany were already "under the control of the true believers" (indeed, the rabbis of both towns were among the 1759 converts; two-thirds of the Busk Jews apostatized, and Jewish sources confirm that almost all the town's Jews accepted Frank's leadership).[11] The request to establish a colony for the converted Sabbatians also appeared in the supplication to the king; in Warsaw, the project took on a more concrete shape. Many representatives of the Polish nobility expressed their readiness to accept a certain number of neophytes on their estates and provide for them and their families. One of them, Prince Jabłonowski, argued that the Frankist colony should be granted autonomy and given full political and financial support "so that it may follow the example of the populous and rich province of Paraguay, which took its beginning from some fifty savage families converted and civilized by the Jesuits."[12]

Other noblemen, however, reckoned that the converts should be dispersed over a larger territory. The Frankists sought to maintain the unity of the group and were reluctant to accept the offer of settlement on private estates, fearing that before long, they would decline into serfdom. They repeatedly asked to be allowed to remain together and demanded settlement on lands belonging to the Crown. The king was rumored to favor the idea; some bishops also offered to settle the converts in the Church's *jurydyki*, ecclesiastical enclaves that adjoined Poland's bigger towns.[13] Frank pointed out that the converts originated not only from Poland but from Wallachia, Moldavia, Hungary, and even Turkey proper; not knowing the Polish language or the customs of the kingdom, they would inevitably perish should they be separated from one another.[14] The promise to persuade foreign Jews to come to Poland-Lithuania and settle there as Christians was clearly Frank's strongest card and the most likely reason that the Polish elites supported him over Krysa: on several occasions, he claimed that if they were allowed to settle together and were granted a measure of political independence, "a multitude of Jews would come to Poland from these countries [the Ottoman Empire and its tributary principalities of Wallachia and Moldavia] to accept the Christian faith."[15] He gave the figure of "no fewer than ten thousand" potential settlers.[16]

Little is known about the character envisaged for the projected colony. Frank demanded total rule over the neophytes and envisioned a strict military

regimen. He was always surrounded by armed guards and forced his followers to train with weapons. He wanted the converts to become soldiers rather
than artisans or peasants and argued that even a small force of Jewish converts
familiar with the borderland territories between Poland and Turkey would be
useful in any eventual conflict between the Commonwealth and the Ottoman
Empire.

Frank's conversion was not a part of his original program but was necessitated by the joint pressure of the rabbinate and the clergy. However, after
the baptism, Frank presented the abandonment of official Judaism as a double
liberation: emancipation from the tyranny of religion and the tyranny of land-
lessness. The Frankists were to become soldiers and the Frankist leaders—
military commanders. It was only natural that they had abandoned Judaism,
since, as Frank put it, "military commanders must not have religion."[17] This
militaristic program was intrinsically linked with the plan to obtain territory
for settlement, and the acceptance of Christianity was the shortest path to
acquiring land. On one occasion, exasperated by the plodding pace of the
negotiations with the clergy, Frank stated that had he had two hundred Jews
able to handle weapons, he could have managed to obtain a permanent abode
for his followers and for himself.[18] He claimed that from the very outset, God's
intention regarding the Israelites was for them to conquer lands rather than
study the Torah. Official Judaism inverted the natural order of things; Frankism was to put things right. Thus, Frank "cursed those who teach the Jewish
laws in that religion. Those who do not have God should study laws. Come
and see, God told Abraham, I give all these *lands* to you and your children.[19]
He did not say that he would give them *laws*."[20]

Gershom Scholem believed that militarism and "Jewish territorialism"
were crucial features of Frankism: the first signaled the culmination of the
process of the birth of "a new type of Jew . . . for whom the world of Exile
and Diaspora Judaism was partly or wholly abolished";[21] the latter "expressed
in a bizarre yet unmistakable manner the desire of his followers for a reconstruction of Jewish national and even economic existence."[22] According to
Scholem, Frank's "personal contribution to the Sabbatian worldview" was the
rejection of the connection between redemption and the return to the Land
of Israel: it was precisely this promise of the "territorial centralization of all
Sabbatians" that drew such a large following. The Frankists originated mainly
from the lowest stratum of Jewish society; they were people from villages and
small towns,[23] the poorest of the poor, "Jewish *Lumpenproletariat*," whose
only dream was the liberation from the oppressive power of the rabbinate.[24]

What Scholem did not state explicitly, but what I maintain follows from his argument, would be that, like any true proletariat, they had nothing to lose but their chains: despite the odium attached to it within the Jewish community, conversion to Catholicism promised social advancement, and the "territorialist program" offered a special bonus and carried a promise of genuine emancipation.

The majority of those who converted in Lwów in 1759–60 were indeed poor and marginal. The Frankist elite consisted of four or five communal rabbis from townlets[25] and several itinerant preachers; the rest were, as the nuncio put it, "total boors and complete paupers."[26] It is indeed likely that many of those who converted had felt oppressed by the Jewish oligarchic establishment and that promises of a better life and permanent settlement would hold special appeal for them. However, the lowest strata of Eastern European Jewry were destitute long before Frank's appearance; never before had poverty led to a mass conversion to Christianity, let alone led Jews from Muslim territories to come to a Christian kingdom to seek baptism. While I agree that militarism and territorialism were crucial elements of Frankism, it seems unlikely that solely the vague and rather uncertain promises of a semiautonomous colony for the converts would suffice to persuade a few thousand Jews to accept the stigma of apostasy or to abandon their homes in the Ottoman Empire and migrate to the Commonwealth to become Christians.

The unprecedented alliance of the Catholic clergy and the rabbinate drove Frank and his Polish followers into a corner and left them no other option than to convert to Christianity. Their brethren who came to Lwów from Turkey and the Balkans, poor and oppressed by the rabbis as they may have been, still had other choices. Nevertheless, they decided to leave everything behind and plunge into total uncertainty. Christian sources agree that even after the Ottoman Jews' arrival in Lwów, it was next to impossible for the clergy to make the final push and induce them to be baptized: in a letter to the nuncio, the administrator of the Lwów archdiocese honestly admitted that the priests' preaching and promises had little influence upon the Sabbatians, and the "majority of them would never convert if not for Frank's imploring and his personal example."[27]

Frank's charisma must have been great indeed, and the territorialist idea might have played a role, yet what tipped the balance was not the unarticulated "desire for a reconstruction of Jewish national and even economic existence." Undoubtedly, the Frankists sought to establish a semi-independent Sabbatian colony in the Diaspora and rejected the idea of rebuilding the Temple in Jerusalem. However, this does not mean that they would have settled in Uganda. The idea of seeking a semiautonomous settlement for both Polish and Ottoman Sabbatians can be understood only in the context of earlier Sabbatian teachings concerning Poland. Scholem already noted in his discussion of "the territorialist program" that the Frankists transferred Sabbatian messianic hopes connected to the Land of Israel to Poland.[28] Frank regarded Poland as "the country promised to the Patriarchs, . . . God's succession and our succession," which he would not abandon "for all other countries, even if they were filled with precious stones."[29] Extraordinary as they might seem, his ideas about the messianic role of Poland were not completely original.

In his *Sefer kav ha-yashar* (1705), the preacher and chronicler Tsevi Hirsh Kaidanover reported a tradition attributed to the Sabbatian prophet Heshel Tsoref of Vilna (1633–ca. 1700). According to Kaidanover, Tsoref taught about the numerological equivalency between the name of biblical Tsefo, grandson of Esau, and the Hebrew name of Poland (*Polin*).[30] Thus Samael, the angelic guardian of Tsefo and Esau, is also the angelic guardian of Poland, which should rightly be called "the Kingdom of Edom." The name Tsefo is etymologically related to the Hebrew word for the North (*tsafon*), which in turn has the same numerical value as the words *Polin Lita* (Poland-Lithuania);[31] according to Tsoref, the phrase from Jer. 1:14 "out of the north an evil shall break forth" hinted that the tribulations directly preceding the coming of the messiah would take place in Poland and that "when the redemption comes, it will start in the country of the north, that is, Poland-Lithuania."[32]

Sabbatian exegesis inverted the traditional meaning of the symbols of Ba'al Tsafon/Tsefo and Esau/Edom, connecting them with redemption rather than with evil and impurity. Heshel Tsoref linked this symbolic complex with Poland, and there is no doubt that this association was known to Frank and many of his followers.[33] Like Tsoref, Frank explicitly equated Poland with "the land of Edom."[34] He claimed that Poland was "the ground for the ascension,"[35] the place where the *Shekhinah*, the Divine Presence, would start to rise from the Exile. This task of raising the *Shekhinah* had been undertaken by Sabbatai Tsevi,[36] who, however, failed to accomplish his mission.

Throughout *The Words of the Lord*, Sabbatai's failure is presented as a failure to go to Poland: "the First [Sabbatai] wanted to go to Esau, and the Second, Signor Santo [Berukhiah], who revealed the Christian state, also wanted to go to Esau, but they could not because Laban and Esau are now in Poland."[37] Frank portrayed his entire mission as "coming to Poland,"[38] which is where "the Day of Judgment will be fulfilled"[39] and where the gathering of the elect would take place: "I am telling you that the Patriarchs and Moses and Aaron and all the kings of Israel and all the chosen ones will come to me to Poland. And the First and Second will come as well. I will teach them with great honor."[40]

Frank managed to attract a large following and to persuade foreign Sabbatians to arrive in Lwów and seek baptism on the basis of the older Sabbatian tradition that associated "coming to Poland" with coming to Esau in the land of Edom directly before the advent of redemption. The rekindling of this earlier Sabbatian tradition allowed Frank to overtake Krysa in the quest for leadership over the Podolian Believers and gave him extraordinary sway among the Sabbatians in all of Eastern and Central Europe: the declarations that he would bring several thousand foreign Jews to Poland were not necessarily exaggerated. Certainly, the Christians took these declarations seriously. The eastern parts of the Commonwealth were sparsely populated, and local landowners constantly vied for new inhabitants of their towns and villages, often offering subsidized or even free settlement and tax incentives. Ostensibly, Frank had a strong bargaining position with Polish clergy and nobility, who were also tempted by his promises to attract a large number of such new settlers into their domains.

Yet the authorities were uneasy about the political and religious implications of having a semi-independent colony of converted Jews on their hands and the possible unrest caused by granting them exceptional status. The nobility were worried that creating a Jewish-Christian settlement close to Turkey would threaten "both the religion they accepted so recently and the good order of the Kingdom."[41] The clergy argued that the Lwów archdiocese alone could not handle the pastoral care of such a large number of new Christians.[42] The militaristic character of the proposed settlement also caused anxiety: Jews coming to Poland from the Ottoman Empire might have been valuable settlers, but they might also have been Turkish spies or infiltrators of dubious loyalties.

Open negotiations concerning guarantees of political autonomy for the projected Sabbatian-Christian settlement between the Frankist leadership and the Christian establishment (and promulgating rumors about such negotiations) were lures for prospective converts: theoretically, all options were on the table. Nevertheless, it is very clear that the authorities never intended to give in to Frankist demands, for Frank's bargaining position was weaker than it seemed. That so much hinged on his personal charisma and the messianic expectations of the Sabbatians concerning his "coming to Poland" was a double-edged sword: it temporarily gave him tremendous power over his followers' souls, but it made it extremely easy to shatter the unity of the group. All that was needed was to sever the bond between Frank and other converts. For the time being, in order to attract a few more neophytes, Frank might have been allowed to revel in a six-horse chariot, and the Jews converting in Warsaw might be given a royal treatment. Before long, however, the party was over.

In November 1759, two recent converts and three catechumens reported to their confessor, Father Gaudenty Pikulski, that Frank's adoption of Christianity was not sincere.[43] The denouncers told Pikulski that Frank had taught about the approaching end of the world and claimed that he had seen the Antichrist in the town of Salonika.[44] The Antichrist would soon perform miracles and persecute the Christians. The coming of the Antichrist was a sign that the final unification of world faiths had started and that soon "there shall be one flock and one shepherd."[45] Allegedly, Frank said to his followers: "You know that Jesus the Lord will come from Heaven for the Last Judgment, and it is true. But you do not understand the explication of these words of the Gospel. Who knows? Maybe He is already in human flesh and will reveal Himself after the end of the persecutions of the Antichrist."[46]

The followers inferred from this that Jesus was hidden in the body of Frank, who was also reported to have received the stigmata. Pikulski sent a copy of the denunciation to the administrator of the Lwów diocese, who forwarded it to Primate Łubieński and the papal nuncio in Warsaw.[47] The revelations aroused a storm among the Christian public. The Warsaw consistory summoned Frank, who denied the accusations and stated that he had heard only rumors about the appearance of the Antichrist in Antioch, but he never actually believed in them.

However, further detrimental testimony started to pile up: another disillusioned follower reported that Frank and his closest entourage appropriated funds donated for all neophytes and that the converted Frankists carried out bizarre ceremonies, worshiping Frank and singing songs in Ladino[48] (the consistory ordered two of the Frankists to sing one such song before the investigators and commissioned a translation).[49] Yet others testified that the Frankists practiced polygamy.[50] Frank was said to demand a true personality cult and to have chosen twelve "apostles" from among his followers.[51] The ecclesiastical authorities carried out a search, which revealed that the name of Jesus in copies of the New Testament belonging to the disciples of Frank was struck out and replaced by the name Jacob.[52]

Most damaging, however, was the public revelation of the fact that before his widely publicized conversion to Catholicism, Frank had silently adopted Islam: Father Pikulski said that this alone would suffice to bring Frank into absolute disrepute.[53] It seems that at least some priests knew about the conversion to Islam before Frank's arrest: they hushed it up temporarily and let it be leaked at the right time. The revelation made it possible to discredit Frank and provided a good reason for denying any request for a separate semiautonomous settlement for the new Christians: rumors about these being Turkish agents suddenly began to look real and dangerous indeed.

On 7 January 1760, Frank was arrested.[54] As the high-ranking clergy began to change their tune and discredit Frank, his longtime interpreter and supporter, Moliwda, suddenly turned against him. The Catholic authorities had been keeping Moliwda under surveillance for quite some time: the priests were well aware of his earlier membership in the sect of Philipovtsy.[55] (The issue of the Philipovtsy was heavily debated in Poland at that time: rumors about their "clandestine and depraved customs" circulated in the capital, and the sect was said to "be infecting the kingdom like gangrene").[56] The Church threatened to expose Moliwda's sectarian past; in exchange for his cooperation against Frank, he was also offered the position of major domo at the court of Primate Łubieński.[57] He revealed other detrimental details about Frankist rituals and obediently accused Frank of practicing magic and believing in metempsychosis.[58] Now he served as a translator for Church investigators, for the interrogations were conducted in Turkish.[59]

Under interrogation, Frank declared his belief in the unity of God, in the Trinity, and in Jesus as divine and human, and professed full agreement between his faith and the Athanasian creed.[60] He stated his belief in the approach of the Last Judgment (arguing from Hos. 3:4 that, since the conversion, the Jews again had "the priests and the altar," which must indicate the fulfillment of the prophecies), but he categorically denied claiming to have seen the Antichrist. He also denied all messianic pretensions, saying that he never claimed to be the messiah and that before being told by Catholic priests, he had been unaware that some of his disciples considered him as such. As soon as he learned about it, he wanted these disciples to leave.[61] He admitted that in a dream he saw Jesus, who commanded him to go to Poland[62] (indeed, such a dream is independently recorded by *The Words of the Lord*).[63] He also acknowledged that he had previously believed that the souls of the wicked perish but said that after the baptism, he accepted the correct doctrine of the immortality of the soul.[64] Finally, he invoked the symbolism of the *erev rav*: on the basis of the verse "there shall be one flock and one shepherd," Frank argued that the Jews who did not accept Christianity together with him were not real descendants of the Israelites but the progeny of the mixed multitude, who had joined the Israelites during the wandering in the desert after the Exodus from Egypt.[65]

Following Frank's arrest and discredit, his backers among the clergy and nobility had to justify their earlier support for the head of the Contra-Talmudists. They claimed that Frank misled them and concealed various unsavory details of his past. Any dreams of a semi-independent colony were quickly shelved: the Frankists were expected to become good Christians and good Poles and to integrate within the surrounding population. The majority of the converts were settled in Warsaw, Krasnystaw,[66] and Zamość (according to Abraham ha-Kohen of Zamość, the Frankist colony in his home city numbered a couple of hundred people).[67] There were also a number of smaller rural Frankist communities: Raphael Mahler found documents about eight such villages near Lublin; according to a contemporary source, they were "earlier inhabited by Jews, now by Contra-Talmudists."[68] Scholars have emphasized the long duration of the Frankist movement, pointing to the existence of a cloistered crypto-Frankist community in the nineteenth century. This needs qualification. While it is true that in Warsaw, a group of hard-core Frankist believers survived well into the nineteenth, and possibly until the early twentieth, century, the other colonies formed for the converts disintegrated very quickly.

None of the communities aside from that of Warsaw played a role in the future development of Frankism. Christian authorities were prepared to lure the converting Jews with promises of autonomy, for they knew that these promises would eventually come to naught, and the converts would be quickly absorbed by the surrounding Christian population. Meanwhile, they were content to attract what might prove to be a large number of new Christians; for this purpose, they supported Frank and allowed for his excesses and abuses of power, even for spreading some messianic fantasies and propaganda among the Jews. This point is important in the context of the common characterization of Frankism as a messianic movement. If Frankism indeed was a mass messianic movement, it was so only during the final four months of 1759. The establishment of an independent Sabbatian-Christian colony "in Edom" would not merely hold promise of social advancement but would signal the gathering of the elect in preparation for the final act of the redemptive drama. The earlier Sabbatian belief in the messianic role of Poland provided the fertile soil, upon which fell Frank's call to come to Edom: it allowed him to persuade the Ottoman Jews to move to the Commonwealth and helped overcome reservations related to apostasy. The apparent fulfillment of such messianic expectations spurred the instantaneous growth of Frank's following: the leader of one of many competing Sabbatian subsects in Podolia suddenly became the focal point of the entire Sabbatian movement.

Yet what had started with a bang quickly ended with a whimper: after his detention, Frank was abandoned by the majority of those whom he had persuaded to apostatize and was left only with a handful of faithful. Never again did he manage to rebuild his following to a level comparable with that of the three months between his conversion and his arrest; never did he cease to lament the lost opportunity and scold his disciples for forsaking him in his hour of trial. If Frank indeed had messianic pretensions, he only voiced them explicitly at that time. His denial of such pretensions during the investigation at the Warsaw consistory was more than a tactical move: in *The Words of the Lord*, the concept of messiah is never applied to Frank himself. Frank's messianic star rose very high, only to fall spectacularly. In later Frankist teachings, messianic claims were applied to someone else entirely.

Cet Obscur Objet du Désir

The investigation at the Warsaw consistory lasted through January and most of February 1760. During the entire investigation, Frank was kept in the Lazarite monastery in the suburbs of the capital. On 26 February, the detainee was quietly dispatched from Warsaw and sent to Częstochowa (some 160 miles from Warsaw). He was placed in specially prepared rooms in a military fortress adjacent to the Pauline cloister at Jasna Góra ("Bright Mount").[69] About a week later, on 1 March 1760, the consistory issued an official proclamation concerning Frank. The proclamation stated that the investigation established the purity of belief of the Jews who had converted to Catholicism and their true faith in the Trinity and in the divinity of Jesus Christ.

However, Jacob Frank's negative influence had led the converts into erroneous beliefs concerning the Second Coming and the Last Judgment. The authorities concluded that Frank should immediately be separated from his disciples, who had been giving him excessive honor. He should be isolated at a secluded location, where he was to remain for an unlimited time awaiting a decision by the Holy See.[70] As the rest of the Frankists had been misled by their leader, the authorities dismissed any accusations against them and called upon all good Christians to give them assistance.[71]

Isolating Frank from his followers was the last element of the strategy devised by Primate Łubieński and the newly appointed papal nuncio in Warsaw,
Bishop Eugenio Visconti. Frank had fulfilled his role as a lure to convert the
Jews to Catholicism; now the Church wanted to break the bond between him
and other converts, thereby neutralizing the impact of his personal charisma
and denying any religious or political claims that he might have had. By May
1760, the Frankist group had left Warsaw and returned to Lwów;[72] the priests
hoped that after being separated from their leader, they would gradually blend
into the surrounding Christian society. In Częstochowa, Frank was initially
forbidden any contacts with the outside world, including his wife and children. Nor was the prior of Jasna Góra given much information about his prisoner. He was only told that Frank was suspected of embracing Islam *after* his
baptism, of creating a sect, and of pronouncing himself a messiah. For these
crimes, he was sent to Częstochowa to await the verdict of the ecclesiastical
authorities.[73]

Łubieński and the nuncio sought to close the matter by keeping Frank
incommunicado; Sołtyk and Załuski's faction wanted to keep it alive and tried
to facilitate contacts between the detainee and his family and followers. In
July 1760, Załuski interceded on behalf of Frank's wife, Hana, so that she
would be allowed to join her husband in the monastery.[74] The intercession was
unsuccessful: the Częstochowa priests even prevented Hana from speaking
to her husband after the death of Frank's firstborn son, Emanuel, in September 1760.[75] Sołtyk also intervened with the prior, demanding that Frank be
given large and comfortable quarters and be allowed to accept guests and send
envoys.[76] Following this intervention, some of Frank's followers managed to
reach their leader in Częstochowa and speak to him through a window.[77]

The situation improved only after a year, when the nuncio and the primate
lost interest in the matter and—despite complaint from the prior, who was no
longer receiving funds for the prisoner's accommodation[78]—forgot about the
Frankists completely. Sołtyk immediately stepped in and underwrote all of
Frank's expenses in the monastery.[79] He allocated special funds for settling the
converts in his diocese and personally undertook to subsidize thirty Frankist
families.[80] Sołtyk's continuous support led to the easing of Frank's conditions
in prison: his wife was allowed to join him in September 1762 (the Frankist
chronicle duly noted that the couple resumed sexual relations on 8 September
of that year). In late 1762 and early 1763, a group of his most faithful followers started to live with Frank in Częstochowa on a permanent basis.[81] Frank
and his entourage attended Catholic services every day, took communion,

and regularly attended confession. They learned Polish and studied the New Testament. However, the Frankists also conducted their own rituals on the ramparts of the fortress. The monks and the pilgrims staying in the monastery noted these rituals,[82] but there is no evidence that anyone tried to prevent them.

Łubieński and Visconti appear to have chosen Częstochowa as the place of Frank's detention for reasons of simple convenience: the Church did not have its own prisons, and Jasna Góra was unique in that its military fortress was under the direct command of the prior of the monastery. However, they did not take the symbolic potency of the location into account. The shrine of Our Lady of Częstochowa, with its miraculous icon of the Virgin Mary (the "Black Madonna"), was one of the most important centers of the Marian cult in the world and the most important religious site for all Roman Catholics in Poland.

According to a legend dating back to at least the early fifteenth century,[83] the Częstochowa icon was painted by Luke the Evangelist on a fragment of the table of the Last Supper and later brought by Constantine the Great from Jerusalem to Constantinople; Lev Danilovich, ruler of Halych-Volhynia, was given the icon by a Byzantine emperor and placed it in his castle in Bełz. Halych was conquered and annexed by the Poles in 1349; some years later, the icon fell into the hands of the governor of the province, Duke Władysław of Opole, who transferred it to Częstochowa and vowed to establish a shrine devoted to its cult. The Jasna Góra sanctuary was founded in 1382; the first recorded miraculous cures associated with the icon happened in the 1430s.[84] Among the inhabitants of the Commonwealth, the Polish victory over the Swedes in 1656 was widely attributed to the special protection of Our Lady of Częstochowa; following the victory, King Jan Kazimierz consecrated his kingdom to the Częstochowa Madonna, whom he proclaimed Queen of Poland.

All subsequent Polish monarchs made a pilgrimage to the monastery to pay homage to the icon. Częstochowa became a major pilgrimage site and the icon an object of ardent devotion, both popular and learned. In 1762, some two years after Frank's arrival in Częstochowa, more than 200,000 pilgrims visited the sanctuary during the period of a month and a half.[85] A book printed a year later brings a meticulous record of more than fifteen hundred miracles that took place at Jasna Góra: the blind recovered their vision, the paralyzed regained use of their limbs, and even a few dead were resurrected.[86]

It is little wonder that a stay at such a spiritually charged location made a deep impression on Frank. The Frankist theses for the Kamieniec and Lwów

disputations were elaborations of older Sabbatian tenets; during his imprisonment at Jasna Góra, Frank developed his own, highly original teachings, in
which he combined elements of traditional Judaism, kabbalah, and Sabbatian
theosophy with motifs deriving from Catholic Mariology as well as products
of his febrile religious imagination. If the Frankist movement as a social phenomenon emerged during the period of mass conversions in Lwów, "Frankism" as a cluster of theological or theosophical ideas elaborated by Jacob Frank
and professed by his disciples was born in Częstochowa.

The miraculous icon of Our Lady of Częstochowa became the heart of
a constellation of interconnected symbols for Frank, and on numerous occasions he acknowledged the special powers of the icon: "Do the kings and
lords go to the portrait of the Maiden in Częstochowa in great humility for
nothing? They are wiser than you, for they see that all powers come from her
and are in her hand. As it was said of Christ that he arose from the dead, so
she will arise from the dust, almost from the dust, and all the kingdoms of the
earth will bow before her."[87]

The phrase "she will arise from the dust" is an allusion to Isa. 52:2: "Shake
yourself from the dust; arise, and sit down, O Jerusalem; loosen yourself from
the bands of your neck, O captive daughter of Zion." The expression "daughter
of Zion" was traditionally taken to refer to the Temple Mount, the section of
Mount Zion on which Solomon's Temple had been located, or was interpreted
as a synecdoche for the Temple itself. Jewish tradition considered the Temple
the earthly abode of the *Shekhinah*, the personified Divine Presence.[88]

The tribulations following the destruction of the Temple were commonly
depicted in the metaphor of the Divine Presence wailing in filth, while the end
of exile was envisioned as Her rising from the dust to a triumphal return home
to the restored Temple.[89] Sabbatian theology described Sabbatai's messianic
mission precisely as the "raising of the *Shekhinah* from the dust" and dated the
beginning of this process for 1657 or 1658; as in mainstream Judaism, its conclusion was to be the rebuilding of the Temple in Jerusalem.[90] Frank, on the
other hand, claimed that "the true Mount Zion" was located in Częstochowa[91]
and linked the rising of the Divine Presence from the dust not with return to
the Land of Israel but with pilgrimages to the icon of the Black Madonna. As
the notion of the *Shekhinah* is crucial for understanding this element of his
teachings, a brief summary is in place here.

The Aramaic word *shekhinta* is an abstract noun meaning literally "the act
of indwelling" or "being present" and was initially employed by the Targumim
(ancient Aramaic translations of the Hebrew Bible) to express the concept of

God's presence at a particular place or during a particular event, perceivable to men. Hence, for instance, *Targum Onkelos* (second century C.E.) rendered the biblical verse "And let them make me a sanctuary; that I may dwell among them" (Exod. 25:8) as "And they shall make a Sanctuary to My Name, that My Presence [*shekhinti*] may dwell among them."[92] Early rabbinic literature used the Aramaic term (or its Hebrew equivalent, *shekhinah*) roughly in the same way, describing the Divine Presence inhabiting first the Tabernacle and then both Jerusalem Temples, or accompanying the People of Israel in the exiles of Egypt and Babylon; following the destruction of the Second Temple, the *Shekhinah* again went into exile together with the Jews, to return in messianic times.[93]

While depictions of God's indwelling on earth were at times brazenly anthropomorphic (which provoked rationalist Jewish thinkers to try to downgrade the Divine Presence to the status of a created being), early sources in no way indicated the *Shekhinah's* gender, save for the feminine grammatical gender of the Hebrew and Aramaic forms denoting "indwelling." With the rise of kabbalah in the late twelfth and early thirteenth centuries, portrayals of the *Shekhinah* acquired distinctly womanly characteristics for the first time, and the notion of the God's Presence became identified with the feminine aspect of the Godhead. The symbolism of the indwelling began to overlap and interplay with gender symbolism: as kabbalah developed, the *Shekhinah* became the Divine Woman, as it were, "incarnating" in the women of the earthly world: "For the *Shekhinah* in the time of Abraham our father is called Sarah and in the time of Isaac our father is called Rebecca and in the time of Jacob our father is called Rachel."[94] The symbol of the female God's Presence ultimately absorbed attributes of previously existing independent feminine images present in biblical and postbiblical Judaism such as the Congregation of Israel (*knesset Yisrael*), the Daughter of Zion (*bat Tsiyon*), and Divine Wisdom (*hokhmat Elohim*, Sophia).

Gershom Scholem has interpreted the emergence of the feminine *Shekhinah* as an internal Jewish development: the consequence of the exegetical identification of God's Presence with the gendered notion of the Congregation of Israel, which simultaneously feminized the *Shekhinah* and raised Israel to the level of a mystical body, akin—but not genetically connected—to the Christian concept of the Ecclesia as the Corpus Christi.[95] He also conjectured that the kabbalistic concept might have been the primordial Great Mother archetype expressed in the preexisting Jewish symbols.[96] More recently, Arthur Green has argued that the female *Shekhinah* was "a Jewish response to an adaptation of the revival of devotion to Mary in the twelfth century Western church."[97] For Green, the uniqueness of the kabbalistic notion consists not in the plain fact that the *Shekhinah* became a woman but in her representations as a female consort of the male God of Israel combined with individual piety devoted to a feminine figure interposed between the male worshiper and the male God.[98] Thus, in a striking parallel to the Virgin Mary, the kabbalistic *Shekhinah* became both the bride of God and the agent of creation of the lower worlds, the representation of both the collective (the Congregation of Israel) and the individual (the soul of a kabbalist), both virgin and mother, and a mediatrix acting in both directions: bringing the life force down to earth and receiving the prayers and good deeds of humanity.[99]

Whatever the genealogy of the feminized concept of the Divine Presence in late twelfth-century kabbalah, it is clear that by the seventeenth century, some kabbalists had become acutely aware of similarities between the Jewish concept of the *Shekhinah* and Christian conceptions of the Virgin Mary.[100] A case in point is the Sabbatian Abraham Miguel Cardoso, who remarked that "although most of their prayers . . . they direct to Jesus, they augment their devotions and extol also Mary his mother, and they call upon her and praise her, and she corresponds to the Holy *Shekhinah*."[101] Yet Frank went much further than any other Jewish thinker, Sabbatian or otherwise. At the very beginning of his stay at the Jasna Góra monastery, he had the following dream:

> In Częstochowa, I saw in a dream that a doe came to me and changed herself into a Maiden of a particular beauty, and I led you before her. . . . And this Maiden, at the time when you entered the baptism, was pleased as a mother with her children and very much desired that you would go in wholeness and be devoted yourselves to her love. . . . But now, if you are worthy and she extends her hand, I will accept whomever she puts in my hand. If you are worthy that she open this gate in which we hope to enter, you will see the House of God. Now I will show you its gate.[102]

In Jewish tradition, the "doe of dawn" (*ayelet ha-shahar*, Ps. 22:1), whose outspread horns resemble the rays of the rising sun, became the focus of extensive and complex allegorical interpretations. Early midrash treated the doe as a soteriological emblem and compared the steady yet almost imperceptible approach of the dawn to the coming of redemption, which also arrives in barely discernible stages.[103] The motif introduced by the rabbinic aggadot[104] was further developed by the Zohar.

According to a Zoharic myth, the doe is the most merciful of all animals of the world and gathers food for all of them. In search for food, she goes first to the Mount of Darkness, where she encounters a twisted serpent; from there, the doe and the serpent proceed to the Mount of Light [*tura de-nehora*] together. Upon their arrival, God sends another serpent, which attacks the first one, thus saving the doe. When she descends from the Mount, she is pregnant: she runs and conceals herself so that other animals cannot find her. Yet she has a narrow womb, suffers great pains, and is unable to give birth. When she crouches to deliver, God again sends a snake, which bites her genitals twice, thus loosening the tightness. The first time, blood comes out; the second time, water: "all the animals in the mountains drink, and she is opened and gives birth."[105]

The text of the Zohar portrayed the doe as a symbol of the *Shekhinah*; later Zoharic strata (*Ra'ya mehemna*) supplemented the story with the idea that as a result of the snake's two bites, the doe gave birth to two messiahs, the messiah son of Joseph and the messiah son of David.[106] Subsequent interpreters explained the birth pangs suffered by the *ayalah* as the tribulations preceding the advent of the messiah(s), whom they termed "the son(s) of the doe of dawn," "son(s) of the *Shekhinah*," "one(s) born through the bite of the snake."[107] Lurianic kabbalah held this complex of motifs to be the greatest of mysteries and a source of the gravest danger for those who study it; according to the tradition, Luria was punished by the death of his son for daring to expound the secret of the "two fawns of the doe."[108]

Yet the subversive successors of Lurianism, the Sabbatians, were undeterred: their exegesis promptly linked the Zoharic myth of the *ayalah* to the messiah Sabbatai Tsevi, who came to be presented as the offspring of the doe/*Shekhinah* (*tsevi* means "deer" in Hebrew) and simultaneously as the serpent that bit her womb (the Hebrew words *mashi'ah* [messiah] and *nahash* [serpent] are isopsephic equivalents).[109] The most comprehensive Sabbatian discussion of this cluster of symbols can be found in Israel Hazzan of Kastoria's *Commentary on the Midnight-Vigil Liturgy*, which I mentioned in the Introduction to this volume.[110] Hazzan portrayed the Sabbatai-snake as the lover of the doe-*Shekhinah*. He interpreted the serpent's bite as an equivalent to the sex act and simultaneously as a symbol of "the donning of the turban, coiled like a serpent."[111]

Thus the founding deed of Sabbatianism—the conversion to Islam—

became equated with the sexual union with God's Presence, and the Zoharic Mount of Darkness was taken to represent the Muslim religion. However, for Hazzan, Sabbatai was not only the lover of the *Shekhinah*, who followed her to the Mount of Darkness, but also the first of her two sons, destined to enter the faith of Ishmael; the other son would enter the faith of Edom. Thus, during the first stage of redemption, Sabbatai Tsevi impregnated the *Shekhinah* and fathered himself as the first redeemer; the second stage involves the birth of another messiah, who is supposed to become a Christian (Hazzan did not know the identity of this messiah).

The *Shekhinah*, in turn, is not only the divine mother of the messiahs and passive recipient of Sabbatai's seed; she herself is the messiah (since her sufferings are the same as his),[112] as is the serpent (according to the verse of the Zohar "when Israel is in exile she [the *Shekhinah*] moves like a serpent").[113] In the end, all the actors in this divine drama are united and equated with one another: "the Blessed Holy One, His *Shekhinah*, and the Beloved Son AMIRa"H [Sabbatai Tsevi] are incorporated as one, with no division or distinction among them."[114]

It is not clear how much and what exactly Frank knew of earlier traditions concerning the doe and the *Shekhinah*. He was probably unfamiliar with Hazzan's commentary, for, had he known it, he would most probably have cast himself in the role of the doe's younger son, who is supposed to convert to Christianity. However, he certainly knew other Sabbatian traditions identifying the messiah Sabbatai with the Divine Presence. As he noted: "You said about the First One [Sabbatai Tsevi] that he was like the *Shekhinah*."[115] He also knew the Zoharic myth of the *ayalta*:[116] the Frankist dicta paraphrased elements of it and evoked the motifs of blood and water gushing from the doe[117] and of her concealment.[118]

In one respect, Frank's reading of the Zohar departs from earlier interpretations. Although the doe of the Frankist dicta still represents the Divine Presence, its symbolism acquires an additional shade of meaning here: the *ayalta* has come to symbolize not the *Shekhinah* as such, but Her failed and destitute state: "As I told you, she is now in a very filthy and bitter place; as I also told you, she is *ayalta*, which means: she is now in the form of an animal and must be relieved from that bitterness. If you were good, it would happen through you that she would shed the animal shape and [assume] a human form."[119]

In Frank's dream from Częstochowa, the *Shekhinah*, imprisoned in the animal form of the doe, turns into the Maiden, that is, becomes human. *Panna* (the Maiden) is one of the most common Polish appellations of the Virgin Mary, and Frank must have heard the phrase *Święta Panna*, Holy Maiden, repeated daily by the pilgrims praying before Our Lady of Częstochowa. Although Frankist sources do not make this connection explicitly, one might surmise that Frank could not have failed to notice that the climax of the Zoharic story of the doe takes place in the Mount of Light [*tura de-nehora*], while his own place of imprisonment and the place of Mary's most ardent worship was the cloister named Jasna Góra (the Bright Mount). What he did say explicitly was that the Maiden, which his dream identified as the human form of the *Shekhinah*, God's Presence on earth, is already "hidden in the portrait" of the Black Madonna.[120] The nucleus of his teaching was not any parallel or correspondence between the *Shekhinah* and Mary but the idea that the former somehow transformed into the latter.

Christian doctrine (in both its Catholic and Orthodox forms) posited that, since the birth of Jesus, aural revelations granted to the Jewish prophets have been surpassed by God's palpable presence among the humans, thereby lifting the prohibition against making graven images and opening the possibility of His graphic depiction. Christian veneration of material representations of the divine is thus rooted in the reality of the Incarnation: since immaterial and formless God chose to make Himself accessible in the corporeal form, worship should also be accorded to plastic images adequately affording His corporeality. The reality of the Incarnation (and the reality of the hypostatic union of the two natures of Christ), in turn, is guaranteed by Mary, who, as a truly human mother, gave her son Jesus a truly human body. Accordingly, Catholic and Orthodox Mariology developed in close connection with the debate concerning the visual portrayal of the Deity and the cult of icons.

Along the same lines, Frank established an *iunctim* between iconic worship and pictorial representation of God, on the one hand, and the extolment of the feminine principle, on the other. In full accordance with the Church's doctrine, he claimed that the advent of Christianity established legitimacy and necessity of the cult of icons: "What did Christ show? Just one thing: that everyone should pray to a painted picture."[121] He also linked the veneration of images with the cult of the Virgin. In Częstochowa, the Frankists were urged to contemplate the Black Madonna icon for several hours every day, "just as the Jews look at the moon at the New Moon Festival,"[122] and even to buy little reproductions of the miraculous icon widely sold to the pilgrims coming to Jasna Góra; they were to shut themselves for three nights in a secluded room and recite a special prayer there, while kneeling before the paintings.[123]

Frank was clearly fascinated by the Częstochowa icon and the worship accorded to it by the pilgrims coming to the monastery. He developed a deep interest in Christian Mariology and picked up customary Marian appellatives and expressions from Polish prayers. One of his dicta describing the *Shekhinah*-Maiden contains three standard Catholic salutations to Mary: Eternal Maiden (Semper Virgo), Queen of Heaven (Regina Coeli), and Lady of Assistance (Auxilium Christianorum).[124] The characteristic idiom of these expressions leaves no room for doubt that Frank gleaned them from prayers or sermons that he heard in Częstochowa; for instance, the word *wspomożycielka* (Lady of Assistance) is a highly technical term of Catholic discourse, which is virtually never used in everyday Polish and appears only in the works of theologians, Polish versions of the Litany of Loreto, and novenas to the Virgin. However, from Frank's perspective, Christian Mariology was also imperfect. The Virgin Mary is for Christians an especially elevated human being, who served as a medium of the divine incarnation in man's flesh; Frank's Maiden herself was the divinity incarnated.

To put it in a nutshell, unlike Christianity, Frankism was not about a male God who took a human body upon himself through a human woman, but about a feminine goddess who acquired a human form. This has immediate relevance to Frank's understanding of the Częstochowa icon: in a somehow paradoxical way, Frank combined the Jewish concept of the *Shekhinah*, which placed the female principle of the Godhead in concrete spatiotemporal dimensions (such as the Jerusalem Temple), with Christian hyperdulia accorded to the icons of the Virgin Mary: the painting of the Black Madonna of Częstochowa became for him not a plastic depiction of the sacred femininity but a location of her actual "indwelling."

Frank appropriated elements of Catholic Mariology but departed from Christian doctrine in two crucial respects: he claimed that the Maiden was an element of the Godhead (and not, as the Christians would have it, the human mediatrix Virgin Mary); and he declared that She was actually present (and not only pictorially represented) in the Częstochowa icon. From his perspective, Christianity discovered the human face of God and realized that it is the face of a woman. However, as Frank emphasized on numerous occasions, the Christians knew the face of the Maiden only "in a picture,"[125] meaning that the Christian notion of the Maiden—although superior to the Jewish notion of the *Shekhinah*—was also partial and incomplete: it was based on the revelation of the female Divine Presence in human form but not in human body. While the painting of Our Lady of Częstochowa was, for Frank, the true dwelling place of the *Shekhinah*, the Presence indwelt in an inanimate object:

the icon. The soteriological sense of Frank's coming to Częstochowa was "to liberate" the Maiden from the icon and thus to bring the revelation of divine femininity to accomplishment. As Frank announced, when this happened, the "Maiden who is there [that is, the miraculous icon] . . . will lead you [the Frankists] to another Maiden."[126] The identity of this other Maiden is known from Frankist dicta and other documents. The final and complete revelation of Frankism amounts to the true incarnation of the divine Maiden in a true human maiden: Eve Frank.

Frank's only daughter was born a year or so before the beginning of his activity in Poland. (Frank's first son, Emanuel, died in infancy; his two other sons, Roch and Joseph, are hardly mentioned in Frankist documents and did not play any role in the development of the sect.) From the very outset, Frank presented her as a semidivine being and a future leader of the group: when she was only six months old, he told the disciples to "know that she is a queen." He emphasized: "Do not think that I call her the queen on account of her beauty; she is really a queen in her very essence."[127] Wherever she appeared, she was accompanied by a cortège of the daughters of prominent Frankists, who were trained to attend to all her needs.[128] Her Jewish name, Rachel,[129] was one of the most common appellations of the *Shekhinah* (after the famous image of Rachel weeping for her children going to exile in Jeremiah 31)[130] and the name of the beloved bride of the biblical Jacob; the Frankist dicta often portrayed the redemption or "deliverance" as a union of Jacob and Rachel. (Actual incestuous relations between Jacob Frank and his daughter, Rachel, became the stuff of rumors and made an impact on several literary works inspired by the history of Frankism but are not directly attested by any Frankist source.) Her Christian baptismal name, Zofia (Sophia),[131] linked her with the biblical figure of the Divine Wisdom, God's earliest creation, who "was set up from everlasting, from the beginning, even before the earth" (Prov. 8:25) and guided all further creations.[132]

The Words of the Lord mentions neither name, usually referencing her by the honorific *Imość* or *Jejmość* (Her Highness, the Lady). In some later dicta and in *Various Notes*, the name Hawacza or Hawaczunia (diminutive forms of the name Ewa, Eve) appears.[133] It seems that the name Eve was adopted sometime in Częstochowa; it is under this name that she appears in most Polish and German sources from the later period and in scholarship. The Rachel-Sophia-Eve triad is laden with theological associations: Frank's only daughter came to epitomize the Divine Presence, the Wisdom of God, and the Mother of Humanity.

On her arrival in Częstochowa, Eve Frank was approximately fifteen years old. Her beauty was said to be striking; her dark complexion and deep brown eyes charmed numerous visitors to the monastery. According to *The Words of the Lord*, a Polish nobleman who paid a visit to Frank and his family after praying in the chapel of the Black Madonna looked at Eve and remarked: "I would much more readily believe that this is the Holy Mother and the True Virgin."[134] Another "rich young lord" asked for permission to kneel before Eve and kiss her feet.[135]

Step by step, an actual cult of Eve was introduced. The Frankist dicta give detailed directions of the way an initiate should behave in order to be "worthy to come to the Maiden": he should come dressed in white and fall on his face without raising his eyes toward her, then kiss her feet, then stand up with his hands folded without looking at her, and then slowly look at her but without looking her directly in the face. Finally, he will be allowed to kiss her hand; she will address him as "brother" and ask about his dearest wish, to which he will answer with a phrase from the Song of Songs 5:2, "Open to me, my sister, my love!"[136] The text of this dictum seems to treat the ritualized "coming to the Maiden" as a description of a vision rather than a rite that took place in the material world. However, we know from the memoir of Moses Porges, a young Frankist from Prague who visited the Frankist court in Offenbach in 1798, that during the last stages of Frankism, precisely this ritual was performed when approaching Eve.[137] The pictorial element was transferred onto Eve as well: while at the beginning of their stay at Jasna Góra, the Frankists were told to purchase miniature copies of the Black Madonna icon, later on they were given miniatures of Eve Frank.[138]

The revelation of the Maiden was the foundation stone of Frank's soteriology. Frankist rejection of normative Judaism was rooted precisely in the failure of the Jewish religion to truly appreciate the female facet of the Godhead and the messianic dimension of femininity: "All the Jews are now suffering tribulations, despair, and misery, for they trust in the coming of the messiah in a form of a man, not in the advent of the Maiden."[139] Although Judaism had developed a concept of *Shekhinah*, it recognized the feminine aspect of God only in its "failed animal state" and—consequently—strayed into the erroneous concept of a masculine messiah: "How could you think that the messiah would be a man? That may by no means be, for the foundation is the Maiden. She will be the true messiah. She will lead all the worlds."[140] Sabbatianism partly corrected this misconception: if we are to believe the Frankists, a rumor circulated among the Sabbatian believers that Sabbatai Tsevi was secretly a woman.[141] In accordance with the program first voiced at the grave of Nathan of Gaza, Frank's aim was to make this secret known and to "make in the flesh everything that has been in spirit."[142]

The Christian paradox of the Incarnation consists in the belief that the Virgin Mary is the mother of her human son, Jesus, and, at the same time, the daughter of her divine son, consubstantial with God, the creator of all being. In the Sabbatian commentary of Israel Hazzan, the messiah-redeemer Sabbatai Tsevi was the lover and son of the *Shekhinah* and therefore, in a sense, his own father. In Częstochowa, Frank developed a doctrine in which he was the physical father and a partner (metaphorical or not) of his daughter Eve, the true messiah of the Frankists.

Chapter 7

The Fall of Edom

The Bar Confederation

The first two years of Frank's stay in Częstochowa were relatively uneventful, but at the end of the Seven Years' War, external developments began to have an impact on the prisoner. The conclusion of fighting marked a change of the political climate in Europe and the inception of a new system of alliances. Russia wanted the weakened Polish-Lithuanian Commonwealth to become a subsidiary ally in the great alliance of Northern powers consisting of, beside herself, Prussia and Denmark. Although such an alliance made much sense militarily and politically, it was bound to ruffle the sensibilities of many of the *szlachta*:[1] a large section of Polish nobility naturally opposed bringing their country into a league of non-Catholic states directed against the traditional Catholic allies of the Commonwealth such as France. King Augustus III Wettin died in October 1763, and the election of his successor was a showdown between the pro- and anti-Russian parties.[2] Even before the king's death, Frank sensed the winds of change. On 1 March 1764, he wrote to Nuncio Visconti, presenting himself as a faithful believer in Jesus living in full agreement with the teachings of the Church, and requested immediate release from the monastery. Should the nuncio, however, decide not to set Frank free, the petitioner asked for larger quarters and additional funds. (He remarked that he had been prevented by the Częstochowa priests from receiving alms from his former disciples and had used up all the money he had been given by Catholic pilgrims coming to Jasna Góra.)[3]

Frank's appeal to the nuncio was the first fissure in his relationship with

Bishop Kajetan Sołtyk. His erstwhile protector was not merely a high-ranking cleric with a penchant for using the blood libel as a tool of fund-raising; he was also one of the leaders of the conservative pro-Saxon, anti-Russian faction in Poland. During the 1763–64 election, Sołtyk was actively involved in efforts to seat another Wettin, Augustus III's son Frederick Christian, on the Polish throne, and he forcefully opposed the election of the Russian-supported candidate, a former lover of Catherine the Great, Stanisław Poniatowski.[4] (Stanisław was the hope of the forces of change and campaigned on a clear mandate of reforming the inefficient system of government; he was elected in September 1764 under the name Stanislaus Augustus, after the Saxon party was thrown into disarray by the unexpected death of Frederick Christian in November 1763). While Sołtyk was officially reconciled with the king, he continued to work quietly against Poniatowski and his Russian patrons.[5] Before long, the bishop became a symbol of opposition to the reformist policies of the Crown. The most conspicuous bone of contention (partly real and partly a pretext) was the so-called dissident issue.

One consequence of the advance of the Counter-Reformation in the Polish-Lithuanian Commonwealth was the gradual encroachment on the rights and privileges of non-Catholic Christians. Step by step, the religious dissidents (*dissidentes de religione* or *różnowiercy*), as they were called in Poland, were banned from holding state offices, disenfranchised, and restricted in public worship. In search of support, they began to make appeals to foreign non-Catholic monarchs, who, in turn, often found it advantageous to utilize the religious cleavages between different segments of the Commonwealth's population to further their own agendas.[6] In September 1730, on the occasion of the renewal of the Potsdam treaty of 1720, King Frederick Wilhelm of Prussia and Czarina Anna Ivanovna of Russia signed a supplementary protocol guaranteeing the protection of their kingdoms' Polish coreligionists, the Protestants and the Eastern Orthodox, respectively.

The policy of support for the dissidents was continued by both powers throughout the first half of the eighteenth century and reached its peak in the 1760s: a few months before her ascension to the throne in September 1762, Catherine the Great proclaimed herself the "protectress of the Orthodox Faith" in Poland-Lithuania.[7] For Russia and Prussia, the dissident issue was arguably the most powerful instrument of the "divide and conquer" strategy and a useful excuse to meddle in the matters of the Commonwealth at will. For the new king, it was the source of permanent difficulty, which necessitated constant navigating between the Scylla of acceding to ever increasing foreign demands

and the Charybdis of offending the sensibilities of the Catholic clergy and nobility. For the king's enemies, it was the flagship issue in the battle against the
reformers: any concession on behalf of the dissidents could be immediately
portrayed as a betrayal not only of religious but of national interests. Stanislaus Augustus and the proponents of religious tolerance were presented as bad
Catholics and as foreign puppets.

The dissident debate climaxed in 1765–66, when Catherine the Great instructed the Russian ambassador in Warsaw, Prince Nikolay Vassilievich Repnin, to demand complete freedom of confession in public life for the Eastern
Orthodox subjects of the Polish king.[8] The reaction coalesced around Bishop
Sołtyk, who—just before the October 1766 session of the Sejm—composed
a series of circular letters to the Catholic rulers of Austria, Saxony, France,
Spain, Sardinia, and others calling upon them to set up a league for the defense of the ruling religion in Poland.[9] During the sittings of the Sejm, the
bishop—despite the opposition of the king and Primate Łubieński—brought
the issue to the forefront of the proceedings and proposed an ultraconservative
anti-dissident bill.[10]

The move provoked the ire of the reformers, who were repelled by the
bishop's reactionary views and also felt that linking the debate on religious tolerance to issues of everyday governance of the kingdom would kill any efforts
to modernize the latter. Yet the step taken by Sołtyk made him a hero among
conservative nobility, who widely praised the bishop for daring to stand up
to the Russians. Repnin became his public and fervent enemy. A year later,
he decided to teach the bishop and his supporters a lesson and abandoned
any pretense of noninterference in lawmaking in the Commonwealth: Russian troops entered Poland as protectors of the rights of the dissidents. Before
the opening of the October 1767 Sejm, Sołtyk, Załuski, and two other anti-
Russian senators were kidnapped on Repnin's order and deported to the city
of Kaluga, some 120 miles from Moscow.[11]

A minor reform was introduced by the Coronation Sejm after the election of Stanislaus Augustus: the command of the Jasna Góra fortress was taken
from the Paulines;[12] after 1764, the prisoner of Częstochowa was no longer
under the direct jurisdiction of the Church. Frank clearly sensed that the tide
was beginning to turn and that, in counting on the alliance with the conservative section of Polish clergy, he was betting on a losing horse: whatever the
appearances might have been, open defiance of the Russians was not a viable
option for any party in the politically and militarily weak Commonwealth.
Clearly impressed with the power of the Russians and the rise of the pro-

Russian party in Poland, Frank sought contacts with the winning side and began to consider a conversion to Eastern Orthodoxy. He stated: "Thus you did not understand now, when I sent you from this state to Russia, that there must certainly be there a greater, more precious and a higher state. The great Patriarchs and the pillars of the world were waiting for this state; and those words that you have from of old 'Dear is the scent which comes to me from the north'[13] refer to that religion."[14]

Frank probably gleaned his first inklings of Eastern Orthodoxy from the Old Believer Moliwda. According to *Various Notes*, in June 1765 the leader of the Frankists "started to talk about Muscovy and Greek [Orthodox] religion."[15] In the same month, he sent three emissaries to Moscow. In December, they reached Smolensk, where they obtained letters of recommendation from the local archimandrite. From Smolensk, they proceeded to Moscow, and after a six-week stay returned to Warsaw in March 1766; in the Polish capital, they established direct contact with Repnin.[16]

Jewish sources confirm that the mission of the three Frankist emissaries to Moscow indeed took place, but they ascribe the events to December 1767–January 1768.[17] A letter from Baruch me-Erets Yavan to Rabbi Jacob Emden describes how the Frankists established contacts with representatives of the Russian military in Poland and through them with the Smolensk archimandrite. They told him that their leader, Jacob Frank, currently imprisoned in the Częstochowa monastery, had determined on the basis of the study of kabbalistic books that Greek Orthodoxy (*emunat Yevani[m]*) was the true religion. Accordingly, they expressed the wish to convert to the faith of the Russians and requested the release of their leader from the monastery. Armed with letters of recommendation from the archimandrite, they arrived in Moscow, where they stated that Frank had come to Poland from Muslim lands in order to spread true Orthodox Christianity among the Jews, but had been jailed by the Catholics. If he were to be set free, they promised, twenty thousand Jews would convert to Eastern Orthodoxy.

The timing of the Frankist emissaries' mission was not lucky, however. Concurrently to their arrival in Moscow, their powerful enemy, the *shtadlan* Baruch me-Erets Yavan, also came to the Russian capital. Yavan deployed all his skills to thwart the Frankist stratagem. First, he spoke to the Polish ambassador in Moscow and other Polish nobles present at the court of Catherine. He portrayed the mission of the Frankists as a betrayal of Catholicism and a plot against the Commonwealth and encouraged them to have the prisoner of Częstochowa beheaded for high treason and apostasy. Parallel to his lobbying the Poles, Baruch Yavan approached the Russians as well. The *shtadlan* presented Frank as an infamous opportunist, changing religions and loyalties according to changing circumstances and stated that, while Frank claimed to have been victimized and unjustly imprisoned for religious reasons, in truth "he had no religion whatsoever but [professed] evil deeds and twisted ways, made himself an idol and permitted incest."[18] Finally, Yavan warned that the true intention of the Frankists was to obtain a territory close to Turkey so that they could collaborate with the Ottoman enemies of Russia.[19]

The dating of the mission to Russia in January 1766 by the author of *Various Notes* is either an error or an intentional distortion; the embassy almost certainly took place exactly two years later, as attested by Baruch me-Erets Yavan (Baruch's letter is dated 10 April 1768, and the accuracy of this date can be corroborated by its author's references to contemporary events such as the imprisonment of Sołtyk and other senators by Repnin).[20] The *shtadlan's* two-directional strategy aimed parallelly at the Poles and the Russians proved successful: the Russians expelled the emissaries from Moscow, and Frank's position in Poland became precarious.

The plans for conversion to Eastern Orthodoxy were shelved, and their very existence was concealed from all but the most intimate circle of Frankists. Frank and his closest followers went straightaway into damage-control mode and tried to restore their credentials as good Roman Catholics. Immediately after their return from Moscow, two of the emissaries were dispatched to Podolia with "the last call [upon the Jews] to enter the religion of Edom."[21] Echoes of this call were preserved in two missives composed at that time and later incorporated into the so-called Red Letters.

In 1800, some ten years after his death, Frank's disciples sent circular epistles to European Jewish communities (I shall discuss the circumstances of these dispatches in Chapter 9).[22] Because of the color of the ink in which they were written and the symbolic association between the biblical kingdom of Edom and the Hebrew word *adom* ("red"), these epistles came to be known as the "Red Letters." Incorporated in them were two shorter missives written by Frank in Częstochowa in 5527 (1766–67) and 5528 (1767–68).[23]

Frank's first letter was composed a few months before the arrival of his envoys in Moscow, and the other shortly after their return. The first epistle was addressed to the Jews of Brody. Composed in an ornate mixture of Hebrew and Aramaic, collating biblical and Zoharic allusions and quotations, the letter predicted imminent doom for the Jewish communities of Poland, especially "Kraków and its surroundings," and an approaching war between "the nation of the sons of Edom" (Poland) and another "rebel nation" (Russia or, more likely, the Cossacks). As a result of this war, the letter stated, the Jews would suffer terribly: "the corpses shall lie like dung on the ground, and dogs shall lick their blood."[24] The only escape for the Jews will be conversion: "anyone who has the spark of the seed of Abraham, Isaac, and Jacob must enter into the holy faith of Edom, and whoever will accept this creed with love will be saved from all [the persecutions]."[25]

The second epistle, addressed to "all Jewry" (*klal Yehudim*), developed the same message. Again, Frank warned of impending tribulations and predicted the increased hatred of the Jews by "all dukes and princesses of the world."[26] There will come troubles, he stated, the likes of which have never been seen in the world, and the Jews will find no safe haven in any country, great or small. He concluded by saying that before the wheel of the world can make a full circle, the Laws of Moses must be "exhausted" and Jacob must fulfill the promise given to Esau;[27] in order for the promise to be fulfilled, he repeated, "anyone who is of the seed of Abraham, Isaac, and Jacob must follow the holy creed of Edom [*ha-dat ha-kdosh[a] shel Edom*]."[28]

In Jewish tradition, "Edom," the land of Esau, is a common general term for Christianity.[29] As noted in the previous chapter, Sabbatian tradition dating back to Heshel Tsoref identified the Land of Edom with Roman Catholic Poland. Consequently, in the Frankist dicta, the terms "Esau" and "Edom" came to refer specifically to Roman Catholicism, especially in juxtaposition with Eastern Orthodoxy (usually termed "Yavan," Greece, or simply "Moscow").[30] In *The Words of the Lord*, Frank often referred to Jacob's promise to Esau from Gen. 33:12–17. In the biblical narrative, when Esau and Jacob met after Jacob's departing from Laban's and the fight with the angel, Esau wanted his brother to travel with him. Jacob told Esau to go first and that he would follow. However, while Esau went to Seir, Jacob went to Succoth, and the brothers did not meet until Isaac's funeral (Gen. 35:29). Frank understood his mission as a fulfillment of the unfulfilled promise given by Jacob to Esau,[31] called his conversion to Catholicism "the path to Esau,"[32] and described his program in terms of a quest for the reunion of the brothers.

In the missives from Częstochowa, the call upon "anyone who has a spark of the seed of Abraham, Isaac, and Jacob" to accept the creed of Edom was meant to distinguish between the descendants of the "true" Israelites and the progeny of the mixed multitude—the Egyptians who joined the Israelites during the Exodus and, as such, did not stem from the Patriarchs. In Frank's letter, the formula of true Israelites denoted the Sabbatians, in contrast to the anti-Sabbatian rabbis, but its use also seems to insinuate that the time of the ultimate test had come: as it was impossible to distinguish externally between those Jews who were truly of the seed of Abraham, Isaac, and Jacob and those who originated from the mixed multitude, the acceptance or rejection of Catholic Christianity makes possible a clear delineation between the two camps, thus separating the redeemed from the rejected.

However, the timing of the letters makes matters more complicated. Ben-Zion Wacholder, who edited and translated the Red Letters into English, claimed that Frank had expected his messages to be intercepted by the Catholic Church: while most of the letters are written in an abstruse Aramaic that only people highly familiar with the Jewish esoteric tradition could decipher, "assertions that urge the Jews to be baptized are formulated in simple Hebrew, which would have been understandable to the Church censors."[33] If we accept Wacholder's suggestion, we may interpret the 1767–68 appeals to "all Jewry" to convert to Roman Catholicism as a part of Frank's effort to deflect the attention of the Polish priests from his idea of embracing the "schismatic" faith of the Russians or—after the failure of the Moscow mission—part of his attempts to convince the clergy that he had not betrayed Catholicism, as Baruch Yavan claimed in Moscow.

Alternatively, it is possible that the smokescreen tactic was directed not at the priests but at Frank's own disciples. Aleksander Kraushar and Jan Doktór have both noticed that Frank strived to conceal his negotiations with the Russians and their collapse from the majority of his followers.[34] Given the role that the idea of "coming to Poland/Edom" played in the earlier Sabbatian theology of Heshel Tsoref and the likelihood of success in persuading Sabbatians to convert to Catholicism in Lwów, it is easy to imagine that some Catholic Frankists might have seen his overtures toward Russia and Eastern Orthodoxy as dangerous vacillation or even betrayal. Indeed, one of the very few mentions of the Moscow mission in *The Words of the Lord* (composed in the 1780s) relates that some Frankists "murmured against it."[35] In another place, Frank attributed the failure of the embassy to the intervention of God's providence: had it succeeded, he claimed, "the Muscovites would have taken away wives and children" from among Frank's followers.[36] It seems clear that in later times, Frank tried to erase the memories of the mission to Moscow or to present its failure as a providential success; the two letters of Częstochowa appear to have been his first attempt in that direction.

Frank's calls upon the Jews to convert to Catholicism in 1767 and 1768 should be seen as a part of the propaganda campaign that he launched after the breakdown of negotiations concerning the conversion to Eastern Orthodoxy. Nevertheless, the apocalyptic tone of the letters is real enough. The period was one of extreme turmoil. Russian troops were roaming through the Commonwealth. Among the Polish nobility, rival factions were engrossed in an increasingly nasty power struggle involving attempts to push openly partisan legislation through the Sejm, mudslinging campaigns in the local and foreign press, appeals to foreign powers, and occasional outbursts of violence. One of the administrative changes introduced after the coronation of Stanislaus Augustus particularly affected the Jews: the abolition of the Council of Four Lands.[37]

For the king, the move was merely a minor element in an ambitious package of fiscal reforms. (The idea was to have all subjects of the Crown, including the Jews, pay their taxes directly as individuals rather than through the representations of their respective corporations or estates). However, leaders of the Polish Jewry saw it as the destruction of Jewish legal and religious autonomy. The memoirist Ber of Bolechów has described the reform as "the great change brought about . . . with the purpose of humiliating the people of Israel, and of depriving them of what little honor they had always enjoyed since the time they came to settle in Poland nine hundred years ago";[38] Baruch me-Erets Yavan's trips to Moscow were part of the council's efforts, although formally it no longer existed, to influence the king through his Russian patrons to rescind the decree of abolition. But the worst was yet to come: a Cossack revolt erupted in May 1768, reviving memories of the Chmielnicki uprising and causing the Jewish communities in the eastern part of the country immeasurable suffering. After the massacre at Uman in June of that year, Frank's statements about unburied corpses and the lack of safe havens by no means sounded like mere metaphors.[39]

With the rise of tensions between different ethnic and religious groups, the nobility—often guided by their foreign backers—began to organize confederations aimed at the defense and furtherance of their group interests. In March 1767, the non-Catholic *szlachta* formed two confederations for the protection of the rights of the dissidents: the Lutherans convened in Toruń (Thorn) and the Calvinists and Eastern Orthodox in Słuck.[40] The Catholics responded with the Radom Confederation three months later[41] and—more forcefully—with the formation of a general confederation in the town of Bar in February 1768.[42]

Polish historians disagree in assessing the Bar Confederation: for some, it represented a paroxysm of reactionary forces rallied against badly needed political reforms, religious tolerance, and ideas of the Enlightenment; for others, it embodied a patriotic effort to defend the endangered independence of the country. The confederation was directed against the king (it declared his election invalid and claimed that the Commonwealth had been in a state of interregnum since the death of Augustus III), and against the Russians (the confederate soldiers immediately began attacking Russian garrisons in Poland); its ideology had an arch-Catholic, ultraconservative character and aimed at the preservation of the privileged status of Catholicism as "the ruling religion in Poland," as well as at the defense of the traditional liberties of the *szlachta*.

The confederation exhibited a curious combination of shrewd strategic thinking and rather wild religious and ideological enthusiasm. The strategy of the uprising was based on direct support from Turkey (the Porte declared war on Russia in September 1768) and indirect assistance from France (the French sent money, military advisers, and guaranteed informal treaties between the *szlachta*, the Ottomans, and the Crimean Khanate); the support of these two powers gave the enterprise a reasonable chance of success. Yet any planning was undermined by the confederates' refusal to develop branches of the army that were regarded as beneath the dignity of the nobility (such as infantry and artillery as opposed to cavalry), their inability to agree on unified leadership, and—most significant—the impact of spiritual and ideological factors on any decision making. The fighters saw battles as an opportunity to flaunt religious symbols, they suffered losses defending sacred places lacking any military significance, and they believed that their success depended on piety rather than pragmatic considerations. Many of them saw themselves as waging an apocalyptic battle against the demonic forces of darkness. In a sense, it was a conflict between the vanishing world of chivalric culture and the emerging world of modern warfare: sabers clashed with cannons. The confederate *szlachta* became a laughingstock for Frederick the Great, who wrote a vitriolic pamphlet, *La guerre des confédérés,* against them; but they were praised by Rousseau in his *Considérations sur le gouvernement de Pologne.*

Marian devotion played a particular role in the spirituality of the Bar Confederation: at its very inception, the confederates vowed to spread the cult of the Virgin. The Częstochowa Madonna was of special importance for their ideology, as was the Jasna Góra shrine-fortress for their military strategy: the proclamation of the confederation already contained a point about restoring "this place famed by miracles and devoted to the splendor and honor of the Queen of Poland"[43] to its proper glory. The confederate soldiers adorned their banners and gorgets with images of Our Lady of Częstochowa and composed numerous songs and prayers invoking Her special protection.[44] In September 1770, they marched into the Jasna Góra fortress, which they successfully defended against a Russian attack a couple of months later.

The Frankist sources contain few direct mentions of the presence of the confederates at the monastery: the dicta describe advice given by Frank to one of the soldiers during the defense of the fortress against the Russians,[45] and *Various Notes* records that after entering Częstochowa, "the confederates conspired against Her Highness [Eve]."[46] The scarcity of direct references notwithstanding, the Bar Confederation was of paramount importance for Frank, who incorporated the fighting in Częstochowa into his teachings and—like the confederates themselves—elevated its meaning to truly apocalyptic proportions. He returned to the myth of the *ayalah* and interpreted the motif of the blood gushing from the doe as a symbol of the bloodshed during the confederate warfare: he claimed that much blood had to be shed before the *Shekhinah* could shake off the dust[47] and rise into the world,[48] and before the gates guarded by the Maiden could be opened.[49] He called upon all Frankists to come immediately to Częstochowa; the carnage war was a sure sign of the approaching *eschaton* and the premonitory token of the final revelation of feminine divinity, also attested by the symbolism of the confederates' banners.

Alas, real femininity was less accommodating to the Frankist prophecies: in February 1771, Frank's wife, Hana, suddenly died.[50] Frank scolded his disciples who tried to mourn her (claiming that they should celebrate instead)[51] and introduced new ceremonies honoring femininity: a month after Hana's death, he performed a ritual in which he sucked at the breasts of the wives of two of his followers.[52] Yet this time, the disciples, some of whom had believed in Hana's immortality, revolted; most of them fled from the monastery (one of them even leaped from the ramparts), and Frank was left alone. He spent a year in total isolation from everyone but his daughter, Eve.[53]

The 1768–72 fighting saw changes in the fortunes of all parties involved. In the early stages, when Russia became embroiled in a war with Turkey, the prospects of the confederation seemed promising. But the Russian campaign against the Turks was victorious, and the confederates' chances dwindled quickly. A botched attempt to kidnap King Stanislaus Augustus made them vulnerable to accusations of regicide and made the support of European courts unsustainable.[54] Ultimately, Suvorov's army got the upper hand in Poland. The remnants of the confederates gathered in Częstochowa, where they found a temporary haven, but the old fortress was no longer able to withstand a sustained assault. With the fall of Jasna Góra on 18 August 1772, the Bar Confederation collapsed.[55] About two weeks before that date, on 5 August, the Convention of Saint Petersburg decreed the First Partition of Poland.

For Polish Jewry, the partition was devastating: the largest Jewish community in the world was split into four separate entities, each existing within a different political and legal framework, developing its own institutions, encountering different challenges, and pursuing different goals. Ber of Bolechów interpreted the partition in the context of the struggle between Edom and Israel:

> In that, or the following year, that is, in 527 (1767), the prophecy of Ezekiel, contained in chapter 25, verse 14, was fulfilled: "And I will lay my vengeance upon Edom by the hand of my people Israel." For in that year began the confederation, that is, a revolt against the Crown and the Senate [Sejm] in Warsaw. . . . Then the Polish people and their kingdom were deprived of all honor, and the verse was fulfilled: "And I will lay my vengeance upon Edom"—that is, the Polish nation, Gentiles being called Edom"—"by the hand of my people Israel"—that as they dealt with Israel, so were they dealt with.[56]

Frank drew upon the same symbolism. He claimed that he had predicted the partition at the very beginning of his stay in Częstochowa[57] and stated:

> You must know and understand that all kingdoms are sustained by some powerful thing. The proof of this is that all the Israelites derived their power through maintaining the Temple, and as soon as the Temple was destroyed, they were immediately exiled. So it is in Poland: the great power of their guard was in Częstochowa because of that great guardian who serves Her, as it is written: "The maidservant has inherited the property of her mistress."[58] And when we came there, the country was divided and the words of Balaam were fulfilled, *Wehoio Edom iereischo,* Edom will be passed on as an inheritance,[59] which has not ever happened since Poland became Poland.[60]

The Zohar links the phrase from Proverbs about "a maidservant who is heir to her mistress" (Prov. 30:23) with the exile of the *Shekhinah* and Her replacement by the female demon, Lilith.[61] In the context of the previous discussion, the dictum can be taken to associate this motif with the occultation of the Divine Presence in the Częstochowa icon: the *Shekhinah* was not simply present but was imprisoned in the portrait, as it were. To effect the final liberation of the feminine principle from the portrait, even the mighty kingdom of Edom must crumble. Frank invoked a mishnaic statement about all kingdoms turning to heresy in the footsteps of the messiah[62] and concluded: "And you see with your own eyes that all religions change and go beyond the borders laid down by their ancestors. It is already a few years since I told you that Poland would be divided into four parts. . . . And the rest [of countries] will also be divided."[63]

Whether or not Frank predicted the partition, his disciples understood that the division of Poland represented an event of fundamental messianic importance. They flocked back to Częstochowa, abased themselves before their leader and Eve, and were punished.[64] The commander of the Russian garrison at Jasna Góra, General Bibikov, treated Frank with respect.[65] Several years after the fall of Częstochowa, Bishop Joseph Garampi, then papal nuncio in Warsaw, recounted his conversation with Bibikov: "When I asked what happened to the neophyte Frank, I was told that [in Częstochowa] he attended the Holy Mass every day and gave all appearances of piety. For the rest of the day, he studied Jewish books and devoted himself to writing. General Bibikov enjoyed very much talking to him (as did later Prince Golitsin).[66] Even more he enjoyed Frank's daughter, a modest girl who never left her father. Later, on arriving in Warsaw, Bibikov dispatched an order to release Frank from the monastery."[67]

Apparently, although the Russians had rejected the offer of bringing the Jews into the fold of Eastern Orthodoxy, they had plans for the Frankists. After his release, Frank promptly left for Warsaw. In the capital, he was given passports by the ambassadors of the three partitioning powers. Equipped with these documents, Frank left Poland in mid-March 1773 for Moravia, the northernmost province of the Habsburg Empire. He stated: "Because of my daughter, I must now come to the country of the emperor, so that she might learn the language and the ways of kings."[68]

Frankism in Moravia

Eve's linguistic training might have been important, but the real reason for Frank's settlement in the Habsburg Empire was the connection with Sabbatianism in the region. Frankism had begun to spread in Moravia practically concomitant with the expansion of the movement in Poland, and the province had a rich Sabbatian tradition dating back to the late seventeenth century. Among rabbinic opponents of Sabbatianism, Moravia had been widely considered a stronghold of heresy: Rabbi Jacob Emden even devised a gematria to the effect that the numerical value of the Hebrew letters in the verse "there is none that does good, no, not one" (Ps. 14:3) was equivalent to the numerical value of the letters in the Hebrew term *Mehrin* (Moravia).[69] The most prominent among the Moravian Frankists was the Dobruschka family of Brünn.

The first member of this family to settle in Brünn was Jacob Moses, known as Wimer or Opotschner, who came from Dobruschka, a small town near Königgrätz in Bohemia. He arrived in Brünn in 1730, and—although Jews were forbidden to live in the city[70]—he was given permission to settle there and to deal first in precious stones and jewelry, and later also in spices and tobacco. In 1750, Dobruschka was granted a monopoly on the tobacco trade in all royal cities of Moravia and leased a tobacco factory in Mährich-Neustadt.[71]

Jacob Moses Dobruschka was a widower and brought his two children, Salomon and Esther, to Brünn. Esther married Adam Oppenheimer of Vienna, a relative of the well-known court purveyor Samuel Oppenheimer; the marriage multiplied family fortunes and opened new avenues of profitable trade.[72] Salomon married Schöndl, daughter of Löbl Hirschl of Rzeszów and Güttel Jacobi of Prossnitz; at the time of the marriage of Salomon and Schöndl, their parents-in-law lived in that town.[73] In 1755, Salomon Dobruschka was granted permission to collect the Jewish entry tax to Brünn; after his death in 1774, the concession was renewed on behalf of his wife.[74] Scholem suggests that Salomon Dobruschka was a Sabbatian; however, we know that he was sufficiently observant to apply for permission to conduct religious services in his house.[75]

Schöndl Dobruschka, famous for her beauty, was known as a patroness of the Moravian Sabbatians.[76] Jacob Emden, who reserved for her the epithet of "the whore of Brünn,"[77] sometimes portrayed her as the leader of all Sabbatians in Moravia.[78] Schöndl and Salomon Dobruschka had twelve children.[79] After the death of her husband in 1774,[80] Schöndl conducted a salon, where not only Jews but also prominent Christians gathered. Among them was an officer of the Dragoons, Vizekreishauptmann of the Brünn district Ferdinand Geißler. A love affair developed between Geißler and Schöndl's eighteen-year-old daughter, Blümele. In October 1775, Blümele and her sixteen-year-old brother, Gerstl, informed the authorities of their request to receive baptism. The authorities consented, and Blümele and Gerstl were baptized on 21 November 1775.[81] Other children quickly followed suit: Moses, Jacob Naftali, Joseph, and David converted in December of the same year; the eldest son, Carl, had been a Christian since 1764.[82] Three younger daughters, Sara, Gilt and Esther, were baptized in 1791.[83] In the end, only two of the twelve children remained Jewish.

The conversions involving the Dobruschka family deserve more detailed attention. Arthur Mandel believed that the baptisms of the younger Dobruschkas took place at Frank's direct instigation.[84] It is certain that some two months after Frank's arrival in Moravia, in May 1773, eight Jewish families (thirty people) converted to Roman Catholicism in Prossnitz.[85] Among those baptized was the rabbi of the Dobruschka family, Salomon Gerstel, and his three sons.[86] However, we have no evidence that the Frankists called upon the Jews of the Habsburg lands to convert prior to 1800. Hence, we cannot be sure if Frank's direct encouragement triggered the baptisms in Prossnitz, if his arrival sparked them (without any explicit appeals to convert), or if they simply coincided with his arrival in the region. Whether or not there was Frankist propaganda in support of apostasy in Moravia in the 1770s and 1780s, the region clearly did not witness a wave of conversions similar to the one that affected Poland in the late 1750s and early 1760s.[87] Indeed, the structure of Frankism in the Czech lands differed from that in Poland, where the majority of Frank's followers became (at least outwardly) Roman Catholic, for the greater part of Moravian and Bohemian Frankists remained (at least outwardly) Jewish.

Gershom Scholem attributed this development to sociological factors: "[T]he majority of the Sabbatians in Podolia were members of the lower class and few of those converted were educated. The Sabbatians in Germany and the Austro-Hungarian Empire were largely from a more wealthy background and many of them were men of considerable rabbinical learning."[88] Scholem's claim is only partly true: some Frankists in the Habsburg monarchy did indeed belong to the richest Jewish families, which was certainly not the case in Poland. The issue of education is, however, more complicated. Communal rabbis were among the Frankists who converted in Lwów in 1759, and the formulation of the points for the disputations attests to substantial Jewish knowledge.

If there was indeed a difference in the respective educational backgrounds of the Czech and the Polish Frankists, it lay not so much in the lack of *Jewish* learning among the latter, but in the presence of *Gentile* education among the former. The Polish Frankists were not deficient in rabbinic scholarship, but it appears that only a minority had had contact with the non-Jewish world prior to their conversion. In contrast, many Moravian Frankists were fairly acculturated before they joined the movement.

In order to appreciate fully the role and the meaning of conversions to Christianity in Moravian, and later in Bohemian and German, Frankism, we must place the phenomenon in a wider historical frame. We do not encounter celebrated mass conversions similar to those that took place in Salonika in 1683 or in Lwów in 1759 in the history of Sabbatianism in Bohemia, Moravia, and Germany. Instead, we find single, private, or often clandestine baptisms and, most interestingly, *rumors* of conversions surrounding the most important personalities of the movement. A case in point is Rabbi Jonathan Eibeschütz. Contemporary Christian theologians believed that he was a "secret proselyte [to Christianity] and half Christian,"[89] and Christian groups disseminated accounts of his clandestine baptism.[90]

Similarly, stories about secret conversions circulated around Schöndl Dobruschka.[91] In her case, the stories were untrue. Not only did Schöndl not convert, but she vigorously opposed the acceptance of Christianity by her children Blümele and Gerstl "without a real religious motive," and she even took the Geißlers to court, protesting against the conversion of minors without the consent of their parents.[92] As for the children of Rabbi Jonathan Eibeschütz, although none of them converted, most of them took Christian names.[93] Schöndl Dobruschka also took the name Katharina.[94]

Insofar as the case is representative, we may say that the Sabbatians of the generation of Schöndl Dobruschka adopted a Christian façade for the sake of social mobility but shunned actual baptism. This also indicates another aspect of the difference between Polish and Moravian-Bohemian branches of Frankism: while Jewish acculturation or upward mobility in eighteenth-century Poland presupposed becoming clearly and unequivocally Roman Catholic, the situation in the Habsburg monarchy and especially in the German lands permitted greater social fluidity and less rigidly defined identities.

The consequence was twofold. First, in Poland it was difficult even for a converted Jew or his children to be fully integrated into non-Jewish society. Polish pamphlets emphasize the Frankists' maintenance of a cloistered community long after their conversions. Despite their rise in social status, Polish Frankists could never dream of a career similar to that of the jurist and reformer Josef von Sonnenfels (who, by the way, also came from a Sabbatian family).[95]

Second, the break with their Jewish background was necessarily exceptionally rapid and violent in Poland. As far as the Frankists were concerned, the rupture was intensified by accusations and schemes surrounding the disputations. Those who converted in Lwów and Warsaw in 1759 broke virtually all contacts with the Jewish community. In contrast, eighteenth-century Habsburg history knows numerous cases of Jewish converts and their children who, despite the change of faith, retained links with their former religion and community. In many ways, Frankist converts from Poland were similar to medieval Jewish apostates, who were hostile to Judaism and its customs. By contrast, at that time many Jewish converts in the Habsburg monarchy had much more neutral (if not friendly) attitudes. Sonnenfels is again a case in point.[96] But even Sabbatian and Frankist converts from Bohemia and Moravia apparently did not sever all ties with mainstream Judaism.[97]

As I have said, the older generation of Moravian Sabbatians exploited the façade of Christianity but stopped short of accepting baptism. The younger generation did not have similar qualms: all but two of Schöndl's children converted, despite her clear misgivings. The most talented among the children was certainly Moses, born in Brünn on 12 July 1753. In May 1775, he married Elke Joß, an adopted daughter of Joachim Edler von Popper.[98] Popper (born as Hayyim Bresnitz) was an important Viennese financier who owned numerous factories and companies and had a substantial share in the Austrian tobacco monopoly.[99] He was also the *Primator* of the rural Bohemian Jewry, and his daughter was perhaps the best Jewish match in the Czech lands. Some eight months after the wedding, on 17 December 1775, Moses, Elke, and their daughter, Maria Anna, converted to Roman Catholicism in the Prague cathedral of Saint Vitus and were given the names Franz Thomas, Wilhelmine, and Marianna, respectively.

Upon hearing of the conversion, Popper disinherited his daughter, and Dobruschka did not receive the promised dowry.[100] Franz Thomas sued his father-in-law, and the proceedings dragged on for many years.[101] Meanwhile, Franz Thomas was given a temporary post at the censorship office in Prague and received an annual salary of five hundred guldens.[102] Following in the footsteps of both his father and his wife's father, he was also involved in the tobacco trade.[103]

On 25 July 1778, Moses and Elke, together with other children of the Dobruschka family, were ennobled. Adolf Ferdinand Edler von Schönfeld, an important Prague Freemason and publisher, bestowed the titled name upon the Dobruschkas.[104] Moses Dobruschka (Franz Thomas von Schönfeld) became acquainted with the circle of reformers surrounding Joseph II and enjoyed some favor with the emperor, to whom he dedicated enthusiastic poetic eulogies.[105] The reformers gathered around Michael Denis, who translated the famous forged epic of MacPherson, *Songs of Ossian*, into German. Dobruschka was employed as an assistant to Denis and became acquainted with a group of former Jesuits who had found a new home in Freemasonry.[106] His Masonic connections developed and resulted, toward the beginning of the 1780s, in his involvement in the creation of the Order of Asiatic Brethren. I shall return to the history of this order in the next chapter. For now, I shall concentrate on the links between the Dobruschka family and Jacob Frank.

Some contemporary accounts—and also much later secondary literature—claim that Moses Dobruschka was Frank's nephew. This rumor probably arose because, upon his arrival in Brünn, Frank presented himself as Schöndl's brother.[107] Fritz Mauthner, who himself came from a Frankist family from Bohemia, reported gossip that Moses and David Dobruschka were Frank's sons.[108] Fritz Heymann went so far as to claim the real Jacob Frank "ended up in the dungeons of the Częstochowa fortress," while the "Jacob Frank" who lived in Brünn and Offenbach was, in fact, Moses Dobruschka.[109] Although such a masquerade is completely impossible, Heymann did manage to establish a convincing family connection between Frank and the Dobruschkas and determine that Schöndl was a maternal cousin of Frank.[110]

The family bond was strong, and Frank's stay in Brünn was, from the outset, associated with the Dobruschkas. Some accounts even claim that he lived in the city "under the name of Dobruski or Dobruschka."[111] The maskil Lazarus Bendavid, who had an opportunity to meet Frank on the occasion of the coronation of Leopold II in Frankfurt, also believed that his name was "Dobruski."[112] As for Moses, the Frankist chronicle records that "in 1783, Schönfeld accused the Lord [Frank] before the nobles, and he tried to incite everyone, but it was he who was taken to prison for a year."[113]

It is impossible to say whether this cryptic remark refers to Moses or to one of his brothers, or to what exactly it does refer. Even if it does refer to Moses and hints at a conflict within the sect, the issue must have been resolved later. An anonymous denunciation against the Bohemian Frankists sent in 1799 to the mayor of Prague states that during Frank's funeral in Offenbach in 1791, Moses Dobruschka was offered the leadership of the sect but declined and went to France to take part in the Revolution.[114] Along the same lines, Georg Forster noted that the Frankists had thought that forty-nine days after his death, the soul of Frank would incarnate in "his nephew" (apparently Moses) through a kind of "Tibetan metempsychosis."[115]

Practically all sources agree that Frank chose to reside in Brünn after his release from Częstochowa because of the connection with the Dobruschkas. Toward the end of March 1773, Frank arrived in Brünn.[116] He was accompanied by eighteen people; none of the men who had been leaders of the Frankists during the disputations in Poland now belonged to his entourage.[117] Initially, Frank took lodgings at the guesthouse "Zum blauen Löwen," but after a couple of days, he rented a house belonging to a certain Ignatz Pietsch in Obrovitz.[118] Shortly after his arrival, Frank presented passports from the Austrian, Russian, and Prussian ambassadors in Warsaw.[119] He informed the authorities that he originated from Smyrna, had traveled from Poland, and wanted to settle in Brünn. He also requested permission to visit Vienna for a week, together with his daughter, and to send four of his domestic staff back to Warsaw.[120]

Initially, the authorities were cautious. Count Carl Friedrich von Zollern, the prefect of the Brünn district, asked the Moravian Gubernium for instructions. Suspicion was raised by the fact that Frank traveled with an entourage that was unusually large for a neophyte and in which his only companions were other baptized Jews.[121] The Frankists were also presumed to be Prussian spies.[122] The governor ordered Zollern to investigate more thoroughly. Zollern interrogated Frank, who presented himself as a merchant forced to leave Poland because of the adverse effect on trade created by current political disturbances. He stated that he owned large numbers of horses, sheep, and cattle near Czernowitz and had some possessions in Smyrna, whence he received revenues every three years. He said that he had no intention of following any trade or of working in Brünn and would live from his own means. Zollern also determined that Frank and his people behaved properly and lived within their means, without contracting any debts. Accordingly, the governor allowed "the neophyte Joseph Frank to settle in Brünn freely and without any restrictions."[123]

For over a year, the authorities did not concern themselves with Frank. Then, on 31 July 1774, Zollern received a letter from the supreme chancellor of Austria, Count von Blümegen.[124] The chancellor asked Zollern to investigate Frank's activities and to determine whether he was organizing a sect.[125] He was also worried by rumors that Frank had presented himself as a messiah.[126] Zollern sent the chancellor a copy of his earlier letter to the governor of Moravia, and added that Frank was behaving very well: every day he attended mass, confessed, took communion, and succeeded in converting some local Jewish families to the "true faith."[127] His proselytizing among the Jews was carried out under the direct supervision of the local parish priest and gave no reason to suspect any sectarian activity.[128] Zollern believed that the suspicions toward the Frankists were the result of a campaign of slander conducted against Frank by Bohemian and Moravian Jews and should therefore be ignored.

The intervention from Vienna was indeed based on accusations disseminated by Frank's Jewish opponents.[129] Blümegen was informed that Frank had been arrested in Warsaw in 1760 because he claimed to be a new messiah, preached the coming of Elijah, and considered himself a newly born Antichrist. The denunciation that caused the most stir was written by an erstwhile follower from Poland who had become disenchanted with Frank. On 7 September 1776, Jacob Galiński, a former rabbi of Gliniany near Lwów, sent a letter to Maria Theresa, in which he accused Frank of "immoral behavior and acts against human nature," of extorting money from his followers, and of involvement in various subversive plots as well as spying on behalf of Russia. He also stated that Frank's only companions were converted Jews and that the Frankists formed a close-knit sect that only superficially adhered to the Christian religion.

Despite the initial anxiety it had caused, in the end the Austrian authorities decided to ignore Galiński's denunciation, which returned it to the sender, suggesting only that he might pursue a civil case against Frank.[130] In response, Galiński sent another petition, this time to the local authorities in Brünn. In the second letter, he emphasized that his request was inspired by truly religious motives and demanded a confrontation with Frank.[131] Galiński's second set of accusations was forwarded to Vienna with a note requesting advice. However, this time, too, the chancellery refused to intervene: on 7 October 1776, Blümegen replied that "the denunciation of Jacob Galiński against the Polish neophyte Jacob Frank should be disregarded" but that the Moravian Gubernium should keep an eye on Frank and report every suspicion to the Royal Chancellery.[132]

Oskar Rabinowicz has attributed the indifference of the authorities to their enlightened attitude in matters of faith, resulting in the "refusal to be dragged into religious controversy."[133] Kraushar, in turn, has ascribed the failure to respond to Frank's influence at the court in Vienna.[134] Although the gaps in the sources do not allow us fully to confirm Kraushar's hypothesis, I am inclined to concur with his opinion. Frank certainly did have connections in Vienna at that time. In the following chapter, I shall discuss Frank's activities in the Habsburg Christian milieu.

Chapter 8

The Vagaries of the Charlatans

Wolf Eibeschütz and Jacob Frank: Early Parallels

To understand the development of Frankism in the 1770s and 1780s, we must first discuss Frank's most important rival for the leadership of Eastern European Sabbatians: Wolf, the youngest son of Rabbi Jonathan Eibeschütz. The links between Wolf and the Frankists went back to 1755, the very year when Frank's activity in Poland began. In that year, at the request of his father, Wolf, who was then fifteen years old, undertook a journey to the Balkans, Podolia, Moravia, and Hungary.[1] During his journeys, he reportedly met Frank[2] as well as one of the most important participants in the Kamieniec and Lwów disputations, Solomon Shorr.[3] In Moravia, he associated with the Dobruschka family. He also had contacts with the *ba'ale kabin*, the disciples of the leader of the Dönmeh, Berukhiah, and—either in a formal Jewish ceremony or according to some mystical Sabbatian rite—he married Berukhiah's daughter or granddaughter.[4]

Graetz, with his customary irony, described Wolf Eibeschütz as a "small-scale Frank [*ein Frank im Kleinem*]."[5] Aside from the direct influences and borrowings in doctrinal matters, there are clear phenomenological parallels between Wolf and Frank. Comparisons between the two already appeared in the earliest testimony. An anti-Sabbatian account from *Sefer shimush* said that Wolf and Frank were as similar as two drops of water. Thus, Wolf "could not write even a word in the Holy Language without a blunder and three mistakes," while Frank was "incapable of speaking and of any language; he only stuttered and whistled and cried like a rooster, and so anybody who was not well accustomed to him could not understand anything."[6] Wolf was "possessed by an evil spirit, and he had a sickness of falling to the ground [epilepsy?] and fell on earth and was saying the words of kabbalah," while "an evil spirit entered Frank and . . . he fell on the ground and revealed secrets and mysteries." Wolf wore "Turkish robes" and a turban during midnight prayers; so did Frank.[7] As with Frank, during the Sabbatian ceremonies, the letters of the Name of God shone on Wolf's chest, and the smell of the Garden of Eden surrounded him during his prayers.[8]

Quasi-shamanistic trances involving falling on the ground and revealing kabbalistic mysteries typified earlier Sabbatian prophets. For instance, it was reported that Heshel Tsoref—in a manner very close to that of Frank and Wolf some hundred years later—who was seen by his adherents as a man of exceptional wisdom and by his adversaries as a semiliterate (or completely illiterate) boor, also entered trances that allowed him to reveal the deepest secrets of the Zohar, which he could not otherwise have known or understood.[9] Frank's and Wolf's predilections for Oriental dress also originated in their shared Sabbatian heritage. In 1671, Sabbatai Tsevi demanded that his followers wear turbans; *yom ha-mitsnefet* ("the day of the turban") became a festival for the believers,[10] and there are numerous testimonies about various Sabbatian groups wearing turbans during special prayers. Likewise, wife-swapping ceremonies and dances around a naked woman were Turkish Sabbatian rites imported to Europe.

In 1755, Frank returned to Podolia as an emissary of the Dönmeh of Salonika and an anointed inheritor (or even a reincarnation of the soul) of Berukhiah. If the conjectures from the Introduction are correct, his wife was the daughter of Levi Tova, leader of one of the most prominent groups of Dönmeh. During his youth in the Ottoman Empire, he experienced ecstatic trances, had visions, engaged in magical therapeutic practices, and learned the art of reading peoples' deeds and destinies from their physiognomies. As noted, after one such trance, the "young and vain boor" Frank metamorphosed into Hakham Jacob Frank, head of a *bet midrash* in Salonika expounding mysteries of the Torah. Upon his arrival in Poland, he presented himself as a miracle worker; he caused heavy stones to fly in the air or to float on the surface of a river, made an ox speak mysteries in a human tongue, and revived the dead.

When Frank came to Lwów, local Jews were advised by their rabbis to lock themselves in their houses and not to look at his face, so that he would not cast a spell upon them.[11] In his early activities, he claimed to be guided by higher spiritual powers, saying that he could see a flame over the heads of the prospective disciples whom he was preordained to accept; he said that he had refused to take on those above whose heads he did not see the flame, although some of them had offered large sums of money.[12]

In the first stages of his activity, Frank carried on in the Sabbatian tradition of prophets, charismatics, magicians, and miracle workers. Frank's later story, however, was not that of a simpleton turned sage, thanks to miraculous powers or a direct prophetic revelation. Important as these must have been at the beginning of his path, trances and revelations played no role in Frank's later career. Descriptions of ecstatic séances such as the one from *Sefer shimush* invariably refer to his *Wanderjahre* in the Ottoman Empire: the period before Frank came to Poland and converted to Christianity, the period before Frank became Frank. The visions of a flame over the heads of his followers disappeared as soon as the Frankists became Christian.[13] Following his conversion, Frank became something else entirely.

Wolf's contacts with the disciples of Berukhiah during his journeys to the Balkans and especially his alleged marriage with Berukhiah's daughter or granddaughter are clear indications of his attempts to tap into the same Sabbatian tradition. It seems that from 1755 to 1760, Wolf presented himself as a transmitter of secret Sabbatian beliefs from the Ottoman Empire and the Balkans to Eastern Europe and, accordingly, competed with Frank for the leadership of Podolian and Moravian Sabbatians.[14] Here is a description of what happened to Wolf one winter night in the Moravian city of Brünn:

> At the time of the Hanukkah, Wolf pointed to eight lights against the firmament, and when Christmas Eve [*leil kuti*] arrived, he said: "Lo and behold! The entire world, even the great sages tell us to play cards on this night, but we will not do so. We will be destroying the *kelippot!*" And he took a violin and started to sing songs and cried a great cry. And Wolf told the people who were there with him to look through the window, and they saw a pillar of fire [*amuda denura*] coming from the heavens to the earth. And he also told them: when I call you, fall on your faces, because the power of destruction is great and you might be destroyed. And there were also sounds and lightning.[15]

The motif of the pillar of fire standing between the heavens and the earth is, of course, familiar from the book of Exodus, where God led the Israelites through the wilderness with a pillar of a cloud by day and a pillar of fire by night.[16] In the midrashim, this form of epiphany has been identified with that of the *Shekhinah*, the Divine Presence; thus, for instance, in *Pirke de-Rabbi Eliezer*, Abraham recognized the place chosen for the sacrifice of Isaac when he saw the Glory of the *Shekhinah* standing atop Mount Moriah in the form of the pillar of fire.[17]

According to Lurianic kabbalah, the sin of the first man caused the *Shekhinah* to move up to heaven; Her subsequent descent has been associated with the ascending movement of the Patriarchs and of Moses: the rise of Abraham, Isaac, Jacob, and Moses brought the *Shekhinah* closer to earth again.[18] The descent of the Divine Presence into the emanation has been further described as her garbing herself in the *sefira malkut* associated with the messiah; according to the Zohar, one of the first signs of the arrival of the messiah is the appearance of a pillar of fire extending from heaven to earth and visible to all nations.[19] Sabbatai Tsevi occasionally identified himself with the *Shekhinah*, and the Sabbatian inversion of fasts into feasts was motivated by the "rejoicing in the honor of the bride that has thus been revealed."[20] His prophet, Nathan of Gaza, also associated Sabbatai's messianic claims with the appearance of the pillar of fire.[21] Later Sabbatian prophets and messianic pretenders described their mission and tried to legitimize their claims by causing the descent of the Shekhinah in the form of the pillar of fire.

The testimony describing the pillar of fire descending upon Brünn is undated, but we know that it describes events that took place during Wolf's return journey from Eastern Europe to Altona (at the end of the 1750s) and that the phenomenon occurred on a Christmas Eve, which came close to, or even overlapped with, Hanukkah. I believe that the pillar of fire and the lights and sounds on the sky were, in fact, Halley's Comet and the accompanying meteorite storm, which were first officially recorded by the amateur astronomer Georg Palitzsch of Dresden exactly on Christmas, 25 December 1758 (in 1758, the first day of Hanukkah coincided with the Christmas Eve). Wolf clearly wanted to use the appearance of the comet to gain a following and to confirm his messianic mandate. His efforts to attain the leadership of the Sabbatians in Eastern and Central Europe intensified a year later, in 1759—the year of the conversion of the Frankists in Poland.

Following the wave of baptisms in Lwów in August 1759, Eibeschütz called on the converts not to lose their Sabbatian faith and promised to come to them with a large group of fellow believers ("and the priests in Podolia boasted that Rabbi Jonathan himself would come with four hundred—and some say five thousand—people, and they were saying that the converts had received letters from him promising that he would come and would be as they are and that his son [Wolf] was paving the way for him").[22] Wolf's efforts to take control of the sect climaxed after the Frankists were "abandoned" by Frank during his arrest and imprisonment in Częstochowa.[23] Reportedly, at the beginning of the 1760s, a group of disciples, deprived of Frank's leadership, proclaimed Wolf Eibeschütz their leader.[24] Emden mentioned also that in Nagyvárad, Wolf attempted to organize a gathering of all the "unclean," including the "converts from Poland" (the Frankists).[25]

The Rise of Wolf Eibeschütz

Wolf Eibeschütz's attempts between 1755 and 1760 to take over the leadership of the Eastern and Central European Sabbatianism were unsuccessful. As a Sabbatian leader, young Eibeschütz can be described not so much as a "small-scale Frank" but as a "failed Frank": despite all his efforts, the movement in formation around him did not gain momentum. Whether because of insufficient personal charisma, or tactical errors, or simple bad luck, Wolf did not manage to unify splintered Sabbatian groups the way Frank did. In the course of his travels, young Eibeschütz contracted large debts and had to return to Altona, where his father had to publish his unfinished commentary on *Shulhan arukh*, *Kereti u-feleti*, in order to pay the son's creditors.[26] However, within a couple of months, his financial situation miraculously improved and Wolf purchased one of the most impressive properties in the city:

> He bought a large house and estate, a field and a garden full of exquisite and fine fruit trees. And he hired many painters and artisans and ordered them to rebuild the external wall from the side of the street, which was old, crooked, and crumbling. And he had it built tall and beautiful, with decorations made of precious stones and images of lion and wolf and his name *gvul benyamin*[27] carved upon the wall. Inside the garden, he had a wall of glass built; all the trees and plants were eradicated, and parterres made with arrangements of colored porcelain taken from broken china. He also had a wine cellar carved, inside of which there was a basin of water with engravings representing scales of sea creatures and conches, as it is customary among great lords. In the house, he had figures of naked courtesans dancing with lovers and hunting scenes of the priests of the goddess of the ancient Greeks, Venus. In his room (where, as he

claimed, the *Shekhinah* had descended on him), he hung a painting of a young man and woman embracing each other. In the garden, he also placed costly sculptures of marble and alabaster, statuettes of the Virgin with the child and of other known [Christian] saints. And he had a great chronograph [*keli sha'ot*], which is called *Wanduhr* [wall clock] . . . and which was decorated with the images of all the deeds of Jesus [*kol ma'ase talui*].[28]

In his new estate, Wolf began to host lavish parties and established a private house of study headed by one of his friends or followers, Moses ben David of Podhajce.[29] He "began to conduct himself ostentatiously and flamboyantly [*linhog atsmo be-gedulot u-nifla'ot*], purchased lands and properties . . . and bought himself various human pleasures [*ta'anuge bne adam*]."[30] He had a splendid equipage harnessed with expensive horses and a brigade of servants wearing special liveries.[31] His luxurious lifestyle quickly devoured even considerable resources, the gaudy parties aroused the indignation of the Jewish community, and the house of study came to be regarded as an almost open center of heretical Sabbatianism.

Soon the mounting debts made it necessary to auction off the mansion,[32] revealing to everyone's eyes Wolf's collection of *objets d'art*, including sculptures and paintings widely regarded as alien to the spirit of Judaism, idolatrous and immoral. The visitors also found a Sabbatian manuscript, a kind of manifesto.[33] The discoveries caused a considerable upheaval among pious Jews and compromised the position of the chief rabbi, who—encouraged by other rabbinic leaders—decided to send his son away.[34] In March 1762, Wolf left Altona, leaving behind a whiff of scandal and a trail of unpaid debts. He traveled in a new, gold-leafed carriage accompanied by two lackeys; the coachman sounded a trumpet, and a crowd gathered to witness the magnificent spectacle.[35]

Wolf Eibeschütz's Sabbatian doctrines, expounded in the manuscript found in his house, have been masterfully reconstructed by Yehudah Liebes. From the perspective of the present discussion, however, more important than his teachings or beliefs are Wolf's appearance, patterns of behavior, even mannerisms. While the theme of Sabbatianism is prominent in the majority of Jewish accounts concerning young Eibeschütz, another element is equally important: parallel to the accusation of Sabbatian heresy, Wolf was accused of unseemly, scandalous, or indecent conduct. Few of the testimonies attributed Wolf's misadventures to Sabbatian antinomian theology; most simply pointed to his appallingly lax morals, especially the sexual ones.

At the end of the day, it was impossible to tell whether stories about Eibe-schütz's *liaisons dangereuses* with a married Jewish woman,[36] married and un-married non-Jewish women,[37] orgies and alleged incestuous relations with his sister,[38] or his habit of entertaining guests while sitting between two girls with his hands on their bosoms[39] indicated his adherence to Sabbatian antinomian-ism or to licentiousness or even perversion. Even if these stories were exagger-ated, and regardless of the motives underlying his actions, Wolf's conduct was totally unacceptable to the Jews of Altona. What most shocked and bothered pious members of the community was not only (and even not especially) his heretical belief: in most Jewish sources, Wolf was not even rebuked because of his Sabbatianism, but for behavior blatantly not befitting a Jew.

It was not uncommon among medieval and early modern Jews to imitate patterns of dress and behavior of their Christian neighbors. Indeed, there is hardly an element appearing in the testimonies about Wolf that does not appear in accounts about other Jews of the period. Contemporary writers bemoaned the decline of morals and the widespread adoption of non-Jewish customs by the Jews. Thus, for instance, the well-known preacher Tsevi Hirsh Kaidanover complained that "nowadays" Jewish women "came to dress provocatively, not at all like daughters of Israel, so on the street one cannot distinguish between a Jewish woman and a [Christian] noblewoman or one belonging to the towns-people"; they "walk with stretched-out necks"[40] and "bared breasts."[41] He also chastised Jewish men for shaving their beards, adopting non-Jewish names, eating forbidden food and drinking nonkosher wine, hunting animals for sport, and even for learning French.[42]

Other sources also mention eighteenth-century Jews who lived in lavish houses, fancied expensive clothing and jewelry, and traveled in coaches ac-companied by footmen.[43] Wolf belonged to the upper stratum of the Jewish society, which—like its Christian counterpart—loved to make an ostentatious display of wealth and power. Since the Middle Ages, European Jewish com-munities had enacted sumptuary laws against luxury and ostentation. Com-munal regulations placed restrictions on the manner of dress, the wearing of jewelry, the number of guests permitted to attend festive meals, and so on. As Robert Bonfil has demonstrated in his study of the Jews in Renaissance Italy, the reason that Jewish sumptuary laws were initially enacted was not so much for fear that Jews would mix with Gentiles, as it was preoccupation with not attracting attention or standing out: "[T]he idea was not to spark the envy of the Christians, who might have been tempted to impose high taxes."[44]

Indeed, such feelings were expressed also by Kaidanover and in some testimonies pertaining to Wolf Eibeschütz: after seeing his house as described above, a member of the Altona community admonished Rabbi Jonathan to make his son "be on guard from the envy of the Gentiles."[45] However, most accounts concerning Wolf did not refer to the possible adverse reactions of the non-Jews but attacked his "un-Jewish" appearance and behavior. Thus, for instance, one testimony stated that "he had his domestic staff wear special clothes according to the customs and laws of the Gentiles [*ke-hok ve-ke-dat ha-umot*]" or that he "sat in [his carriage] without a hat, as it is customary among the Gentiles [*ke-hukkot ha-umot*], and his overall tendency was to present himself as a nobleman or an adviser to the king [and] to follow [the Gentiles'] ways."[46]

The wording of these accounts is significant in its making explicit use of the concept of *hukkot ha-goy* (literally, the laws or customs of the Gentiles). The concept is of biblical provenance (Lev. 20:23: "you shall not walk in the manners of the nation [*hukkot ha-goy*], which I cast out before you"), and its original meaning referred to specific types of sexual immorality practiced by the Egyptians and the Canaanites.[47] In rabbinic literature, however, the notion was extended to copying or emulating non-Jewish customs and practices in general. Of course, as such, the concept of *hukkot ha-goy* became open to countless interpretations. Early halakhists tended to adopt a lenient view, applying the notion to the *religious* conduct of the Gentiles and often emphasizing the absurdity of banning certain practices simply because they were also carried out by non-Jews.

However, a stricter interpretation gradually emerged: nineteenth-century halakhists, facing the crisis and decomposition of the traditional Jewish society, extended the scope of *hukkot ha-goy* in such a way that the concept came to cover such practices as using an organ in the synagogue, hunting animals, playing music, not growing a beard, or wearing a tie.[48] Wolf Eibeschütz's case is perhaps the best illustration of this gradual process of change and illustrates the complex interplay of mid-eighteenth-century Sabbatianism with wider forces of secularization and assimilation. The son of the arguably most prominent rabbi of the period became an assimilationist *avant la lettre*: Wolf Eibeschütz became a non-Jewish Jew.

After leaving Altona, young Eibeschütz went back to Moravia and reestablished contacts with the Sabbatian network in Brünn, Prossnitz, and Holleschau. Initially, he seemed to have been gaining a following. But before long, his creditors—new and old—caught up with him. He quietly fled Moravia and arrived in Vienna,[49] where he established contacts with prosperous financiers and high society: fluent in French, he was seen socializing with people of rank and was reportedly received at audiences with Maria Theresa and Joseph II.[50]

Through his contacts in the Austrian financial world, Wolf found favor with a "very important statesman" who became his patron.[51] After a sojourn in the Habsburg capital, he moved to Dresden and became a court agent (*Hoffaktor*) of Elector of Saxony Frederick Augustus. He resumed his hedonistic lifestyle, rubbing shoulders with members of the Saxon elite, rebuilding his art collection, establishing a curiosity cabinet and a treasure house compared by one source—perhaps somewhat exaggeratedly—to the famous Grünes Gewölbe of Augustus the Strong.[52] The same source also reported that "during this time, [Wolf] did not behave at all like a Jew: he ate prohibited foods and publicly violated the Sabbath."[53] He purchased a manor in the vicinity of Dresden and a palace in the city itself.[54] He was known as "Baron von Eibeschütz," "Baron von Adlersthal," or simply "the baron," and Christian noblemen "thought he was one of them."[55]

Baron von Eibeschütz and Count von Frank

Stories about Wolf's baronial title demand some clarification. Following the mass conversion after the Lwów disputation of 1759, many of the Polish Frankists were promoted to nobility. Their ennoblement was based on an obscure Lithuanian law of 1588, which gave the prerogatives of the *szlachta* to baptized Jews and their offspring.[56] The baptismal records from 1759 and 1760 already made use of this law: names of the neophytes mentioned for the second time, as godparents of other converts, were usually preceded by the epithet *generosus* or *nobilis*.[57] The issue of the ennoblement of the converted Frankist was then taken up by the 1764 Sejm. The bill *Concerning the Neophytes* stated: "It became frequent in Poland that some neophytes covet prerogatives of the *szlachta*. Out of their innate cunning and greed, they push for offices and possessions with harm done to native noblemen."

The Sejm revoked noble privileges granted to recent Jewish converts to Christianity and equated them with the burghers.[58] However, already during the next session of the Sejm, Lithuanian deputies demanded "out of compassion" restoration of the nobility of some distinguished and commended neophytes. The bill listed names of the forty-eight ennobled converts and granted the king the right to promote ten more every year.[59] None of these names seemed to be in any way connected to Frank. Many recent Jewish converts in Poland, including some of those who were baptized in Lwów in 1759, lost their noble status in 1764 (although some of the families were ennobled again few years later). However, the noble status of Frank and his closest entourage was unchallenged.

The legal system of the Holy Roman Empire did not have an equivalent to the Lithuanian statute of 1588 invoked in the case of the Polish Frankists, and Jewish conversions in the Habsburg monarchy never resulted in automatic ennoblement. Generally, nobility was a Christian prerogative: the *Primator* of the Bohemian Jewry and the father-in-law of Moshe Dobruschka, Joachim Popper, was probably the first confessional Jew to be raised to noble status by the emperor.[60] However, Popper's situation was in every way unique. Even baptism did not ensure ennoblement for Jews lacking his stature. Indeed, the difficulties encountered by Christianized Jews seeking noble titles in the 1770s might have deterred the Frankists from conversion in the Habsburg lands, as noted in the previous chapter. In light of this, accounts of Wolf Eibeschütz's ennoblement and his rank of baron need to be examined carefully.

Rabbi Jacob Emden described how Wolf, after leaving Altona, traveled in an equipage accompanied by lackeys bearing his coat of arms on their liveries: "a golden rooster called capercaillie."[61] It was said that Eibeschütz claimed that he had been granted the title of baron by the ruler of Altona, the king of Denmark,[62] in exchange for providing the Danish crown with a substantial, long-term, interest-free loan. According to Emden, however, "all this was completely false": Eibeschütz promised only to contribute a small amount to a loan offered to the king by several of the Jewish financiers of Altona, he never made good on his promise, and his writ of ennoblement belonged to another aristocrat and was obtained by Wolf through "deceit and bribery."[63] On the basis of this writ, Wolf purportedly presented himself to Empress Maria Theresa as a Danish nobleman and was treated as such by Habsburg aristocrats; significantly, Emden did not link Wolf's spurious ennoblement with any allegations of conversion to Christianity.

Elements of this story filtered through to various anecdotal accounts. The maskil Lazarus Bendavid stated in 1812 that Wolf Eibeschütz "had ostensibly [*äußerlich*] converted to Christianity and lived in Dresden under the name Baron von Eubeschütz [*sic*]."[64] In 1858, Gutmann Klemperer reported—and dismissed—a version according to which the Danish writ of ennoblement belonged to Rabbi Jonathan; his son Wolf was said to have obtained a copy illegally and to have used it for his own machinations.[65]

According to Yeshashakhar Beer (1857), on his arrival in Vienna, Wolf presented a passport in the name of Wolf Jonathan von Eibeschütz and claimed to have been ennobled by the king of Denmark. He also stated that he had purchased a barony (*Rittergut*) near Dresden; as a Danish nobleman residing in the Holy Roman Empire and wishing to engage in various businesses in the Habsburg territory, he petitioned Maria Theresa to be granted the imperial title of baron, and the designation "von Adlersthal" added to his name. While the authorities initially looked upon this petition favorably, and some of Wolf's supporters among the aristocrats began to accord him the title, a more detailed investigation revealed that his Danish ennoblement was spurious and the petitioner was turned down. In connection with the Austrian investigation, Beer mentioned that Wolf "had told the priests of the empress that he would convert to Christianity in Dresden, but now they realized he had not done so."[66]

As Bernhard Brilling has demonstrated, while many details of these anecdotal accounts are inaccurate, young Eibeschütz indeed was offered the title of baron by Joseph II.[67] In July 1776, Wolf petitioned the emperor. He stated that he owned an estate in Priesnitz, near Dresden, and intended to purchase more properties in German lands. He claimed that he *could have* obtained a writ of barony from the king of Denmark, but he preferred to seek the title from the Holy Roman Empire. In Wolf's petition, the issue of his religious affiliation went unmentioned.[68] Joseph II accepted the plea, and a patent for "Jonas Freiherr Wolf von Adlersthal" was issued by the Habsburg administration. However, before Wolf managed to lay hands on the document, the authorities realized that the petitioner had concealed his Jewish origins and demanded that the patent should not be accorded to him "before he publicly acknowledges his entering the Christian faith."[69] After some hesitation, Wolf decided to remain faithful to Judaism and never collected the writ of nobility.

Nevertheless, he told Elector Frederick Augustus of Saxony that he had been granted the title by the Empire; he stated that "current circumstances" did not allow him to make this fact public and only requested certain freedoms not ordinary allowed to the Jews. Thus, for instance, Wolf was given permission to live outside of Dresden's city walls (a privilege normally restricted to Christians) and to use the name Adlersthal. Official Saxon documents consistently referred to him as "Hoffaktor Wolf Jonas Adlersthal, also known as Eibeschütz."[70] Among the Jews, the conviction that Wolf indeed possessed a noble title was so strong that the first version of his marriage contract referred to him as "Herr Baron von Adlersthal hochwohlgeboren aus Dresden." In this particular case, Wolf insisted that the contract be revised to include only the name Wolf Jonas Adlersthal.[71] But popular opinion (both Jewish and Christian) persistently credited him with the title of baron and, in some cases, linked acquisition of the title with conversion to Christianity. Aside from official occasions, Wolf did nothing to quell these rumors; he even seemed to promote them. His lifestyle definitely offered food for such speculations. In Dresden, he became a familiar figure among the city's elites. No longer a Sabbatian leader, he became a fake aristocrat and, on occasion, a fake Christian.

Fascinating in itself, the story of Wolf's pursuit of barony becomes even more interesting against a wider backdrop. Wolf's petition was not the only request for a noble title by a Jew that the Habsburg authorities had to consider in 1776. A few months before being approached by Wolf, Joseph II received a petition from Jacob Frank. Frank's contacts with the emperor began a year earlier: on 19 and 21 March 1775, he was admitted, accompanied by Eve, to audiences with Joseph II; and on 22 March with Maria Theresa.[72]

After the audience with Maria Theresa, Frank visited Schönbrunn and rented lodgings in the Graben. He swam in the Danube and, accompanied by "two Cossacks and eight uhlans with standards," went for a stroll in the Prater.[73] As the Frankist chronicle had it, "the whole city was amazed."[74] A year after this first visit to Vienna, Frank moved to the city for several months and applied to the emperor for the title of count of the Holy Roman Empire. As had been the case with the petition of Wolf Eibeschütz, Joseph II initially seemed to welcome this request and ordered Chancellor Kaunitz to write to the Austrian resident in Warsaw, Revitzki, to learn more about Frank's background.[75] Revitzki responded that he did not have detailed information but only recalled rumors about Frank being a swindler who played the role of the messiah among the Jews, many of whom—even though he had been exposed—still believed in him and gave him money.[76]

A few weeks later, he inquired at the Warsaw Nunciatura and obtained a copy of the correspondence of Bishop Serra with the Holy See and minutes of Frank's interrogation at the ecclesiastical court in 1759. He forwarded both documents to Kaunitz,[77] and the emperor decided to turn Frank down.[78]

Within less than three months (April–July 1776), Joseph II received both Wolf Eibeschütz's request to become a baron and Frank's to become a count of the Empire; it is possible—although not directly confirmed by any source— that the kaiser made a connection between these two cases. Of course, Frank's situation was different from Wolf's: he was officially a Christian and a Polish nobleman. Although Frank's noble status was never formally recognized in Austria, it was taken for granted in the correspondence between Revitzki and Kaunitz. Because he had previously been ennobled, Frank was able to seek the higher rank of count, skipping the lesser one of baron—no small feat, if accomplished. But even the failure to obtain the title of count and the exposure of Frank's past did not ruin his prospects in the Habsburg monarchy. Although his petition was rejected, his noble status was uncontested; occasionally, he seemed to have implied that he was at least a "baron," and he was often thought to be one by Jews and Christians alike.

The Viennese court also did not turn its back on Frank after his failed bid to obtain a title. Frank was granted three audiences by Joseph II in 1777[79] and, on numerous occasions, visited the emperor in military encampments.[80] In November 1781, Russian Grand Duke Paul (traveling under the name Graf du Nord) visited the Frankists in Brünn together with the kaiser.[81] When meeting the emperor, Frank was usually accompanied by his daughter, and rumors about Joseph's alleged affair with Eve started to circulate.[82]

Possessing a noble rank had legal and practical consequences and was an important symbol of status. For Wolf Eibeschütz, the false barony was a passport to the salons and a valuable business asset in his dealings with Christian aristocrats and financiers. As such, Wolf's case was not common but by no means unique. In November 1775, Benjamin Hönig, scion of an important family of Moravian tobacco traders (also having Sabbatian leanings), converted to Christianity, against the will of his father and his wife, who decided to remain Jewish, and he adopted the name Christoph Bienenfeld.

Within a month after the baptism, Hönig was denounced to the authorities as an insincere Christian who continued to practice some Jewish customs or even had secretly returned to Judaism. What is more, he had assumed—without any royal authorization—the name Baron Hönig von Bienenfeld. Even though the authorities launched an initial investigation and Hönig had to flee to Saxony for a few months, the matter was soon dropped; in the early 1780s, he lived in Vienna as a Christian nobleman, and neither his religious confession nor his noble status was questioned.[83] It seems that among Christian aristocrats with whom Wolf Eibeschütz and Benjamin Hönig associated, the pretense of a title and conversion were as good as a real ennoblement and a real baptism.[84]

Eibeschütz and Hönig were rich and powerful Jews who had business dealings with even richer and more powerful Christians; their spurious noble ranks were marketing strategies utilized for social climbing. Fake ennoblements of prominent Jews might have been polite fictions that facilitated contacts and created an illusion of equality. Whereas Eibeschütz and Hönig never dared to use the titles in formal contexts or official documents, they might have been allowed to indulge their personal vanity on more informal occasions. Moreover, Hönig's self-styled title *sounded* like a joke: it is highly unlikely that anyone took the noble pretensions of Baron Honey of the Field of Bees seriously. Hönig could play an aristocrat, but it was obvious to everyone that he was only playing one.

Wolf Eibeschütz's and Benjamin Hönig's aspirations to nobility were expressions of their efforts to advance in non-Jewish society. While they both came from Sabbatian backgrounds, in their later careers they operated mainly in Christian milieus. Frank's situation was more complicated. He became a Christian and a Polish nobleman but also continued to be a leader of a Jewish sect, some members of which converted, while others remained within the formal framework of Judaism. If his pursuit of the title of count was an exercise in social mobility, it also had an impact on internal affairs within the circle of his followers. The Frankists developed a peculiar "mythology" of nobility: the noble titles granted to some of them in the wake of their conversion in Poland were also treated as status symbols within the group, and external manifestations of noble rank became one of the most important semantic codes employed in Frank's teachings. Contemporary accounts mentioned that the Frankists who converted in 1759 immediately began to dress in *żupans* (long gowns worn by Polish *szlachta*) and to buckle on sabers.[85] The traditional dress of Polish nobility became the standard garb of the Frankists, and the symbolic significance of donning the *żupan* and especially of wearing the saber was invoked by Frank on numerous occasions.[86]

The leader of the Frankists always conducted himself with ostentatious splendor and attached utmost importance to outward emblems of rank and status; most of these emblems derived from the culture of the nobility. Thus, for instance, Frank rode in an equipage pulled by six horses[87] (a privilege restricted to the pope and the emperor), wore a ceremonial sword, and was accompanied by uniformed honor guard. He was fully aware that such appropriations of symbols of nobility and his general pompousness attracted much derision and hatred; he claimed that "he was a thorn in the eyes of the Jews because of his baptism and in the eyes of the peoples [the non-Jews][88] because of the pomp of his conduct and for the grandeur of his cavalcade made of hussars and uhlans."[89]

Frank identified Polish magnates with the biblical commanders of Esau—

one of the most important symbols in his teachings.[90] The appellation by which he was called by his followers—*Pan* (Lord)—was an honorary title referenced to the nobles of Poland-Lithuania; the appellation of his daughter and wife—*Jejmość*—was a traditional honorific of Polish noblewomen. Rumors about Eve's affair with Emperor Joseph II might or might not have been true, but Frank certainly hoped for a noble match and claimed to have conducted secret negotiations to that effect: once he maintained that he had received a request for Eve's hand from the recently widowed Prince Adam Czartoryski;[91] on another occasion, he spread the word about her betrothal or even marriage to Prince Jerzy Marcin Lubomirski.[92] Among the soteriological promises that he made to his disciples, a prominent role was played by "turning all Israelites into knights"[93] and "respect in the eyes of all Polish magnates."[94] These promises culminated in a vision of the inversion of the emblems of hierarchy between the Jews and the nobility:

> You have read in your teachings that in the future times, Esau will wear the Jewish costume that we use now, such as the veil, bands,[95] etc., . . . but when you catch him you will be able to knock him down from the place where he stands to the place where you stood, and you will inherit his place, and he will stand in yours. I accepted you . . . so you would be lords [*abyście wy byli panami*], as it is said: "I will make them lords over the entire globe of the earth."[96] I wanted to tour with the whole Company from one country to another in equipages with horses wearing beautiful and lavish trappings. Everywhere we would have taken their place and they would have started to study the [Mosaic] Law.[97]

The inversion of the positions of the nobility and the Jews, in which the former turn to the Torah study and the latter travel around in costly equipages, was part of Frank's teachings about the eschatological "inversion of everything." For now, however, another aspect of the Frankist romance with nobility is important. Frankist sources meticulously documented signs of respect shown to the leadership of the sect by Polish and German noblemen, and Frank stated on many occasions that "great lords will come and will ask to speak with us, to be in my court, or at least near my court."[98]

Alas, whereas many curious aristocrats might have been willing to pay visits to Frank and show their admiration to the celebrated convert and his beautiful daughter, Christian nobles were not particularly eager to join the

ranks of the Frankists. But one great lord did indeed became a member of
Frank's court: Prince Jerzy Marcin Lubomirski, heir to one of the most distinguished magnate families in Poland. Born in 1738 and educated in École des
Cadets-gentilshommes in Lunéville, the prince became the youngest major-
general in the army of the Polish Crown. Prospects of an illustrious military
career suffered the first setback in 1757, when he deserted the command in
order to abduct and elope with a woman without the consent of her parents.
Still, Lubomirski was given a second chance: his tactical genius was recognized
by Frederick II, who appointed him a general in the Prussian military and gave
him command of a unit fighting in Silesia during the Seven Years' War.

However, the prince—who in the meantime divorced, remarried, and divorced once more—deserted again, joined the Russian irregulars, and became
chief of a band of brigands that attacked his erstwhile Prussian comrades in
arms, as well as passing merchants. Captured by the Poles, he was condemned
to death for desertion and banditry; the sentence was commuted to life imprisonment and eventually rescinded entirely. After his release, he joined in 1768
the Bar Confederation (the city of Bar was a property of the Lubomirskis), was
given the rank of field marshal, and became one of the most important leaders
of the uprising against the Russians. After the fall of the confederation, he again
switched sides, became a member of the Partition Sejm and a participant in a
committee whose task was to set new borders of the Commonwealth. After
the First Partition of Poland, Lubomirski lived in Warsaw in infamy, squander-
ing his gigantic fortune: in 1781, his debts reached the astronomical sum of
2,699,288 złotys; he officially was declared bankrupt and published the famous
Table of Debts, listing hundreds of people to whom he owed money.[99]

Lubomirski was arguably the most notorious—and certainly the most
colorful—character of eighteenth-century Polish history. Scion of an aristocratic family dating back to the fourteenth century, he was heir to one of
the largest fortunes in the Commonwealth. He managed to fritter his wealth
away; he was an adventurer and a libertine, a multiple deserter and multiple
divorcé, turncoat, gambler, and a leader of an arch-Catholic patriotic uprising,
who, among his enemies, earned the nickname "Martin Luther the apostate."

Oddly enough, Lubomirski's fate intertwined with that of Frank from the
outset. The first command he deserted was in Kamieniec Podolski, and the
prince witnessed the 1757 disputation in that city. In 1759, 150 converted
Frankists were settled on the estates of the Lubomirskis. In 1771–72, Lubomirski stayed—together with other Bar confederates—in the Częstochowa mon-
astery-fortress where Frank was imprisoned. Finally, in 1786, the ruined prince

approached Frank about becoming commander of his militia. The request was conveyed through the imperial privy councillor, Count Friedrich Karl Johannes Lichnovsky, who "mentioned to Mr. Frank the most difficult situation in which His Highness has found himself."[100] According to Lichnovsky, Frank responded that he "would be delighted to offer Your Highness the command of his personal guard, and thus contribute the splendor of Your Highness's name to the honor of his court."[101] A meeting between the parties was a contest of fancy and fashion: Frank appeared in a red silk *żupan* set with ermine and a tall fur hat adorned with heron feather and a brilliant-studded clasp, with a large diamond star shining on his chest. Lubomirski wore a white, gold, and red parade uniform of a general, with numerous decorations, including the Order of Saint Hubertus on a sash. Both gentlemen displayed "the most exquisite politeness and chivalry."[102]

Following the meeting, Lubomirski was offered—and accepted—the position of commander of Frank's guard. The prince was overjoyed and could "hardly contain his happiness": he was given "the best quarter in town, an equipage, and an adjutant with the rank of colonel."[103] He designed special uniforms for Frank's hussars, uhlans, and Cossacks, and presided over military maneuvers in which all the young Frankists had to participate. Becoming a commander in chief of Frank's personal militia was not much of an advancement for the general in the armies of Frederick II; still, the job alleviated the financial hardships of the bankrupt prince and provided a social environment for the generally ostracized adventurer.

At Frank's court, Lubomirski set up an orchestra, taught dance and polite conversation, and organized "live tableaus," in which the Frankists staged scenes from the Bible and Greek mythology. Not surprisingly, it was also reported that he had an affair with Eve, or even—according to some sources—became her husband. While the marriage between Eve and Prince Jerzy never in fact took place, the Frankists did spread the rumor concerning their betrothal, thereby building a legend of her aristocratic connections.[104]

For the Frankists, Prince Marcin opened a window for the European high culture and latest fashion. The employment of Lubomirski crowned Frank's pursuit of the trappings of nobility: he might not have succeeded in obtaining the title of count of the Holy Roman Empire, but he did manage to buy himself an authentic Polish prince. Lichnovsky correctly read Frank's aspirations: the leader of the Frankists sought to raise the status of his court by adding a true great aristocrat to it (the interesting side effect of the affair being that Lubomirski became the only non-Jewish Frankist). However, the glitter of noble rank and aristocratic connections was only one element of Frank's broader pursuit. This wider scheme can best be understood by reference to the figure of the charlatan.

The Conundrum of the Charlatan

Lazarus Bendavid, who, as noted, alleged that the son of Rabbi Jonathan had converted to Christianity and called himself a baron, believed that Wolf's supposed conversion and noble rank were merely instruments to be used in the "numerous charlataneries [*manche Charlatanerien*]" in which he was involved. Bendavid got it right: fake aristocracy and fake Christianity were indeed part of a wider pattern of Wolf's charlatanry, and the concept of the charlatan offers an invaluable key to the understanding of the fortunes of both Wolf Eibeschütz and Jacob Frank. As the *Encyclopédie* put it, charlatanry is "the vice of him who strives to recommend himself, or things belonging to him, as being endowed with imaginary qualities."

While charlatans obviously existed in every age and "every class had its charlatans," in some periods charlatanry was particularly prominent and widespread.[105] According to the author of the most comprehensive study of subject, Grete de Francesco, charlatanry was especially likely to appear in the periods of social, cultural, and scientific change, in which empirical research outran theory, and the rapid development of technology eluded the abilities of its conceptualization, let alone the possibilities of explaining it to the general public. In other words, charlatanry was likely to hold sway whenever the "fringe of the inexplicable" became especially large and the gap between those in the know and the rest of the population particularly wide.

The case in point was Wolf Eibeschütz seeing the descent of the *Shekhinah* in Halley's Comet. The reappearance of the comet toward the end of 1758 was the first time that its advent had been accurately predicted—by Halley and Clairant. All of Europe eagerly awaited its arrival, and the occurrence provoked considerable millenarian and apocalyptic speculation. Young Eibeschütz almost certainly expected it, having read about it in Christian newspapers or other publications. Wolf's prediction of the descent of the *Shekhinah* brings to mind Mark Twain's Connecticut Yankee predicting an eclipse of the sun. It was a textbook example of charlatanry: Eibeschütz used his foreknowledge of an imminent natural event in order to make an impression on the less knowledgeable, naïve, and gullible audience.

In a similar vein, after his return to Altona, Eibeschütz tried to ward off creditors by resorting to a "supernatural" means of making money. He took a bag of gold coins and had the coins smelted and the gold refined. Then he began to spread the rumor that he had mastered the science of alchemy and knew how to change copper into gold; the high-quality gold in his possession was reported to have been obtained through the alchemical process of sublimation. Altona's moneychangers thought that they had gotten wind of easy money and provided Wolf with funding, hoping to receive pure gold in exchange in the future. Indeed, a few days later, they were given bars of "gold," which were actually bars of copper plated with a layer of gold. When the moneychangers realized that something was wrong, they were told that the alchemical process was slow, the gold was still in an almost spiritual state, and, for a period of time, it should be locked in a chest without access to air until it fully materialized. Meanwhile, Wolf demanded more credit, and it was extended to him.[106]

Jacob Frank also devoted time to alchemy[107] and established a special laboratory at his court for this purpose.[108] The laboratory was said to produce large quantities of Hoffman's Liquor (a mixture of ethanol and ether), which Frank consumed daily, believing that it would make him immortal.[109] In the course of his experiments, he invented "Drops of Gold," which were supposed to be a cure for every illness.[110] The cure was produced at the Brünn court and distributed to needy Frankists elsewhere. In the Frankist sources, there is only one mention of someone actually taking the drops; sadly, before long, the patient died.[111] However, Frank continued to claim that "the wisdom of alchemy came from the *shed*.[112] Whoever drinks this Water of Gold can come to power and to Life."[113] He also made frequent use of alchemical imagery, telling his disciples, for instance, that as "the whole world seeks and desires to make gold, so I desire to make pure gold out of you."[114]

The importance of alchemy can be gathered from the fact that he derided his Sabbatian former teachers precisely for not mastering its mysteries: "On the 10th of October [17]84, the Lord, dressed in white, said: If I knew at least that you had achieved the wisdom of making gold, then I would say nothing to you. And that is what I told Rabbi Issahar and Mordechai. I will not believe that you are chosen, unless I see that you possess that wisdom."[115]

Wolf Eibeschütz's and Frank's alchemical pursuits (and their scams utilizing the belief in alchemy) were highly characteristic for their epoch. In the second half of the eighteenth century, alchemy enjoyed a special vogue and became a favorite pastime of both rich and poor. It was practiced in all European capitals and major cities. It attracted the attention of the crowned heads and the nobility, but it was also widespread among the lower strata of society. According to Georg Forster, around 1785 in Warsaw alone, there were two thousand active alchemists, "the number simply stunning for one city, even a large one."[116] In 1768, August Fryderyk Moszyński, great pantler of the Kingdom of Poland during the reign of Stanislaus Augustus, wrote a special memorandum detailing the tricks of the quacks who pretended to possess the secret of transmutation and warning the Crown not to stake its economy on the promises of the alchemists.[117] The document clearly suggests that Stanislaus Augustus *did* entertain the possibility of replenishing the coffers of the kingdom through the services of alchemists.

Indeed, needy rulers of the eighteenth century were constantly offered such services by wandering alchemists. Thus, Giacomo Casanova demonstrated his alchemical skills to Prince Charles of Courland and wrote for the prince a long description of the Magnum Opus.[118] The Comte de Saint-Germain knew how to "ameliorate" gems: on the request of Louis XV, he made pearls grow and removed flaws from diamonds without diminishing their weight or size;[119] he also offered to Frederick II a secret of transforming fine stones into precious ones.[120] In Warsaw, Josef Balsamo *vel* Cagliostro gained the king's attention: while teaching local alchemists how to fabricate pearls, he was caught (by the very same Moszyński) trying to fake an alchemical transmutation of a quantity of mercury into an ingot of silver.[121]

Wolf's and Frank's exploits resemble those of other personalities of the age. As with the affairs involving Casanova, Saint-Germain, or Cagliostro, their teachings and experiments were directed toward a public that already harbored beliefs and expectations about the nature and possibility of the alchemical process. But Casanova, Saint-Germain, and Cagliostro were much more than wandering alchemists selling their services to the needy and greedy. They belonged to the informal pan-European guild of the itinerant charlatans, whose members drifted from court to court, rotated from salon to salon, exchanging experiences, swapping mistresses, and underwriting one another's false bills of exchange. The knowledge of alchemy was only one of an international charlatan's many tools of the trade. Stefan Zweig gave the following description of his other features:

> They hear of a court, and in a trice they flock thither, the adventurers, in hundreds of masks and disguises. No one can tell you whence they come. . . . They wear brilliant uniforms, said to be those of

some Indian or Mongolian army; and they bear pompous names, false as the jewels they flaunt on their shoe buckles. They speak all languages; claim to be the familiar friends of rulers and other people of importance. . . . They devise a new trick for each court. In one, they let it be given out that they are Freemasons and Rosicrucians; in another, where the ruler has a lust for money, they claim to be extraordinarily well versed in the law of transmutation and in the writings of Theophrastus. To a prince whose chief interest is in the fair sex, they offer their services as pimps; to one who has warlike ambitions, they present themselves as spies; to a ruler with a taste for literature and the arts, they introduce themselves as philosophers and poetasters. They snare the superstitious with horoscopes; the credulous with schemes for enrichment; the gamblers with false cards; and the unsuspicious with a veneer of good breeding. But whatever role they choose, they are careful to invest it with an aroma of mystery which will make it more interesting than ever.[122]

The second half of the eighteenth century was the golden age of the charlatans: the most important representatives of this type were contemporaries and often knew one another. Zweig's description brings together the elements of the ideal type of eighteenth-century charlatan: his penchant for exotic oriental clothing, delight in fancy titles, multilingualism, bogus genealogies, his claim to have mysterious connections with ruling elites and secret societies, the ability to provide the most desired goods and services, the aura of mystery. To these, there might be added three other crucial facets: characteristic vicissitudes between extreme poverty and extreme wealth (or, on a different plane, a curious combination of radical asceticism and equally radical hedonism), a programmatically itinerant lifestyle, and a fundamentally pagan worldview.

Already Georg Forster saw Frank as yet another incarnation of the type of wandering charlatan cum alchemist cum adventurer who populated the salons and courts of the European Enlightenment.[123] The epithet "Jewish Cagliostro" was applied to Frank in the unpublished novel of Julian Brinken[124] and in the memoirs of Fritz Mauthner.[125] The parallel was further developed by Peter Beer, who pointed out the striking resemblances between Frank and Cagliostro, noting the ostentatious luxury of their dress, fake princely titles, and pompousness of their manners and conduct[126] (in this context, it should be mentioned that a testimony described Cagliostro as "looking like a Podolian ox"[127]—given Frank's origins and physiognomy, not a small similarity

indeed). Finally, Harris Lenowitz has argued that "the tradition of the charlatan . . . best configures [Frank] and his deeds."[128]

Undoubtedly, there are far-reaching parallels between Frank (and Wolf
Eibeschütz) on the one hand, and European charlatans, on the other. Wolf's
and Frank's turbans and Turkish costumes might have come from the Sabbatian tradition, but they also clearly resembled Cagliostro's "Coptic" dress
or the robes that Casanova wore during the ceremony meant to force gnomes
to bring treasures to the surface of the earth.[129] All charlatans liked to make a
show during their travels and fancied lavish equipages preceded by mounted
trumpeters; the trajectory of their travels covered most of Europe and parts
of the Ottoman Empire. Just as Joseph Balsamo became Count Alessandro di
Cagliostro or, on occasion, Count Pellegrini, and Giacomo Casanova became
Chevalier de Seingalt, so Wolf Eibeschütz became Baron von Adlersthal, and
Yankiev Leibowicz became Baron or Count von Frank. Both Wolf and Frank
were—or appeared to be—multilingual; both provided various services to the
rulers, and both were said to have mysterious connections.

The key element, rightly emphasized by Zweig, was "the aroma of mystery" with which the quack imbued his appearance and all his actions. With
respect to Jewish charlatans, this point assumes a special dimension. In her
paper on the attribution of secrecy and perceptions of Jewry, Elisheva Carlebach describes how secrecy constituted a recurrent and inevitable motif in
medieval and early modern Christian discourse on the Jews and Judaism.
She argues that even though in the eighteenth century, a "paradigm shift"
occurred and descriptions of the Jews became more realistic, thereby partly
replacing the "suspicion of secrecy" by "delight in difference," the fundamental perception of the Jews did not change during the Enlightenment,
and Jews continued to be seen as "trying to hide their inherent and essential
difference."[130] While Carlebach's conclusions seem contradictory (she argues
both for the radical "shift of paradigm" and for the fact that the "fundamental perception" remained intact), she has touched upon an important issue.
A paradigm shift with regard to the Christian association of the Jews with
secrecy undeniably occurred in the eighteenth century. However, this shift
did not transform the rejection of the Jews based on the attribution of arcane
qualities, teachings, and practices into acceptance based on a more realistic
perception.

Indeed, if there was "delight in difference" with regard to the Jews among
some circles of eighteenth-century Christian society, it was stimulated precisely
by the fascination with the secrets of the Jews. Among the upper echelons of

a society that—in the words of Leibniz—"delighted in getting to know things uncanny," secrecy turned into mystery: the very same qualities that repulsed anti-Jewish theologians of the Reformation often inspired philo-Semites of the Enlightenment. "The secret" became "the esoteric," and Jewish esoterica became part of what Krzysztof Pomian termed "the culture of *curiosité*."[131]

To be sure, Christian interest in kabbalah and Jewish esoteric lore can be traced back at least to fifteenth-century Florence. However, early Christian kabbalah was the province of a small group of erudite scholars; in the eighteenth century, it became a fad. Many important personalities actively pursued their interest in secret teachings of Judaism. To give only two prominent examples from the geographic idea of Frank's activity: Count Heinrich Brühl, who played such an important role in the early development of Frankism, owned one of the largest kabbalistic libraries in Europe; and the mistress of Augustus the Strong, Countess Cosel, not only studied kabbalah with a Jewish teacher but was reported to have secretly converted to Judaism.

If the "aroma of mystery" was one of the most important qualities of the eighteenth-century charlatan and Jews were seen as repositories of mysteries, no wonder that kabbalistic studies and other Jewish secrets became favorite components of the charlatan's persona. Casanova's links with the Jews and kabbalistic pursuits will be discussed below. Rumors about Cagliostro's Jewish extraction multiplied[132] (and the name Balsamo might have derived from the term *ba'al shem*). He himself publicly claimed to be a pupil of Shmuel Falk, the *ba'al shem* of London.[133] Saint-Germain was reported to be fluent in Yiddish,[134] and, among various parentages ascribed to him, "a Portuguese (or an Alsatian) Jew" figured prominently.[135]

Both Cagliostro and Saint-Germain were believed by many to be the newest incarnations of the immortal Wandering Jew.[136] Regardless of whether these Jewish links and lineages were true, they were believed to be true by the public: the demonic Kalifalkzherston, protagonist of Empress Catherine the Great's anti-Masonic satire *Obmanshchik* (The deceiver), was an intentional conflation of Cagliostro and Falk and was recognized as such by at least some of the play's spectators[137] (incidentally—or perhaps not so incidentally— *Obmanshchik* was translated into Polish by the interpreter of the Frankists during the Kamieniec and Lwów disputations, Antoni Kossakowski *vel* Moliwda).[138]

Against this backdrop, Wolf Eibeschütz's and Frank's contacts with the Christians appear in a different light. In contrast to many other charlatans, they both *were* authentic Jewish kabbalists who could play upon their origins and education and who often capitalized on the Christian vogue for Jewish esoterica. In the context of the discussion of the international charlatans, the best illustration of this issue is the contact between Frank and Casanova.

Frank and Casanova

Giacomo Casanova was much more than one of the many eighteenth-century charlatans: he was the theoretician and eulogist of their way of life, as well as the historian of their guild.[139] On the pages of his memoir, *Historie de ma vie*, we encounter Saint-Germain, Cagliostro, and a plethora of minor quacks. He also had some knowledge of Hebrew, numerous contacts with Jews (including intensive contacts with the "beautiful Leah"),[140] and a lifelong interest in things Jewish.[141] At the age of sixteen, he successfully defended a doctoral dissertation in canon law on the subject *Utrum hebrei possint construrere novas synagogas.*[142]

In addition to all this, he was an avid practitioner of various occult disciplines and claimed to be thoroughly acquainted with kabbalah.[143] In winter 1758, when Halley's Comet was shining in the heavens, Casanova was in Paris, embarking on one of his greatest schemes. Upon arriving in the city, he was invited to visit a great lady, the Marquise d'Urfé. During a polite conversation, the marquise expressed her deepest regret that, as a woman, she could never enter communication with elemental spirits. However, she added, there was a secret process through which a hermetic adept could cause a female soul to reincarnate into the body of a male offspring of the union between a human man and a semidivine woman. Surely, she hinted, it was not beyond Casanova's powers to perform such a union and to produce such a child.

Indeed, the operation was not beyond Casanova's powers: after long preparations, he managed to perform the union with the septuagenarian lady and to relieve her of a significant portion of her fortune.[144] But before he could embark on his arduous task, the elemental spirits themselves had to be consulted. Here is a description of Casanova's first conversation with the marquise:

> Madame d'Urfé's greatest chimera was believing in the possibility of conversing with what are called "elemental spirits." She would have given everything she possessed to acquire the art. . . . Confronted with me, . . . she thought she had reached her goal. [She asked]: "Does he [the spirit] know what secret I lock in my soul?" "Certainly, and he must tell it to me if I question him." "Can you

question him whenever you please?" "Whenever I have paper and ink; and I can even let you question him yourself. . . . Write a question addressed to him, as if you were putting it to a mortal. . . . Trembling with joy, Madame d'Urfé writes her question; I put it into figures, then into a pyramid as always, and I make her obtain the answer, which she herself puts into letters. She finds only consonants, but by a second operation I make her obtain the vowels, which she combines with the consonants, and she has a perfectly clear answer, which surprises her. I left her, taking with me her soul, her heart, her mind, and all her remaining common sense.[145]

The numerical oracle employed by Casanova during the Marquise d'Urfé affair is mentioned in several places in *Historie de ma vie*. Sometimes, Casanova explicitly disparaged its importance and admitted that he had stretched the calculations so that they produced the desired answer.[146] Often, he regarded it as a valuable tool to impress women. On other occasions, he treated its predictions with utmost seriousness and had recourse to it in making the most important decisions of his life.[147] He claimed to have learned the oracle from a hermit living on Monte Capegna; his patron, Signor Bragadin, identified it as "the Key of Solomon, known to the uninitiated as kabbalah."[148] However, nowhere in the text of his memoirs did Casanova explain the details of the procedure. Such an explication appears only in one place in his entire extant oeuvre.

On 23 September 1793, about a year and a half after Jacob Frank's death, Casanova wrote his daughter, Eve: "For a long time, I have had in my possession a numerical *Kab-Eli*, through which I can arrive at an answer (expressed in Arabic numerals) to any question that I had put in the same numerals. As I am sure you well know, the *Kab-Eli*, which means the Mystery of God, is not the same as kabbalah [*Cab-ala*], which allows only a more or less inaccurate glimpse into divine secrets. I have asked my *Kab-Eli* about you . . . and nothing that pertains to your father or to you yourself is unknown to me."[149]

Casanova followed with a detailed description the calculations necessary to obtain the answer, and concluded: "For twelve years, since my consecration, the spirit that guards this secret has been the guardian of my fortune and my guidance in all my enterprises. It was him who protected me from misfortune during the critical nineteen months in Paris. [I have been] as diligent a student of this vast discipline as your late father."[150]

The secrets of Casanova's numerology need not concern us here; indeed, they seem to have more to do with "Kab-Eli" than with Jewish kabbalah.[151] More significant, Casanova's letter to Eve clearly refers to the direct acquaintance between Frank and the Venetian adventurer: the letter was written in response to Eve's earlier communication, and in its body Casanova gently admonished Frank's daughter for "neglecting him for many years."[152] Unfortunately, no earlier correspondence between either the leader of the Frankists or his daughter and Casanova is extant.

The only scholar who attempted to establish an actual link between Frank and Casanova was Fritz Heymann, who stated that the two met in Vienna in 1784.[153] The Frankist chronicle does not mention any trips to this city between November 1781 and May 1786,[154] and it seems unlikely that a meeting in Vienna really took place. Heymann's claim was based on the improbable hypothesis that "Frank" from Brünn was, in fact, Moses Dobruschka, who indeed might have visited Vienna in 1784. The meeting must have happened elsewhere. The most likely location is Brünn. Casanova visited the city first in January 1784 and then on 30 June 1785.[155] He stayed with his friend Count Maximilian Joseph Lamberg (1729–92), who recommended Casanova to his acquaintance Johann Ferdinand Opitz (1741–1812).[156]

Casanova maintained a lively correspondence with both men; accompanied by Lamberg, he visited the Masonic lodge "Zur aufgehenden Sonne im Orient" in Brünn.[157] "Zur aufgehenden Sonne" was founded in 1782 as an "aristocratic" lodge; aside from Maximilian Lamberg and his brother Leopold, it counted among its members Count (later Prince) Karl Joseph von Salm-Reifferscheidt,[158] leader of Moravian Rosicrucians, and two members of the Mittrovský clan, which—as I mentioned in the previous chapter—supported converted Jews and acted as patrons of the Dobruschkas.[159] Casanova also had dealings with other Freemasons and benefactors of the Dobruschkas—namely, the Schönfeld family, who were printers, and from whom Moses and his siblings derived their Christian name. It was Dobruschka's godfather, Johann Ferdinand Edler von Schönfeld, who published *Soliloque d'un penseur*[160] and *Historie de ma fuite des prisons de la Republique de Venise*[161] and who, after protracted negotiations, refused to sponsor the publication of *Icosameron*.[162]

Casanova's letter to Eve alluded to Frank being a famous kabbalist and a fellow student of esotericism. The Venetian was an avid Freemason who believed that "every young man who travels, who wishes to know society, who does not wish to be inferior to another and excluded from the company of his equals in the age in which we live, should be initiated into what is called Freemasonry."[163] All his travels to Brünn were connected to the Habsburg Masonic scene.[164] The meeting between Frank and Casanova took place in a very specific milieu of Bohemian and Moravian Freemasonry. It was characteristic of the region that the ideas of the Enlightenment found little scope at the university level and were mainly transmitted through private institutions, especially the lodges of Freemasonry and its derivatives.[165] Among the latter, the "higher rites" were particularly prominent: Rosicrucian lodges multiplied, and the Bohemian Crown was probably the most important center of the Illuminati outside Bavaria.[166] No wonder the presence of Frank's court in Brünn provoked keen interest in Christian aristocrats devoted to mystical and esoteric pursuits. Before long, the Frankists developed contacts with secret societies.

Frankism and Secret Societies

In the words of J. M. Roberts, "in sheer numbers, there probably have never been so many secret sects and societies in Europe as between 1750 and 1789."[167] The connection between the Frankists and these groups has been elaborated in the works of Jacob Katz and Gershom Scholem; the focus of their investigation was the Order of Asiatic Brethren. The order known initially as Die Ritter (or Brüder) des Lichts and later as Die Brüder St. Johannes des Evangelisten aus Asien in Europa was founded in Vienna in 1780 or 1781 with the avowed purpose of creating a Masonic organization accepting both Jews and Christians in its ranks.[168] The central figures in the founding of the order were an impoverished Bavarian aristocrat, Hans Heinrich von Ecker und Eckhoffen, and Moses Dobruschka. Franz Joseph Molitor, who wrote his account of the history of the Asiatic Brethren in 1820, described the beginnings of the order:

> Die Brüder des heiligen Johannes aus Asien initially called themselves "Die Brüder des Lichts." The known leaders of the order were a certain Schönfeld, who had a great knowledge of Hebrew and Chaldean . . . and Eckhof; both of them lived in Vienna. Schönfeld was a grandson of the famous rabbi Eibeschütz from Hamburg, who was a member of the sect of Sabbatai Tsevi. After the baptism, Schönfeld became a court librarian in Vienna and inherited many rare manuscripts from his grandfather, upon which he based the rites of the Brüder des Lichts. Because of his origins and because of his knowledge deriving from these manuscripts, there was always a

connection to the sect of Sabbatai Tsevi, which had many followers
in Poland, Hungary, and Bohemia.[169]

Of course, Moses Dobruschka was not Rabbi Jonathan Eibeschütz's
grandson. However, it is true that Dobruschka developed a unique syncretic
Masonic rite mingling traditionally Christian Masonic concepts with elements
of esoteric Jewish lore and incorporating portions of Eibeschütz's Sabbatian
treatise *Va-avo ha-yom el ha-ayyin* into the ritual.[170] The syncretic character of
the order derived, according to Scholem, from Dobruschka's roots in a Sabbatian environment, where the distinctions between the two religions were
already blurred to a significant extent. Similarly, the rites of the order included
ceremonies, which, from the Jewish perspective, had a very strong antinomian
flavor, such as a ritual feast on pork and milk. In Scholem's view, these elements should not be attributed to the Christian members' desire for the Jews
to accommodate to the prevailing dietary habits of the non-Jewish society;
rather, they are indicative of the Sabbatian doctrine of ritual violation of the
principles of Mosaic Law.

In addition to the impact of Sabbatian theology on the doctrines and
rites of the order, there were also direct contacts between its members and
the Frankists. It was reported that Dobruschka brought some recruits to the
order to Frank's court in Brünn for initiation.[171] Aside from the Dobruschkas,
the previously mentioned Hönig family from Brünn and Prague was also involved in the enterprise.[172] Another ideologue of the order, Ephraim Joseph
Hirschfeld, although he did not come from a Frankist family, later moved
to the Frankist stronghold Offenbach, where he wrote his most important
work.[173]

Christian members of the Asiatic Brethren were given Hebrew names,
and various offices were designated by Hebrew terms. In addition to Christian holidays such as Christmas and the Day of Saint John the Apostle, the
Asiatics also celebrated the anniversaries of the birth and death of Moses and
Shavuot.[174] As Molitor explained, the intention behind these practices was "to
bring about religious unity by leading Christianity back to its Jewish form."[175]
Among the members were important Christian dignitaries (Prince Lichten-
stein, Count Westenburg, Count Thun), wealthy Jewish financiers from Vienna (Nathan Arnstein, Bernhard Eskeles),[176] and Rabbi Baruch ben Jacob
Schick from Shklov, who was the Hebrew translator of Euclid, a *dayan* in
Minsk, and a reformer of Russian Jewry.[177] In Silesia, the Asiatics established
the lodge Pythagoras in Troppau.[178] Indeed, the order might have been re-

sponsible for the transmission of the Jewish kabbalistic symbols that can be found in the murals in the castle in Uherčice.[179]

On the basis of the history of the Asiatic Brethren, Katz and Scholem argued that in the mid- and late eighteenth century, Freemasonry constituted the only form of a "neutral platform" accessible to both Jews and Christians; it allowed "for sociability and even the cultivation of values despite the gulf between existing religious churches and denominations."[180] Accordingly, "Jewish efforts to secure emancipation ran parallel with the history of their relations with the Freemasons."[181] If the Frankists were indeed "persecuted" by both Jewish and Christian religious establishments, they could hope to find refuge in an organization that "adopted a universalistic position, claiming that there was fundamentally only one religion common to all mankind."[182]

While Katz's and Scholem's accounts of the Asiatic Brethren offer an interesting perspective on the links between Sabbatians and Frankists (and the Jews in general) and eighteenth-century European Freemasonry, it must be said that within the framework of the Masonic history, the order was, at best, a highly controversial fringe phenomenon. From the very outset, the Asiatics were subjected to fierce attacks not only by enemies of Masonry but by prominent Austrian and Prussian Freemasons.

In July–September 1782, an international Masonic gathering convened in Wilhelmsbad. The aim of the convention was clearly to define the aims and the purpose of existence of the Masonry, to unify splintered Masonic and para-Masonic groups, and to clear up the confusion regarding conflicting and often contradictory rites and traditions. A significant part of this effort was to cleanse Masonry of unwelcome political influences and elements contaminating its Christian character. The Asiatics figured high on both scores: some of the convention's participants considered the order a "treacherous concoction of the Jesuits and a secret hideaway of ex-Jesuits";[183] others denounced it as an "impure source" polluting the flow of the truly Christian esotericism.[184]

A protest filed at Wilhelmsbad denounced Ecker as a false Christian and as a magician consorting with occult powers.[185] The fact that in the lodges of the Asiatics, Christian aristocrats rubbed shoulders with Jews made things even worse: the theoretical interest in kabbalah did not necessarily translate into the willingness to interact socially with Jews of flesh and blood. The attacks upon the order continued after the convention. Two of the attackers were particularly zealous: the Grand Master of the Austrian lodges, Prince Johann Baptist Karl von Dietrichstein; and a prominent Mason, Ignaz von Born.[186] As the Illuminati affair was developing concurrently, Dietrichstein and Born managed to persuade Joseph II to promulgate the *Freimaurerpatent* (1785), which placed Freemasonry under the emperor's protection but greatly reduced the number of permissible lodges.[187]

The *Freimaurerpatent* was a death sentence for the Asiatic Brethren in the Habsburg monarchy. Within a year, the Asiatics relocated from Austria to Schleswig. Around that time, Dobruschka left the order.[188] He settled in Vienna and started to make a fortune by furnishing supplies for the Austrian army in the Balkans. He might also have switched allegiance and joined the Illuminati,[189] since from 1786 to 1790, former members of this order were the dominant force of Moravian Masonry.[190] Dobruschka was acting under the patronage of Count Johann Baptist Mittrovský, whose nephew Johann Nepomuk attempted to transform Czech Freemasonry into a platform of support for the enlightened absolutism of Leopold II around 1791.[191]

It is beyond the scope of my analysis to dwell on the later fortunes of Moses Dobruschka and the subsequent history of the Asiatic Brethren.[192] If the real impact of the Frankists (and other Jews) upon Freemasonry was limited, the widespread perception inflated and mythologized their role. In 1781, Great Pantler August Moszyński wrote another note for King Stanislaus Augustus:

> I became convinced that there existed in the past, and maybe exists to this day, wisdom unknown to the present-day scholars; its subjects are things natural, which are commonly considered supernatural, and also traditions regarding cycles of change undergone by our planet, and finally the knowledge less inaccurate than ours of the Divine Being. . . . It is said that these teachings are contained in a Chaldean book called "The Zohar" [*le Zoar*]. However, they are expressed there in a way so convoluted and allegorical, and so demanding the knowledge of the numerical values and etymologies of the [Hebrew and Aramaic] words, that only very few Jews understand [the Zohar]. Among these who do, Falk and Frank are often mentioned; they know enough to be able to perform purely physical experiments, which however seem supernatural to people who witness them and are considered pure charlatanry by scholars who hear of them. . . . It is likely that after the destruction of the [Second] Temple, remnants of this priestly knowledge were dispersed in the Orient . . . among the Arabs . . . who transferred its tidbits to the Crusaders, especially the Templars, who in turn passed them over to

their inheritors; in the last century, the latter reappeared under the name of Freemasons.[193]

Moszyński's memo illustrates the ambiguity felt by devotees of European esotericism with regard to Jews and Judaism: on the one hand, its adherents believed Jewish secret lore to be a necessary link in the chain of transmission of the ancient wisdom; and on the other, they considered it *only* a link that was surpassed by later developments. Whereas many Freemasons might have had a side interest in the esoteric tradition of Judaism, in Jewish kabbalah they saw at best a "preface" to its Christian counterpart—just as in the "Old Testament," they saw but a preface to the New.

Still, in the late 1770s and early 1780s, Freemasonry was facing an internal crisis and dwindling membership: the hermetic craze and the infinite multiplication of degrees, systems, and rites were expressions of both the crisis itself and of attempts to overcome it. The most common response to the predicament was to search for the "Unknown Superiors," "true" initiates, transmitters of the "authentic" tradition. If Jewish kabbalistic lore was often scorned as only an introductory stage of true Christian esotericism, no one could deny its ancient roots and authenticity. The search for Oriental mysteries naturally involved contacts with those who could be seen as having borne these mysteries through the ages. Along these lines, Moszyński's memo exemplifies the growing perception that Falk and Frank were purveyors of kabbalistic secrets to Freemasons. Falk was considered by Christian theosophists "the Prince and Grand Priest of all Jews,"[194] and he might have been the prototype for the major protagonist of Lessing's "Dialogues for Freemasons," *Ernst und Falk*.[195] According to Marsha Schuchard, he "played a significant role in an ambitious effort to develop a new form of Judeo-Christian Freemasonry, in which there would be no conversionist pressures."[196] In light of the attacks on the Asiatic Brethren and other lodges accepting Jews, these "ambitious efforts" should not be overestimated.

Schuchard's imaginative description of the eighteenth-century Jewish-Christian international Masonic network reads more like a positive fantasy of modern enthusiasts of multiculturalism than a historical reconstruction. It is true that *a few* of the prominent Masons believed that the Craft might have been the route to the emancipation of the Jews without forcing them to convert to Christianity.[197] What was more significant was that even those who did not cherish such views sought channels of transmission of authentic kabbalistic teachings that might bring a solution to the crisis of European Freemasonry.

Some delegates to the Wilhelmsbad convention saw such a channel precisely in Falk's teachings: his fame and influence upon adherents of Christian
esotericism hugely exceeded his real status and importance as a Jewish kabbalist. Falk's unexpected death in autumn 1782 put an end to these hopes.[198]
I believe that after 1782, his position was partly taken by Frank. At the earliest stages of the Frankism, its leader already demonstrated admirable skill
in accommodating his strategies and teachings to the expectations of various
pressure groups. Caught between the Polish clergy and the Jewish rabbinate,
he managed to find a middle way. The Church expected a large Jewish conversion, and Frank—within two years—delivered. He was able to present heretical Jewish tenets as Christian truths to the Churchmen and to adapt Christian
ideas to the expectations of his Jewish followers.

The development of Frankism in the late 1770s and the 1780s again attested to his abilities. At the early stages of the development of the movement,
Frank utilized Christian millenarian teachings about the ultimate conversion
of the Jewish people and presented himself as a kind of apostle to the Jews;
however, during the later period, the Frankists began to use the surrounding "mythology" of secret societies and to develop relations with Freemasons.
Frank's first biographer, Hipolit Skimborowicz, mentioned in his unpublished
account of the history of Polish Freemasonry that Frank called upon his followers in Poland to seek contacts with Polish and Russian Freemasons.[199] Baptized Frankists were said to have flocked to the Masonic lodges following the
French Revolution.[200]

If Frankism clearly had some impact upon Freemasonry its derivatives,
more important (and also more interesting) was the opposite process: the influence of secret societies and their mythology upon Frankism. This process
had a twofold character. First, some of the most important tenets of Frank's
teachings were shaped by the encounter with European esotericism (to the
extent that the "gods of Freemasonry" were incorporated into the Frankist
pantheon).[201] Second, on the social and political level, Frankism was increasingly being seen through the prism of the interchange with Masonic (and
anti-Masonic) obsessions of the age. While in the 1750s and 1760s, Frankism was first perceived as a sect within Judaism and then as a movement on
the border between Judaism and Christianity, its expansion in the 1770s and
1780s was defined by the reformulation of its tenets in terms of something
that can best be called a secret society. This perception became dominant in
the early nineteenth century. Marcus Jost, in his *Geschichte der Israeliten*, described the Frankists as "a sort of an order,"[202] while Count Edward Raczyński

defined the Frankists as a "sect, which seems to have a secret aim and whose members are initiated according to various ranks or grades, similar to the ones of Freemasonry."[203]

Frank's involvement in the world of secret societies had a political dimension as well. In 1781, Joseph II concluded an alliance with Russia that was aimed at the partition of the Ottoman Empire, and the annexation of Crimea by Russia two years later sparked messianic speculations among the Sabbatians in Turkey.[204] We might assume that some of these ideas filtered through to the Frankists; *The Words of the Lord* stated cryptically, "In the year 1783 began the last days."[205] Shortly thereafter, Frank again turned his attention to the Ottoman Empire. The Frankist chronicle registers seven embassies to and from Istanbul from April 1785 until June 1786.[206]

The Frankists also developed contacts with the Judeo-Christian sect of "Abrahamites" in Bukovina.[207] As the prospects of Austro-Turkish war loomed, the idea of utilizing the Frankist network of contacts in the Ottoman Empire seems to have been floated again. Reportedly, Frank had conversations with Joseph II regarding the Jews being armed by Austrians and used against the Turks.[208] There is some indication that the concept of giving the Frankists an autonomous area in captured Ottoman territory, raised for the first time in Poland in 1759, began to be considered again.[209]

The extant sources do not allow us to say much more. Whatever happened, something must have gone wrong. Frank quarreled with Joseph II, who ordered a detailed investigation into the affair of the Brünn court by the local commissioner of police. The inquiry did not reveal any wrongdoing, demonstrating to the emperor only the "pure fanaticism of the Jews who hold the Pole Frank a prophet."[210] However, following the investigation, Joseph instructed the leader of the Frankists to send away all his foreign followers and pay all his debts.[211] After desperate fund-raising among followers in Constantinople, Warsaw, and Prossnitz, Frank paid all his creditors and left the Habsburg monarchy on 12 February 1786, heading for Frankfurt am Main.

Chapter 9

The Ever-Changing Masquerade

Das Gotteshaus in Offenbach

The last quarter of the eighteenth century saw the decline of Frankism as it had existed during Frank's time. Although Frankist communities survived long into the nineteenth century, the movement lost much of its homogeneity and splintered into disparate groups. At that time, Frankism had three main focal points: Offenbach, where Frank lived the last four years of his life and where he established the court that served as a pilgrimage center for followers from different countries; Warsaw, where the majority of the converted Frankists lived; and Prague, whose importance grew as that of Offenbach waned.

Accounts pertaining to this period attest to the birth of rumors, legends, and stories that surrounded the sect and its leadership (and that also found their way into later scholarship). Offenbach's citizens knew very little about Frank's origin, teachings, and intentions. Nor did the residents of Warsaw, although better informed, always retain a clear recollection of the events surrounding the two disputations that had taken place more than thirty years earlier. They had virtually no knowledge of Frank's whereabouts and fortunes after he left Poland, and their opinions were based on interactions with the second generation of converts, who were already deeply integrated, *mutatis mutandis*, into Polish society. Polish and German accounts of the last years of Frank's life and the years following immediately thereafter add little new information regarding Frankist doctrine. They do, instead, provide an opportunity to analyze the formation of the movement's collective memory and the way that the Frankists sought to present themselves to the surrounding non-Jewish society.

Frank left Brünn for Frankfurt am Main, where he met Prince Wolfgang

Ernst II of Isenburg-Birstein. Contact with the prince might have been established through Masonic channels prior to Frank's arrival: the prince was a Rosicrucian, and, through a relative of his who was married to Baron Bender, the commandant of the Olmütz fortress, he had numerous connections with Freemasons and Illuminati in Brünn.[1] It is also possible that Frank first met Wolfgang Ernst through Joseph II, to whom the prince served as an adjutant.[2]

Initially, Frank was granted permission to come to Offenbach together with sixteen people.[3] It was agreed that the Frankists would settle in the unused castle belonging to the prince and that they would be exempted from the jurisdiction of the local police. Some accounts also claim that, along with the castle, Frank was granted the title of baron, which he used in Offenbach. As the castle needed refurbishment, Frank stayed temporarily in the nearby village of Oberrad. More of his followers came to join him there, and his entourage began to grow, reaching between two and three hundred people.[4] On 3 March 1787, when the castle was ready to accommodate residents, Frank finally moved in.[5]

The manner of Frank's entry to the city provided rich material for gossip and speculation. According to a report written in 1866 by the grandson of an eyewitness, the Frankists arrived in five equipages surrounded by riders. A mounted herald, escorted by two pages dressed in green and gold, led the procession. Frank himself, accompanied only by his interpreter and dressed in a high fur cap and a long red cape, adorned by a diamond-studded clasp, followed in a coach pulled by six horses. His coach was followed by another, carrying Eve, who wore a costly green dress embroidered with pearls and diamonds. Armed, uniformed guards surrounded the whole procession. Among the guards rode Roch and Joseph, Frank's two sons, wearing the insignia of high-ranking Russian officers. On Frank's arrival, the gate of the castle opened and a precious carpet was spread on the ground. The entourage fell on its knees as one man, and Frank and his daughter entered the castle.[6] In Częstochowa, Frank promised that "the Maiden" would open for the Frankists "the gate to the House of God." Accordingly, the Offenbach castle, Eve's residence, was dubbed the *Gotteshaus*.

The Frankists' life in Offenbach began at once to follow a strict regime. No one had free access to the castle. Heavy curtains covered the windows. A section of the castle was turned into an alchemical laboratory, where mysterious experiments took place. The yard in front of the building became a parade ground on which military maneuvers were executed; every day, young Frankists could be seen training with weapons. On the rare occasion when someone from outside of the sect was permitted to enter the castle, he would be escorted to a guarded room, where Frank, always accompanied by an interpreter, sat on an ottoman smoking a water pipe. While his followers wore Western uniforms, Frank always dressed according to the "Turkish" fashion: he wore yellow slippers, long, wide, red trousers, and a Turkish caftan set with ermine. A high fur cap was always set upon his head.[7]

Every day at four o'clock, a carriage with outriders left the castle for the nearby forest, where religious ceremonies were conducted. The carriage was reportedly accompanied by children wearing red and white turbans, by armed pages in Polish and Hungarian uniforms, a little Chinese man carrying a sun umbrella, and "a curious procession of half-Turks, Greeks, Poles, Hungarians, and Armenians." Eve sat in the second carriage with a boy dressed up as Amour holding a small bow and quiver. Their coach was escorted by young women in "Amazon" uniforms with solar emblems on their garb, and accompanied by three men, one bearing the emblem of a wolf, another of a deer, and a third wearing a golden crescent on his chest. The whole parade was led by a "waterman," who sprinkled the road in front of Frank's coach.[8] The windows of both carriages were kept covered with thick green curtains. It is reported that on one occasion, the curtain fell down and Frank was seen wearing the attire of the Jewish High Priest, with the Urim and Thummim on his chest.[9]

Because there was not yet a Roman Catholic church in Offenbach, Frank traveled to the nearby village of Bürgel on Sundays and Catholic holidays to attend services. When the Frankists used the Bürgel chapel, armed sentries barred outsiders from entry.[10] It was noticed that during the Catholic service, Frank never bared his head and that he prayed prostrate on a carpet.[11] The Frankists also took daily ritual baths, in summer in the river Main,[12] and in winter in a bathhouse, which they refused to share with either Jews or Christians.[13]

Aside from the daily parade and the trips to Bürgel, Frank seldom strayed from the castle. His only noteworthy public appearance during the Offenbach period was a trip to Frankfurt for the coronation of Leopold II, where he stunned the public with his Oriental splendor and was treated as one of the peers of the Empire. In contrast, Eve often ventured out to visit local residences and established some contacts with Offenbach's polite society. She was always vague about her past, but her cultivated manners, piano playing, skills at embroidery, and fluent French led people to assume that she came from an aristocratic background. Offenbach's poor also praised her generosity: she gave alms and supported various charitable cases. A special secretary was assigned to deal with written requests for assistance, and a large portion of the Frank family revenue was allocated to philanthropy. Contributions for ecclesiastical purposes were particularly generous, and the first Roman Catholic chapel in Offenbach was established and decorated thanks to Eve's assistance.[14]

In Offenbach, Frank's health gradually deteriorated. In 1788 and 1789, he suffered two strokes but recovered, only to succumb to a third attack on 10 December 1791. Frank's "departure" was no less pompous than his arrival. Bells were rung in all the churches of Offenbach. The body lay in state on a catafalque surrounded by silver candelabra for two days. The coffin was upholstered with red satin and adorned with golden crowns. Frank was dressed in his red robe and ermine mantel, with a diamond star on his chest. His hands grasped a golden cross. On the third day, the procession left the castle. Two hundred women, all dressed in white, with white ribbons in their hair, carried candles. The coffin followed, borne by pages in white and surrounded by armed guards, wearing white armbands on their sleeves. They were followed by Frank's sons, Prince Lubomirski with a large star of the order of Saint Hubertus on his chest; and Eve's equipage, escorted by the Amazon guards. Other male members of Frank's court brought up the end of the procession.[15] It was explained to the curious public that on his deathbed, Frank forbade his following to wear black clothes as a sign of mourning.[16]

Early nineteenth-century newspaper reports and memoirs are difficult to verify. For the most part, the accounts were written not by eyewitnesses but by their children and grandchildren. Some elements are clearly distorted—it is, for instance, very unlikely that Frank was ever surrounded by a crowd of the "Chinese, half-Turks, Greeks, Poles, Hungarians, and Armenians." Other aspects correspond to credible testimonies from earlier phases of the movement: while still in Poland, Frank had the habit of lying flat on a carpet during Catholic services and would entertain his guests while sitting cross-legged on pillows and smoking a water pipe. Many details are confirmed by sketches and etchings executed during Frank's lifetime that clearly show Frank's "Turkish" and Eve's "European" manner of dress. These also attest to the presence of children wearing turbans and of the waterman in their entourage and document many details of the funeral description quoted above.

My aim is not to verify the factual accuracy of the early accounts of Frankism in Offenbach but to analyze the way in which these accounts presented the movement and, correspondingly, the way the Frankists presented themselves to the public. Although often distorted and exaggerated, these early reports demonstrate how—for the first time since the inception of the movement—

Frankism was removed from its original Jewish context. Observers in Poland and Moravia knew the true origins of Frank and his following. In contrast, Offenbach's residents and visitors to the city—with very few exceptions— genuinely did not know who the Frankists were or where they came from. The Frankists in Offenbach were known as "Poles" ("Pohlen" or "Polacken"),[17] while Frank was referred to as "Baron von Franck,"[18] "the Old Lord" ("der alte Herr"),[19] or "the Polish prince" ("polnischer Fürst," "Polackenfürst").[20] Their noble status and their Polish origin were never questioned. Even when the first reports on the Jewish background of Frankism reached Offenbach, the major- ity of the town's residents refused to accept them; as one irate burgher put it: "According to Lady Eve von Franck's own testimony, the Old Lord was the foster father of the three children. The claim, voiced in the article 'Der heilige Herr,' which depicts the von Franck family as converted Jews and goes so far as to claim that Lady Eve's former Jewish name was 'Rachel,' is completely unfounded; neither the family nor, especially, Lady Eve von Franck ever dis- played in their personalities, manners, and conduct anything that would seem remotely Jewish. Eve Frank's manners were that of a born princess."[21]

Clearly, people in Offenbach simply did not want to believe that "their" Baron von Franck was, in fact, a converted Jew.[22] Those who thought that the Frankists belonged to the Polish nobility assumed that their stay in Offenbach was linked to the partitions of the Commonwealth: "One more word about Of- fenbach. We saw there many of that strange sect whose patriarch was buried last year with royal pomp and exotic ceremonies. They form a separate community; about a thousand of them, I was told, partly armed. . . . The most reasonable of many contradictory assumptions seems to be that these are some wealthy fami- lies of Polish nobility who left Poland on account of the internal disorders in re- cent years. In order to wait undisturbed for the time for their safe and profitable return to their motherland, they have adopted the form of a religious sect."[23]

The normative religious status of the group went unchallenged. The Frank- ists observed all the Catholic holidays, baptized their children, and buried their dead in the Catholic cemetery. It was noted, however, that the Frankists must have belonged to a sect, since, in addition to Christian ceremonies, they observed many other religious customs.[24] Of course, the ostentatious wealth of Frank's court, as well as its exotic rituals, bred gossip and speculations. No one seemed to know Frank's true identity, and no one could understand his re- lationship with Prince Wolfgang Ernst.[25] However, the local population could not believe that a ruling prince would allow an unknown adventurer to stay in his castle and to keep an armed guard.[26]

Some pointed to Rosicrucian or Illuminati connections.[27] Others emphasized the possibly sectarian character of the Frankist group and noted the tradition of religious tolerance characteristic of the House of Isenburg-Birstein: the prince whose ancestors had offered asylum to the Waldensians and the Huguenots was thought likely to grant refuge to a members of another allegedly persecuted religious minority.[28] Yet others thought that the impoverished prince badly needed cash and had sold the castle to the fabulously rich Frank for the sum of three million guldens.[29] This last line of thought, however, led to other questions. The sources of Frank's wealth remained unclear. The Frankists did not undertake any paid work in Offenbach, and it was noted that every few weeks, coaches filled with barrels of gold arrived from the East.

All this led to the reawakening of the legend of the royal ancestry of the Frank family. The legend was already in circulation while the Frankists were in Brünn. However, the story did not gain a proper footing until they settled in Offenbach. Some believed that Frank was really the dethroned Czar Peter III, miraculously rescued. Others could not come to terms with the inexplicable discrepancy between Frank's Oriental dress, awkward manners, and inability to speak proper German,[30] and Eve's fluent French, mastery of music and embroidery, and skill at holding a cultivated conversation. It was believed that Eve, or, in another version, Eve and her two brothers, were in reality the illegitimate children of Czarina Elisabeth and Prince Alexiey Rasumovsky.[31]

Rumor had it that Frank had been appointed by the Russian Royal House as the children's guardian and that Prince Wolfgang had received a large sum in exchange for offering him asylum. It was assumed that the barrels of gold, which arrived regularly in Offenbach, came from Russia. Frank's death did not inhibit the spread of the legend. Indeed, even the children of the 1759 converts who came from Poland to Offenbach in the last decade of the eighteenth century were told that the "von Frank family descends from a great monarch":[32] the Jewish origins of the leaders were concealed even from some of the second or third generation of the followers of Frankism, to whom the legend of royal ancestry was marketed.

The financial situation of the Frankist court began to deteriorate rapidly. Eve incurred numerous debts with local merchants while the transports of money no longer arrived as frequently as before and ceased altogether around 1796. Local gossip promptly connected this to the death of Catherine the Great.[33] As the creditors refused to go away, Eve, Roch, and Joseph posted an announcement in January 1800 saying that on the invitation of the Russian Royal House, Roch von Frank would leave for a six-month journey to

Petersburg in order to obtain funds to satisfy all creditors. Although Roch did not bring back any money, the trip strengthened the belief in mysterious connections with the Russian court. The rumors intensified when the Frankists were visited in Offenbach by Czar Alexander I on his way from the Battle of Nations in 1813.[34]

However, the finances of the Franks were already in catastrophic condition. Joseph Frank died in 1807 and Roch in 1813, and the leadership of the court was left solely in the hands of Eve. At that point, the legend of the royal lineage of Frank's family was virtually the only way to ward off her creditors. Eve's cutlery was engraved with the monogram "E.R.," which was supposed to stand for "Eve Romanovna,"[35] and she started to sign letters to creditors with the same initials.[36] Finally, the debt reached the sum of 800,000 guldens, and Eve was put under house arrest.[37] The court proceedings against Eve ceased with her death on 7 September 1816. Although the creditors went away empty-handed, the legend of the royal lineage persisted. The entry in the books of Offenbach's Catholic parish reads: "Den 7. September starb Fräulein Eva von Franck Romanowna und wurde den 9. ejus[dem] men[sis] begraben, alt ohngefähr 56 Jahr."[38]

Local mythologies develop according to their own logic, and it would be beyond the scope of the present discussion to dwell too long on the posthumous life of Frankism in Offenbach. More important in the present context is that in Offenbach, we find yet another demonstration of the Frankist ability to accommodate to surrounding customs and to fulfill the expectations of the public. The Offenbach version of Frankism fed on early romantic sentiments. Sectarian and magical features are not only much more pronounced than they had been in earlier phases of the movement but also seem to have been emphasized by the Frankists themselves. Whereas in Poland the Frankists tried to mask their sectarian character and to give the impression of being faithful Christians, in Offenbach, they created a kind of sectarianism for sale in order to satisfy the taste for religious exotica. If earlier the parallel was drawn between Frank and the adventurers of the Age of Enlightenment such as Cagliostro, it was now replaced by the comparison to Kaspar Hauser, the mysterious foundling of allegedly royal descent.[39] Frank's court was known to Goethe, who described it as a "masquerade,"[40] and also to Bettina Brentano, who remarked in a letter:

> [Offenbach] has changed into some kind of a magical tale. . . . A
> mystical nation wanders the streets in strange, colorful clothes, old

men with long beards, wearing purple, green, and yellow robes, young beautiful boys in gold, one half of the leggings green, the other one yellow or red. They ride horses with silver bells on their necks; in the evenings they play guitars and flutes under the window of their beloved. . . . A prince at the head of these people, with silver beard and long white robes, rests on luxurious carpets and pillows in front of the gates of his castle, surrounded by his court. Each person wears the emblem of his function and status.[41]

The romanticization of Frankism shortly before Frank's death and in the following years went deeper, however. In the last decade of the eighteenth century, Frankism had profoundly changed its character. This change found its expression in two main sources: the Red Letters and a manuscript titled *The Prophecies of Isaiah.*

At the very end of the century, the Frankist leadership in Offenbach dispatched circular epistles to Eastern and Central European Jewish communities. Some were written in red ink; on this basis, Peter Beer, the first scholar to analyze the dispatches, coined their name, under which they became known also in later scholarship.[42] The first copies reportedly started to circulate around 1798,[43] but most of the letters can be dated to January 1800. The epistles included a full text of two letters written by Frank during his imprisonment in Częstochowa in 1767–68, which I discussed earlier, a short commentary thereupon, and another lengthy message signed by three "elders" of the Offenbach court: Franciszek Wołowski (Solomon ben Elisha Shorr), Michał Wołowski (Nathan ben Elisha Shorr), and Jędrzej Dębowski (Yeruham ben Hananiah Lippman of Czarnokozienice). The message was addressed to "the entire House of Israel" and purported to be a "final warning" to heed Frank's calls in the Częstochowa letters; it predicted terrible catastrophes about to befall the Jews and claimed that the "the faith of Edom" would soon become the only refuge for the Jewish people.

Drawing upon talmudic and midrashic material, the signatories stated that the imminent tribulations heralded the advent of the messiah, whose coming demanded the abolishment of the Torah and "turning the entire kingdom to heresy."[44] Jewish tradition commonly understood this talmudic phrase as a reference to the takeover of pagan Rome by Christianity, and the Frankists interpreted it as describing the necessity for all Jews to become Christians. They portrayed the founder of their sect as the incarnation of the biblical Patriarch Jacob, who "went to Edom" (that is, embraced baptism), thereby fulfilling the promise given to Esau and showing the way for the people of Israel. Quoting the Zoharic statement that "Jacob our father did not die,"[45] they maintained—nine years after his funeral—that Frank "surely is not dead."[46]

This was probably intended to counter the spread of the news of his demise among Sabbatian believers in remote countries, but it also served as the justification and legitimization of Eve's leadership of the movement: once Frank was relegated to the purely spiritual sphere of the immortals and, as it were, "canonized," Eve was to hold all the powers in the material world. Accordingly, the epistles stated that Jacob had "found Rachel" and presented Frank's daughter as the fulfillment of messianic expectations and the key figure in the profound political changes that were about to occur.[47] This political aspect of the letters was arguably their most pronounced dimension: Gershom Scholem interpreted them as a "mystical theory of revolution."[48]

The Red Letters did not exert much influence upon Jews; the main Jewish response to them, Rabbi Eleazar Fleckeles's *Ahavat David*, will be discussed in the next section. However, they aroused anxious reactions among the non-Jewish authorities. In 1786, Habsburg authorities in Hungary were already expressing fears that the "so-called Frankist sect [*Frankische Secte*] attempts to create confederations among the Jews. Under the guise of the opposition to the Talmud, they undermine the Roman emperor and praise the Turkish rule."[49] The Red Letters revived these fears. Although the dispatches were sent from various places so as not to attract too much attention,[50] copies were discovered and investigations were launched. On 28 February 1800, the Austrian royal commissioner of Western Galicia, Count Frederick Trauttmannsdorff, wrote to the minister of state and police, Count Johann Anton Pergen, reporting proclamations that had inspired unrest among the Jews. He also contacted the governors of the Prussian and Russian partitions of Poland and requested information about similar proclamations in the areas under their rule.[51]

The Russians had already embarked upon their own investigation. In early March of 1800, the governor of Podolia, Kiev, and Wolhynia, Count Ivan Vasilyevich Gudovich, was handed a copy of an intercepted letter addressed to the Jewish community of Kamieniec Podolski. He had it translated into Russian. Although he determined that the letter contained "nothing exciting or disturbing the peace," except the call for the Jews "to join a new sect called Edom" (the translator either missed or intentionally misrepresented the allusion to Christianity), the governor decided to pay close attention to developments among the Jewish population of the province.[52] Emperor Paul I was informed about the investigation and ordered Gudovich to keep an eye on the

Jews and to ascertain if "under the veil of religion they do not conceal other dangerous relationships."[53]

The Russian and Austrian authorities were worried by the Red Letters' obscure allusions to wars and bloodshed (which might well have been interpreted as calls to arms to liberate Poland from the partitions) and the sheer scale of their dissemination: the Russians intercepted at least twenty-four copies of the Red Letters addressed to the communities of Podolia and Wolhynia,[54] while the Austrians seized forty copies at the Kraków main post office alone.[55] In response to Trauttmannsdorff's writing, the Russian civil governor of Lithuania, Friesek, prepared a short account of the Frankists, mainly based on a chapter in Calmanson's recently published *Essai sur l'état actuel des Juifs de Pologne et leur perfectibilité* (1791).[56] However, he satisfied himself with stating that Frankism was some kind of scheme to extort money from naïve Jews.[57]

At that juncture, the third partitioning power, the Prussians, also entered the fray. The Prussian resident in Warsaw was informed that "a new sect is attempting to take control of the synagogues in the former Poland" and told to "keep close watch on the spread of this suspicious sect and to inform the Royal Cabinet about any new developments."[58] Frederick Wilhelm himself took an interest in the affair and instructed his *chargé d'affaires* in Frankfurt, Councillor Formey, to conduct an investigation in Offenbach.[59] Formey's preliminary report focused on the financial aspects of the movement and—like Friesek's account—portrayed the Frankists as a scam: the so-called Baron Frank had been given permission to settle in Offenbach because of the impression that he was rich and could contribute to the economic well-being of the city.

Indeed, at first the group received large sums, which always arrived in barrels full of cash, bypassing the banking system. However, after Frank's death, it turned out that he had been an impostor and a bankrupt who had contracted large debts. His daughter tried to save the situation by claiming that she was "a natural sister of the Russian czar" and insisted upon being addressed as princess, though the investigation launched by the local authorities revealed that Eve Frank had no connection whatsoever to the Russian royal family.[60]

The authorities in Berlin were not satisfied with the report and urged that the inquiries be deepened and accelerated.[61] This demand produced a supply: Formey's second report concentrated on the political elements: the sect was said to use religious enthusiasm (*religiöse Schwärmerey*) as a cover for unknown political purposes. The councillor reported that the prince of Isenburg let the Frankists become "a veritable state within the state [*statu*(*s*) *in statu*]."[62] He gave a detailed description of the military organization of the Offenbach court and conjectured that the young Frankists' training with weapons might be preparation for an uprising aimed at liberating Poland from Prussian rule.[63] Roch Frank's trip to Saint Petersburg and rumors that the barrels of gold had been sent from Russia also raised suspicions that Frankism might be a Russian anti-Prussian plot. Formey described how the Frank siblings sent circular letters to the Jewish communities of former Poland. According to him, the letters called for the unity of different religions under the common leadership of a sect called Edom; the sect was to consist of Jews and Christians, removing any differences between these two religions.[64] The report concluded: "In these times, the sect's political aims deserve special attention. Yet at this point, it is impossible to say anything specific about these aims. The Frankist sect [*Franckeshe Secte*] is rumored to be in close contacts with the Freemasons, Illuminati, Rosicrucians, and Jacobins. . . . However, so far we have not managed to discover any such links, either by written correspondence, or personal connections, or any other means. Neither did we find . . . signs of contact with French, German, or Polish [subversive] propagandists."[65]

Formey's inability to establish connections between the Frankists in Offenbach and subversive political movements and societies did not allay Frederick Wilhelm's concerns; shortly after receiving the councillor's report, the king issued the following rescript:

> In 1767 and 1768 and also later, a certain Frank traveled to Moravia, to Olmütz and other towns and, although his means remained unknown, lived in great luxury. The man was then thought to be leader of a sect or the secret agent of an unknown power. Recently, there have appeared proclamations of a previously unknown Jewish sect, which intends to unify different synagogues under its control; in these proclamations, Joseph Frank is also considered head of the sect. As in the present times, everything that relates to secret societies, associations formed under unknown auspices, religious and political enthusiasms [*religiöse und politische Schwärmereyn*], demands double attention, and especially as there are also numerous testimonies that the secret societies always operate in silence and darkness, each using for its own purpose the means of the propagandists of the Jacobin crimes and atrocities; the presence of the Jews in so many countries can be employed in accord with time and opportunity as a means of spreading their treacherous tenets. . . . Therefore, we order the proclamations of the new sect that calls itself Edom

and comes from the vicinity of Offenbach, Düsseldorf, and Dud-
erstadt, and other places where the aforementioned Frank acted
be investigated and that the government be immediately informed
about the activities, tenets, and aims of the Sect of Edom, and of
everything that has the slightest connection with the late Frank and
his so putative daughter.[66]

The pendulum swung: parallels with secret societies or links to them,
which, during the Moravian phase of Frank's activity, served as a magnet for
curious aristocrats, began to work to the Frankists' disadvantage. What had
been thought of as appealing and innocent exotica before the French Revolution now became associated with the dangers of Jacobinism.

It is of particular interest that in describing the Frankists, Formey used
the phrase "a state within the state." The formula, coined against the Huguenots in the mid-seventeenth century, gained wide currency some hundred
years later, when it became commonly employed first against the Jesuits and
then against the Freemasons.[67] In Fichte's analysis of the revolution in France
(1793), the phrase acquired distinctly anti-Semitic overtones: "A mighty state
stretches across almost all the countries of Europe, hostile in intent and engaged in constant strife with everyone else . . . this is Jewry."[68]

In the last decade of the eighteenth century, Prussian administration officials used the formula "a state within a state" in their debates about proposed
reforms and the potential abolishment of restrictions against the Jews;[69] it is
possible that Formey—who was a Prussian administration official—knew of
these debates. If not, he was certainly familiar with the usage of the phrase
with reference to Freemasons. Representatives of the three partitioning powers who become involved in investigations concerning the Red Letters saw
Frankism not as a religious but essentially as a political phenomenon. Frank,
earlier portrayed as a false messiah, came to be suspected of being the "secret
agent of an unknown power." The Frankists were presented as a transnational
spy network. Frankist doctrine and rituals were assumed to be masks conceal-
ing the true political (and most likely revolutionary or subversive) face of the
movement.

In internal Frankist sources, this shift from the religious to the political
dimension found its fullest expression in the book *The Prophecies of Isaiah*. The
manuscript, which was composed sometime after the French Revolution,[70]
is now lost, but large portions of it are reproduced in Kraushar's book on
Frankism. Its full title read: *Proroctwa Izaiiaszowi [sic], wielkiemu Prorokowi,*

jednemu z członków Świętego Sanedrin [sic], przy jego Tabernakulum, przez wiel-
kiego Szaday z białej magii objawione (Prophecies revealed to Isaiah, the great
prophet, one of the members of the Holy Sanhedrin, at his Tabernacle, by the
Great Shadday of the white magic). The book presents a collection of revelations concerning the end of days "given by the Lord [Frank] to Isaiah, that
is to say, to himself through his external image."[71] The poetics of the work is
very different from that of *The Words of the Lord*: the register is much more
formal, the style elevated, and the text abounds in biblical allusions and paraphrases. The imagery draws mainly upon Lamentations, the book of Isaiah,
and the Revelation of Saint John, presenting an apocalyptic vision of impending wars and catastrophes: countries will be overrun and made desolate, cities
ruined and burned, harvests destroyed.[72] The Frankists attempt to dissociate
themselves from any link to subversive secret societies. Thus the manuscript
attacks "dishonest Masons"[73] and states that "all these false fishermen, who try to
lure people to various sects, associations, and societies, will be exposed and punished."[74] Yet concrete political references and predictions, very scarce in *The Words
of the Lord*, are abundant in *The Prophecies of Isaiah*. Biblical peoples and locations
are identified with present-day nations and countries. The text comments upon
the revolutionary unrest in France ("the Land of the Philistines") and the death of
Louis XVI ("King Ahaz"),[75] foretells disasters awaiting Germany ("Egypt"),[76] and
a great war with the Turks ("Elom").[77]

Messianic hopes, earlier connected to Poland, are now tied to Germany
and Austria: "All Egyptians [Germans] will come to the Lord, will follow him,
and will call for him and cry for him. Then the Lord will have mercy upon
them and will bring them all to Life. . . . Then Egypt will unify with Assyria
[Austria], and the true Israelites will be the unifying point between the Assyr-
ians and the Egyptians."[78]

On several occasions, the text refers to the forthcoming fall of the Holy
Roman Empire and the papacy. The disintegration of official Christian institutions, however, does not mean that Christianity as such will collapse. To
the contrary, it is the non-Christian religions that will be abolished: "The om-
nipotent God will suddenly, in one day, link the head with the tail; He will
destroy and eradicate all religious systems, customs, and rites, and bring everything under the rule of Christendom."[79] Since the Jews, who have been long
deceived by their leaders,[80] have become the nation that is most unholy and
most remote from God,[81] the breakdown of the non-Christian religions refers
first and foremost to Judaism: "The false religion of the Israelite nation" will be
completely eradicated,[82] and all Jews will convert to Christianity.[83]

Frank never looked for followers outside the Jewish fold, nor was he interested in aggressive proselytizing. *The Prophecies of Isaiah* departs from that
policy and proclaims the ultimate recognition of Frank by members of other
religions: "The time will come when numerous foreigners from different countries and nations, and especially from Greece [Russia], will join the chosen
ones. They will come straight to the house of Jacob, and it will be revealed that
they serve him, whom the worshipers of Jacob serve, and that they—among
other peoples—also worship only the true Jacob."[84]

Frank—to whom *The Prophecies of Isaiah* refers as "the true" or "the second" Jacob—is deified: "You of the House of Jacob! Of the House of the
second, hidden Jacob! Approach [him] and reveal to the entire world that
you saw your God, your Jacob, in human form."[85] He has the power to re-
deem the sins of the peoples[86] and is the "Lord of eternal life."[87] Frank went
to Germany to "shed his human form and clothe himself in divinity, so that
he could triumph over death."[88] A new aeon will begin with Frank's second
coming; he will soon return to earth to judge all nations.[89] Then will follow
the final revelation of "the true Rachel"[90] (Eve): "He will lead us on his holy
path of Jacob, where none can be perplexed, none can fall, because from this
holy Zion, from this double cave, from this mountain, she will reveal herself.
She! She will abolish all the laws and will pronounce the first, unknown word
of God, which will permeate the New Jerusalem."[91]

In comparison with *The Words of the Lord*, *The Prophecies of Isaiah* sounds
banal and derivative: the colorful world of Frank's tales was replaced by a
common stock of apocalyptic images. The book was composed by epigones
who could not match the originality of Frank's imagination. The degeneration
of the doctrine was paralleled by changes in the social profile and the style of
the leadership of the sect. The changes that took place at the Offenbach court
after Frank's death closely follow the classical Weberian paradigm of the rou-
tinization of charismatic authority.[92] Since Frank's leadership was based on his
personal qualities, by its very nature it was unstable and could be maintained
only in direct contact with his followers.[93]

Consequently, after his death, the leadership of the court had to be institutionalized. In full accordance with Weber's model, this institutionalization
took on a threefold form. First, Frank's children and a few of their closest
associates appropriated controlling powers and economic advantages, at the
same time eliminating the potential and existing opposition of other followers. Second, a canon of Frankist teachings was instituted. In this process, some
elements present in the documents from Brünn were discarded, and Frank's

biography was given its canonical form, often employing quite far-reaching distortions. Finally, the membership of the group as well as the recruitment of new members was regulated to suit the needs of the new leadership and the new structure of the sect.[94]

The account of Moses Porges, who arrived in Offenbach from Prague in 1798, attests to these developments. Porges's adventure with Sabbatianism began when, at the age of fourteen, he was initiated into the sect in Prague. Three years later, he was sent to Offenbach. Porges's testimony documents social developments corresponding to the doctrine expounded in *The Prophecies of Isaiah*. At that time, Frank was indeed considered divine, and a section of the Offenbach castle was dedicated to his cult.[95] The daily life of the residents of the court was minutely regulated, with specific times allocated to military training, prayer, and various other obligations. Everyone was given a special function and a uniform. Visitors were expected to bring costly offerings to Frank's children and were sometimes forced to donate all their possessions.

Only Frank's sons engaged in orgiastic practices; common members of the court were forbidden to have any contacts with the opposite sex at all. Other antinomian activities were strictly regulated, and rulers of the court charged a fee for permission to perform them. For example, Porges was allowed to cut his beard on the Sabbath and paid a fee of six hundred florins for this privilege.[96] Iron discipline was introduced. Nevertheless, disillusionment with Frank's children was growing, and escapes from the court grew more frequent. Some of the deserters were caught and severely punished.[97] Many believers were set on leaving the court but had been robbed of the means by which to return to their faraway homes.[98]

Porges mentions the compilation of *The Prophecies of Isaiah*, ascribing the book to Abraham, Akiba, and Joseph Wehle from Prague.[99] He also offers a few remarks on the Sabbatian doctrine that was taught in Prague. Until the time of his initiation, Porges was a fully observant Jew. On the day of his fourteenth birthday, he was told that "next to the Torah there is a holy book called the Zohar, which reveals the mysteries that are only hinted at in the Torah; it summons us to spiritual perfection and shows us how to achieve it. There are many fine men devoted to the new teaching, with salvation from spiritual and political oppression being their purpose, their aim."[100]

He was also informed that there appeared "a messenger from God by the name of Jacob Frank," who revealed himself as the messiah and promised "spiritual and physical salvation and especially life eternal." In an attempt to contain him, Christian authorities imprisoned him in the fortress of Częstochowa. Following his release, he converted to Christianity together with his family and most of his followers; the aim of the conversion was to "liberate the *Shekhinah* from Roman bondage." After the conversion, he lived in Prossnitz under the name Baron Frank.[101]

The distortions of Frank's biography are interesting. Porges's initiation took place in 1794, some three years after Frank's death. It seems that by this time, the Prague Sabbatians already had their own version of the history of his life. In Porges's account, Frank's conversion is placed after the liberation from Częstochowa and is given a kabbalistic interpretation as a redemptive act undertaken in order to "liberate the *Shekhinah* from Roman bondage." The account also lays stress on the choice to convert: "Conversion to a different religion is an important step, with lasting influence on the life of the individual concerned. Taken out of conviction, this step should be regarded as respectable; taken out of the delusion of a passion that can be only satisfied this way, it must end in misfortune and bitter regret, once the passion is gone and replaced by calm reasoning."[102]

This idea of a voluntary conversion in order to "liberate the *Shekhinah*" does not appear in *The Words of the Lord*. According to Porges's testimony, Frank was assigned a messianic role, although this was something he had explicitly denied in his own teachings. The Zohar, criticized by Frank on numerous occasions, was held in the highest esteem. Kabbalah was treated with utmost seriousness. Indeed, Porges's course of study included the doctrine of the *sefirot*.[103] It is also noteworthy that Frank's derision of Sabbatai Tsevi seems to have been removed from the doctrine taught after his death: in *The Words of the Lord*, Sabbatai was always mentioned disdainfully; in Offenbach, Porges was taught about "Shabbatai Melekh Mashi'ach" (Sabbatai Messiah the King).[104]

As the structure of power within the Offenbach court changed, there arose a need to reformulate the doctrine so as to legitimize the new leadership. On the basis of the Red Letters, *The Prophecies of Isaiah*, and the testimony of Moses Porges, we conclude that after Frank's death, most of his theological innovations were discarded and his followers returned to a traditional form of Sabbatianism. The differences between the teachings of Frank and the earlier Sabbatian tradition, as attested by Frank's ideas from Częstochowa, were effaced and the more radical tenets of the doctrine expounded in Frank's sayings suppressed. The highly unconventional soteriology of *The Words of the Lord* was replaced by much more traditional "spiritual and physical salvation and especially life eternal." The deification of Frank resulted in the neutralization of the most original elements of his message. Excesses were tamed: at Eve's court, "sexual intercourse or marriage was strictly forbidden."[105] What was left was unoriginal and banal political preaching.

Frankism for Literati: Prague

The doctrinal changes and the politicization of Frankism reflect the shifting of the power center of the movement to Prague. *The Prophecies of Isaiah* was composed by members of the Wehle family, longtime leaders of the Prague Sabbatians. It seems that after Frank's funeral, the majority of the Polish followers—except, however, the few very important personalities who were involved in the composition of the Red Letters[106]—left Offenbach. Klaus Werner, who analyzed the parish books of the Offenbach Catholic community, has demonstrated that in 1791–92, the number of baptisms, burials, and marriages of people having Polish names immediately drops and then almost vanishes within the next couple of years.[107] The vacuum left by the departure of the Polish Frankists was immediately filled by new arrivals from Prague.

During Frank's lifetime, Frankism spread in Moravia, but there is no evidence of his gaining any following in Bohemia. However, the region, and especially Prague, had a strong, independent Sabbatian tradition that predated Frank's appearance and was connected to Jonathan Eibeschütz and his pupils. In contrast to Poland, where Frankism took the form of a public movement sweeping through the lower strata of the Jewish society, Bohemian Sabbatianism of the same period was a kind of family religion cultivated by a number of well-established, wealthy, and, to all appearances, perfectly orthodox people. Some of the most prominent Prague Jewish families, such as the Porgeses, the Mauthners, and the Zerkowitzes, were known to be Sabbatians.[108]

Conversions to Christianity, similar to those in Poland and even Moravia, occurred seldom. The Prague Sabbatians were not very numerous,[109] but because of their economic and social standing, they enjoyed a very strong position within the Jewish community. Although the Sabbatian leanings of some of the city's most prominent families had been a matter of rumor since at least the 1720s, the issue was treated by Jewish authorities as an open secret. Reportedly, the Prague Sabbatians even had their own synagogue and a house of study, which taught the Bible and the Zohar, as opposed to the Talmud.[110] Since, in contrast to the Polish Frankists, they did not engage in open propaganda and their external moral conduct was impeccable, the chief rabbi of

Prague, Ezekiel Landau, preferred to avoid open confrontation. In October 1758, on hearing the news of the renewal of Frank's activity in Poland, he issued a *herem* against the Sabbatians. However, the excommunication was explicitly directed against the open Sabbatianism of Podolia.[111] As for the crypto-Sabbatians of Prague, Landau let the matter rest.[112]

Coincidentally or not, Frank's demise in 1791 and Landau's death in 1793 were followed by the rise of the Prague Sabbatians' public profile. Around that time, they established connections with the Offenbach court and became Eve's main financial supporters. As attested by Moses Porges, among others, Offenbach became a regular pilgrimage center for the sons of the Prague families. As the matter could no longer be ignored, Ezekiel Landau's successors, the three *Oberjuristen* Michael Bachrach, Eleazar Fleckeles, and Samuel Landau, came to the decision to stop closing their eyes to the activities of the Sabbatians and to engage in open polemics. In autumn 1800, a writ of excommunication was printed and posted on the doors of the synagogues of Prague.

The writ consisted of two parts. The first one repeated the text of the anti-Sabbatian ban of 1726, which had been issued after the affair connected to the heretical manuscript *Va-avo ha-yom el ha-ayyin* (ironically, the 1726 ban was signed by, among others, Rabbi Jonathan Eibeschütz and the senior of the Wehle family, Aaron Beer Wehle). The other part of the writ touched upon the outbreak of heresy in Prague in the final years of the eighteenth century. The rabbis attributed the rekindling of Sabbatianism (or perhaps the rise of its public profile) to "Jacob Frank (may his name be erased, may the name of the wicked rot), who had ostensibly embraced Christianity, yet then it turned out that he did not really accept its precepts, but only deceived and incited people to follow his own wicked religion [*emunato ha-resha'ah*]. He was imprisoned in the fortress of Częstochowa, set free by the Russians, and since then has been followed by fools and simpletons."[113]

In 1798–1800, Fleckeles, who was the most active in the anti-Sabbatian action, delivered three famous sermons in the Neuschule, Meislschule, and Klausschule. Portions of these sermons were printed, with the permission of the Austrian censorship, under the title *Ahavat David*.[114]

The anti-Frankist rabbinic works produced during the disputations in Poland were directed against heretics openly proclaiming their heterodox beliefs. By contrast, the main targets of *Ahavat David* were people whose external orthodoxy was not to be questioned. Fleckeles saw the biggest danger precisely in the hypocrisy of the Prague Sabbatians, who regularly attended synagogues and practiced charity, giving the deceitful impression that they were faithful

Jews.[115] Yet, under the veil of their sham piety, the Sabbatians engaged in secret antinomian rites: they practiced necromancy,[116] masturbated and then smeared the whole body with the semen,[117] permitted or even encouraged incest,[118] practiced wife swapping and group sex,[119] advocated a complete sexual freedom,[120] and "permitted perjury, theft, and adultery."[121]

In addition to antinomianism, Fleckeles accused the Sabbatians of breaking with the normative Jewish interpretative tradition by concentrating their attention only on non-legalistic and kabbalistic works and ignoring or rejecting the rabbinic halakhic canon: "they deal solely with the aggadot . . . and the great light of Gemara and the codifiers never shone upon them";[122] "they do not study Gemara and *Shulhan arukh* but occupy themselves only with aggadic midrashim and fragments of the Zohar."[123] The rabbi's wrath was also triggered by the fact that in Sabbatian circles, women studied kabbalah together with men.[124] According to Fleckeles, the aim of the sect was to bring about the total destruction of the Jewish religion;[125] because of the false messianic claims of Sabbatai, Berukhiah, and Frank, the advent of the true messiah had been postponed.[126]

Fleckeles's accusations—those concerning antinomianism and those referring to illicit kabbalah and its study—echoed the charges voiced during the 1756 investigation in connection with the Lanckoronie affair but did not touch upon any practices and doctrines introduced specifically by Frank during the later stages of the development of Frankism. The only Frankist documents known to the Prague chief rabbi were the Red Letters, which Fleckeles explicitly denounced for unsubstantiated eschatological speculations, poor knowledge of the Jewish textual canon, and miserable command Hebrew.[127] It is clear that he did not know of any theological or ritual innovations attributable specifically to Frank. Either the teachings and practices of the Prague Sabbatians around 1800 did not differ substantially from the Podolian variety of Sabbatianism that preceded Frank's appearance fifty years earlier, or, more likely, the rabbi based his charges on earlier anti-Sabbatian literature and not on firsthand knowledge. Nevertheless, Fleckeles's preaching reached a receptive audience. As the members of the Sabbatian group were among the richest and best-connected citizens, their position generated much resentment: the anti-Sabbatian campaign in Prague had an aspect of "class struggle," which was completely lacking elsewhere. Shortly after the sermons were delivered, riots erupted in the city, and, although Fleckeles did not mention any names, the mob apparently knew very well whom to assault. During the funeral of a known Sabbatian, a crowd attacked the procession and the body was profaned.[128] It seems that women were especially targeted: there was turbulence in the female section of one of the Prague synagogues, and many of the wives and daughters of known Sabbatians were insulted or attacked on the city's streets.[129]

In response to the rabbinic incitement and constant harassment, one leader of the Prague Sabbatians, Löw Enoch Hönig von Hönigsberg, wrote a petition to the police commissioner complaining about the discrimination faced by the group.[130] In Hönigsberg's petition, there was no mention of Sabbatai Tsevi, Frank, or any other Jewish heretical leader. His account was anti-rabbinic, but not explicitly pro-Sabbatian: he identified himself as "a speaker for the progressive party that is persecuted by the orthodox fanatics."[131] Hönigsberg appealed to the principles of tolerance, rationalism, and equality.[132] Praising the ideals of the Enlightenment, he attacked any form of religious extremism and challenged the rabbis' monopoly on the reading and interpreting of texts of the Jewish canon.[133] While, he claimed, "a treasury of wisdom is buried" in the Talmud, Hönigsberg argued that rabbinic interpretation turned it into "the most harmful and poisonous book."[134]

Löw Enoch von Hönigsberg was a son-in-law of Jonas Wehle, usually recognized as leader of Prague Sabbatianism. He wrote a large number of esoteric letters, homilies, and exegetical tracts expounding the secrets of Sabbatianism.[135] A full account of these writings would require a separate study. Here, I shall only concentrate on elements of Hönigsberg's works that shed light on the relationship of the Prague group to Frank and his teachings.

The epistles and sermons of Löw Enoch von Hönigsberg were composed between 1800 and 1803.[136] They were addressed to the Prague Sabbatian group, called by the author "the Holy Community" (*heilige Gemeinde*) or the "Association of Believers" (*Vereinigung der Gläubigen*).[137] This group—in accordance with the earlier Sabbatian paradigm—Hönigsberg counterpoised with the "mixed multitude" (*erev rav*): non-Sabbatian nonbelieving pseudo-Jews, whose lack of faith attested that their souls originated among not among the true Israelites but the Egyptians.[138] Even a cursory glance at the manuscripts reveals deep differences between Hönigsberg's writings and *The Words of the Lord*.

Two elements are particularly conspicuous. The first is the pronounced presence of elements of contemporary non-Jewish high culture, expressing itself, for instance, in quotations, paraphrases, and references to major personalities of the European Enlightenment. Thus Hönigsberg mentions Leibniz and Rousseau or utilizes Kantian (*Schwäche der theoretischen Vernunft*)[139] and Hegelian terminology (*Weltgeist*).[140]

Second, the traditional Sabbatian conceptual framework, almost completely discarded in *The Words of the Lord*, is here preserved intact: for instance, Sabbatai Tsevi (whose true messiahship is acknowledged on numerous occasions) is referred to as "AMIR"H,"[141] and the distinction between the *torah de-beri'ah* and *torah de-atsilut* is utilized and elaborated upon.[142] Both ideas belong to traditional Sabbatian discourse but do not appear in *The Words of the Lord* or any other Frankist text. Very few specifically Frankist terms are present (Frank's "Big Brother" appears in Hebrew parlance as *ha-ah ha-gadol*).[143] However, concepts to which the Frankists had attached a very specialized meaning are used completely conventionally in Hönigsberg's writings, without any trace of awareness that they had been discussed by Frank: the concept of Edom lacks the specialized meaning that it had acquired in Frank's dicta and is used in full accordance with the mainstream Jewish tradition as a general term for Christianity.[144] Frank himself is not mentioned by name but referred to by the abbreviation H"F; Moses Porges's testimony decodes this abbreviation as *heiliger Vater*, "Holy Father."[145] Some Christian accounts of the Offenbach court confirm that Frank indeed was so called in the final years of his life or shortly after his death, but the term itself does not appear in any internal Frankist source.

The departure from Frank's universe of discourse is attested not only by terminology but also by the theological content of the Prague epistles and sermons. A case in point is one of the most important Sabbatian notions, that of faith, which is completely absent from *The Words of the Lord*, but which builds a conceptual axis of Hönigsberg's theosophy.[146] Hönigsberg juxtaposes the internal certainty of the Kantian religion of reason, with its triad of the existence of God, immortality of the soul, and moral freedom,[147] and the Sabbatian notion of paradoxical faith that is, by its very nature, refuted by historical experience. The disappointments of their messianic expectations are presented as tests of the ability of the people of Israel to withstand external failures and retain their faith; faith is compared to the human soul (*nefesh ha-Adam*), and a person without faith "is not a [real] human being."[148]

In the context of the notion of faith, the persecution of the Sabbatians by the rabbinic authorities in Prague is presented as a test and at the same time as a blessing: "We should thank God that the few of us were taken from mixed multitude . . . and that they themselves excluded us from their midst. . . . [This was done] for our happiness."[149] Only the believers have "the true religion."[150] The idea of the redemptive value of a voluntary apostasy, also known from Porges's testimony, is discussed.[151] However, Hönigsberg rejects the conversion to Christianity precisely because it is Christianity, not Judaism, that is the true religion. The Prague group should stay within the Jewish fold in order to strengthen their paradoxical faith: "There is a need for a special group of people (and not only single individuals) who are—with the greatest piety and fear of God—prepared to undergo all sorts of persecutions for the sake of the Holy Faith. This group will be formed by faith [*emunah*]."[152]

Happiness and redemption are found in Christianity, but Sabbatians should remain Jewish until the last stage of history. This stage will be characterized by the downfall of all institutionalized religions and a period of general unrest. Its first sign is the demise of the secular power of the Church (secularization of Church property during the reforms of Joseph II in Austria and the French Revolution), but the author also expects the imminent downfall of all political and religious structures, and especially of the empire and the papacy: "The *Weltgeist* demands now that all these divine structures collapse . . . The nobles, princes, and dukes will all fall; in one day, thirty thousand dominions will be destroyed."[153] In a fragment that reads like a paraphrase of *The Prophecies of Isaiah*, Hönigsberg argues that the fall of the authorities will lead to the exaltation of the true mountain of God (Isa. 2:3) and the forthcoming revelation of the Virgin.[154]

This last idea is the only element of Hönigsberg's preaching that clearly derives from Frank's teachings. Large sections of Hönigsberg's writings are devoted solely to the issue of the forthcoming revelation of the Virgin and the liberation of the feminine principle. In a section titled "Einige wichtige Bemerkungen be-Megillat Esther (A few important comments on the Scroll of Esther),[155] Hönigsberg presents Esther as a model (*Vorbild*) of redemption but argues that the true nature of femininity could not have been properly appreciated in biblical times. Esther's duplicity is to be an example for the behavior of the Sabbatians, who should constantly operate on the boundary between Judaism and Christianity.[156] Drawing upon the example of Boaz and Ruth,[157] Hönigsberg praises the active behavior of women and lauds their sensuality, arguing that "the redemption of the world requires the emancipation of women and the revelation of their true sensuous nature, which has so far been kept in seclusion."[158] This call for the liberation of the senses culminates in the sermon titled "Something for the Female Sex," which was recently published from the manuscript by Ada Rapoport-Albert and Cesar Merchan Hamman.

"Something for the Female Sex" begins with what reads like a fragment of *The Words of the Lord*: "This is a very great thing, the beginning of everything good in the world. . . . You will be well aware that the personification of the

Shekhinah, from now on better called the Holy Virgin, is the gateway to God and to all divine treasures."[159] However, Hönigsberg's main concern is not the theological discussion of the feminine principle of the Godhead but a political program to improve the social position of women and the liberation of their true nature, which is "entirely disposed to sensuality."[160]

The aim is freeing the woman from the captivity to which she has been subjected by oppressive religious systems (such as, first and foremost, Islam and Judaism) and the gradual assumption of a more leading and active role by women; the avowed political ideal is a female ruler (such as Catherine the Great of Russia),[161] while the desired sexual model is the one whereby the woman chooses and actively pursues the man.[162] In other sermons, Hönigsberg toned down this last element: liberated sexuality, which is praised with regard to biblical characters, is not accepted with regard to believers themselves. Hönigsberg defends the group of believers from the accusations of sexual misconduct raised by Fleckeles and argues for a strictly puritan morality (which, again, brings to mind Moses Porges's memoir and the prohibition of sexual contacts at the Offenbach court after Frank's death). As in the case of the conversion to Christianity, he believes that although liberated sexuality is the aim, the time of the full revelation has not yet come. Thus, for the present, believers should abide by conventional mores.

The Prague group in general, and the writings of Löw Enoch von Hönigsberg in particular, may be an excellent point of departure for a study of Jewish Enlightenment in Eastern and Central Europe. However, as this summary has shown, the version of Sabbatianism upheld in Prague differed substantially from the teachings of Frank as expounded in *The Words of the Lord*. As I have already mentioned, the Prague Sabbatians came from a social milieu completely different from that of their Polish or Moravian counterparts. This was reflected not only in their economic and social standing but also in their upbringing and intellectual horizons. Frank's dicta, whatever their sources and inspirations were, certainly did not draw upon "the words of Kant, the philosopher."[163]

Hönigsberg, in turn, "achieved a certain amount of proficiency in Hebrew and German literature,"[164] studied Kant, Hegel, Leibniz, Mendelssohn, and Rousseau, and published papers in the organ of the maskilim, *Ha-me'assef*.[165] Similarly, Moses Porges read Mendelssohn, Lessing, and Schiller, as well as "historical and geographical works."[166] Even more important, both Hönigsberg and Porges valued and displayed their education while Frank tended to downplay his own learning in favor of intuitive, folk wisdom.[167]

In the works of Hönigsberg, Sabbatianism acquired an intellectual finesse that is lacking in Frank's dicta. On the other hand, the epistles of Hönigsberg do not have the primal, archaic power of *The Words of the Lord*. In Prague, Sabbatianism—along the lines of the earlier tradition of Hayon and Eibeschütz—was confined to a narrow intellectual elite. Frankist antinomian leanings were almost completely absent. Sabbatianism—against all odds—came to be regarded, in an enlightened fashion, as a system of ethics,[168] and the Prague group emphasized the full agreement of their conduct with conventional morality.[169] A strong anti-rabbinic tendency existed in early Frankism but had disappeared completely by the time that *The Words of the Lord* was composed: in Frank's sayings, the rabbis are hardly mentioned and rabbinic opposition was not an immediate context for the development of Frankism in Brünn and Offenbach. After 1760, rabbinic Judaism had ceased to be a point of reference for Frank: he defined himself much more in terms of differences from other Sabbatian groups or from Christians than from the rabbis. In contrast, the apologetic anti-rabbinic element is one of the most pronounced features of Prague Sabbatianism.

Indeed, the Prague "Frankists" were so different—both in terms of the professed teachings and doctrines and the social makeup of the group—from the Polish and Moravian followers of Frank that it might be asked if the term "Frankism" is appropriate at all.[170] Most of the specifically Frankist elements present in Hönigsberg's teachings seem to have been appropriated from oral external testimonies and accommodated to the needs of an independent, older, Sabbatian tradition.[171] As there is no indication whatsoever of any contacts between the Prague Sabbatians and the immediate followers of Frank during his life, it is doubtful that this line of development grew out of his teachings. Frank is presented in the writings of the Prague Sabbatians in a manner closer to the works of the rabbinic opponents of the movement than to the doctrine expounded in *The Words of the Lord*: he is seen as a continuator of the Sabbatian tradition, and his name is used in the same breath with those of Sabbatai and Berukhiah.

As many scholars have already noted, the opponents of Sabbatianism not only helped to keep the heresy alive but also kept various splinter groups together. The homogeneity of eighteenth-century Sabbatianism is, to a large extent, grounded in the rabbinic perception of the movement as homogeneous. Indeed, it is the heresiologists, not the apologists, who make distinctions among deviant sects. I strongly believe that the Prague group posthumously appropriated Frank and that they may be called "Frankists" only in the sense that after Frank's death, its members incorporated him into their pantheon. They supported Eve Frank financially and made pilgrimages to the Offenbach court. Like Porges's memoir, Hönigsberg's letters confirm that all Prague Sabbatians were expected to embark upon the "holy path to Offenbach [*heilige Weg nach Offenbach*],"[172] to walk all the way on foot, and to make donations to Eve.[173] For the Prague believers, the Offenbach court acquired the status of a holy place: "Abraham and Sarah's *bayit* [house] was then the only House of God in this world . . . exactly as now the true House of God is here."[174]

Yet for both Porges and Hönigsberg, the actual pilgrimage culminated in bitter disillusionment: the former fled the Offenbach court and abandoned his Frankist beliefs; the latter returned to Prague "almost deranged" with disappointment and nearly lost his faith in Eve.[175] Eve Frank might have been worshiped as the incarnation of the *Shekhinah*, but even the most faithful believers had trouble coming to terms with the incarnation of the feminine principle of the Godhead as a malicious spinster who ran an establishment that squeezed money from the naïve. It is little wonder that Hönigsberg's vindication of the female sex does not discuss the divinity of Eve (indeed, it does not mention her at all) but focuses instead on the sexual emancipation of the Prague Jewish bourgeoisie.

Frankism for Burghers: Warsaw

Warsaw had become the most important Frankist center in Poland by the time of Frank's imprisonment in Częstochowa. Some key figures of the Kamieniec and Lwów disputations had settled there, and although a few of them (including the chief disputant of 1757 and 1759, Yehudah Leyb Krysa) assimilated into Catholic society very quickly and severed their ties to the sect, others maintained close contacts with Frank and continued to support his court, first in Brünn and then in Offenbach. As the Warsaw community became more established, it gained relative independence from the leadership of the sect in Germany. Shortly before his death, Frank reportedly sent his secretary, Antoni Czerniewski, with a special delegation to Warsaw.[176] According to a manuscript quoted by Kraushar, Czerniewski was ordered to tell the "abandoned *machne*" (the company) that "*Jankiew lo mes* [Jacob did not die].[177] Lo and behold! Jacob is a true and living God, he is alive and will live forever."

The manuscript also referred to the growing dissent among the followers in Warsaw; the journey of Frank's secretary was apparently meant to address their concerns. Evidence concerning Czerniewski's mission is circumstantial: the trip is not mentioned in the usually detailed Frankist chronicle, and Kraushar refers to his source in a footnote as "a contemporary manuscript."[178] If the mission indeed took place, it might be seen as an attempt to strengthen ties between the Warsaw "company" and the Offenbach court or as Frank's effort to keep the Warsaw sectarians in check. But even if it is a later interpolation, it suggests that Kraushar's nineteenth-century informants were aware of the widening gap between the Frankists in Poland and those in Germany. As for Czerniewski, we know that although he was in Offenbach during the last few months of Frank's life (he bought a house on behalf of Frank),[179] shortly after the funeral, he left the city and moved to the Bukovina, where he became a leader of the sect known as the Abrahamites.[180]

I would venture to speculate that at least some of those who left Offenbach after Frank's funeral had either been disappointed by the death of the supposedly immortal Frank, or refused to accept Eve's leadership. Indeed, the steady stream of money that had flowed from Warsaw to Offenbach during Frank's life dried up relatively soon after his death. Another factor might have been a conflict with the newcomers from Prague. Hönigsberg in his writing explicitly derides "the *mahna* that left for Warsaw."[181] In any case, a large group of Frank's followers from Offenbach, including some important personalities, arrived in Warsaw in 1791 and strengthened the already powerful community living in that city. According to contemporary accounts, the Warsaw Frankists were quite numerous. Jacob Calmanson, who wrote a report about the state of Polish Jewry in 1791, observed that there were a "very large number of members of this sect, in particular in Warsaw."[182] An anonymous pamphlet printed in the same year estimated the total number of baptized Frankists living in Warsaw at six thousand and in the whole of Poland at 24,000.[183]

We possess no documents produced by the Warsaw Frankists, and there are no reports that such documents ever existed. Instead, we have at our disposal a number of anti-Frankist pamphlets produced in the last quarter of the eighteenth century; the pamphlets shed light on the way the Frankists were seen by their Christian neighbors and may serve as a basis for an analysis of how this perception might have influenced the group.

Warsaw enjoyed the crown-bestowed privilege *de non tolerandis Judaeis* from 1527.[184] However, the ban was never strictly enforced, and some Jews lived in the city throughout its history. A large number of Jews began to settle in the capital in the 1760s and 1770s. They usually lived on nobles' estates, which were jurisdictional enclaves exempted from municipal authority.[185] A census of Warsaw's Jewish population recorded in January 1778 listed 3,512 Jews in 1,260 households.[186] Driven by fear of economic competition and by ordinary anti-Semitism, the nascent Polish bourgeoisie attempted simultaneously to rid the towns of Jews and to control their economic activity.[187] Contemporary economic works and popular literature are rife with anti-Jewish arguments and tend to link the economic decline of the towns to the increase of Jewish economic activity in the territory of the Commonwealth.[188] In most cases, Polish burghers were victorious in their power struggle against Jewish merchants: King Stanislaus Augustus confirmed all privileges *de non tolerandis Judaeis* issued since the sixteenth century, and some forms of anti-Jewish legislation were adopted in most large towns and cities.[189] However, the appeals to anti-Jewish laws did not work against the Frankists, who were nominally Christians.[190]

Accordingly, around 1790, among the Warsaw mercantile class, the focus shifted from general anti-Jewish to anti-Frankist polemics: as Józef Ignacy Kraszewski has stated, "the fear of so-called Frankists who had recently converted was probably greater than of the true Israelites."[191] Kraszewski also quoted a pamphlet, *O prawach konfraterniom i cechom służącym* (On the laws of the confraternities and guilds), that targeted "the sectarian neophytes of Frank [who] deprive the burghers of means to a livelihood in every way" and reproduced fragments of a project of an anti-Frankist bill proposed by Warsaw's city council in 1790.[192]

In 1790 and 1791, an anti-Frankist propaganda campaign was launched in Warsaw. If we are to believe the pamphleteers, the Frankists in Warsaw were present in such numbers that "one could not walk a street or enter a house without running into a neophyte."[193] The pamphlets focused on the disproportionate influence that the sectarians exerted on commerce and social life. The Frankists were accused of using their connections to monopolize certain professions or branches of trade: they had reportedly completely taken over Warsaw's breweries and distilleries, as well as the tobacco monopoly. Many were lawyers: a sensational report by Eduard Jellinek, attesting to the continuous presence of the Frankists in Warsaw as late as the 1880s, claimed that in the mid-nineteenth century, one seldom met a lawyer or a notary who did not come from a Frankist family.[194] However, the greatest emphasis was placed on the Frankists' activity in trade. The pamphlet *List przyjaciela polaka . . . wyjawiający sekreta neofitów, poprawy rządu wyciągające* (Letter of a Polish friend revealing secrets of the neophytes for the good of the government) contains a list of products supplied by Warsaw neophytes:

The neophytes trade in vodka, strong and normal beer, Hungarian, French, and Rhenish wine, English ale, Champagne, Hungarian and Polish mead, cherry liqueur, raspberry liqueur, punch, and various other liqueurs. Neophytes sell all kinds of goods such as cheese, butter, lard, fat, meat, eggs, flour, onions, garlic, sulfur, kindling wood, starch, litmus, gunpowder, pomade, tobacco, splinters, brooms, shoemaker's wax, tar for carriages, bread, rolls, soap, candles, oil, vinegar, ginger, pepper, saffron, bay leaves, English herbs, cloves, flowers, saltpeter, nutmeg, salt, Dutch and Swedish herrings, raisins, almonds, figs, dates, syrup, honey cakes, torts, cooked food, biscuits, lamprey, eels, sturgeon, olives, capers, smoked sausage, caraway, anise, lemons, sugar, paper, wax, chalk, paints, needles, materials, ribbons, tapes.[195]

The lexicon of the anti-Frankist literature is revealing. The sectarians are usually designated as the *meches* (pl., *mechesy*).[196] So far as I was able to determine, the word had not appeared in the Polish language before it was used in the anti-Frankist pamphlets in the early 1790s. The nineteenth-century dictionaries of Samuel Bogusław Linde (1854) and Maurycy Orgelbrand (1861) do not contain entries on *meches*, but we know from contemporary novels and occasional works of, for example, Józef Ignacy Kraszewski that the word was in fairly wide use by the 1850s. The 1904 *Dictionary of Polish Language* compiled by Jan Karłowicz, Adam Krysiński, and Wacław Niedźwiecki features an entry on *meches* where the word is defined as: "a convert, converted Jew, neophyte" and derived from the Hebrew word *mekhes*, meaning "custom," "rent," or "fee." However, this etymology does not make much sense. Ignatz Bernstein proposes a more interesting and likely etymology, arguing that *meches* is really a Hebrew abbreviation for *mi-Kat Signor Santo* (of the sect of Signor Santo).[197]

Another commonly employed term is *neofita* (neophyte). In the anti-Frankist literature, the term acquired a meaning quite distant from its etymological sense and earlier usage. The term did not mean simply a convert from one religion to another but necessarily a recent convert from Judaism to Catholicism. At the beginning of the 1790s, the word "neophyte" became tantamount to "freshly converted follower of Frank." In this context, neophytes are presented as a special, separate class of people, defined by religion, with application to various apprehensions.

The pamphlet *Katechizm o Żydach i Neofitach* (Catechism about Jews and neophytes, 1791) asks: "Who is a neophyte?" and answers: "A neophyte is neither Jew nor Christian, who worships his Patriarch, at first Frank and recently his son, who was educated at the expense of the society of the neophytes."[198] The brochure argues that the neophytes operate in a legal vacuum; since they are "neither Jews nor Christians," they manage to escape the control of Jewish as well as Polish authorities. Other publications, too, consider Frankism as a kind of separate religion, a peculiar mix of Judaism and Christianity. Although nominally Roman Catholic, the Frankists are reported to circumcise their children[199] and keep the Shabbat,[200] they do not submit to the confession of sins,[201] they have separate burials,[202] and they do not take wives from other religions.[203] They are fanatically devoted to their patriarch, to whom they constantly send money, depriving their homeland thereby of precious resources.[204] Their morals are also dubious: they have a kind of *ius primae noctis* and send their daughters to Frank for defloration.[205] At least one pamphlet variant associates the neophytes with free thought and radical politics and places Frank in the same category as Voltaire and Jansen.[206]

The anti-Frankist literature focuses mainly on social and political issues. Virtually all the pamphleteers declare their adherence to the principle of freedom of belief and attack Frankism not for its theological aberrations but because of the Frankists' unfair edge in economic competition or their dubious political loyalties.[207] Although some of the brochures are openly anti-Semitic and attack "Jewish" features of the Frankists, mocking their dress, their awkward Polish accent, and other mannerisms, there seems to have been a growing feeling that they should be treated as a group within Christianity rather than as an offshoot of Judaism.

This perception became a commonplace in the early nineteenth century and gained official recognition in the special ukase on "Israelite Christians" issued by Czar Alexander I on 25 March 1817.[208] The document created a special committee whose aim was to look after the existing "Israelite Christians" as well as to further conversions of the Jews to Orthodox Christianity and to establish agricultural colonies in Crimea for the converts. Although the project was never implemented, the idea of a mass deportation of Polish Jews to Crimea was later broached on several occasions.[209] In the context of these projects, the Frankists were clearly distinguished from other Jews and treated as a kind of a paradigm for future developments.

Although there is evidence that the Frankists as a distinct social group existed into the 1880s and that Kraushar and other historians consigned the sect to premature death to please the descendants of the converts, who had already assimilated, it is very unlikely that Frank's doctrine was still taught in its original form at that time. The surfacing of the earlier closely guarded manuscripts can be linked to the gradual evaporation of the religious dimension of the movement: there was no longer any esoteric program that needed to be preserved and transmitted.

I believe that the anti-Frankist polemical literature, in conjunction with the suspicion of association with radical politics and subversive societies, caused the Warsaw Frankists to abandon most of the tenets to which they had earlier adhered. Orgiastic elements were replaced by traditional bourgeois morality. The radical elements of Frank's teachings were suppressed, and the group eventually turned into a kind of mutual aid association, in which the connections initially established within the sect were used to facilitate business enterprises.

The End

In the nineteenth century, the history of Frankism began to overlap with its historiography. Eduard Jellinek's report on the continuous presence of the Frankists in Warsaw, mentioned in the previous section, caused a considerable sensation and was published in several languages.[210] Other reports appeared in the Polish press as well.[211] Grandchildren of the converts of 1759 were very sensitive about the issue of their origins. For example, Kazimierz Zalewski, a popular playwright and a friend of historian of Frankism Aleksander Kraushar, always carried a genealogical document with him, attesting to his descent from an old Polish family.[212] Therefore, they tried to counteract the spread of gossip by creating an "official" history of the movement. The first Polish monograph on Frankism, written by the priest Hipolit Skimborowicz in 1866, was commissioned by the Frankist Wacław Szymanowski.[213] In 1893, the conservative writer Walery Przyborowski compiled printed accounts of the movement in another monograph. Despite the author's solid right-wing or even anti-Semitic credentials, his book was published pseudonymously. That, along with his generally favorable attitude toward Frank, raised suspicions that he had been "hired by the Contra-Talmudists."[214]

In the case of Przyborowski, these rumors are impossible to verify. In the case of Aleksander Kraushar, there is direct evidence that the descendants of the Frankists selected him for the task of writing a sanctioned account of the sect, supplied him with manuscripts, and sponsored his research trips to Vienna and Offenbach.[215] Kraushar's mission was twofold: to draw a clear line between the excesses of Frank and his early supporters and the flawless conduct of their children and grandchildren; and to ensure that the history of the movement would be seen as closed. Accordingly, the introduction to his book contains the following statement: "The descendants of the first followers of the 'Lord' became true and faithful Christians and citizens of their country. In the second generation, they had already severed all ties to the tenets proclaimed by the agitator, and today, after the passing of more than five generations, their grandchildren have nothing in common and wish to have nothing in common with their historical past. The historian of Frankism must not . . . try to complicate unnecessarily the events already finally closed and attempt to project them onto the present."[216]

Kraushar's position was generally accepted, and the majority of scholars ignored reports about the existence of Frankism in the nineteenth century. In 1904, the prolific anti-Semitic writer Teodor Jeske-Choiński published a kind of directory of converts to Roman Catholicism in Poland, titled *Neofici polscy* (Polish neophytes). He praised the contribution of the Frankists to Polish society and claimed that the second and third generations of the sectarians had become "true Catholics and true Poles."[217] His book has a chapter on converted Frankists but does not contain the names of some of the best-known Frankist families. It was well known that Jeske-Choiński funded the publication of his work with hush money extorted from some rich converts for omitting their names;[218] rumors that the descendants of Frank's followers attempted to bribe or to silence the historians dealing with the subject circulated in the 1930s and occasionally resurface even today.[219]

Various parties who had an interest in keeping the matter alive counteracted the efforts of the Frankists' grandchildren to bury their past. Polish anti-Semites vied with one another in pinning down one or another public figure of allegedly impeccable lineage as a "Frankist" or, alternatively, in defending the purity of Christian blood of national heroes rumored to be "tainted" by Frankist ancestry. Debates about the Frankist origins of Poland's greatest poet, Adam Mickiewicz, and greatest composer, Frédéric Chopin, were particularly stormy.[220]

Political powers also attempted to use the history of Frankism for their own purposes. In this regard, the lead was taken by the Russians. Alexander I's interest in the sect has been already mentioned; his Warsaw spy, Macrott, was instructed to inform the czar regularly about everything pertinent to the sect.[221] In 1845, Julian Brinken started publishing a serialized novel on Frank in the periodical *Biblioteka Warszawska*; the publication—largely fictionalized but based on some firsthand oral accounts—portrayed Frankism as a Jesuit plot and compared Frank to Ignatius Loyola.[222] Brinken gave an account of Frank's biography and followed the development of the sect until his own times.

The last chapter described secret Frankist conventicles in Prussian-occupied Warsaw. Only the first three chapters appeared, and the publication was halted after the intervention of Maria Szymanowska née Wołowska, who was a renowned pianist and tutor to Alexander's I daughter, a friend of Goethe, the mother of Mickiewicz's wife, Celina, and a member of the powerful Shorr-Wołowski clan, which had played such an important role in the development of Frankism.[223] However, in the 1890s the czarist authorities gained possession of the manuscript and published a Russian translation under the official imprint of the Ministry of Interior.[224] Brinken's book was distributed alongside the much more famous and influential work by Jacob Brafman, *Kniga pro kagale* (1869), thus creating an early antecedent of the Protocols of the Elders of Zion. As noted, a Russian translation of the protocol of the Lwów disputation containing the blood libel accusation was used in 1913 during the Beilis trial.[225]

The efforts of the descendants of Frank's followers, anti-Semitic campaigns against Jewish converts, and the involvement of governments and other official institutions all contributed to the shifting of attention from the religious to the political aspects of Frankism. In 1815, Bartłomiej Michałowski, a Polish nobleman who reportedly had met Frank personally, summed up the Frankist enterprise:

> [Frank's] reform did not have a religious but a social character. His sectarians not only did not reject the Mosaic Law, but they did not even discard the most important additions of the Talmud. I believe that they did not introduce any novelty but only rejected some fantasies of the rabbis. . . . Frank wanted to reconcile the Jewish religion with Christian civilization and mores. He wanted the Jews to be integrated into the countries they inhabit in order to become citizens without accepting the dominant religion; that is, to become like other dissidents. In one word, he wanted the Jew to be a citizen of Mosaic faith similar to a Roman Catholic in Russia or a Protestant in France.[226]

Michałowski's account is clearly distorted; however, the idea that Frankism served as a vehicle of emancipation became a commonplace in the histori-

cal literature on the subject and was shared by most historians of the movement, from Graetz to Scholem, regardless of their often negative assessment of
Frank's personality and actions. Interesting and insightful as it is, this perception inadvertently placed Frankism in a teleological frame, whereby developing events necessarily led to a preordained purpose.

In this work, while agreeing that Frankism had important political consequences, I hope to offer a more nuanced perception than the dominant
one by focusing on the religious aspect of Frankism and on the interactions
between the Frankists and other groups and bodies, Jewish and Christian.
Frank's teachings were not a fixed and homogeneous creed of emancipation
but a diverse and eclectic body of beliefs, drawing upon diverse traditions and,
in Protean fashion, created and re-created in response to constantly changing
circumstances and needs.

If we judge the movement in terms of its explicitly formulated aims, the
Frankist enterprise was a failure, which is far from meaning that it was not historically significant. Projects of autonomy and legalization of the special status
of the group were rejected. While academic discourse is not the appropriate
venue for deciding whether the theological aim of drawing the redemption
closer was a success, Frank himself was at least skeptical in this regard.

What makes Frankism interesting is the originality of Frank's teachings and
the diversity of responses to the movement among Jews and non-Jews alike. I
believe that a major reason that Frank became the unchallenged leader of his
movement, exercising almost absolute power upon his followers, was his flexibility: the ability to adjust his teachings and actions to rapidly changing circumstances and needs and to the expectations of various and diverse audiences.

Frankism challenged what its contemporaries—both Jewish and
Christian—considered the natural order of things: the mutual boundaries
of different religions, established religious principles, traditional social structures, patterns of social advancement and mobility, and symbolic hierarchies.
In a sense, it demonstrated that there were not really two separate societies, Christian and Jewish, but rather two agglomerations of heterogeneous
social groups. It forced the Jews to redefine the understanding of their own
religion and their self-perception vis-à-vis the Christians. It changed the way
that Judaism was seen among the Christians by demonstrating the internal
heterogeneity and complexity of the Jewish world. Whether seen as an aber-
ration, a movement of social unrest, or a theological innovation, it affected
Jewish-Christian relations and revamped the mutual attitudes and perceptions
of everyone concerned.

Current and Historical Place Names

Current names are given in parentheses; historical alternate names are given in square brackets.

Brünn (Brno) [Brunno]
Buczacz (Buchach)
Chocim (Khotyn) [Hotin]
Czernowitz (Chernivtsy)
Gliniany (Hlyniany)
Holleschau (Holešov)
Iwanie (Ivano)
Kamieniec Podolski (Kamianets-Podilskyi) [Kamenets-Podolsk]
Lwów (Lviv) [Lemberg, Leopolis, Lvov]
Nadworna (Nadvirna)
Podhajce (Pidhaytsi)
Prossnitz (Prostějov) [Prostist]
Rohatyn (Rohatyn)
Smyrna (Izmir)
Żółkiew (Zhvohkva) [Zholkva]

Abbreviations

AGAD	Archiwum Główne Akt Dawnych, Warsaw
AJG	Archiwum Jasnej Góry, Częstochowa
AMB	Archiv Města Brna, Brno
ASV	Archivio Segreto Vaticano, Vatican City
BC	Biblioteka Czartoryskich, Kraków
BJ	Biblioteka Jagiellońska, Kraków
BN	Biblioteka Narodowa, Warsaw
Bod	Bodleian Library, Oxford
BPL	Biblioteka Publiczna im. H. Łopacińskiego, Lublin
BT	Babylonian Talmud
BUW	Biblioteka Uniwersytecka w Warszawie, Warsaw
GStA	Geheimes Staatsarchiv Preußischer Kulturbesits, Berlin
HUCA	*Hebrew Union College Annual*
JNUL	Jewish National and University Library, Jerusalem
MGWJ	*Monatsschrift für Geschichte und Wissenschaft des Judenthums*
MZA	Moravský Zemský Archiv, Brno
PVAA	*Pinkas va'ad arba aratsot* (*Acta Congressus Generalis Judaeorum Regni Poloniae 1580–1764*), ed. Israel Halperin (Jerusalem, 1945), 2nd edition, revised by Israel Bartal (Jerusalem, 1991)
RA	*Rozmaite adnotacje, czynności i anekdoty Pańskie*, Jan Doktór (ed.). (Warsaw, 1996)
SAD	Staatsarchiv Dresden
SAO	Staatsarchiv Offenbach
UA	Unitätsarchiv, Herrnhut
ZSP	Zbiór Słów Pańskich w Brünnie mówionych, BJ, Ms. 6968/9; BPL, Ms. 2118

Notes

PREFACE

1. I have discussed various recensions of the manuscripts of these works and dealt with their dating, authorship, language of composition, and so on in Maciejko, "The Literary Character and Doctrine of Jacob Frank's *The Words of the Lord*."

2. Hillel Levine titled his edition *Ha-kronika: Te'udah le-toledot Ya'akov Frank ve-tenu'ato*.

3. Doktór, ed., *Rozmaite adnotacje, przypadki, czynności i anekdoty pańskie*.

4. Doktór, ed., *Księga słów Pańskich: Ezoteryczne wykłady Jakuba Franka*.

INTRODUCTION

1. Carlebach, *Divided Souls*, 12.

2. For the development of the martyrdom ideal, see Yuval, *Two Nations in Your Womb*, esp. 135–204.

3. For the most recent contributions on the Jewish conversion in Poland, see Fram, "Perception and Reception of Repentant Apostates in Medieval Ashkenaz and Premodern Poland"; and Kaźmierczyk, "Converted Jews in Kraków, 1650–1763."

4. Liebes, "Ha-tikkun ha-kelali shel R' Nahman mi-Breslav ve-yahaso le-Shabbeta'ut," in *Sod ha-emunah ha-Shabbeta'it*, 238–61, esp. 251–52.

5. Dov Baer ben Samuel, *In Praise of the Baal Shem Tov*, trans. and ed. Ben-Amos and Mintz, 59.

6. Ibid., 59.

7. Agnon, "Ein Wort über Jakob Frank, 56–57.

8. Exod. Rabbah 18:10; see also Mekhilta de-R. Simeon b. Yohai, 12.

9. Exod. Rabbah 42:6.

10. Num. Rabbah 15:25; and Midrash Tanhuma (Vilna, 1885), Beha'alotekha, 35.

11. BT Beitsah 32b.

12. Zohar 1:28b.

13. Ibid.

14. Ibid.

15. Ibid.

16. Zohar Hadash, 645, 31d.

17. Zohar 1:25a–25b.

18. Zohar 1:25b.

19. Zohar 2:191a, passim.

20. Tikkune Zohar, Tikkun 19.

21. Zohar 1:25b.

22. Zohar 3:153a–b.

23. Baer, "Ha-reka ha-histori shel Ra'ya Mehemna," esp. 1–5, 18–19, 31–35; and idem, *A History of the Jews in Christian Spain*, 1:270–77.

24. Scholem, *Sabbatai Sevi*, 206–7.

25. Ibid., 207.

26. Scholem (ed.), *Be-ikvot mashi'ah*, 59–61; and idem, *Sabbatai Sevi*, 226.

27. Scholem, *Sabbatai Sevi*, 283; cf. Freiman, *Inyane Shabbatai Tsevi*, 60.

28. Ibid., 747.

29. Scholem discusses this text as the "Commentary on the Psalms." I accept the correction of the translation of the title suggested by David Halperin in a paper delivered at the meeting of Association for Jewish Studies in Washington, D.C., in December 2008.

30. Scholem, *Sabbatai Sevi*, 867; idem, "Perush mizmore tehillim mi-hugo shel Shabbeta'i Tsevi be-Adrianopol," in *Mehkare Shabbeta'ut*, 122–23.

31. The words of the Sabbatian Abraham Yakhini; see Scholem, "Ha-tenu'ah ha-Shabbeta'it be-Polin," in *Mehkarim u-mekorot le-toledot ha-tenu'ah ha-Shabbeta'it ve-gilgulehah*, 79.

32. For a fuller account of Sasportas's position, see Chapter 2 in this volume.

33. Ber Birkenthal of Bolechów, *Sefer divre binah*, Jerusalem, JNUL, Ms. Heb 28° 7507, 222.

34. Liebes, "Hibbur bi-lashon ha-Zohar le-R' Wolf ben R' Yehonatan Aybeshits al havurato ve-al sod ha-ge'ullah," in *Sod ha-emunah ha-Shabbeta'it*, 77–102, esp. 78, 82, 85, 94.

35. See Emden, *Sefer shimush*, 83ʳ, on the basis of Zohar 3:124b; cf. also ibid., 86ʳ; idem, *Sefer hitabbkut*, 29ʳ; *Edut be-Ya'akov*, 37ᵛ; and *Megillat sefer*, ed. Kahana, 184.

36. Emden, *Sefer shimush*, 77ᵛ.

37. An attempt to define the role of Sabbatianism in forming the boundaries of Judaism has been made by Liebes in his "Shabbeta'ut ve-gevulot ha-dat."

38. Scholem, *Sabbatai Sevi*, ix.

39. Ibid., 128.

40. Ibid., 161.

41. Ibid., 145, 837.

42. Ibid., 464, 508–9.

43. Ibid., 142.

44. Carlebach, *The Pursuit of Heresy*, 80.

45. Ibid., 174–78.

46. See Emden, *Sefer torat ha-kena'ot*, 82; idem, *Sefer hitabbkut*, 88; and idem, *Edut be-Ya'akov*, 66ʳ⁻ᵛ, passim; see also Carlebach, *The Pursuit of Heresy*, 177–82.

47. I have discussed this aspect of the controversy in my "The Jews' Entry into the Public Sphere."

48. See Maciejko, "Baruch me-Erets Yavan and the Frankists."

49. Rabbinic courts (sing. *bet din*)

50. For Podolia under Turkish rule, see Kołodziejczyk, *Podole pod panowaniem tureckim.*

51. Bałaban, "Z zagadnień ustrojowych żydostwa polskiego," 44–45.

52. The edict was published in *Arkhiv jugo-zapadnoj Rossii* (Kiev, 1863), vol. 5, pt. I, 101.

53. Archiwumu Państwowe w Krakowie, Archiwum Tarnowskich z Dzikowa, 386, fol. 583 DD. Uniwersał Jerzego Przebendowskiego Podskarbiego W[ielkiego] Kor[onnego], Radom 21 VI 1719. I am grateful to Adam Kaźmierczyk for giving me a copy of this document, soon to be published.

54. See Isaac Abravanel, *Nahalat avot* (Venice, 1545), 20ᵛ; for the use of the title in the early modern period, see Katz, *Tradition and Crisis: Jewish Society at the End of the Middle Ages,* trans. Bernard Cooperman (New York, 1993), 142–43, 167–68, 198–99.

55. Scholem, "Ha-tenu'ah ha-Shabbeta'it be-Polin," 101, 106.

56. Benayahu, "Ha-'havurah ha-kedoshah,'" 136–37.

57. Ibid.; see also Krauss, "Die Palästinasiedlung der polnischen Hasidim und die Wiener Kreise im Jahre 1700."

58. Benayahu, "Ha-'havurah ha-kedoshah,'" 137.

59. Emden, *Edut be-Ya'akov,* 50ᵛ; and *Torat ha-kena'ot,* 70.

60. Emden, *Edut be-Ya'akov,* 50ᵛ; and *Torat ha-kena'ot,* 70.

61. See Wirszubski, "Ha-mekkubbal ha-Shabbeta'i Moshe David mi-Podhayyts."

62. Scholem, *Halomotav shel ha-Shabbatai Rʿ Mordechai Ashkenazi.*

63. Emden, *Sefer hitabbkut,* 96ᵛ; *Torat ha-kena'ot,* 128; and *Akitsat akrav,* 8ʳ.

64. See Chapter 6 in this volume.

65. Emden, *Edut be-Ya'akov,* 51ᵛ; and [Joseph Prager], *Sefer gahale esh,* Oxford, Bod, Ms. 2187, 1:69ᵛ.

66. The fast of the Ninth of Av was abolished by Sabbatai Tsevi; see Scholem, *Sabbatai Sevi,* 509, 615, 643, passim. Celebrating on the Ninth of Av was one of the most important and widespread Sabbatian rituals.

67. Ber of Bolechów, *Divre binah,* 185.

68. Ibid., 186.

69. Ibid.

70. *RA,* no. 1.

71. Ber of Bolechów, *Divre binah,* 189. During the investigation before the Warsaw consistory in 1760, Frank himself stated that he had been born in Korolowka. See Kraushar, *Frank i frankiści polscy,* 1:39.

72. Pikulski, *Złość żydowska przeciwko Bogu i bliźniemu, prawdzie i sumieniu, na objaśnienie talmudystów, na dowód ich zaślepienia i religii dalekiej od Prawa Boskiego przez Mojżesza danego,* 317.

73. The identification of Moses Meir as Frank's uncle appears in the text of the ban of excommunication against the Frankists pronounced in Prague; see the final chapter of this volume.

74. See Kraushar, *Frank i frankiści polscy*, 1:40.

75. B. Lewis and J. F. P. Hopkins, "Ifrandj or Firandj," in P. Bearman et al. (eds.), *Encyclopaedia of Islam*, 3:1044

76. *RA*, no. 2.

77. *ZSP*, nos. 3, 4, 854.

78. Scholem, *Sabbatai Sevi*, 901–14; and Liebes, "Yahaso shel Shabbata'i Tsevi le-hamarat dat," in *Sod ha-emunah ha-Shabbeta'it*, 20–34.

79. Awedyk, *Opisanie wszytkich dworniejszych okoliczności nawrócenia do wiary s. Contra-Talmudystów albo historia krótka ich początki i dalsze sposoby przystępowania do wiary s. wyrażającą*, 7. The conjecture was first suggested by Doktór, *Śladami mesjasza-apostaty*, 142, who, however, failed to provide historical arguments in its support.

80. For the overview of the beginnings of the Dönmeh, see Scholem, "The Crypto-Jewish Sect of the Dönmeh (Sabbatians) in Turkey," in *On the Messianic Idea in Judaism*, 142–66; and Ben-Zvi, *The Exiled and the Redeemed*.

81. Galante, *Nouveaux documents sur Sabbetai Sevi*, 72.

82. Hagiz, *Shever poshe'im*, quoted in Scholem, *Major Trends in Jewish Mysticism*, 316.

83. For this group, see esp. Scholem, "Berukhiah: Rosh ha-Shabbeta'im be-Saloniki," in *Mehkare Shabbeta'ut*, 321–89.

84. *Karet* (Hebr. extirpation or excision) signifies an automatic punishment at the hands of heaven for transgressions that are too severe for a human legal system to handle; for the thirty-six categories of sins incurring the *karet*, see BT Keritot 1:1.

85. *ZSP*, no. 1013.

86. Ibid., no. 48.

87. Ibid., no. 3. For Rabbi Mordechai in the Frankist sources, see ibid., nos. 26, 27, 40, 48, 49, 527, 707, 854, 946, 1013; for his other Sabbatian activities, see Scholem, "Ha-tenu'ah ha-Shabbeta'it," 95; and *Halomotav shel ha-Shabbeta'i*, passim.

88. Emden, *Sefer shimush*, 83ʳ.

89. *RA*, no. 7. I am informed by Hadar Feldman that a Ladino song called "Signor Mostro" is listed in one of the manuscripts containing songs and prayers of the Dönmeh currently housed at the Ben-Zvi Institute in Jerusalem.

90. Ibid., nos. 6, 7.

91. *ZSP*, nos. 16, 381.

92. Ibid., no. 25. For Sabbatai's parallel deed, see Scholem, *Sabbatai Sevi*, 145.

93. *ZSP*, no. 16.

94. Ibid., no. 19, 512. For a parallel deed of Sabbatai, who trampled the Torah scroll, see Scholem, *Sabbatai Sevi*, 671.

95. A full description of this pilgrimage existed in an early version of the Frankist chronicle, as quoted in Skimborowicz, *Żywot, skon i nauka Jakóba Józefa Franka ze*

spółczesnych i dawnych źródeł oraz z 2 rękopisów, 47, but was discarded in later redactions of *Various Notes*. The visit in Skoplje is also attested by *ZSP*, nos. 39, 40.

96. *ZSP*, no. 548.

97. See, e.g., *ZSP*, no. 263.

98. See [Prager] *Sefer Gahale esh*, 31ᵛ.

99. Ibid., no. 255.

100. Kraushar, *Frank i frankiści polscy*, 1:56–57.

101. *ZSP*, no. 1039.

102. Ber of Bolechów, *Divre binah*, 189.

103. Emden, *Meirat eyna'im*, 1ʳ; and idem, *Petah eyna'im*, 15ᵛ. The connection between the description in *Divre binah* with that of Emden was first made by Scholem in "Berukhiah: Rosh ha-Shabbeta'im," 374–75.

104. *RA*, nos. 8–13.

105. For the parallel between Malakh and Frank, see Dubnow, "Yakov Frank i ego sekta khrictianstvuyushchikh," 78; and idem, "Istoriya Frankizma po novootkrytym istochnikam," 108.

106. On Zalman Naftali Shorr and the halakhic importance of this work, see Tchernowitz, *Toledot ha-poskim*, 3:258–60.

107. Rapoport-Albert, "Al ma'amad ha-nashim ba-Shabbeta'ut," in Rachel Elior (ed.), *Ha-halom ve-shivro*, 1:143–327, esp. 163–66.

108. For the Shorrs' genealogy and connections, see Bałaban, *Le-toledot ha-tenu'ah ha-Frankit*, 1:122.

109. Baruch Yavan sent the text of the prayer to Rabbi Jacob Emden, who printed it with substantial changes, introducing derogatory puns and replacing all commendations with dysphemisms; see Emden, *Sefer shimush*, 7ʳ⁻ᵛ.

110. Yavan to Emden, 21 December 1755, in *Sefer shimush*, 4ᵛ.

111. *ZSP*, no. 1256.1 A Turkish (Ladino) Sabbatian prayer containing the phrase *Mi dio barach io* was printed from a Dönmeh manuscript by Isaac Ben-Zvi, "Kuntrasim be-kabbalah Shabbeta'it mi-hugo shel Berukhiah," *Sefunot* 3–4 (1960): 372. For more on this prayer, see Scholem, "Berukhiah: Rosh ha-Shabbeta'im," 370–71.

112. The credo of the Dönmeh was printed in English translation by Scholem, "The Crypto-Jewish Sect of the Dönmeh," 157; the quotation from it appears in the Frankist dicta in an appendix to *ZSP* titled *Dodatek Słów Pańskich w Brunnie mówionych*.

113. Scholem, "The Crypto-Jewish Sect of the Dönmeh," 160.

114. Dubnow, "Yakov Frank i ego sekta," 18.

115. Scholem, "A Sabbatian Will from New York," in idem, *The Messianic Idea in Judaism* (New York, 1995), 355 n. 4.

116. *ZSP*, no. 1051.

117. Ibid., no. 799.

118. Ibid., no. 1256.

119. Awedyk, *Opisanie*, 3–4.

120. Emden, *Sefer shimush*, 82ᵛ.

121. Awedyk, *Opisanie*, 4.

122. Emden, *Sefer shimush*, 82ᵛ.

123. Graetz, *Frank und die Frankisten*, 2.

124. *Encyklopedia kościelna* (Warsaw, 1874), 5:595, s.v. "Frank."

125. Kraushar, *Frank i frankiści*, 2:185.

126. Scholem, "Redemption through Sin," 127.

CHAPTER I

1. Scholem, "Mitsvah ha-ba'ah ba-averah," *Knesset* 2 (1937): 347–92. In English, "Redemption through Sin," trans. Hillel Halkin, in *The Messianic Idea in Judaism and Other Essays on Jewish Spirituality* (New York, 1971), 78–141.

2. For various contradictory accounts of the Lanckoronie incident, see Skimborowicz, *Żywot, skon i nauka Jakóba Józefa Franka*, 11–12; Graetz, *Frank und die Frankisten*, 26–28; Sulima, *Historya Franka i Frankistów*, 58–64; Kraushar, *Frank i frankiści polscy*, 1:70–73; Bałaban, *Le-toledot ha-tenu'ah ha-Frankit*, 1:116–18; and Doktór, *Śladami mesjasza apostaty*, 152–55.

3. *RA*, no. 17.

4. *ZSP*, no. 1311.

5. Prov. 11:22.

6. Amos 2:8.

7. Emden, *Sefer shimush*, 78ᵛ–79ʳ.

8. Ibid., 78ᵛ.

9. *Ma'aseh nora be-Podolia* was first printed as an appendix to Emden's edition of Saadia Gaon's *Sefer ha-pedut ve-ha-purkan* (Altona, 1769), 27–30. It was reprinted by Bałaban in "Studien und Quellen zur Geschichte der Frankistischen Bewegung in Polen," 52–57, and in *Le-toledot ha-tenu'ah ha-Frankit*, 2:297–305.

10. Bałaban, *Le-toldedot ha-tenu'ah ha-Frankit*, 2:298.

11. Ibid.

12. Ibid., 2:299.

13. Ber of Bolechów, *Divre binah*, 190–93.

14. Kleyn, *Coram iudicio recolendae memoriae Nicolai de stemmate Jelitarum a Dembowa Góra Dembowski*, sig. F. The existing foliation is unreliable; I provide instead the numbers of the signatures.

15. Ibid.

16. Ibid., sig. F1; cf. Luke 23:4.

17. Kleyn, *Coram iudicio*, sig. F1.

18. Awedyk, *Opisanie*, 9–10, mentions Rabbi Falik of Lanckoronie among the Frankists who converted in 1759.

19. In his numerous polemical publications, Emden printed letters, official pronouncements of rabbinic authorities, and testimonies concerning Sabbatianism. To the

extent that modern scholars were able to verify the content of the documents published by Emden, they were reproduced with great precision; see, e.g., Leiman, "When a Rabbi Is Accused of Heresy: R. Ezekiel Landau's Attitude toward R. Jonathan Eibeschütz in the Emden-Eibeschütz Controversy," 3:192; and Liebes, "Meshihiyuto shel R' Ya'akov Emden ve-yahaso le-Shabbate'ut," in idem, *Sod ha-emunah*, 198–211, esp. 198–99, 209.

20. Ya'ari, *Toledot hag Simhat Torah*, 124–25.

21. Zohar 3:256b.

22. Scholem, *Sabbatai Sevi*, 159.

23. Ibid., 160, 400.

24. Kleyn, *Coram iudicio*, sig. F2, I3.

25. *RA*, no. 46.

26. For examples, see Rosman, "The Role of Non-Jewish Authorities in Resolving Conflicts within Jewish Communities in the Early Modern Period," 53–65 and references therein.

27. Kleyn, *Coram iudicio*, sig. D7, E2. The fact that the initiative belonged to the rabbis is confirmed also by Awedyk, *Opisanie*, 15, and by Ber of Bolechów, *Divre binah*, 197.

28. Kedar, "Canon Law and the Burning of the Talmud," 79–83; and Shatzmiller, "Ha-kefirah ha-albigenzit be-eyne ha-Yehudim bne ha-zeman." I am grateful to Professor Joseph Shatzmiller for his suggestions regarding this point.

29. Innocent IV, *Commentaria* on the *Decretales*, as quoted in J. Cohen, *The Friars and the Jews*, 97.

30. J. Cohen, *The Friars and the Jews*, 98.

31. Kleyn, *Coram iudicio*, sig. E2. The bull *Antiqua iudaeorum improbitas* was issued on 1 July 1581.

32. Ibid., sig. E1.

33. Ibid.sig. D5–D6.

34. Ibid., sig. D5.

35. *RA*, no. 18.

36. Emden, *Sefer shimush*, 3ʳ.

37. Kraków, Archiwum E. Baziaka, Indeks akt konsystorskich lwowskich z lat 1624–1759, 1756, 1039ʳ. I am grateful to Adam Kaźmierczyk for pointing out this source to me.

38. The Vatican, ASV, Archivio della Nunziatura Apostolica di Varsavia, 94, Relazione della Causa e Processo di Frenk, fol. 153ʳ. I have published this letter as an appendix to my "Baruch me-Erets Yavan and the Frankist Movement," 354.

39. Ibid.

40. Emden, *Sefer shimush*, 3ʳ, 19ᵛ.

41. For Łyszczyński, see Andrzej Nowicki, "Pięć fragmentów z dzieła 'De non existentia dei' Kazimierza Łyszczyńskiego (według rękopisu Biblioteki Kórnickiej nr 443)," *Euhemer* 1 (1957): 72–81 .

42. Ber of Bolechów, *Divre binah*, 193.

43. *RA*, no. 20. *RA* mistakenly dates this event for mid-April. In 1756, the Fast of Esther fell on 15 March.

44. Kleyn, *Coram iudicio*, sig. D6.

45. *RA*, nos. 21–23.

46. Bałaban, *Le-toledot ha-tenu'ah ha-Frankit*, 1:117.

47. Emden, *Sefer shimush*, 6ᵛ.

48. Ibid.

49. Ibid., 5ᵛ, 6ᵛ.

50. The Vatican, ASV, Archivio della Nunziatura Apostolica di Varsavia, 94, Relazione della Causa e Processo di Frenk, 154ʳ.

51. Emden, *Sefer shimush*, 6ᵛ.

52. Ibid., 5ᵛ–6ʳ.

53. The Vatican, ASV, Archivio della Nunziatura Apostolica di Varsavia, 94, Relazione della Causa e Processo di Frenk, 154ʳ.

54. Emden, *Sefer shimush*, 6ᵛ.

55. Ibid., 6ʳ⁻ᵛ.

56. Ibid., 6ʳ.

57. Patai, *Sex and Family in the Bible and the Middle East*, 139–45.

58. See Shai, "Neti'ot antinomi'ot be-etika shel hayye ha-ishut be-kat ha-Donmeh," 236–91.

59. Emden, *Sefer shimush*, 6ʳ.

60. Ibid.

61. Ibid., 6ᵛ.

62. Ibid.

63. Jewish law deems divorce in cases of adultery mandatory.

64. Ibid., 7ʳ.

65. Uriel da Costa, *Exemplar Humanae Vitae*, in Carl Gebhardt (ed.), *Die Schriften des Uriel da Costa* (Amsterdam, 1922), 113–14.

66. The text of the ban was published by Joseph Cohen Tsedek, "Herev pifi'ot," *Otsar Hokhmah* 1 (1859): 21–22.

67. This document was stored in the archives of the Hamburg Jewish community but was destroyed during World War II. A summary and the signatures of the rabbis are given in Matthias Grunwald, *Hamburgs deutsche Juden bis zur Auflösung der Dreigemeinden 1811* (Hamburg, 1904), 124. The signatures fully overlap with those on "Herev pifi'ot"; see n. 66 above.

68. I have made suggestions about the reasons for these different attitudes in my "Baruch me-Erets Yavan and the Frankists," 344–45.

69. Izak Lewin, *Klątwa żydowska na Litwie w XVI I XVII wieku*, 39, 55–56, 81–82.

70. Ibid., 3.

71. Ibid., 10–11.

72. Calmanson, *Uwagi nad nineyszym stanem Żydów Polskich y ich wydoskonaleniem*, 28.

73. *PVAA*, 495.

74. Ibid., 125.

75. Lewin, *Klątwa żydowska*, 44, and references therein.

76. Scholem, "Ha-tenu'ah ha-Shabbeta'it be-Polin," 109.

77. Emden, *Edut be-Ya'akov*, 55ᵛ.

78. Idem, *Akitsat akrav*, 6ʳ, 20ᵛ.

79. The text of the herem can be found in idem, *Aspaklaria ha-me'ira*, and *Sefer hitabkut*, 95ʳ; cf. also his *Petah eyna'im*, 15ᵛ and *Akitsat akrav*, 13ʳ.

80. Scholem, "Ha-tenu'ah ha-Shabbeta'it be-Polin," 79.

81. Ibid., 82.

82. *PVAA*, 496; and Lewin, *Klątwa żydowska*, 44–45.

83. Carlebach, *The Pursuit of Heresy*, 11.

84. A text of such ban from 1791 was published by Isaac Lewin, "Ein Bannfluch," 162–66.

85. See, e.g., Emden's *Shevirat luhot ha-even*, 31ᵛ, about copies of *Va-avo ha-yom el ha-ayyin*, "in the hands of kosher Jews." Emden himself was a collector of Sabbatian writings.

86. Carlebach, *The Pursuit of Heresy*, 184. For Sabbatian rites involving masturbation during the prayer, see Liebes, "Hibbur bi-lashon," 98, and references therein.

87. Ibid., 192.

88. For the excommunication of these five communities, see Emden, *Sefer shimush*, 2ᵛ, 3ʳ, 78ᵛ. Rabbis Falik of Lanckoronie, Wolf of Krzywcze, and Nathan of Busk were among the 1759 converts; see Awedyk, *Opisanie*, 9–10.

89. Isaac of Biała to Emden, 22 September 1756, *Sefer shimush*, 2ᵛ.

90. Ber of Bolechów, *Divre binah*, 193–94.

CHAPTER 2

1. Scholem, *Sabbatai Sevi*, 566–67.

2. This point has been first made by Tishby in his "Al mishnato shel Gershom Shalom ba-heker ha-Shabbe'aut," in *Netive emunah u-minut* (Jerusalem, 1964), esp. 258–62. Scholem "remained unconvinced of the validity of [Tishby's] strictures"; see *Sabbatai Sevi*, 566 n. 252.

3. Sasportas, *Tsitsat novel Tsevi*, ed. Tishby, 39; and Goldish, *The Sabbatean Prophets*, 133.

4. Shatz-Uffenheimer, "Tsitsat novel Tsevi u-madurato ha-shlemah," in *Ra'ayon ha-meshihi me-az girush Sefarad*, 139–61.

5. Goldish, *The Sabbatean Prophets*, 131–51.

6. Ibid., 143.

7. Sasportas, *Tsitsat novel Tsevi*, 4; and Scholem, *Sabbatai Sevi*, 142.

8. Sasportas, *Tsitsat novel Tsevi*, 43. In the text, "my faith"; cf. Goldish, *The Sabbatean Prophets*, 143.

9. Sasportas, *Tsitsat novel Tsevi*, 113; see also Scholem, *Sabbatai Sevi*, 582.

10. Sasportas, *Tsitsat novel Tsevi*, 115.

11. Ibid., 131.

12. Ibid., 205.

13. Ibid., 256; cf. Scholem, *Sabbatai Sevi*, 718.

14. BT Sanhedrin 99a–b. For the discussion of both terms, see Maimonides, *Hilkhot teshuvah*, chap. 3.

15. Goldish, *The Sabbatean Prophets*, 143, 145–46.

16. Scholem, *Sabbatai Sevi*, 489.

17. Sasportas, *Tsitsat novel Tsevi*, 166. Cf. Scholem, *Sabbatai Sevi*, 582; Goldish, *The Sabbatean Prophets*, 137.

18. See, e.g., Sasportas, *Tsitsat Novel Tsevi*, 98, 115, 131, and passim.

19. Ibid., 83, 98.

20. Ibid., 7.

21. Scholem, *Sabbatai Sevi*, 489, 697. Nantava's writings are based on Nathan's apocalypse; see Introduction in this volume; cf. Scholem, *Sabbatai Sevi*, 224, 274.

22. Lev. 3:4. The sentence paraphrases the words of Nathan of Gaza; see Introduction in this volume; and Scholem, *Sabbatai Sevi*, 226.

23. Zohar 3:282a. I partly rely on the translation provided in Tishby, *The Wisdom of the Zohar*, trans. David Goldstein (Oxford, 1985), 3:1436.

24. Sasportas, *Tsitsat novel Tsevi*, 180–81.

25. Idel, "Saturn and Sabbatai Tsevi," esp. 191–99. For important corrections to Idel's interpretation of Sabbatai's own views on Saturn and on Nathan of Gaza, see Elqayam, "Leidato ha-sheniyah shel ha-mashi'ah." For Christian astrology linking the ascension of Saturn with the rise of Jewish false prophets, see Zafran, "Saturn and the Jews," esp. 18–19.

26. Sasportas, *Tsitsat novel Tsevi*, 93; cf. Scholem, *Sabbatai Sevi*, 647 n. 155.

27. Sasportas, *Tsitsat novel Tsevi*, 99–100; see also Yerushalmi, *From Spanish Court to Italian Ghetto*, 354.

28. See, e.g., the Munich Ms. quoted in Steinschneider, *Polemische und apologetische Literatur in arabischer Sprache*, 362.

29. For Jewish views, see Halbronn, *Le monde Juif et l'astrologie*, 142; and Idel, "Saturn and Sabbatai Tsevi," 180–81 and references therein.

30. See, e.g., Paul L. Maier, "Herod and the Infants of Bethlehem," in *Chronos, Kairos, Christos II* (Winona Lake, Ind., 1998), 171

31. Sasportas, *Tsitsat novel Tsevi*, 80.

32. Hagiz, *Shever poshe'im*, 17, 61.

33. On the lack of references to Sasportas in Hagiz, see Carlebach, *The Pursuit of Heresy*, 150.

34. Goldish, *The Sabbatean Prophets*, 131.

35. The first full edition was published only in 1954 by Isaac Tishby.

36. Tishby, introduction to Sasportas, *Tsitsat novel Tsevi*, 42.

37. Emden (ed.), *Kitsur tsitsat novel Tsevi*.

38. *PVAA*, 359–60. Graetz's statement in *Frank und die Frankisten*, 33 n. 3, that Abraham was the president of the council is erroneous.

39. Emden, *Edut be-Ya'akov*, 70 [50]ʳ.

40. Ibid., 52ᵛ; and *PVAA*, 398.

41. Emden, *Edut be-Ya'akov*, 55ᵛ; and *PVAA*, 396–97.

42. [Joseph Prager], *Sefer gahale esh*, Oxford, Bod, Ms. 2187, 2:206ʳ–208ᵛ.

43. Emden, *Shevirat luhot ha-even*, 1ᵛ.

44. Abraham Yoski to Emden, 11 August 1756, in idem, *Sefer shimush*, 2ᵛ.

45. He was the son of the rabbi of Prossnitz, who persecuted the Sabbatian Leibele and sided with Emden from the very beginning; see Emden, *Edut be-Ya'akov*, 67ᵛ–69ᵛ; 70 [50]ʳ, 74 [54]ʳ⁻ᵛ, passim.

46. Isaac of Biała to Emden, 7 December 1756, *Sefer shimush*, 3ʳ. Isaac of Biała does not refer to the Lanckoronie incident but to the event in Lwów involving the Sabbatian Samuel of Busk; see Chapter 1 in this volume.

47. Abraham Yoski to Emden, 11 August 1756, in Emden, *Sefer Shimush*, 2ᵛ.

48. Ibid., 7ᵛ.

49. Isaac of Biała to Emden, 22 September 1756, ibid., 2ᵛ.

50. Abraham of Zamość to Emden, 20 September 1756, ibid., 2ʳ.

51. Kleyn, *Coram iudicio*, sig. D7–E; see also Kraushar, *Frank i frankiści polscy*, 1:77.

52. Num. 32:17.

53. Baruch Yavan to Emden, 28 September 1756, in *Sefer shimush*, 3ᵛ (the 1760 date of this letter is a misprint).

54. Emden, *Edut be-Ya'akov*, 49ᵛ.

55. Abraham of Zamość to Emden, 26 December 1756, in idem, *Sefer shimush*, 1ᵛ.

56. Abraham stated that he had intended to send to Elyakim a responsum on the issue of an *agunah*; Elyakim took up this issue in an undated letter published by Abraham Berliner in *Otsar Tov*, a supplement to the *Magazin für Wissenschaft des Judenthums* 15 (1888): 9–14.

57. Emden, *Megillat sefer*, ed. Kahana, 185; cf. BT Sanhedrin 39b.

58. Yerushalmi, *From Spanish Court to Italian Ghetto*, 340–47; and Kaplan, *From Christianity to Judaism*, 214–15.

59. Emden, *Kitsur tsitsat . . .*, 1ʳ; *Edut be-Ya'akov*, 35ʳ, where he compares himself to Sasportas; *Sefer shimush*, 18ʳ, where he says he continues Sasportas's line of argument.

60. Idem, *Sefer shimush*, 15ʳ.

61. Ibid.

62. In fact, 5:17–18.

63. Emden, *Sefer shimush*, 15ᵛ–16ʳ.

64. Ibid., 15ʳ.

65. Ibid.

66. Ibid., 17ᵛ.

67. In a note, Emden gives a reference to 1 Cor. 7:17.

68. Emden, *Sefer shimush*, 16ʳ–17ᵛ.

69. Gen. 9:4–7; cf. BT Sanhedrin 56a.

70. For the development of this attitude, see Jacob Katz, *Exclusiveness and Tolerance*, 162–64.

71. Emden, *Ets avot*, 40ʳ–1ᵛ.

72. Cf. Jer. 2:3.

73. Emden, *Sefer shimush*, 20ʳ–1ᵛ.

74. Greenberg, "Rabbi Jacob Emden," 354–55, 363; Schacter, "Rabbi Jacob Emden," 515.

75. Willi, "Das Christentum im Lichte der Tora," 260.

76. Emden, *Megillat sefer*, 97.

77. Schacter, "Rabbi Jacob Emden," 514–15 and notes therein.

78. I am grateful to Hayyim Hames for bringing this work to my attention and for providing me with a typescript of his unpublished paper on it.

79. See BT Gittin 40b.

80. Hames, "And on This Rock I Will Build My Community," 6; and Carlebach, *The Pursuit of Heresy*, 109–10.

81. Oxford, Bod, Ms. Michael 259. The Michael collection includes manuscripts and printed books from Emden's personal library.

82. E.g., "'Aktus Apostolorus': *Hoda'at Ba'al Din*," Ms. Oxford, 54, vs. *Sefer shimush*, 16ʳ; "'Poil/Paul/Paulo': *Hoda'at Ba'al Din*," 48–49, vs. *Sefer shimush*, 16ᵛ–18ᵛ; and "'Timotius': *Hoda'at Ba'al Din*," 50, vs. *Sefer shimush*, 16ʳ.

83. E.g., Matt. 5:17–19: *Hoda'at Ba'al Din*, 20, vs. *Sefer shimush*, 16ʳ; 1 Cor. 7:18: *Hoda'at Ba'al Din*, 49, vs. *Sefer shimush*, 16ᵛ, 17ᵛ; and Acts 16: *Hoda'at Ba'al Din*, 54, vs. *Sefer shimush*, 16ʳ⁻ᵛ.

84. *Hoda'at Ba'al Din*, 45–49, vs. *Sefer shimush*, 17ʳ⁻ᵛ.

85. *Hoda'at Ba'al Din*, 16, 20, 23, 44–54, vs. *Sefer shimush*, 16ʳ–18ʳ.

86. The best-known examples are Shem Tov Shaprut's *Even bohan* and Profiat Duran's *Kelimat ha-goyyim*.

87. Hames, "And on This Rock I Will Build My Community, 5.

88. Ibid., 8.

89. Partial English translations were published by Fasman, "An Epistle on Tolerance by a 'Rabbinic Zealot'"; and by Falk, "Rabbi Jacob Emden's Views on Christianity." A partial German translation appeared in Willi, "Das Christentum im Lichte der Tora."

90. Emden, *Sefer shimush*, 17ᵛ.

91. Carlebach, *The Pursuit of Heresy*, 10.

92. Megerlin, *Geheime Zeugnisse vor die Wahrheit der Christlichen Religion*, introduction.

93. Emden, *Sefer shimush*, 19ᵛ–20ʳ.

94. Leiman, "When a Rabbi Is Accused of Heresy: The Stance of Rabbi Jacob Joshua Falk in the Emden-Eibeschütz Controversy," 438.

CHAPTER 3

1. Awedyk, *Opisanie*, 17.

2. ZSP, no. 114; see also Pikulski, *Złość żydowska przeciwko Bogu i bliźniemu*, 828.

3. Awedyk, *Opisanie*, 16.

4. The manifesto was published in Kleyn, *Coram iudicio*, sig. M7–N5.

5. See Elżbieta Aleksandrowska, "Antoni Kossakowski h. Ślepowron," *Polski Słownik Biograficzny*. Wrocław, 1968–69, 14:261–62.

6. Adam Darowski (ed.), *Pamiętniki Józefa Kossakowskiego*, 21

7. Ibid., 53.

8. Juliusz Gomulicki, "Athos i królewska ptaszarnia," 181–91

9. Darowski, *Pamiętniki*, 53.

10. Władysław Konopczyński (ed.), *Diariusz Sejmu Ordynaryjnego 1748*, 167, 252.

11. See Kraushar, *Frank i frankiści polscy*, 1:129–30.

12. Ber of Bolechów, *Divre binah*, 195.

13. Ibid., 197.

14. Abraham of Szarogród, "Ma'aseh nora," in Bałaban, *Le-toledot ha-tenu'ah ha-Frankit*, 300; see also *RA* 22.

15. Kedar, "Canon Law and the Burning of the Talmud," 81.

16. Kleyn, *Coram iudicio*, sig. E2.

17. Rosenberg, "Emunat hakhamim," 293.

18. Kaplan, "'Karaites' in Early Eighteenth-Century Amsterdam," 238.

19. Ibid., 254, 262.

20. J. Van den Berg, "Proto-Protestants?," 35. For a review of early modern Christian interest in the Karaites, see Popkin, "The Lost Tribes, the Caraites and the English Millenarians."

21. Kaplan, "Karaites," 242.

22. Ibid., 261–62.

23. Ibid., 277.

24. Bałaban, "Karaici w Polsce," in *Studia historyczne* (Warsaw, 1927), 66, 74; and Mann, *Texts and studies in Jewish history and Literature*, 2:1013, 1015, 1069, 1058.

25. Bałaban, "Karaici w Polsce," 15, 39.

26. Mann, *Texts and Studies*, 2:663–64, 788, 1033.

27. Ibid., 719; see also Emden, *She'elat YAVe"Ts*, II, question 152.

28. Mann, *Texts and Studies*, 2:1215, 1337; and see Neubauer, *Aus der Petersburger Bibliothek*, 143.

29. Mann, *Texts and Studies*, 2:1013, 1015.

30. Dubnow, *Pinkas va'ad ha-kehillot ha-rashiyyot bi-Medinat Lita*, 151, 165, 203, 204, passim.

31. Mann, *Texts and Studies*, 2:1295; see also 810.

32. Bałaban, "Karaici w Polsce," 16, 19, 39, 41.

33. Zajączkowski, "Na marginesie studjum Bałabana 'Karaici w Polsce'"; and idem, "Przywileje nadane Karaimom przez Królów polskich," 22.

34. Bishop Serra to Cardinal Torrigiani, 4 April 1759, the Vatican, ASV, Segr. di Stato, Polonia, 271, 388ʳ.

35. Theiner (ed.), *Vetera Monumenta Poloniae et Lithuaniae gentiumque finitimarum historiam illustrantia maximam partem nondum edita ex tabulariis vaticanis deprompta col-*

lecta ac serie chronological disposita (Rome, 1864), 4:164; cf. the Vatican, ASV, Segr. di Stato, Polonia, 272, 60ᵛ–61ʳ.

36. For accounts of the Kamieniec debate in earlier scholarship, see Skimborowicz, *Żywot, skon i nauka Jakóba Józefa Franka*, 13–17; Graetz, *Frank und die Frankisten*, 34–38; Sulima, *Historya Franka i Frankistów*, 69–94; Kraushar, *Frank i frankiści polscy*, 1:84–94; Bałaban, *Le-toledot ha-tenu'ah ha-Frankit*, 1:137–51; and Doktór, *Śladami mesjasza apostaty*, 158–65.

37. *RA*, no. 24 (erroneous date of 6 September).

38. The first grant of Jewish rights in Poland was issued by Bolesław the Pious in 1264, and subsequently confirmed many times. This privilege formed the basis of later privileges issued in the Polish-Lithuanian Commonwealth. The extended versions of Kazimierz Jagiellończyk (1453) and Stefan Bathory (1585) include a provision that legal jurisdiction over Jews belongs exclusively to the king or the *wojewoda*. For the texts of the privileges, see Bloch, *Die General-Privilegien der polnischen Judenschaft*.

39. *Kuryer Polski*, 2/1757, col. 3.

40. Ber of Bolechów, *Divre binah*, 197–98.

41. Kleyn, *Coram iudicio*, sig. E4.

42. Ber of Bolechów, *Divre binah*, 203.

43. The manifesto was first published by Kleyn, "Manifestatio quorunda Judaeorum Contra Thalmud," in *Coram iudicio*, sig. M7–N5. A Hebrew translation from Polish, together with supporting arguments (not reproduced in Kleyn) and an extensive commentary, was published by Emden in his *Sefer shimush*, 31ʳ–70ʳ.

44. A Frankist source gives a date of 2 June; see *RA*, no. 26.

45. Awedyk, *Opisanie*, 69. Bałaban has claimed that the debate was conducted in Yiddish; see his "Studien und Quellen," 210. Weinryb, in turn, argued that it was in a "mixture of crude Polish-Ukrainian"; see his *The Jews of Poland*, 247. I do not know what the basis of Bałaban's and Weinryb's ideas is.

46. *Kuryer Polski*, 29 (1757,) col. 3.

47. *Hildesheimer Relationskurier*, 144/1757, quoted in Lewinsky, "Zur Geschichte der Juden in Polen und Russland während des 18. Jahrhunderts," 201.

48. Kobielski's account was printed as *List Jaśnie W[ielmożnego] J[ego] M[ości] Xiędza Biskupa Łuckiego y Brzeskiego do Starszych uczonych Całey Synagogi Brodzkey* in his *Światło na oświecenie narodu niewiernego, to iest Kazania w Synagogach Żydowskich miane* (Lwów, 1746). The *List* has a separate pagination.

49. Kobielski, *List*, 18–21; see Wurm, *Z dziejow żydowstwa brodzkiego za czasow dawnej Rzeczypospolitej*, 52–54; and Hundert, *Jews in Poland-Lithuania in the Eighteenth Century*, 67–72.

50. Doktór, *W poszukiwaniu żydowskich kryptochrześcijan; dzienniki ewangelickich misjonarzy z ich wędrówek po Rzeczypospolitej w latach 1730–1747*, 228.

51. Kobielski mentions Bishop Antoni Dembowski's involvement in the introduction to his *Światło na oświecenie*, [7]. He does not specify the character of this involvement.

52. Maccoby, *Judaism on Trial*, 76.

53. Kleczewski, *Dissertacya albo mowa o pismach żydowskich i Talmudzie podczas wal-nej dysputy Contra-Talmudystów z Talmudystami pod rządem J. W. Imci księdza Szczepana z Mikulicz Mikulskiego, obojga praw doktora, archidjakona i kanonika archikatedralnego, ad-ministratora generalnego metropolii lwowskiej agitującej się na sesji czwartej, miana we Lwowie Roku Pańskiego 1759* (n.d.), 32; and Pikulski, *Złość żydowska*, passim.

54. Chazan, *Barcelona and Beyond*, 58.

55. See references to Luria and Cordovero in Kobielski, *Światło na oświecenie*, [35–40]; and *List pasterski*, 7–9.

56. Maccoby, *Judaism on Trial*, 19.

57. Freiman, *Inyane Shabbatai Tsevi*, 96.

58. Scholem, "Iggerot Natan ha-Azzati al Shabbeta'i Tsevi ve-hamarato," in *Mehkarim u-mekorot*, 241.

59. Sasportas, *Tsitsat novel Tsevi*, 190; see Scholem, *Sabbatai Sevi*, 691.

60. Abraham Cardozo, "Drush zeh eli ve-anvehu," in Scholem, *Mehkarim u-mekorot*, 350–54; cf. Cardozo, *Selected Writings*, trans. D. J. Halperin, 206–16.

61. Hayon, *Oz le-Elohim*, 1^{v}.

62. Ibid., 7^{r}.

63. Emden, *Mitpahat sefarim*, 1.

64. Ibid.

65. Katz, "Post-Zoharic Relations between Halakhah and Kabbalah," in idem, *Divine Law in Human Hands*, 27.

66. Idem, "Halakhah and Kabbalah as Competing Disciplines of Study," in *Divine Law*, 56–87, esp. 79–80.

67. Bans of 1671, 1687, and 1753 (twice); see Chapter 1 in this volume.

68. Kleyn, *Coram iudicio*, sig. G; the detail about the converts is in Pikulski, *Złość żydowska*, 23, 43.

69. Pikulski, *Złość żydowska*, 36. The fragment appears only in the 1760 edition. I am grateful to Jan Doktór for bringing to my attention the discrepancies between two different editions of Pikulski's book.

70. [Prager], *Sefer gahale esh*, 1: 53^{v}, 64^{v}-65^{r}; cf. Carlebach, *The Pursuit of Heresy*, 191.

71. Emden, *Edut be-Ya'akov*, 50^{v}, passim.

72. [Prager], *Sefer gahale esh*, 1: 53^{v}, 60^{v}; cf. Perlmuter, *Rabbi Yehonatan Aybeshits ve-yahaso el ha-Shabbeta'ut*, 46; and Carlebach, *The Pursuit of Heresy*, 191.

73. Emden, *Edut be-Ya'akov*, 50^{v}.

74. According to D. Kahana, *Toledot ha-mekkubbalim, ha-Shabbeta'im, ve-ha-Hassidim*, 2:123–26, Hotsh was a "Sabbatian ascetic"; Scholem states in his *Major Trends in Jewish Mysticism*, 421 n. 74, that he belonged to the "Lurianic wing of Sabbatianism"; in an entry on Hotsh in *Encyclopaedia Judaica*, Scholem argued that Hotsh was not a Sabbatian at all.

75. *Nahalat Tsevi*, introduction, quoted after Baumgarten, "Yiddish Ethical Texts and the Diffusion of the Kabbalah in the Seventeenth and Eighteenth Centuries," 86.

76. See the letters of Abraham ha-Kohen of Zamość and Isaac of Biała in Emden, *Sefer shimush*, 2^{r–v}.

77. In the original *sefer* (book). Tishby corrects the reading into SP"R, which is a widespread abbreviation for Sefer Pardes Rimonim; see Tishby, "Ha-ra'ayaon ha-meshihi ve-ha-megamot ha-meshihi'ot be-tsemihat ha-hassidut," *Zion* 32 (1967): 4 n. 19.

78. Cohen Tsedek, "Herev pifi'ot," 27.

79. Such restrictions were placed on the study of philosophy already by the rabbinic council of Montpellier in 1272. The parallel between the 1272 and 1756 restrictions has been discussed by Dubnow; see his "Yakov Frank i ego sekta." Cf. Idel, "Le-toledot ha-issur lilmod kabbalah lifne gil arba'im," esp. 14–15; idem, "Perceptions of Kabbalah in the Second Half of the Eighteenth Century," 61.

80. M. Kahana, "Mi-Prag le-Prossnitz: Ktiva hilkhatit ve-olam mishtaneh me-ha-Noda bi-Yehuda le-Hatam Sofer," 9–10. I am grateful to Maoz Kahana for sharing his work with me.

81. This position was fully expressed in a responsum of Rabbi Ezekiel Landau, *Noda bi-Yehuda* (Prague, 1776), *Yore de'ah*, 141, no 74. As Maoz Kahana has demonstrated, this responsum was written in February 1756: a few weeks after the Lanckoronie affair, some two months before the *herem* of Brody. Landau was a graduate of the Brody *kloyz* and was in touch with many of the signatories of the ban. Although the text of the responsum was not printed until many years later, the timing of its composition hardly seems coincidental: it is likely that Landau's position was known to the excommunicators and the wording of the *herem* appears to reflect his characteristic style; see M. Kahana, "Mi-Prag le-Prossnitz," 8–10.

82. Emden, *Mitpahat sefarim*, 20, 107.

83. Emden, *Sefer shimush*, 4^r.

84. *ZSP*, no. 707.

85. Ibid., no. 1088.

86. Ibid., no. 331; cf. also nos. 307, 320.

87. Ibid., no. 421.

88. Pikulski, *Złość żydowska*, 60–62.

89. Mopsik, *La cabale*, 10.

90. Wirszubski, *Pico della Mirandola's Encounter with Jewish Mysticism*, 162, 169.

91. Blau, *The Christian Interpretation of the Cabala in the Renaissance*, 100.

92. See Kleczewski, *Dissertacya*, 10–11; and Pikulski, *Złość żydowska*, 108.

93. Reuchlin, *On the Art of the Kabbalah (De Arte Cabalistica)*, trans. M. and S. Goodman, 97.

94. Pikulski, *Złość żydowska*, 133; see also 18, 46, 48, 145, and passim; and Kleczewski, *Dissertacya*, 10–11, 108.

95. Wirszubski, *Pico della Mirandola*, 108.

96. Chazan, *Daggers of Faith*, 181.

97. Galatino, *De Arcanis Catholicæ veritatis*, 23^v. The idea that the Jewish elite actually knew of the messiahship of Jesus and of the Trinitarian character of the Godhead

but suppressed this knowledge from the Jewish masses is of patristic provenance; see, e.g., Hippolytus, *Adversus haereses*, 9, 25. However, it was Galatino who linked these ideas to the Zohar.

98. Pikulski, *Złość żydowska*, 37; and Awedyk, *Opisanie,* 3.

99. One of the most important anti-Sabbatian works was written by Joanicjusz Galatowski, Rector of the Kiev Academy and archimandrite of a monastery in Chernichov; see Scholem, *Sabbatai Sevi*, 596.

100. See Bałaban, "Sabataizm w Polsce," 87–88.

101. Bałaban quotes an official edict of King Jan Kazimierz forbidding the Jews to march with Sabbatai's portraits and a pastoral letter of Stanisław Sarnowski, bishop of Przemyśl, condemning the marches as a "new Jewish malice offending the Divine Majesty"; see ibid., 88–89; see also Scholem, *Sabbatai Sevi*, 596–97.

102. See Galas, "Nieznane XVII-wieczne źródła polskie do historii sabataizmu," 2:177–82; and Świderska, "Three Polish Pamphlets on Pseudo-Messiah Sabbatai Tsevi," 212–16.

103. E.g., Pikulski relies on Jakub Radliński, *Prawda chrześcijańska od nieprzyjaciela swego zeznana, to iest traktat Rabina Samuela pokazujący błędy żydowskie około zachowania prawa Mojżeszowego y Przyścia Messyaszowego,* which, in turn, reprints the aforementioned epistle of Bishop Sarnowski on 391–93.

104. Pikulski, *Złość żydowska*, 37.

105. Awedyk, *Opisanie,* 3.

106. See, e.g., Pikulski, *Złość żydowska*, 828.

107. Kleyn, *Coram iudicio*, sig. A1–5.

108. Ibid., sig. G-H.

109. Ibid., sig. I1; cf. Pikulski, *Złość żydowska*, 829–30.

110. Ibid., sig. H5.

111. Emden, *Sefer shimush*, 79^v.

112. See Ya'ari, "Srefat ha-Talmud be-Kamnits Podolsk," 297.

113. Kleyn, *Coram iudicio*, sig. H1.

114. Ibid., sig. I5.

115. The full text of the verdict is in ibid., sig. M4–M6.

116. Ibid., sig. H5.

117. Emden, *Sefer shimush*, 79^r.

118. Ibid., 79^v.

119. *Kuryer Polski*, 49/1757, [col. 2].

120. Emden, *Sefer shimush*, 81^v; and idem, *Megillat sefer*, 188.

121. Emden, *Sefer shimush*, 79^{r-v}.

122. Ibid., 79^v.

123. Emden, *Sefer shimush* 79^{r-v}; 79^v–80^v, 82^r; and Abraham of Szarogród, "Ma'aseh nora," in Bałaban, *Le-toledot ha-tenu'ah ha-Frankit*, 303–4.

124. Emden, *Megillat sefer*, 188.

125. *ZSP*, 1631. The fragment is missing in the extant manuscripts. It is quoted by

Mieses, *Polacy,* vi. I did not manage to substantiate Dubnow's claim that Elisha Shorr was among those killed; see Dubnow, "Yakov Frank i ego sekta," part 3, *Voskhod* 4 (1883): 91.

126. Ber of Bolechów, *Divre binah,* 222; the fragment has been censored by Brawer.

127. *RA,* no. 23.

128. Chocim was the border town between Poland and Moldavia, the tributary state of the Ottoman Empire. While Moldavia was never fully incorporated by the Ottomans and remained outside of the *eyalet* system, the Porte had garrison rights and exercised complete control over the state's foreign policy.

129. This is the only source that mentions Frank's Muslim name.

130. The Vatican, ASV, Nunz. di Varsavia, 94, Relazione, 149ᵛ.

131. BT Berahot 60b.

132. Ber of Bolechów, *Divre binah,* 221.

133. Doktór, *Śladami mesjasza-apostaty,* 157–59, 195–96; see also *ZSP,* nos. 22, 23, 1017. Frank indeed stated that the followers of Berukhiah in Salonika "did not want to help him with anything, being afraid that . . . he would not go away."

134. *RA,* no. 29.

135. Ibid., no. 32.

136. Ber of Bolechów, *Divre binah,* 223.

137. Kraushar, *Frank i frankiści polscy,* 1:99.

138. *ZSP,* nos. 21–24.

139. Ber of Bolechów, *Divre binah,* 222.

140. Emden, *Sefer shimush,* 82ʳ.

CHAPTER 4

1. Bałaban, *Le-toledot ha-tenu'ah ha-Frankit,* vol. 2

2. Dubnow, "Yakov Frank i ego sekta," part 3, *Voskhod* 4 (1883): 90–116, esp. 101–10; part 4, *Voskhod* 5 (1883): 44–67, esp. 44–48.

3. See, however, Yuval, *Two Nations in Your Womb,* 184–88.

4. Po-Hsia, *The Myth of Ritual Murder,* 204.

5. Ibid., 208.

6. Węgrzynek, *"Czarna legenda" Żydów,* 9.

7. Ibid., 11.

8. Simon Dubnow, *History of the Jews in Russia and Poland: From the Earliest Times until the Present Day,* trans. I. Friedlander (Philadelphia, 1946), 1:172

9. See Tazbir, "Anti-Jewish Trials in Old Poland," 233–45; and Guldon and Wijaczka, *Procesy o mordy rytualne w Polsce w XVI–XVIII wieku.* Guldon and Wijaczka have established that in Poland between 1547 and 1787, there were eighty-one cases of ritual murder accusations. It is generally accepted that the existing lists of ritual murder accusations are incomplete.

10. Bartoszewicz, *Antysemityzm w literaturze polskiej XV–XVII wieku;* and Tollet,

"La littérature antisémite polonaise de 1588 à 1668," *Revue française d'histoire du livre* 16 (1977): 73–105.

11. See, e.g., Johann Christian Wagenseil, *Der denen Juden fälschlich beygemessene Gebrauch des Christen-Bluts* in his *Benachrichtigungen wegen einiger die Judenschaft angehenden wichtigen Sachen*, part 1, 126–206.

12. Eisenmenger, *Entdecktes Judenthum*, 2:220.

13. Frankel, *The Damascus Affair*, 48.

14. See Tazbir, "Anti-Jewish Trials in Old Poland," 233–34; Bałaban, *Zur Geschichte der Juden in Polen* 35–40; and idem, "Epizody iz istorii ritual'nykh protsessov i antievreiskoi literatury v Polshe," 163–81.

15. See Rowlands, *Witchcraft Narratives in Germany*.

16. For an analysis of the social background of the blood libel accusations in the Middle Ages, see Graus, *Pest, Geissler, Judenmorde*.

17. Wyporska, "Male Witches in the Polish-Lithuanian Commonwealth," 246. I am grateful to Wanda Wyporska for allowing me have a typescript of her thesis.

18. Baranowski, *Procesy czarownic w Polsce w XVII i XVIII w.*, 30.

19. Wyporska, "Male Witches in the Polish-Lithuanian Commonwealth," 73.

20. Józef Andrzej Załuski, *Objaśnienie błędami zabobonów zarażonych oraz opisanie niegodziwości, która pochodzi z sądzenia przez próbę pławienia w wodzie niecnych czarownic, jako takowa próba jest omylna . . . aby sędziowie poznali niepewność takiej próby, a spowiednicy wierzących takim próbom z błędu wyprowadzić mogli* (Berdyczów, 1766); and idem, Info[rmation] touch[ant] les Juifs, leur Talmud et les Infanticides par J. Z[ałuski] Ev[êque] de K[iovie] à l'occasion de l'infanticide commis récemment dans son Diocèse, Warsaw, Biblioteka Narodowa, Ms. 3208.

21. Żuchowski, *Process kryminalny o niewinne Dziecie Jerzego Krasnowskiego . . . okrótnie od Żydów zamordowane* ([Sandomierz], 1713 [1720]), 64.

22. The Vatican, ASV, Arch. Nunz. di Varsavia, 94, Relazione della Causa e Processo di Frenk, 67ʳ.

23. However, in Poland, the number of male witches was higher than in the West. See Wyporska, "Male Witches in the Polish-Lithuanian Commonwealth," chaps. 1–2.

24. The best examples of this line of argument are Hugh Trevor-Roper, *The European Witch-Craze of the Sixteenth and the Seventeenth Centuries*; and A. Dworkin, *Woman Hating*

25. See, e.g., Macfarlane, *Witchcraft in Tudor and Stuart England*; Roper, *Oedipus and the Devil*; and Brauner, *Fearless Wives and Frightened Shrews*.

26. Frankel, *The Damascus Affair*, esp. 157, 185–91, 214–30.

27. *Dielo Beilisa: Stenograficheskii otchet* (Kiev, 1913). A collection of documents from the Polish blood libel trials was edited during the Beilis trial by Vladimir Kuzmin, *Materyaly k voprosu ob obvinienich Evreev v ritualnych postupleniach* (Saint Petersburg, 1913). The arguments from the Frankist disputation of 1759 were quoted by the prosecution.

28. See Thomas of Monmouth, *The Life and Miracles of Saint William of Norwich*, 15, 93–94; see also lxxi, lxxix.

29. See Strack, *Das Blut im Glauben und Aberglauben der Menschheit*, 239–50. The

most prominent exceptions are Brenz, *Jüdischer abgestreiffter Schlangenbalg*, and Kirchner; see n. 30 below.

30. Kirchner, *Jüdisches Ceremoniel* [*sic*] *oder Beschreibung derjenigen Gebräucher, welche die Juden sowol inn: Als ausser dem Tempel, bey allen und jeden Fest-Tagen, im Gebet, bey der Beschneidung . . . in acht zu nehmen pflegen*, 150–52; for Kirchner and his conversion, see De Le Roi, *Die evangelische Christenheit und die Juden unter dem Gesichtspunkte der Mission geschichtlich betrachtet*, 1:405. Kirchner's idea that Jewish women need Christian blood in childbirth is based on Eck, *Ains Judenbüechlins Verlegung*. Kirchner's anti-Semitic publication was reprinted in Germany by the Reprint-Verlag Leipzig in 1999; the blurb on the cover introduces the book as "having a special place among the old Jewish[!] literature," since it "demythologizes the seemingly mysterious Jewish religious ceremonies and demonstrates the origins of the customs and mores in the text of the Old Testament."

31. Po-Hsia, *The Myth of Ritual Murder*, 208.

32. See, e.g., the Regensburg case of 1474; and Strack, *Das Blut*, 192. Other examples are in the Ganganelli report; see below.

33. Ber of Bolechów, *Divre binah*, 316.

34. Börner, *Auserlesene Bedanken der theologischen Facultät zu Leipzig*, 613–22; and Goldberg, "Leipziger Theologen gegen die Ritualmordprozesse," 65–72.

35. See, e.g., Regulus, *Czarownica powołana abo krótka nauka y przestroga z strony czarownic zebrana zrozmaitych Doktorów tak wprawie Bożym iako y świeckim biegłych dla ochrony y poratowania sumnienia, osobliwie na takie Sądy wysądzonych*; Czartoryski, *Instructio circa judicia sagarum judicibus eorumque consiliariis accomodata Romae primum 1657*; and Gamalski, *Przestrogi duchowne sądziom inwestygatorom i instygatorom czarownic*.

36. Maciejko, "Christian Accusations of Jewish Human Sacrifice in Early Modern Poland."

37. Pikulski, *Złość żydowska*, 705.

38. I have published a Latin text of a deposition made by Serafinowicz on his deathbed. The text partly overlaps with what we know about Serafinowicz's first manuscript, but it also introduces new elements. It does not have a form of almanac; see Maciejko, "Christian Accusations of Jewish Human Sacrifice."

39. Żuchowski, *Process kryminalny o niewinne Dziecie Jerzego Krasnowskiego . . . okrótnie od Żydów zamordowane*, 79; and Pikulski, *Złość żydowska*, 760–61.

40. Pikulski, *Złość żydowska*, 773–74; and Żuchowski, *Process*, 111–12.

41. Żuchowski, *Process*, 32, 113, claims that the Jews wanted to hold a dispute with Serafinowicz in order to kill him.

42. The affidavit is dated 22 May 1712 and is currently housed in the Archiwum Państwowe w Poznaniu, Act Castr. Kcyniensia, T. 58, fol. 655, non vidi; see also Bałaban, *Le-toledot ha-tenu'ah ha-Frankit*, 1:53.

43. See Bałaban, "Ein Autodafe in Lemberg im Jahre 1728," *Skizzen und Studien*, 71–76

44. Idem, "Ritual'nyi protsess v Poznani," *Evreska Starina* 1 (1913): 469–81.

45. Decree in Kuzmin, *Materialy*, 134–59; see Galant, "Zhertvy ritual'nogo obvineniia v Zaslavii v 1747 g," *Evreska Starina* 2 (1912): 202–18.

46. Galant, "Ritual'nyi protsess v Dunaigorod v 1748 g," 272–83.

47. Gelber, "Die Taufenbewegung unter den polnischen Juden in XVIII Jahrhundert," 227; Guldon and Wijaczka, *Procesy o mordy rytualne*, 60–64; and Bałaban, "Studien und Quellen," 39–41.

48. Bałaban, "Studien und Quellen," 42–43; and Guldon and Wijaczka, *Procesy*, 61.

49. Rudnicki, *Biskup Kajetan Sołtyk*, 15–18.

50. See the letters of the Danish ambassadors in Warsaw, Beregard, and Haxthausen, quoted in Bałaban, "Studien und Quellen," 44. The future Polish king, Stanislaus Augustus Poniatowski, who was at that time in Amsterdam, repeated the same information and expressed his indignation; see *Pamiętnik Króla Stanisława Augusta*, 1:81.

51. There is some confusion as to the name of the emissary: while he himself signed letters Elyakim ben Asher Zelig of Jampol, some Christian sources call him Jacob Selek or Selig. Elyakim's presence was noticed by the Polish colony in Rome; see Loret, *Polacy w Rzymie w osiemnastym wieku*, 85–90. Loret states that Elyakim went to Rome twice, first in 1756 and then "shortly before the end of the Lwów disputation." Bałaban, who analyzed the bills for accommodation in Rome submitted to the Council of Four Lands, believes that it was one long trip, lasting from 1758 until 1760; see Bałaban, "Studien und Quellen," 46.

52. Cecil Roth (ed.), *The Ritual Murder Libel and the Jew*, 67. The original Italian text was first published by Israel Loeb, "Un mémoir de Laurent Ganganelli sur la Calomnie du Meurtre Rituel," *Revue des Etudes Juives* 18 (1889): 185–211; a corrected version was published by Stern, *Die Papstlichen Bullen über die Blutbeschuldigung* (Berlin, 1899), 37–143.

53. Ibid., 26.

54. Rudnicki, *Biskup Kajetan Sołtyk*, 23.

55. *Błędy talmudowe od samychże żydów uznane y przez nową sektę siapwscieciuchów, czyli contratalmudystów wyiawione* (Lwów, 1758).

56. Ibid., [3ʳ].

57. Ibid., [6ᵛ⁻ʳ].

58. See Doktór, *Śladami mesjasza-apostaty*, 163; idem, "Saloniki—Częstochowa—Offenbach," 37 n. 24.

59. Warsaw, BN, Ms. 540, Kajetan Sołtyk, Złość żydowska, 47ᵛ–52ʳ.

60. Sołtyk, *Złość żydowska w zamęczeniu dzieci katolickich przez list następujący y dekreta grodzkie wydana* (Lublin, ca. 1761). *Błędy talmudowe* was also reprinted as *Krótkie zebranie obrządków żydowskich i ich ku chrześcijanom wieczna nienawiść z okazji nowej sekty kontrtalmudystów* (Vilna, 1759). Majer Bałaban had a copy of this edition belonging to Bishop Sołtyk, with Sołtyk's handwritten comments; see Bałaban, "Studien und Quellen," 44 n. 3.

61. Sołtyk, *Złość żydowska w zamęczeniu dzieci katolickich przez list następujący y dekreta grodzkie wydana* (Lublin, 1774). The only extant copy of this edition is housed at the Jagiellonian Library in Kraków, shelfmark 67084/I. *Błędy talmudowe* is reprinted on 20ʳ–34ʳ and is titled "Talmuty [sic] błędów Żydowskich."

62. Majer Bałaban already suggested that Sołtyk was behind keeping the blood libel alive and rekindling the Frankist affair. However, Bałaban was unaware of the existence of

the pamphlet *Błędy talmudowe*. He knew Sołtyk's book *Złość żydowska* but had only the edition of 1772, which does not include any Frankist-related material; see Bałaban, "Studien und Quellen," 44 n. 3. Accordingly, he failed to make a connection between Sołtyk and the first ritual murder accusation ascribed to the Frankists.

63. Kleyn, *Coram iudicio*, sig. R7–S4; see also Horn, *Regesty dokumentów i ekscerpty z Metryki Koronnej do historii Żydów w Polsce, 1697–1795*, 118.

64. Kraushar, *Frank i frankiści polscy*, 1:167.

65. Roth, *The Ritual Murder*, 90.

66. Ibid., 93.

67. Ibid., 90.

68. Ibid., 94.

69. Ibid., 32.

70. For the text of this supplication, see "Suplika Żydów Wiarę Świętą Katolicką przymuiących" ([Lwów], 1759). There is also a separately printed Latin version: *Supplex Libellus a Judaeis fidem catholicam amplectentibus et baptismum expetentibus Illustrissimo et Reverendissimo DD Łubieński Archiepiscopo Leopolienski [sic] nunc celsissimo nominato principi primati porrectus.*

71. "Z Łowicza d. 18 Junii," *Kuryer Polski* 26 (1759): cols. [1–12], reprinted in Pikulski, *Złość żydowska*, 158–61; see also the Vatican, ASV, Segr. di Stato, Polonia, 272, 56ᵛ–59ʳ.

72. For the account of the opening of the debate, see "Z Lwowa d. 18. Julii," *Kuryer Polski* 30 (1759): cols. [15–17]; and Pikulski, *Złość żydowska*, 171.

73. "Z Lwowa d. 19. Septembris," *Kuryer Polski* 40 (1759): col. [3].

74. Pikulski, *Złość żydowska*, 279–80.

75. The protocol is housed in the Vatican Secret Archives, Segr. di Stato, Polonia, 271, 56ᵛ–87ʳ, and reprinted (with some modifications) in Pikulski, *Złość żydowska*, 153–91. The Hebrew text in Ber of Bolechów, *Divre binah*, 289–313, is an abridged translation from Pikulski.

76. To retain the flavor of the original, I am giving the Hebrew transliterations as they appear in the official protocol of the disputation from 1759.

77. *Shulhan arukh, Orah Hayyim* 472, not 412; probably a misprint.

78. See *Ture zahav* on *Orah Hayyim* 472, 8: the usage should be given up on account of false accusations.

79. Maimonides, *Yad hazaka, Hilkhot akkum*, 89, 4.

80. Pikulski, *Złość żydowska*, 173–74.

81. Maimonides, *Hilkhot hamets u-matsa*, 88.

82. Pikulski, *Złość żydowska*, 179.

83. The Frankists translated *Orah Hayyim* 460, 60, *al yade*, "by" as *przy*, "in the presence of."

84. Pikulski, *Złość żydowska*, 181–82.

85. Ibid., 183–84, 185–87.

86. Leviticus 17. The Jews, of course, brought this point; see below.

87. Pikulski, *Złość żydowska*, 190.

88. BT Ketubbot 60a: "human blood, however, is not forbidden but permitted."

89. Maimonides, *Hilkhot ma'akhalot assurot* 86, 4.

90. See also *Mishnah bikkurim*, 2, 7.

91. See Leiman, "Rabbi Jonathan Eibeschütz's Attitude toward the Frankists," 148–49.

92. Ber of Bolechów, *Divre binah*, 312.

93. Serra to Torrigiani, 7 November 1759, in Theiner (ed.), *Vetera Monumenta Poloniae et Lithuaniae gentiumque finitimarum historiam illustrantia maximam partem nondum edita ex tabulariis vaticanis deprompta collecta ac serie chronological disposita*, Rome, 1864 (1679–1775), 4:155.

94. Serra to Torrigiani, 1 August 1759, in Theiner, *Vetera Monumenta*,151.

95. Ibid.

96. Serra to Torrigiani, 15 August 1759, in ibid., 152–53. The nuncio considered the accusation as "very improbable"; see a letter dated 5 December 1759, ibid., 156.

97. This is stated by the contemporary pamphlet *Myśli z historyi o Kontra-Talmudystach wiernie, krótko, y zupełnie zebraney, z okazyi nastąpioney od Zwierzchności, z temiż Kontra-Talmudystami w dyspozycyi, na zawstydzenie żydowskiego urągania, Z przyłączonemi uwagami o stanie teraźniejszym Chrześcijanów pomieszanych z Żydostwem, oraz z przestrogami bardzo potrzebnemi i pożytecznemi przez pewnego wydane* (Zamość, 1761), 6ᵛ.

98. Serra to Torrigiani, 7 November 1759, in Theiner, *Vetera Monumenta*, 155.

99. Serra to Torrigiani, 1 August, 1759, in Theiner, *Vetera Monumenta*, 152.

100. Serra to Torrigiani, 15 August 1759, in Theiner, *Vetera Monumenta*, 153.

101. Serra to Torrigiani, 13 February 1760, in Theiner, *Vetera Monumenta*, 158.

102. Ibid.

103. Ibid., 166.

104. Vatican, ASV, Segr. di Stato Polonia, 152ᵛ.

105. Władysław Łubieński, *Mèmoires pour serv[ir] à l'historie de Juifs convertis*. The manuscript of Łubieński's account was burned together with other manuscripts belonging to the National Library in Warsaw after the uprising of 1944.

106. Staatsarchiv Dresden, Hausarchiv Friedrich Christian, no. 240, Schreiben an Kurprinz Friedrich Christian von Saxen von Joseph A. Gabelon Graf Wackenbarth-Salmour, 1757–59, 67–71.

107. Leiman, "Rabbi Jonathan Eibeschütz's Attitude toward the Frankists," 145–51.

108. See Strack, *Das Blut*, 191.

109. Leiman, "Rabbi Jonathan Eibeschütz's Attitude toward the Frankists," 145–51.

110. Johann Salomo Semler, *Historischtheologische Abhandlungen: Zweite Sammlung* (Halle, 1762), 398

111. Ibid., 407.

112. Ibid., 391, 414–16.

113. Ibid., 395.

114. Ibid., 402.

115. See Elyakim's letter to the Council of Four Lands, published by Abraham Berliner in *Magazin für die Wissenschaft des Judenthums* 15 (1888): 13

116. See Hadas-Lebel, "Les études hebraiques en France au XVIIIe siècle et la création de la première chaire d'Écriture Sainte en Sorbonne," 93–126, esp. 107–21.

117. Ibid., 100.

118. The Vatican, ASV, Nunz. di Varsavia, 94, Relazione della Causa e Prozesso di Frenk, Response et avis de Mr. L'Abbe L'advocat docteur Bibliotecaire, et Profeseur d'hebreu en Sorbonne, sur le procèes verbal, fait par devant Monsieur Mikulski Chanoine de la Métropolie de Leopol en Pologne et grand Vicaire du Chaptire le Siè300ge vacant en 1759, 4$^{r–v}$.

119. Ibid., 4^v.

120. Ibid., 9^r.

121. For Visconti's worldview, see Ellemunter, *Antonio Eugenio Visconti und die Anfänge des Josephinismus: Eine Untersuchung über das theresianische Staatskirchentum unter besonderer Berücksichtigung der Nuntiaturberichte, 1767–1774.*

122. Roth, *The Ritual Murder*, 29–30.

123. The letter of Cavalchini is housed in the Vatican, ASV, Nunz. Varsavia, 94, 74^r; for the letter of Corsini, see below.

124. Janocki, *Józef Andrzej Hrabia na Załuskach Załuski*, trans. Kantak, 71 n. 28.

125. Ibid., 73 n. 33.

126. Ibid., 30.

127. See Kraushar, *Frank i frankiści polscy*, 1:211; see letter of Józefa [*sic*] Frank to Załuski dated 23 July 1760, Warsaw, BN, Ms. 3260, Józef Andrzej Załuski, Korespondencja z roku 1760, 2:3$^{r–v}$. Hana Frank asked Załuski to intervene so that she could receive Frank's letters from Częstochowa.

128. Turowski, "Polska rajem dla Żydów," 81; Marcin Załuski also took care of Frank's wife during his imprisonment in Częstochowa; see letter of Marcin Załuski to Józef Andrzej Załuski dated 24 October 1760, Ms. 3260, Józef Andrzej Załuski, Korespondencja z roku 1760, 4:93^r.

129. Bałaban, *Le-toledot ha-tenu'ah ha-Frankit*, 2:289.

130. Warsaw, BN, Ms. 3207, Józef Andrzej Załuski, Information touchant les Juifs, leur Talmud et les infanticides par I. Z. E. de Kiovie; Ms. 3208, Józef Andrzej Załuski, Information touchant les Juifs, leur Talmud et les Infanticides par J. Z[ałuski] Ev[êque] de Kiovie à l'occasion de l'infanticide commis récemment dans son Diocèse et de l'objection faite aux Talmudistes de Pologne par les Contre-Talmudistes néophytes en 1759. Sołtyk supplied Załuski with details of the Żytomierz trial and asked him for support in negotiations with the nuncio, see a letter of Sołtyk to Załuski dated 17 May 1760, Warsaw, BN, Ms. 3260, Józef Andrzej Załuski, Korespondencja z roku 1760, 8: 115^r–116^v.

131. For the comparison of the two versions, see Turowski, "Polska rajem dla Żydów," 83–85; and Bałaban, *Le-toledot ha-tenuah ha-Frankit*, 2:285–90. There was also a third, final version titled "La Pologne ditte [*sic*] Paradis des Juifs et Leur Terre, de Promission [*sic*] fourmentée par des Diables incarnés . . . à l'occasion d'un infanticide commis depuis un an au Diocese [*sic*] de Kijovie et au sujet de l'objection de ces crimes atroces aux Juifs

Talmudistes faite tout recemment [*sic*] à Leopol [*sic*] et à Varsovie par les Neophites [*sic*] Anti-Talmudistes, qui sont nos Nouveaux neophytes [*sic*]." This manuscript is lost.

132. Warsaw, BN, Ms. 3207, 11ᵛ–15ʳ. For another list of ritual murders, see Józef Andrzej Załuski, *Cała Polska za złoty, to jest opisanie Polski trojakie, z historii duchownej, z historii cywilnej, z historii literackiej . . . w areszcie smoleńskim r.* 1768, Warsaw, BN, Ms. 3209, 23ʳ–32ʳ.

133. Letter of Hana Frank to the nuncio, the Vatican, ASV, Arch. Nunz. Varsavia, 94, 168ʳ⁻ᵛ.

134. *Processus judicarius in causa patrati cruenti infanticidii per infidels Judaeos seniores synogae Woyslaviencis* (Lublin[?], 1761); Kraushar, *Frank i frankiści polscy*, 1:226–28; and Bałaban, *Le-toledot ha-tenuah ha-Frankit*, 2:285–90.

135. The Vatican, ASV, Nunz. Varsavia, 94, 40ʳ–41ᵛ, 61ʳ. Already Kraushar, *Frank i frankiści polscy*, 1:224–30, and Brawer, *Galitsiah vi-Yehudeha*, 267–69, speculated that the Frankists might have been involved in this trial

136. Lippman of Danzig to Emden, 23 September 1761; Emden, *Sefer shimush*, 88ʳ.

137. *Documenta Judaeos in Polonia concernentia ad Acta Metrices Regni suscepta et ex iis fideliter iterum descripta et extradicta* (Warsaw, 1763). For the details of the background of this publication, see Bałaban, "Studien und Quellen," 45–47.

138. *Documenta Judaeos in Polonia concernentia*, 35; see also a report of Cardinal Corsini, the Vatican, ASV, Segr. di Stato, Polonia, 289, Minutari di lett. del nunzio a Congregazioni Romane ed a diversi, loose file.

139. *Documenta Judaeos in Polonia concernentia*, 41–42.

140. See a letter of Kleczewski to the nuncio, 25 June 1763, the Vatican, ASV, Nunz. Varsavia, 94, 94ᵛ.

141. See Kuzmin, *Materialy*, passim.

142. Bałaban, *Le-toledot ha-tenu'ah ha-Frankit*, 2:290–92.

143. See Frankel, *The Damascus Affair*, 89.

144. As an appendix to the English translation of Isaac Ber Levinsohn's *Efes Damim: A Series of Conversations at Jerusalem between a Patriarch of the Greek Church and the Chief Rabbi of the Jews concerning the Malicious Charge against the Jews of Using Christian Blood* (London, 1841)

CHAPTER 5

1. The edict was published in Pikulski, *Złość żydowska*, 319–23.

2. Kraushar, *Frank i frankiści polscy*, 1:158–60.

3. "Z Lwowa d. 19. Septembris," *Kuryer Polski* 40 (1759): col. [3].

4. Kraushar, *Frank i frankiści polscy*, 1:328–77.

5. Ibid., 1:216–19; Kraushar added nine Jews who converted in Kamieniec in December 1755–March 1759. Some of them might have been Sabbatians; others do not seem to have anything to do with Frankism.

6. Ibid., 1:207–20.

7. For other examples of prominent Frankists missing from Kraushar's list, see Mieses, *Polacy*, 22–23.

8. Such cases are analyzed in ibid., 24.

9. Liber Baptistorum, quoted in Kraushar, *Frank i frankiści*, 1:317.

10. Ber of Bolechów, *Divre binah*, 315.

11. *Myśli z historyi o Contra-Talmudystach*, 6ʳ.

12. Kraushar, *Frank i frankiści polscy*, 1:139.

13. De Le Roi, *Die Evangelische Christenheit und die Juden unter dem Gesichtspunkte der Mission*, 1:341–43. For Kirchoff's account, see below.

14. *Myśli z historyi o Contra-Talmudystach*, 3ʳ.

15. The Vatican, ASV, Segr. di Stato, Polonia 272, 121ʳ⁻ᵛ.

16. Ibid., 175.

17. Ibid., 143ʳ.

18. Ibid., 135ʳ–136ʳ.

19. Ibid., 158ʳ–159ʳ.

20. Pikulski, *Złość żydowska*, 324: "more than 1,000"; Awedyk, *Opisanie*, 91: "almost 2,000."

21. Abraham of Szarogród, "Ma'aseh nora," in Bałaban, "Studien und Quellen," 52–57.

22. Ber of Bolechów, *Divre binah*, 320.

23. Mahler, *Yidn in amolikn Poyln in likht fun tsifern*, 1:62.

24. *Dwór Franka czyli polityka nowochrzczeńców, odkryta przez Neofitę jednego dla poprawy rządu* (Warsaw, 1790), reprinted in Eisenbach and Michalski (eds.), *Materiały do dziejów Sejmu Czteroletniego*, 6:179.

25. Czacki, *Rozprawa o Żydach i Karaitach*, 41. Julian Brinken estimated the figures for 25,000 in the whole of Poland and for 8,000 in Warsaw; Warsaw, BN, Ms. 1345, Józef Frank. Patriarcha Neofitów, 386.

26. Słowaczyński, *Polska w kształcie dykcjonarza historyczno-statystyczno-jeograficznego*, 189.

27. Skimborowicz, *Żywot, skon i nauka Jakóba Józefa Franka*, 20; and Graetz, *Frank und die Frankisten*, 52.

28. Mieses, *Polacy*, 20.

29. Gelber, "Die Taufbewegung unter den polnischen Juden im XVIII. Jahrhundert," *MGWJ* 68 (1924): 236–38.

30. Gelber estimated the total Jewish population of eighteenth-century Poland-Lithuania at 1.5 million. The generally accepted figure arrived at by Raphael Mahler is 750,000 (on the basis of the corrected figures of the fiscal census of 1764–65), some 5.35 percent of the general population of the Commonwealth. Mahler, *Yidn in amolikn Poyln in likht fun tsifirn*, 1:62.

31. For the survey of scholarship on the issue, see Goldberg, *Ha-mumarim be-mamlekhet Polin-Lita*.

32. Ber of Bolechów, *Divre binah*, 218, on the *salvus conductus* [*ktav barzel*] from *Coram iudicio*.

33. Ibid., 221.

34. Maciejko, "Baruch me-Erets Yavan and the Frankists," 333–54.

35. The Vatican, ASV, Arch. Nunz. di Varsavia, 94, Relazione della Causa e Processo di Frenk, 153ʳ⁻ᵛ. I have reproduced a transcription of this document in the Baruch Yavan article; see n. 34 above.

36. Emden, *Sefer shimush*, 16ʳ.

37. The literature on the medieval ideal of martyrdom in response to the pressure is immense; see, e.g., Baer, "Gezerat TaTN"U"; Chazan, *European Jewry and the First Cru-sade*; and Yuval, *Two Nations in Your Womb*.

38. Carlebach, *Divided Souls*, 19.

39. Goldberg, *Żydowscy konwertyci*, 213–14

40. Carlebach, *Divided Souls*, 30–31.

41. For a discussion of this responsum, see Katz, "Kavim le-biografia shel Hatam Sofer," 369.

42. Scholem, *Sabbatai Sevi*, 788.

43. See Ps. 32:6 or Jon. 2:6.

44. Moses Hagiz, *Lehishat saraf* (Hanau, 1726), 3ʳ⁻ᵛ, also quoted in Carlebach, *The Pursuit of Heresy*, 169.

45. Kleyn, *Coram iudicio*, sig. A6, lists him as one of the Contra-Talmudists involved in the Kamieniec affair.

46. *Kuryer Polski* 29 (1759), Z Kamieńca Podolskiego d. 19 Junii, cols. 2–3.

47. A pun on the dictum *sama de-kula meshtuka*, "silence is a medicine for all"; see JT Berahot 9a; *Yalkut Shimoni*, Tehilim 708.

48. Num. 23:9.

49. See *PVAA*, 432 n. 2, R. Ieshehar Berish ben Rabbi Yehoshua.

50. Ezek. 21:8.

51. Emden, *Sefer shimush*, 82ᵛ; sections from this letter have been transcribed in *PVAA*, 432.

52. *PVAA*, 780.

53. Awedyk, *Opisanie*, 100–101; and Kraushar, *Frank i frankiści*, 1:162–65.

54. See the homily of Perets ben Moshe, quoted in Ya'ari, "Le-toledot milhamtam shel hakhame Polin bi-tenu'at Frank," 455–57.

55. Ibid., 495.

56. Emden, *Sefer shimush*, 83ʳ⁻ᵛ.

57. Ibid., 26ʳ.

58. Idem, *Sefer hitabbkut*, 149ʳ–151ʳ, partly transcribed in Graetz, *Frank und die Fran-kisten*, 35.

59. Ber of Bolechów, *Divre binah*, 210.

60. Callenberg, *Bericht an einige christliche Freunde von einem Versuch, das arme jüdi-sche Volck zur Erkäntniss und Annehmung der christlichen Wahrheit anzuleiten*, 14:163.

61. Wirszubski, "Ha-mekkubal ha-Shabbeta'i Moshe David mi-Podhayyts," 189–209.

62. Emden, *Sefer hitabbkut*, 104ʳ; also quoted in Wirszubski, "Ha-mekkubbal ha-Shabbeta'i Moshe David mi-Podhayyts," 209. Wirszubski denies the truth of this testimony.

63. Emden, *Sefer hitabbkut*, 56ᵛ; partly quoted in Wirszubski, "Ha-mekkubal ha-Shabbeta'i Moshe David mi-Podhayyts," 197.

64. For Moses David, see Wirszubski, "Ha-mekkubbal ha-Shabbeta'i Moshe David mi-Podhayyts," 204–5; for Frank, see Chapter 1 in this volume.

65. Wirszubski, "Ha-mekkubbal ha-Shabbeta'i Moshe David mi-Podhayyts," 193–94.

66. Pikulski, *Złość żydowska*, 23.

67. Ibid., 27.

68. For this formula, see Emden, *Sefer shimush*, 15ʳ.

69. Ibid., 19ʳ.

70. See Brockey, *Journey to the East*, 225–26, 291.

71. Pollak, *Mandarins, Jews, and Missionaries*, 37–38.

72. Wolf (ed.), *Menasseh ben Israel Mission to Oliver Cromwell*, 29–31.

73. Emden, *Iggeret bikoret*, in *She'elat YAVe"Ts* (Altona, 1733), 2:24ᵛ

74. Idem, *Birat migdal oz*, 105ᵛ.

75. Prov. 8:34.

76. Emden, *Sefer shimush*, 19ᵛ.

77. Ber of Bolechów, *Divre bina*, 225–26.

78. Ibid. In the manuscript, there is another version of the points, crossed out. I present the alternate version in the footnotes.

79. Ber of Bolechów, *Divre binah*, 226: rest on the Shabbat with the Jews and on Sunday with the Christians.

80. Ibid., 226: that they would study books of the prophets in the holy tongue and also the book of Zohar.

81. Ibid., 226: to prove from the Talmud and the Zohar that Jesus the Nazarene was the true messiah and there will be no messiah for the Jews coming after him. And that the Talmud, because of the greatness of its evil, deserves to be burned.

82. Krętosz, *Organizacja Archidiecezji Lwowskiej obrządku łacińskiego od XV wieku do 1772 roku*, 72.

83. *RA*, 45.

84. Ber of Bolechów, *Divre binah*, 225.

85. See Rymatzki, *Hallischer Pietismus und Judenmission*, 202–9.

86. A Polish translation of excerpts from the 1730–31 Widmann and Manitius report was published by Doktór in *W poszukiwaniu żydowskich kryptochrześcijan: Dzienniki ewangelickich misjonarzy z ich wędrówek po Rzeczpospolitej w latach 1730–1747* (Warsaw, 1999), 162. Because of the oddities of the publishing process, the publication of this excellent translation precedes the publication of the originals, which are still in preparation.

87. Rymatzki, *Hallischer Pietismus*, 207–8.

88. Clark, *The Politics of Conversion*, 7.

89. Rymatzki, *Hallischer Pietismus*, 207.

90. See report of 4 February 1758, Herrnhut, Unitätsarchiv, R.19.B.d.2.a.42, David Kirchoffs Diarium aus Pohlen, 17ᵛ.

91. Herrnhut, Unitätsarchiv, R.16.7. [Lieberkühn], Einige Nachrichten von dem gegenwärtigen Zustand der Juden und den Bemühungen der Brüder ihre Bekehrung zu befördern. A fragment of this report is also quoted in De Le Roi, *Die Evangelische Christenheit*, 1:341–43.

92. Maciejko, "Christian Elements in the Frankist Doctrine," *Gal-Ed* 20: 33–35.

93. Ibid., 29.

94. The letter has been reprinted by Kurt Wilhelm as "An English Echo of the Frankist Movement," 189–91.

95. The most popular edition was *Sefer besorah tovah al pi ha-Mevasher Lukas. Evangelium Lucae ab erudito proselyte Henr. Christ. Imman. Frommano Doc. Med. in linguam ebraeam transferri ea explicari curauit editique Io. Henr. Callenberg* (Halle, 1737).

96. *ZSP*, no. 2097, quoted in Kraushar, *Frank i frankiści*, 1:271.

97. *Volumina Legum*, 6:119, 124–25, 286.

98. Teter, *Jews and Heretics in Catholic Poland*, 139.

99. Koźmian, *Pamiętniki*, 55.

100. Teter, *Jews and Heretics in Catholic Poland*, 5.

101. See ibid., 125–27.

102. Ber of Bolechów, *Divre binah*, 226.

103. "Suplika Żydów Wiarę Świętą Katolicką przymuiących," *Kuryer Polski* 14 (1759): cols. [1–8].

104. *Supplex Libellus a Judaeis fidem catholicam amplectentibus et baptismum expetentibus Illustrissimo et Reverendissimo DD Łubieński Archiepiscopo Leopolienski [sic] nunc celsissimo nominato principi primati porrectus.*

105. The Vatican, ASV, Segr. di Stato, Polonia 272, 35ʳ–40ᵗ.

106. *Supplique présentée à monseigneur l'archeveque de Leopold: Au nom de plusieurs milliers de juifs polonois, hongrois, &c. qui désirent embrasser la foi catholique, & reçevoir le s. baptême* (n.p., 1759?).

107. See Beer, *Geschichte, Lehren und Meinungen aller bestandenen und noch heute bestehenden religiösen Sekten der Juden und der Geheimlehre oder kabbalah*, 2:310.

108. *Memorial de los Judíos de Polonia y de otras varias provincias confinantes de la Turquía presentaron al nuevo Arzobispo de Gnesne . . .* (Zaragoza, 1759).

109. *Memorial de los Judíos de Polonia y de otras varias provincias confinantes de la Turquía presentaron al nuevo Arzobispo de Gnesne, . . . Impreso en Madrid, en la imprenta de los Herederos de la Viuda de Juan Gracia Infanzon, y en Original reimpreso en México en la imprenta de la Biblioteca Mexicana Año De. 1759.*

110. *Memorial, que os Judeos de Polonia, e de outras varias provincias, confinantes da Turquia, apresentaram ao novo Arcebispo de Gnesne* (Lisbon, 1759).

111. Władysław Łubieński, [Że Królestwo Niebieskie podobne jest Gospodarzowi] (Warsaw, 1759). The only copy of this letter I managed to find is housed in Warsaw, AGAD, Archiwum Nuncjatury, 006, 144ʳ–146ᵛ.

112. Wołłowicz's letter was published in the pamphlet *Myśli z historyi*, 20^v–25^r.

113. Łubieński, [Że Królestwo Niebieskie], 144^r.

114. *Myśli z historyi*, 25^r.

115. Serra to Torrigani, 6 June 1759, The Vatican, ASV, Segr. di Stato, Polonia, 272, 33^r–34^r.

116. Serra to Torrigani, July 1759, The Vatican, ASV, Segr. di Stato, Polonia, 272, 114$^{r–v}$.

117. Serra to Torrigani, 1 August 1759, The Vatican, ASV, Segr. di Stato Polonia, 272, 92^r–93^v, a transcript in Theiner, *Vetera Monumenta*, 152.

118. Łubieński's undated letter to Mikulski, The Vatican, ASV, Arch. Nunz. di Varsavia, Relazione della Acta e Processo di Frenk, 94, 60^r–61^v, also transcribed by Theiner, *Vetera Monumenta*, 165.

119. Łubieński, *Mèmoires pour serv[ir] à l'historie de Juifs convertis*, quoted in Kraushar, *Frank i frankiści polscy*, 1:138. The manuscript of Łubieński's account was burned in 1944.

120. *Myśli z historyi*, 16^v–17^v.

121. "Z Łowicza die 23. Junij," *Kuryer Polski* 26 (1759): cols. [11–16]

122. For earlier parallels, see Carlebach, *The Pursuit of Heresy*, 100 (on Hayon).

123. Calmanson, *Essai sur l'état actuel des Juifs de Pologne et leur perfectibilité*, 13; and idem, *Uwagi nad nineyszym stanem Żydów Polskich y ich wydoskonaleniem*, 21–22.

CHAPTER 6

1. The supplication was published as a broadside in 1759 and then reprinted in *Nowiny* 312–13 (1881). For a detailed discussion, see Kraushar, *Frank i frankiści polscy*, 1:165–67.

2. Jeske-Choiński, *Neofici polscy*, 82–84; for an interesting, if difficult to verify, account of the power struggle between Frank and Krysa, see Warsaw, BN, Ms. 1345, Aleksander Bronikowski (Julian Brinken), Józef Frank. Patriarcha Neofitów. Powieść historyczna z drugiej połowy XVIII wieku, 231, 240, 405–6, passim.

3. Jeske-Choiński, *Neofici polscy*, 86.

4. Serra to Torrigani, 28 November 1759, in Theiner, *Vetera Monumenta*, 155.

5. *RA*, 55.

6. Ibid.; and Kraushar, *Frank i frankiści polscy*, 1:169.

7. *Kuryer Polski* 11 (1760): col. 2.

8. According to Pikulski, *Złość żydowska*, 334, approximately thirty people; see also Kraushar, *Frank i frankiści polscy*, 1:176.

9. Emden, *Sefer shimush*, 83^r.

10. ZSP, no. 1707, quoted in Kraushar, *Frank i frankiści polscy*, 1:175.

11. Ber of Bolechów, *Divre binah*, 316; see "Pamiętnik Thulliego," ed. S. Schnür-Pepłowskij, 372.

12. Warsaw, AGAD, Metryka Koronna, Księgi Kanclerskie, 16, 61.

13. Serra to Torrigiani, 14 October 1759, in Theiner, *Vetera Monumenta*, 155.

14. Ibid.

15. Serra to Torrigiani, 5 December 1759, in Theiner, *Vetera Monumenta*, 156.

16. Serra to Torrigiani, 26 December 1759, in Theiner, *Vetera Monumenta*, 157.

17. *ZSP*, no. 1419, in Kraushar, *Frank i frankiści polscy*, 2:333; the dictum has been misquoted and misattributed in Scholem, "Die Metamorphose des häretischen Messianismus der Sabbatianer in religiösen Nihilismus im 18. Jahrhundert," 213.

18. Serra to Torrigiani, 13 February 1760, in Theiner, *Vetera Monumenta*, 158.

19. Cf. Gen. 17:8.

20. *ZSP*, no. 1292.

21. Scholem, "Redemption through Sin," 91

22. Ibid., 127.

23. Idem, "Ha-tenu'ah ha-Shabbeta'it be-Polin," 120–21.

24. Idem, "Die Metamorphose," 209–10.

25. Awedyk, *Opisanie*, 9–10, lists the rabbis Leyb of Brzezie, Wolf of Krzywcze, Israel of Gliniany, Falik of Lanckoronie, Baruch of Rawa. To this should be added Rabbi Nahman of Busk.

26. Serra to Torrigiani, 19 September 1759, in Theiner, *Vetera Monumenta*, 164.

27. Serra to Torrigiani, 31 October 1759, in Theiner, *Vetera Monumenta*, 154.

28. Scholem, "Ha-tenu'ah ha-Shabbeta'it be-Polin," 120–21.

29. *ZSP*, no. 1328, in Kraushar, *Frank i frankiści polscy*, 1:308.

30. Tsefo: $90 + 80 + 6 = 176$; Polin: $80 + 6 + 30 + 10 + 50 = 176$.

31. Tsafon: $90 + 80 + 6 + 50 = 226$; Polin Lita: $80 + 6 + 30 + 10 + 50 + 30 + 10 + 9 + 1 = 226$.

32. Kaidanover, *Sefer kav hayashar*, 336–38.

33. The idea of Poland in Frank's teachings has been analyzed by Schreiner in "Der Messiah kommt zuerst nach Polen," 242–68.

34. *ZSP*, no. 84.

35. Ibid., no. 737.

36. See Scholem, *Sabbatai Sevi*, 164–65.

37. *ZSP*, no. 263.

38. Ibid., nos. 32, 49.

39. Ibid., no. 245.

40. Ibid., no. 1172.

41. Serra to Torrigiani, 31 Oct 1759, in Theiner, *Vetera Monumenta*, 154.

42. Ibid.

43. Pikulski, *Złość żydowska*, 327–33; Hebrew translation in Ber of Bolechów, *Divre binah*, 317–19. Jan Doktór has suggested that the denunciation was orchestrated by Eibeschütz's supporters and based on the rivalry between Frank and Jonathan Eibeschütz; see Doktór, *Śladami mesjasza-apostaty*, 134. While interesting, this is not sufficiently substantiated.

44. In Ber of Bolechów, *Divre binah*, 319: Gog and Magog.

45. In Pikulski, it is a quotation from John 10:16. But in Ber of Bolechów, *Divre binah*, 319, it is given as Zech.14:9: And the Lord shall be king over all the earth; on that day the Lord shall be one, and his name one.

46. Kraushar, *Frank i frankiści polscy*, 1:187.

47. The Vatican, ASV, Nunz. di Varsavia, 94, Relazione della Causa e Processo di Frenk, 150ᵛ, 151ᵛ.

48. Theiner, *Vetera Monumenta*, 157.

49. *RA*, no. 57.

50. Serra to Torrigiani 2 January 1760, in Theiner, *Vetera Monumenta*, 157.

51. Serra to Torrigiani 30 January 1760, the Vatican, ASV, Segr. di Stato, Polonia, 272, 159ᵛ⁻ʳ; choosing the "apostles" is confirmed also by Frankist sources; see *RA*, no. 43.

52. Emden, *Sefer shimush*, 83ʳ.

53. Pikulski, *Złość żydowska*, 336–37.

54. *RA*, no. 57.

55. See Mikulski to Serra, n.d., in Theiner, *Vetera Monumenta*, 164.

56. Antoni Dembowski to Załuski, 27 January 1760, Józef Andrzej Załuski, Korespondencja, Warsaw, BN, Ms. 3261, 1:156.

57. Kossakowski-Moliwda to Załuski, 19 May 1761, Józef Andrzej Załuski, Korespondencja, Warsaw, BN, Ms. 3261, 2:119ʳ⁻ᵛ. In another letter, he was required to confirm that he was a good Christian; see ibid., a letter of Moliwda to Załuski, 22 October 1761, 121ʳ⁻ᵛ.

58. Kraushar, *Frank i frankiści polscy*, 1:182.

59. Ibid., 1:183. See also Serra to Torrigiani, 13 February 1760, the Vatican, ASV, Segr. di Stato, Polonia, 272, 160ᵛ.

60. *Interrogatia et depositions Jacobi Josephi Frenk, recens ad fidem Christianam conversi*, quoted in Kraushar, *Frank i frankiści polscy*, 1:186. The manuscript of the protocol of the investigation quoted by Kraushar was housed in the library of the Piarist convent in Warsaw but has been lost. An abridged version titled "Factum" exists in the Vatican, ASV, Nunz. di Varsavia, 94, Relazione della Causa e Processo di Frenk, 148ʳ–151ᵛ.

61. *Myśli z historyi*, fol. 10ᵛ; Kraushar, *Frank i frankiści polscy*, 1:192–93.

62. Kraushar, *Frank i frankiści polscy*, 1:200; see also the Vatican, ASV, Nunz. di Varsavia, 94, Relazione, 149ᵛ.

63. *ZSP*, no. 32.

64. Kraushar, *Frank i frankiści polscy*, 1:202; see also the Vatican, ASV, Nunz. Varsavia, 94, Relazione, 150ᵛ.

65. Kraushar, *Frank i frankiści polscy*, 1:198.

66. Mieses, *Polacy*, 24.

67. Abraham of Zamość to Emden, 24 October 1760, in Emden, *Sefer shimush*, 84ᵛ.

68. Mahler, "Statistik fun Yidn in der Lubliner Voyevodstve," 6.

69. Częstochowa, AJG, Ms. 1209, Annalium Ordinis S. Pauli i eremitae monachorum sub regula divi Augustini Deo famulantium. Volumen tertium quo (1727–75), 258ᵛ; according to *RA*, no. 58: on 4 February.

70. Corsini to Serra, 17 March 1760, the Vatican, ASV, Nunz. di Varsavia, 94, 161ᵛ.

71. The proclamation was printed as a separate broadsheet [Feliks Paweł Turski], *Uwiadomienie Zwierzchności Duchownej co do osoby Józefa Franka i Żydów przechodzących na wiarę chrześcijańską* ([Warsaw], 1760). Large sections have been reproduced in Kraushar, *Frank i frankiści polscy*, 1:204–6.

72. *RA*, no. 59.

73. Częstochowa, AJG, Ms. 1209, Annalium Ordinis S. Pauli i eremitae monachorum sub regula divi Augustini Deo famulantium. Volumen tertium quo (1727–75), 258ᵛ.

74. Warsaw, BN, Ms. 3260, Józef Andrzej Załuski, Korespondencja z roku 1760, 2: 3ʳ⁻ᵛ.

75. *RA*, no. 62.

76. Sołtyk to Wargawski, 14 July 1761, the Vatican, ASV, Nunz. di Varsavia, 94, 163ᵛ.

77. *RA*, no. 60.

78. Wargawski to Serra, 14 July 1761, the Vatican, ASV, Nunz. di Varsavia, 94, 162ʳ.

79. Sołtyk to Wargawski, 20 July 1761, the Vatican, ASV, Nunz. di Varsavia, 94, 163ʳ–164ʳ.

80. [Kajetan Sołtyk], Relatio status diocesis Cracoviensis anno 1765, the Vatican, ASV, Congregazione del Concilio, Relationes Dioecesum, 272, 28ʳ⁻ᵛ.

81. *RA*, no. 65.

82. Częstochowa, AJG, Ms 748, Memorabilia Celeberrimi Conventus C[lari] M[ontis]. A Capitulo Electivo Provinciali Sub Praesidentia Reverdisimi in Xsto P. Andreaqe Musar Fratrum Eremitarum Ordini S. Pauli Prime S. T. D. Prioris Generalis Meritissuni, 245ᵛ⁻ʳ, 273ᵛ; cf. Baliński (ed.), *Pielgrzymka do Jasnej Góry w Częstochowie odbyta przez pątnika XIX [sic] wieku i wydana z rękopisu*, 397–98.

83. The first extant manuscript describing the legend titled "Translacio tabule Beate Marie Virginis, quam sanctus Lucas depinxit propriis manibus" can be dated to the first half of the fifteenth century. It was published by Szafraniec, "Opis przeniesienia obrazu Matki Boskiej Częstochowskiej z Jerozolimy na Jasną Górę," 196–204.

84. Fijałek (ed.), *Zbiór dokumentów zakonu oo. Paulinów w Polsce*, 1:175.

85. Akta dotyczące obligacj mszalnych, Częstochowa, AJG, 146, 5.

86. Kiedrzyński, *Mensa Nazarea seu Historia imaginis Divae Claromontanae*, 66–383.

87. *ZSP*, no. 778.

88. Num. Rabbah 12:4, 12:6.

89. See, e.g., Nahmanides, *Drush le-Rosh Ha-shanah*, end.

90. Scholem, *Sabbatai Sevi*, 164–65.

91. *ZSP*, nos. 135, 831; see also Kraushar, *Frank i frankiści polscy*, 2:189, 191.

92. J[ohn] W[esley] Etheridge, *The Targums of Onkelos and Jonathan Ben Uzziel on the Pentateuch with the Fragments of the Jerusalem Targum from the Chaldee* (London, 1862), 527

93. BT Megilla 29a; and Rosh Hashanah 31a.

94. Gikatilla, *Sha'are orah (Gates of Light)*, trans. Weinstein, 204.

95. Scholem, "*Shekhinah*: The Feminine Element in Divinity," 160–61.

96. Ibid., 147.

97. Green, "*Shekhinah*, the Virgin Mary, and the Song of Songs," 1–52, esp. 1, 21.

98. Ibid., 15, 19, 26, passim.

99. Ibid., 29, 34.

100. The association became commonplace also in Christian kabbalah; see G. Javary, "A propos du thème de la Šekina: Variations sur le nom de Dieu," in *Kabbalistes Chrétiens* (Paris, 1979), esp. 302–3. For Jewish responses, see Scholem, *Sabbatai Sevi*, 85 n. 130.

101. An untitled text reproduced in Scholem, "Le-yedi'at ha-Shabbeta'ut mi-tokh kitve Kardoso," in *Mehkarim u-mekorot*, 291.

102. *ZSP*, no. 170.

103. Esther Rabbah 10:14; Song of Songs Rabbah 6:25.

104. BT Baba Batra 16b; Midrash Tehillim 22, 42.

105. Zohar 3:249a–b; English translation in Tishby, *The Wisdom of the Zohar*, 1:396–97.

106. Zohar 3:68a.

107. For examples, see Berger, "Ayalta," 1:209–17, esp. 213–15.

108. Liebes, "Tren urzilin de-Ayalta," 113–69.

109. For interpretations touching upon this equivalency, see Scholem, *Sabbatai Sevi*, 235–36, 308 n. 291, 869, passim.

110. For the analyses of this myth in Hazzan, see Elqayam, "Leidato ha-sheniyah shel ha-mashi'ah," 85–166, esp. 121–22; and Halperin, "The Snake and the Ayalta."

111. Elqayam, "Leidato ha-sheniyah," 129.

112. Ibid.

113. Zohar 3:119b.

114. Scholem, "Perush mizmore tehillim," 128–29. See also Hazzan testimony about Sabbatai saying that "there is no division, distinction, or separation whatever" between him and the Godhead; Scholem, *Sabbatai Sevi*, 235.

115. *ZSP*, no. 1452, in Kraushar, *Frank i frankiści polscy*, 2:336. Sabbatai's identification with the *Shekhinah* is attested by many Sabbatian sources; see Scholem, *Sabbatai Sevi*, 908 n. 220.

116. *ZSP*, nos. 169, 801, 817, 1175, 1179, 1254.

117. Ibid., nos. 817, 1254.

118. Ibid., no. 223.

119. Ibid., no. 801.

120. Ibid., no. 614.

121. Ibid., no. 91.

122. Ibid., no. 1153.

123. Ibid., no. 194.

124. Ibid., no. 917.

125. Ibid., no. 1487, in Kraushar, *Frank i frankiści polscy*, 1:252.

126. *ZSP*, no. 597.

127. Ibid., no. 9.

128. See, e.g., *RA*, no. 66.

129. Frank's daughter's Jewish name was recorded in an early, no longer extant, version of *ZSP*, quoted in Skimborowicz, *Żywot i skon*, 44.

130. Scholem, "*Shekhinah*," 145.

131. Kraushar, *Frank i frankiści polscy*, 1:209.

132. See Job 28:13–28; Prov. 8:22–31; also the pseudoepigrapha belonging to the Catholic, but not to the Jewish, canon: Sir. 19:20; Wis. 7:25, passim.

133. *ZSP*, no. 2197; and *RA*, passim.

134. *ZSP*, no. 325.

135. Ibid., no. 329.

136. Ibid., no. 314.

137. See Chapter 9 in this volume.

138. A miniature of Eva has been reproduced in Kraushar, *Frank i frankiści polscy*, 2:frontispiece.

139. *ZSP*, no. 1487, in Kraushar, *Frank i frankiści polscy*, 1:252.

140. *ZSP*, no. 1051.

141. Ibid., nos. 552, 609, 725.

142. Ibid., no. 552.

CHAPTER 7

1. Poland's hereditary nobility.

2. For the 1763–64 election, see Szymon Askenazy, *Die letzte polnischeKönigswahl*.

3. Joseph Frank to Visconti, the Vatican, ASV, 94, Arch Nunz. di Varsavia, 186ʳ.

4. See Rudnicki, *Biskup Kajetan Sołtyk*, 51–83.

5. Ibid., 83–88.

6. Konopczyński, *Fryderyk Wielki a Polska*; Wojciech Kriegseisen, *Ewangelicy polscy i litewscy w epoce saskiej* (1696–1763); and Kraushar, *Książe Repnin a Polska*.

7. Łubieńska, *Sprawa dysydencka 1764–1766*, 9.

8. Kraushar, *Książe Repnin a Polska*, 1:70, 72, 82.

9. Ibid., 89–91; and Rudnicki, *Biskup Kajetan Sołtyk*, 114.

10. See Czeppe, "Biskup Kajetan Sołtyk a innowiercy," 357–64; Rudnicki, *Biskup Kajetan Sołtyk*, 120–44; and Łubieńska, *Sprawa dysydencka*, 109.

11. Rudnicki, *Biskup Kajetan Sołtyk*, 179–89.

12. Kęder, "Jasna Góra wobec przemian politycznych w Rzeczypospolitej w latach 1661–1813," 148–54.

13. A paraphrase of Jer. 1:14, possibly taken from a Sabbatian hymn; see Scholem, "Kuntres me-reshit yame'ah shel kat ha-Donmeh be-Saloniki," in *Mehkare Shabbeta'ut*, 386.

14. *ZSP*, no. 202.

15. *RA*, no. 69.

16. Ibid.

17. Baruch Yavan's letter was published by Rabbi Jacob Emden in his *Sefer hitabbkut*, 81^v–82^v. Large sections of the letter have been reprinted by Graetz, *Frank und die Frankisten*, 33–35; see also Kraushar, *Frank i frankiści polscy*, 1:274–77.

18. Emden, *Sefer hitabbkut*, 82^r.

19. Ibid., 82^v.

20. Ibid., 81^v.

21. *RA*, no. 71. The extant text of *RA* has to "enter the religion etc." Kraushar's recension had to "enter the religion of Edom"; see Kraushar, *Frank i frankiści polscy*, 1:279.

22. Several versions of the Red Letters are known. A letter to the Jews of Brody was used by Peter Beer as a basis for a German translation in his *Geschichte, Lehren und Meinungen*, 329–39. Another one addressed to the Jews of Bohemia was published in Porges, "Texte de la lettre adressée par les Frankistes aux communautés Juives de Boheme," 285. A letter to the Jews of Tartary was published by Vishnitzer as "Poslanie Frankistov 1800 goda," 9–17. Wacholder published yet another one (to the Jews of Hungary), in "Jacob Frank and the Frankists," 265–93. A manuscript copy of a Red Letter is preserved at the Jewish Theological Seminary in New York (Ms. BN 3857).

23. For the discussion of the authenticity of Frank's authorship of the letters, see Wacholder, "Jacob Frank and the Frankists," 267–68. I am convinced by Wacholder's arguments for Frank's genuine authorship.

24. Ibid., 268.

25. Ibid., 269.

26. Ibid., 268.

27. Gen. 33:12–17.

28. Wacholder, "Jacob Frank and the Frankists," 270–71; Hebrew/Aramaic original, ibid., 288.

29. See G. Cohen, "Esau as a Symbol in Early Medieval Thought," 19–48; and Yuval, *Two Nations in Your Womb*, 1–30.

30. See, e.g., *ZSP*, nos. 449, 2121, 2156; and Kraushar, *Frank i frankiści polscy*, 2:379.

31. *ZSP*, no. 939.

32. See, e.g., ibid., no. 584.

33. Wacholder, "Jacob Frank and the Frankists," 276.

34. Kraushar, *Frank i frankiści*, 1:277–78; and Doktór, *Śladami mesjasza apostaty*, 201.

35. *ZSP*, no. 2156.

36. Ibid., no. 1012.

37. See Shmuel Ettinger, "Va'ad arba aratsot," in his *Ben Polin le-Rusya* (Jerusalem, 1994), 174–85; and Israel Bartal, "Politika Yehudit terom-modernit: Va'ade ha-arastot be-mizrah Eyropa," in *Ha-tsiyonut ve-ha-hazarah le-historia: Ha-arakhah me-hadash* (Jerusalem, 1999), 186–194.

38. *Memoirs of Ber of Bolechów (1723–1805)*, ed. Vishnitzer, 142–43.

39. For the revolt of 1768, see Władysław Serczyk, *Hajdamacy*; and Franciszek Rawita-Gawroński, *Historya ruchów hajdamackich*.

40. Kraushar, *Książę Repnin i Polska*, 1:254.

41. Ibid., 1: 292–318.

42. For the Bar Confederation, see, esp., Konopczyński, *Konfederacja barska*; idem, *Konfederacja barska: Wybór tekstów*; Kęder, *Stolica Apostolska wobec Rzeczypospolitej w okresie Konfederacji Barskiej*; and Jerzy Michalski, *Schyłek Konfederacji Barskiej*.

43. Konopczyński, *Konfederacja barska: Wybór tekstów*, 16.

44. For examples, see Janusz Maciejewski et al. (eds.), *Literatura konfederacji barskiej* (Warsaw, 2008), 3:463, 465, 469, 479, passim.

45. *ZSP*, no. 889.

46. *RA*, no. 76, erroneous date (November 1769 instead of 1770); see also *ZSP*, no. 60.

47. *ZSP*, no. 782.

48. Ibid., no. 1254.

49. Ibid., nos. 723, 1179.

50. *RA*, no. 78, erroneous date (1770 instead of 1771).

51. *ZSP*, no. 1595, in Kraushar, *Frank i frankiści polscy*, 1:297.

52. *RA*, no. 79.

53. *RA*, no. 80; see also *ZSP*, no. 60.

54. See Michalski, *Schyłek Konfederacji Barskiej*, 66–70.

55. Ibid., 78–83.

56. *Memoirs of Ber of Bolechów*, 149–50.

57. *ZSP*, no. 316.

58. Prov. 30:23.

59. Num. 24:18

60. *ZSP*, no. 85.

61. Zohar 2:118a–b.

62. Sota 9:15.

63. *ZSP*, no. 429.

64. *RA*, no. 80.

65. Frank's status was discussed with Catholic authorities; see the Vatican, ASV, Segr. di Stato, Polonia, 312, 9^{r-v}; 14^r–15^v.

66. Russian ambassador in Vienna between 1768 and 1784; I did not manage to find any accounts of Frank's meetings with Golitsin.

67. Ignaz Philipp Dengel, *Nuntius Josef Garampi in preussich Schlesien und in Sachsen im Jahre 1776*, 5:239.

68. *ZSP*, no. 808.

69. Emden, *Sefer torat ha-kenaot*, 122.

70. Jews were expelled from five of the six royal cities of Moravia (Brünn, Jihlava, Olomouc, Znojmo, and Neustadt) in 1454 and from Uherské Hradiště in 1514. Until the mid-nineteenth century, the cities were practically closed to Jewish settlement. Jacob Moses and his companion, whose name is not known, were the first Jews to be granted permission to settle in Brünn.

71. Karniel, "Jüdischer Pseudomessianismus und deutsche Kultur," 33.

72. Ibid.

73. Krauss, "Schöndl Dobruschka," 145.

74. Brno, MZA, B1 J2 box 615 1702; AMB, J 57/81.

75. Brno, MZA, B1 J19 box 704 1719, fol. 34; AMB, J 129.

76. Emden, *Sefer hitabbkut*, 24ʳ, 45ᵛ; and Scholem, "Ein Frankist," 83.

77. Emden, *Sefer hitabbkut*, 45ᵛ.

78. See ibid., fols. 32ᵛ, 43ʳ, 50ʳ, 82ʳ.

79. For the Dobruschka family tree, see Ruzička, "Die österreichischen Dichter jüdischer Abstammung Moses Dobruschka," 287.

80. The date of Salomon Dobruschka's death, according to Ruzička, ibid.; Krauss, "Schöndl Dobruschka," 145, believes that Dobruschka died in 1763.

81. See Karniel, "Jüdischer Pseudomessianismus und deutsche Kultur," 35–37.

82. Brno, MZA, B1 J47 box 730/22.

83. Ruzička, 'Die österreichischen Dichter jüdischer Abstammung Moses Dobruschka," 287–89.

84. Mandel, *The Militant Messiah*, 82. Mandel mistakenly dates Moses Dobruschka's conversion to 1778.

85. The list of the families is given in G. Wolf, *Judentaufen in Österreich*, 78.

86. Ibid.; cf. Karniel, "Jüdischer Pseudomessianismus und deutsche Kultur," 35.

87. The material housed in the Moravský Zemský Archiv in Brno documents eleven Jewish baptisms in Moravia in June–August 1759 and eighteen in 1760. I was unable to determine whether these baptisms have anything to do with the Frankist baptisms that took place in Poland around the same time; see Brno, MZA, B1 J47 box 729/1.

88. Scholem, "Redemption through Sin," 135.

89. Megerlin, *Geheime Zeugnisse vor die Wahrheit der christlichen Religionen*, introduction; see also an anonymous booklet, *Kurzer Bericht von dem hochgelehrten Rabbi Jonas und den unter den Juden seinetwegen entstandenen Streitigkeiten*, discussed in Brilling, "Das erste Gedicht auf einen deutschen Rabbiner aus dem Jahre 1752," 38–147.

90. I have published one such account; see Maciejko, "A Jewish-Christian Sect with a Sabbatian Background Revisited," 95–113.

91. Krauss, "Schöndl Dobruschka," 148.

92. Karniel, "Jüdischer Pseudomessianismus und deutsche Kultur," 36–37.

93. See Brilling, "Eibenschütziana," part 2, *HUCA* 37 (1965): 255–73.

94. Mandel, "He'arot-shulayim al aharit toledotehah shel ha-tenu'ah ha-Frankistit," 72; cf. Karniel, "Jüdischer Pseudomessianismus und deutsche Kultur," 38. Schöndl changed her name following the edict of Joseph II of July 1787, obliging the Jews in Austria to take German names. Scholem mistakenly inferred from the change of the name that Schöndl converted to Christianity.

95. Sonnenfels's grandfather, Rabbi Michael Chasid, was a Sabbatian in Berlin; see Friedenthal, "Michael Chasid und die Sabbatianer," 375. More important, Sonnenfels's father was Eibeschütz's pupil in Prague and sent a copy of the manuscript of *Va-avo ha-yom* to Michael Chasid in Berlin; see Emden, *Sefer hitabbkut*, 1ʳ⁻ᵛ; idem, *Beit Yehonatan ha-sofer*, 1ᵛ.

96. Karniel, *Die Toleranzpolitik Kaiser Josefs II*, 519; idem, "Joseph von Sonnenfels," 136.

97. The Dobruschka family kept a strictly kosher kitchen and held a monopoly for supplying Moravian Jews with kosher wine; Brno, AMB, J65/82.

98. See Krauss, *Joachim Edler von Popper*, and Kisch, "Dantons Tod und Poppers Neffen," 65–67.

99. See Krauss, *Joahim Edler von Popper*, 22, 29–31.

100. Ibid., 77.

101. The case continued even after Popper's death in 1795; see Karniel, "Jüdischer Pseudomessianismus und deutsche Kultur," 40; and Kisch, "Dantons Tod," 66. Some of the documents from the case are reproduced in Krauss, *Joachim Edler von Popper*, 106–14.

102. Wölfle-Fischer, *Junius Frey*, 55–56, corrects the contention of Karniel, "Jüdischer Pseudomessianismus und deutsche Kultur," 40, that Dobruschka was given the position of a censor of Hebrew books.

103. Wölfle-Fischer, *Junius Frey*, 56–58.

104. Scholem, *Du frankisme au jacobinisme*, 18.

105. On his literary activity, see Wölfle-Fischer, *Junius Frey*, 61–75; and Karniel, "Jüdischer Pseudomessianismus und deutsche Kultur," 41–46.

106. McCagg, *A History of Habsburg Jews*, 39; and Fischer-Colbrie, *Michael Denis*, 19–23. Although Denis was never a Freemason himself, he was close to many members of Ignatz von Born's lodge, Zur wahren Eintracht.

107. Karniel, *Die Toleranzpolitik Kaiser Josefs II*, 303; cf. Krauss, "Schöndl Dobruschka," 147; and Mandel, *The Militant Messiah*, 79.

108. Mauthner, *Lebenserinnerungen*, 305. For the account of the Frankist origins of Mauthner's family, see 112, 306–7. Moses Dobruschka was born in 1753, long before Frank's arrival to the region.

109. Heymann, *Die Chevalier von Geldern*, 227.

110. Heymann was murdered by the Nazis, and his planned book on Frankism was never published and is probably irretrievably lost. The results of Heymann's genealogical research are preserved in a file titled "Verwandten-Übersicht über die wichtigsten Frankistenfamilien." This file is attached to a letter to Gershom Scholem dated 4 August 1938, which is stored in Scholem's archive in Jerusalem, JNUL, Arc. 4/1599. Some of Heymann's findings were later utilized by Scholem; see his "Ein Frankist," 83; idem, "Ein verschollener jüdischer Mystiker der Aufklärungszeit, 275.

111. Krauss, "Schöndl Dobruschka," 147.

112. See Guttmann, "Lazarus Bendavid," 205–6. Kraushar also mentioned that in Offenbach, Frank started to call himself "Dobrucki"; Kraushar, *Frank i frankiści*, 2:114.

113. *RA*, no. 100.

114. See "Anziege des Anonymus B. gegen die Prager Frankisten vom Jahre 1799," reproduced as Appendix 2 to Žáček, "Zwei Beiträge," 404.

115. Forster, *Sämmtliche Schriften*, 8:169; see also Gordon, "Georg Foster und die Juden," 219–21.

116. Žáček, "Zwei Beiträge," 351.

117. Brno, MZA, B1 1251/F123, Franck, 5ʳ.

118. Trautenberger, *Chronik der Landeshauptstadt Brünn*, 4:113; cf. Balbinder, *Listy z dějin brněnského obchodu*, 154–56.

119. Prussian and Austrian passports have been published in Kraushar, *Frank i frankiści*, 2:271–72. The Russian passport is lost.

120. Brno, MZA, B1 1251/F123, Franck, 14ʳ.

121. Trautenberger, *Chronik der Landeshauptstadt Brünn*, 4:115; and Kraushar, *Frank i frankiści*, 2:6.

122. Karniel, "Jüdischer Pseudomessianismus und deutsche Kultur," 34–35 n. 10. According to some accounts, about 40 percent of Prussian spies working in the Habsburg monarchy during the reign of Maria Theresa were Jewish; see idem, *Die Toleranzpolitik*, 243–46.

123. Part of Zollern's correspondence, as well as other documents pertaining to Frank's stay in Brünn, were published by Rabinowicz, in "Jacob Frank in Brno," 435–45. The transcription is not always reliable.

124. Trautenberger, *Chronik der Landeshauptstadt Brünn*, 4:116.

125. Rabinowicz, "Jacob Frank in Brno," 431.

126. Blümegen's letter in preserved in Brno, MZA, B1 1251/F123, Franck, 20ʳ⁻ᵛ.

127. Mandel, *The Militant Messiah*, 82, links this with the conversion of the Dobruschkas. However, the Dobruschkas did not convert until 1777. It is much more likely that this remark refers to the conversion in Prossnitz of 1773.

128. Trautenberger, *Chronik der Landeshauptstadt Brünn*, 4:116.

129. Žáček, "Zwei Beiträge," 354–55.

130. See Kraushar, *Frank i frankiści polscy*, 2:29–30.

131. Brno, MZA, B1 1251/F123, Franck, 31ʳ⁻ᵛ.

132. Kraushar, *Frank i frankiści polscy*, 2:32.

133. Rabinowicz, "Jacob Frank in Brno," 434.

134. Kraushar, *Frank i frankiści polscy*, 2:29.

CHAPTER 8

1. Löw, "Zur Geschichte der ungarischen Sabbathäer," 4:440–41.

2. Emden, *Sefer shimush*, 18ʳ and 23ᵛ. Eibeschütz's writings and correspondence between Jonathan Eibeschütz and Frank were reportedly circulating among the Frankists in Podolia.

3. See letter of Abraham ha-Kohen of Zamość to Emden, reproduced in Emden, *Sefer shimush*, 84ʳ; Emden, *Sefer hitabbkut*, 23ᵛ. Cf. also Graetz, *Geschichte der Juden von den ältersten Zeiten bis auf die Gegenwart*, 10:404; Liebes, "Hibbur bi-lashon ha-Zohar le-Rabbi Wolf ben Rabbi Yehonatan Aybeshits al havurato ve-al sod ha-ge'ullah," 80.

4. Liebes, "Hibbur," 80; and Scholem, "Berukhiah," 378.

5. Graetz, *Frank und die Frankisten*, 66.

6. Emden, *Sefer shimush*, 82ᵛ–83ʳ.

7. Ibid., 82ᵛ; and idem, *Sefer hitabbkut*, 20ᵛ.

8. Emden, *Sefer hitabbkut*, 48ᵛ.

9. Scholem, "Ha-tenu'ah ha-Shabbeta'it be-Polin," 89.

10. Schatz-Uffenheimer, *Ha-ra'ayon ha-meshihi me-az gerush Sefarad*, 76; and Shai, *Mashi'ah shel gilui arayot*, 240.

11. "Ma'aseh nora," in Bałaban, *Le-toledot ha-tenu'ah ha-Frankit*, 2:297–98.

12. Kraushar, *Frank i frankiści polscy*, 1:183–84.

13. Ibid.

14. Yehudah Liebes has argued that during his trip to Moravia, Wolf accepted the messianic mandate of Frank. According to Liebes, he parted ways with Frank only after the latter's conversion to Christianity; see Liebes, "Ketavim hadashim be-kabbalah Shabbeta'it mi-hugo shel R' Yehonatan Aybeshits," in *Sod ha'emunah ha-Shabbeta'it*, 143–47.

15. Emden, *Sefer hitabbkut*, 40ʳ⁻ᵛ; see also 48ᵛ.

16. Exod. 13:21–22, 14:24.

17. Pirke de-Rabbi Eliezer, 31. In most other midrashim, the vision of Abraham is that of the pillar of a cloud; see Bereshit Rabbah 55:1 and Midrash Tanhuma Noah 11.

18. See Hayyim Vital, *Sefer ets hayyim* (Jerusalem, 1970), 26, part 2; see also Idel, *Ascensions on High in Jewish Mysticism*, 108

19. Zohar 2:7b.

20. For the identification, see Scholem, *Sabbatai Sevi*, 908 n. 220; for the abolition of the fasts in thonor of the descent of the *Shekhinah*, see ibid., 237.

21. Ibid., 927.

22. Emden, *Sefer shimush*, 84ᵛ–85ʳ.

23. Ibid., 54ʳ; see also Liebes, "Hibbur," 95–97.

24. Graetz, "Ezechiel Landau's Gesuch an Maria Theresia gegen Jonathan Eibeschütz," 17–25; Leiman, "When a Rabbi Is Accused of Heresy: R. Ezekiel Landau's Attitude toward R. Jonathan Eibeschütz in the Emden-Eibeschütz Controversy," 185–86; and Klemperer, *Rabbi Jonathan Eibeschütz*, 134 n. 2.

25. Emden, *Sefer hitabbkut*, 51ʳ–52ʳ, 82ʳ⁻ᵛ; cf. also Carmilly-Weinberger, "Wolf Jonas Eibeschütz," 7–26.

26. See Liebes, "Hibbur," 81, and references therein.

27. *Gvul Benyamin* was the title of Wolf's lost book on kabbalah; see Liebes, "Hibbur," 80.

28. Emden, *Sefer hitabbkut*, 19ᵛ.

29. Emden, *Megillat sefer*, ed. Kahana, 201.

30. Emden, *Sefer hitabbkut*, 51ʳ.

31. Ibid.

32. Emden, *Megillat sefer*, 204.

33. This work was frequently cited by Emden (see, e.g., *Sefer hitabbkut*, 26ʳ⁻ᵛ, 27ᵛ, 33ᵛ) but long regarded as inauthentic. However, Yehudah Liebes identified Wolf's treatise

as a part of another manuscript (Jerusalem, JNUL, Ms. Heb. 8° 3100) and published it together with an extensive commentary in his "Hibbur," 77–102.

34. Kwasnik-Rabinowicz, "Wolf Eibeschütz," 268; and Klemperer, *Rabbi Jonathan Eibeschütz*, 134. Ezekiel Landau was one of the Jewish leaders who urged Eibeschütz to send Wolf away.

35. Emden, *Sefer hitabbkut*, 21ᵛ, 30ᵛ–31ʳ; see also Kwasnik-Rabinowicz, "Wolf Eibeschütz," 268–69.

36. Emden, *Sefer hitabbkut*, 53ʳ.

37. Ibid., 21ʳ.

38. Ibid., 21ᵛ.

39. Ibid., 48ᵛ.

40. Isa. 3:16.

41. Kaidanover, *Sefer kav ha-yashar*, chap. 82.

42. Ibid.

43. For examples, see Hundert, *Security and Dependence*, 227–32; and Bałaban, "Zbytek u Żydów polskich i jego zwalczanie," 5–15.

44. Bonfil, *Rabbis and Jewish Communities in Renaissance Italy*, 7.

45. Emden, *Sefer hitabbkut*, 20ʳ.

46. Ibid., 51ᵛ.

47. Jacobs, *A Tree of Life*, 94–98.

48. Ibid., 98.

49. Kwasnik-Rabinowicz, "Wolf Eibeschütz," 274–75; and Klemperer, *Rabbi Jonathan Eibeschütz*, 144.

50. Carmilly-Weinberger, "Wolf Jonas Eibeschütz," 23.

51. Klemperer, *Rabbi Jonathan Eibeschütz*, 144. Bernard Brilling has identified this patron as Count Joseph von Bolza; see his "Eibenschütziana," part 3, *HUCA* 36 (1965): 261–79.

52. Y. Beer, "Toledot bne Yehonatan," 77.

53. Ibid., 80.

54. Ibid., 79.

55. Emden, *Sefer hitabbkut*, 22ᵛ.

56. Kraushar, *Frank i frankiści polscy*, 1:258–69; and Mieses, *Polacy*, 34.

57. Kraushar, *Frank i frankiści polscy*, 1:210–11; and Mieses, *Polacy*, 36.

58. *Volumina legum: Przedruk Zbioru Praw staraniem XX Pijarów w Warszawie od roku 1732 do roku 1782 wydanego* (Petersburg, 1860), 7:39–40. See also a letter of a convert demanding that his noble status be reinstated: Warsaw, National Library, Ms. 3215, 127ᵛ–128ᵛ, reproduced in Goldberg, *Ha-mumarim be-mamlekhet Polin-Lita*, 82–89.

59. *Volumina legum*, 185. A certificate issued by Stanislaus Augustus in Goldberg, *Ha-mumarim*, 90–94. As Mieses has noted, some contemporary observers attributed this to attempts of Stanislaus Augustus to build a party of "new nobility," *Polacy*, 40.

60. Krauss, *Joachim Edler von Popper*, 37–46; and Schnee, *Die Hoffinanz und der moderne Staat*, 3:311, claims that the first one was Israel Hönig, ennobled in 1789.

61. Emden, *Sefer hitabbkut*, 22ʳ; Emden uses a slightly distorted German word, *Auerhuhn*.

62. Ibid. Lit., *sar hofshi*, an attempt to render the German *Freiherr* in Hebrew.

63. Ibid., 22ʳ⁻ᵛ.

64. Guttmann, "Lazarus Bendavid," 205.

65. Klemperer, *Rabbi Jonathan Eibeschütz*, 132.

66. Y. Beer, "Toledot bne Yehonatan," 79.

67. Brilling, "Eibenschütziana," part 3, 261–79 (includes a reproduction of the diploma of ennoblement dated 17 July 1776).

68. The petition is reproduced in ibid., 270.

69. A letter from Vienna to Count von Bolza, dated 16 April 1777, in ibid., 276.

70. See Schnee, *Die Hoffinanz und der moderne Staat*, 2:249.

71. Brilling, "Eibenschütziana," part 3, 278–79.

72. *RA*, no. 90; and Trautenberger, *Chronik der Landeshauptstadt Brünn*, 4:117.

73. *RA*, no. 90.

74. Ibid.

75. Kraushar, *Frank i frankiści polscy*, 2:20.

76. Ibid., 2:272–73.

77. Revizki to the nuncio; see the Vatican, ASV, Segr. di Stato, Polonia, 312, 47ʳ; and Revizki to Kaunitz, 1 April 1776, reproduced in Kraushar, *Frank i frankiści polscy*, 2:273.

78. In Offenbach, Frank reportedly purchased the title of baron together with the castle; see Chapter 9 in this volume.

79. *RA*, no. 97.

80. See ibid., nos. 97, 100, 102.

81. Kraushar, *Frank i frankiści polscy*, 2:36; and Schenck-Rinck, *Die Polen in Offenbach am Main*, 5, 30.

82. Joseph II's putative affair with Eve is a commonplace in later literature; see, e.g., Kraushar, *Frank i frankiści polscy*, 2:37; and Sulima, *Historya Franka*, 192–94, 197, and references therein.

83. Brno, MZA, B1 J47 box 730/32. See Willibald Müller, *Urkundliche Beiträge zur Geschichte der Mähr[ischen] Judenschaft im 17. und 18. Jahrhundert* (n.p., 1903), 148–49, 155; cf. McCagg, *A History of Habsburg Jews*, 34–35; and G. Wolf, *Judentaufen in Österreich*, 80. Wolf Hönig married Salomon and Schöndl's daughter Franziska; cf. Ruzička, "Die österreichischen Dichter," 288. In the 1790s and early 1800s, the Hönig family became one of the most important Sabbatian families in Prague.

84. Jan Doktór reaches a similar conclusion in his *Śladami mesjasza-apostaty*, 140.

85. Schnür-Pepłowski (ed.), "Pamiętnik Thulliego," 372; and Awedyk, *Opisanie*, 92–94.

86. See, e.g., *ZSP*, nos. 826, 829, 955, passim.

87. Ibid., no. 635.

88. The Polish text of *ZSP* customarily uses the word *narody*, "peoples," as a designation for non-Jews. It is, of course, a calque from the word *goyim*.

89. *ZSP*, no. 434.

90. Ibid., nos. 531, 653.

91. Ibid., no. 2202.

92. See below.

93. *ZSP*, no. 169.

94. Ibid., no. 194.

95. Esau = the Christians. The veil and bands are tallit and tefillin; Frank alludes to BT Avodah Zarah 3b: "that in the days of the messiah . . . there will be self-made proselytes who will place phylacteries on their foreheads and on their arms, fringes in their garments."

96. A paraphrase of Zech. 9:10.

97. *ZSP*, no. 1282.

98. Ibid., no. 909.

99. *Tabella długów JO. Xcia Jmci Jerzego Marcina Lubomirskiego, Generała Lieutnanta, kawal[era] or[eru] Ś[więtego] Huberta* (Warsaw, 1781).

100. Zarzycki, *Książę Marcin Lubomirski 1738–1811*, 183.

101. Ibid., 184.

102. Ibid.

103. Ibid.

104. Kraushar, *Frank i frankiści polscy*, 2:120–21; for the rumors concerning Eve's marriage to Prince Lubomirski, see Chomętowski, *Przygody ks. Marcina Lubomirskiego*, 76; Sulima, *Historya Franka*, 246–48; and Warsaw, BUW, Ms. 802, Adryan Krzyżanowski, O dziejowości Talmudu. Dziejowość Antytalmudystów polskich, 54ᵛ.

105. De Francesco, *The Power of the Charlatan*, 7, 13.

106. Emden, *Sefer hitabkut*, 20ʳ. For another account of Wolf's alchemical pursuits, see ibid., 45ʳ.

107. Trautenberger, *Chronik der Landeshauptstadt Brünn*, 4:147–48.

108. Schenck-Rinck, *Die Polen in Offenbach am Main*, 12.

109. A letter to Christian G. Heyne dated 27 December 1791, in Forster, *Sämmtliche Schriften*, ed. Gervinus, 169.

110. The *aurum potabile*, colloidal gold, also known as the "elixir of life," was supposed to cure all diseases.

111. *RA*, no 108.

112. Hebrew for "demon"

113. *ZSP*, no. 1790, quoted in Kraushar, *Frank i frankiści polscy*, 2:362.

114. *ZSP*, no. 254.

115. Ibid., no. 1013.

116. A letter to Christian G. Heyne, dated 14 October 1785, in Forster, *Sämmtliche Schriften*, 271.

117. August Moszyński, "Réflexions sur la science Hermétique présentées au Roi par le Comte Moszyński Stolnik de la Couronne en 1768," Kraków, Biblioteka Czartoryskich, Ms. 809, 955–64.

118. Casanova, *The History of My Life*, trans. Trask, 10:96–97.

119. Cooper-Oakely, *The Comte de St. Germain*, 36–38.

120. Patai, *The Jewish Alchemists*, 472.

121. [August Moszyński], *Cagliostro démasqua à Varsovie, ou relation autentique de ses operations alchemiques et magiques faites dans cette capitale en 1780, par un témoin oculaire.*

122. Zweig, *Casanova*, 31–32.

123. A letter to Christian G. Heyne, dated 27 December 1791, in Forster, *Sämmtliche Schriften*, 169.

124. Brinken, *Józef Frank*, Warsaw, BN, Ms. 1345, 414.

125. Mauthner, *Lebenserinnerungen*, 295.

126. P. Beer, *Geschichte, Lehren und Meinungen*, 2:327.

127. A testimony from *Berlinische Monatsschrift* of 1787, quoted in De Francesco, *The Power of the Charlatan*, 210.

128. Lenowitz, "The Charlatan at the Gottes Haus in Offenbach," 192.

129. Casanova, *The History of My Life*, 3:3–19.

130. Carlebach, "Attributions of Secrecy and Perceptions of Jewry," 128–29.

131. Pomian, *Collectionneurs, amateurs et curieux Paris, Venise*, 2.

132. See, e.g., Goethe, *Italian Journey*, trans. Robert R. Heitner (New York, 1989), 205.

133. Oron, *Mi-Ba'al Shem le-Ba'al Shed*, 55.

134. Patai, *The Jewish Alchemists*, 465.

135. Cooper-Oakely, *The Comte de St. Germain*, 9.

136. Anderson, *The Legend of the Wandering Jew*, 128–31, and references therein.

137. Kazimierz Waliszewski, *The Story of a Throne: Catherine II of Russia* (London, 1895), 301–2; see Oron, *Mi-Ba'al Shem*, 56.

138. Antoni Kosakowski, Katarzyna II carowa rosyjska, *Oszukaniec. Komedia. Tłum. 7 marca 1786*, Warsaw, BUW, Ms. 1069.

139. Zweig, *Casanova*, 37.

140. Casanova, *The History of My Life*, 7:267–78.

141. For a survey of Casanova's encounters with Jews, see Luccichenti, "Casanova e gli ebrei," 23–33 .

142. Casanova, *The History of My Life*, 1:91.

143. See, e.g., ibid., 4:200; and his *Historie de ma fuite des prisons de la Republique de Venise* (Leipzig, 1788), 23.

144. Casanova, *The History of My Life*, 9:45–96.

145. Ibid., 5:118–19.

146. Ibid., 6:9–11.

147. Ibid., 3:273.

148. Ibid., 2:195.

149. Casanova, *Briefwechsel*, ed. Rava and Gugitz, 331–32; the original was first published in idem, *Patrizi e avventurieri, dame e ballerine* (Milan, 1930), 414–17.

150. Casanova, *Briefwechsel*, 333–34; and *Patrizi e avventurieri*, 416–17.

151. The procedure has been analyzed in great detail by Bernhard Marr, "Casanova als Kabalist," in Casanova, *Briefwechsel*, 389–96; and then by W. F. Friedman,

"Giacomo Casanova de Seingalt: The Cryptologist," *Casanova Gleanings* 4 (1961): 1–12. So far as I can tell, it bears no resemblance to any Jewish kabbalistic numerological technique.

152. Marr, "Casanova als Kabalist", 332.

153. Heymann, *Die Chevalier von Geldern*, 228. This information was later repeated, with typical inaccuracies, in Mandel, *The Militant Messiah*, 108–10.

154. *RA*, no. 100.

155. Polišenský, *Casanova a jeho svět*, 97, 115; idem, "Casanova v Čechach," 89–94. For a chronology of Casanova's travels in the later part of his career, see Luccichenti (ed.), *Vita di Giacomo Casanova dopo le sue memorie, 1774–98*, 211–19.

156. The letter of introduction written by Lamberg is reproduced in Giacomo Casanova, *Briefwechsel mit J. F. Opiz*, ed. Kohl and Pick, 272–73.

157. Kroupa, *Alchymie štěstí*, 55.

158. Count Salm-Reifferscheidt is mentioned in the Frankist dicta; see *ZSP*, no. 2225.

159. For the roster of members of the lodge Zur aufgehenden Sonne im Orient, see Kroupa, *Alchymie štěstí*, 209–10.

160. Prague, 1786.

161. Leipzig, 1788.

162. See Polišenský, *Casanova a jeho svět*, 123.

163. Casanova, *The History of My Life*, 3:116.

164. Polišenský, *Casanova a jeho svět*, 115.

165. See Evans, "Moravia and the Culture of Enlightenment in the Habsburg Monarchy," 388–89; and Kroupa, "Die Mährische Gesellschaft und die Französische Revolution," 55.

166. Kroupa, "Die Mährische Gesellschaft und die Französische Revolution," 62; and idem, *Alchymie štěstí*, 80.

167. Roberts, *The Mythology of the Secret Societies*, 90.

168. For the history of the order, see Katz, *Jews and Freemasons in Europe, 1723–1939*, 27–53; and McIntosh, *The Rose Cross and the Age of Reason*, 161–77.

169. Franz Joseph Molitor, "Geschichte des Ordens der Ritter und Brüder Sanct Johannis des Evangelisten, aus Asien in Europa," reproduced as an appendix to Katz, "Hapulmus ha-rishon al kabbalat Yehudim be-kerev ha-bonim ha-hofshim," 204–5.

170. The collection of rites of the order was published as *Die Brüder St. Johannis des Evangelisten aus Asien in Europa oder die einzige wahre und ächte Freimauerei nebst einem Anh. Die Fellersche kritische Geschichte de Freimauererbrüderschaft und ihre Nichtkeit betreffend von einem hohen Obern* (Berlin, 1803). On 265–75, we find partly a paraphrase and partly an exact translation of the eight first leaves of *Va-avo ha-yom el ha-ayyin*; see Scholem, "Ein Frankist," 84 n. 23.

171. Scholem, *Du frankisme au jacobinisme*, 34.

172. Scholem, "Ein verschollener jüdischer Mystiker der Aufklärungszeit," 260; Katz, *Jews and Freemasons*, 32.

173. Hirschfeld, *Biblisches Organon oder Realübersetzung der Bibel mit mystischen Begleitungen*.

174. Scholem, "Ein verschollener jüdischer Mystiker der Aufklärungszeit," 265; and Katz, *Jews and Freemasons*, 36.

175. Quoted in McIntosh, *The Rose Cross and the Age of Reason*, 166.

176. Katz, *Jews and Freemasons*, 32.

177. Scholem, "Ein Frankist," 78. For Rabbi Schick, see Fishman, *Russia's First Modern Jews*, 22–45. Fishman does not account for Schick's Masonic connections. See also Hass, "Żydzi i 'kwestia żydowska' w dawnym wolnomularstwie polskim," 15.

178. Kroupa, *Alchymie štěstí*, 71, 77.

179. Ibid., 77.

180. Katz, *Out of the Ghetto*, 44.

181. Katz, *Jews and Freemasons*, 4. Sonnenfels's Masonic activities again offer an interesting parallel; see Karniel, "Josef von Sonnenfels," 137–38.

182. Katz, *Jews and Freemasons*, 4.

183. Hammermayer, *Der Wilhelmsbader Freimauerer-Konvent von 1782*, 28.

184. Ibid., 41.

185. Katz, *Jews and Freemasons*, 29.

186. McIntosh, *The Rose Cross and the Age of Reason*, 168.

187. See Abafi, *Geschichte der Freimaurerei in Österreich-Ungarn*, 4:143–80.

188. See Katz, *Jews and Freemasons*, 36. Kroupa associates his departure with the promulgation of the *Freimaurerpatent*; see Kroupa, "Die Mährische Gesellschaft," 60.

189. Karniel, "Jüdischer Pseudomessianismus und deutsche Kultur," 41; see, however, Scholem, *Du frankisme au jacobinisme*, 40. There is some evidence that Moses' older brother, Carl, was a member of the Illuminati; Brno, AMB, Trautenberger Nachlaß, T44, box 3, 43–52.

190. See Kroupa, *Alchymie štěstí*, 60; and idem, "Die Mährische Gesellschaft," 55–56. For the Illuminati in Brünn, see Trautenberger, *Chronik der Landeshauptstadt Brünn*, 4:148; Brno, AMB, Trautenberger Nachlaß, T44, box 3.

191. For the patronage of the Mittrovskýs, see Brno, MZA, Archiv Rodiny Mittrovský, G 147 box 32 fols. 12–14; and Kroupa, "Die Mährische Gesellschaft," 60. For Mittrovský's reform of Freemasonry, see Kroupa, *Alchymie štěstí*, 87–96.

192. In 1792, he moved to Strassburg, changed his name to Gottlieb Siegmund Junius Frey, and became very active in the local Jacobin club. Later, he moved to Paris and established connections with François Chabot and Danton. Accused of espionage, he was guillotined together with Danton in April 1794.

193. Moszyński, Mes observations, Kraków, Biblioteka Czartoryskich, Ms. 700, 437.

194. Patai, *Jewish Alchemists*, 456; and Oron, *Mi-Ba'al Shem*, 52.

195. Oron, *Mi-Ba'al Shem*, 57–59; and Schuchard, "Yeats and the 'Unknown Superiors,'" 145.

196. Schuchard, "Yeats and the 'Unknown Superiors,'" 117.

197. McIntosh, *The Rose Cross and the Age of Reason*, 173.

198. See accounts of French and English Freemasons quoted in Schuchard, "Yeats and the 'Unknown Superiors,'" 148–49.

199. Rys historyczny wolnomularstwa polskiego, Warsaw, AGAD, Archiwum Masońskie Skimborowicza II-1/I, 3.

200. Shatzky, *Geshikhte fun jidn in Varshe*, 1:89.

201. *ZSP*, no. 678.

202. Jost, *Geschichte der Israeliten seit der Tage der Maccabaeer bis auf unsere Tage*, 8:134.

203. Raczyński, *Wspomnienia Wielkopolski* (Poznań, 1843), 2:40

204. The idea that 1783 marks the beginning of the end comes up in a homily of Yehudah Leyb Tova published by Molkho and Shatz-Uffenheimer as "Perush lekh lekha"; see also Scholem, "The Crypto-Jewish Sect," 161–62, and "Kuntres mi-reshit yame'ah shel kat ha-Donmeh be-Saloniki," in *Mehkere Shabbeta'ut*, 305 n. 2.

205. *ZSP*, no. 75.

206. *RA*, nos. 101, 103, 108, 109.

207. Bidermann, *Die Bukowina unter österreichischer Verwaltung 1775–1875*, 78–79; cf. also Kassner, *Die Juden in der Bukowina*, 14; Bidermann reports that fifty families of converted Jews gave all their money to "a certain visionary or swindler by the name of Frank."

208. Trautenberger, *Chronik der Landeshauptstadt Brünn*, 4:117.

209. Ibid., 132; Arnsberg, *Von Podolien nach Offenbach*, 23, suggested that "a piece of Turkey" might have been the Land of Israel; this seems very unlikely. The Frankists rejected the idea of the return to the Land of Israel as early as the Kamieniec disputation.

210. Joseph II, handwritten note to Count Pergen, 29 October 1785, Vienna, Allgemeine Verwaltungsarchiv (AVA), Pergen Akten Karton 15 XVI/1. This is the only document of Joseph's attesting to his acquaintance with Frank. I am grateful to Michael Silber for sharing this source with me.

211. *RA*, no. 103; cf. Trautenberger, *Chronik der Landeshauptstadt Brünn*, 4:164. *Rozmaite adnotacje* dates this quarrel to May 1786, two months after the departure to Offenbach. The quarrel must have happened earlier, but it is impossible to establish the exact date. Many contemporary accounts note that Joseph "expelled" Frank, but none gives the reason; see, e.g., Calmanson, *Uwagi nad nineyszym stanem Żydów Polskich*, 25.

CHAPTER 9

1. The connection was made already in contemporary accounts; see Trautenberger, *Chronik der Landeshauptstadt Brünn*, 165; Brno, AMB, Trautenberger Nachlaß, T44, box 3, 21ᵛ.

2. Eginhard Quelle (= Arnold Hirsch), "Das Grab eines Propheten in Offenbach," 21. Most of the newspaper reports quoted in this chapter come from the collection of the Staatsarchiv Offenbach, O 1450/15/2, Frank, Jakob, und die Frankisten. Zeitungs- und Zeitschriftenaufsätze. I am grateful to the curator of the archives, Hans-Georg Ruppel, for his help in obtaining the photocopies.

3. P. Beer, *Geschichte, Lehren und Meinungen*, 325. A report of the Prussian Chargé d'affairs in Frankfurt, Formey, gives the figure of fifty people; see Berlin, GStA, I. HA. Rep. 81 Frankfurt V B No. 23, Wegen der Frankesche Secte zu Offenbach, 3ᵛ.

4. *Festschrift zur 500 Jahrfreier der Zugehörigkeit Oberrads zu Frankfurt am Main*, quoted in Arnsberg, *Von Podolien nach Offenbach*, 26.

5. *RA*, no. 109. Some accounts delay Frank's entry to Offenbach until 1789.

6. For the description of the parade, see Schenck-Rinck, *Die Polen in Offenbach am Main*, 8–9; Anonymous, "Die immerwährende Maskarade," col. 2.

7. Schenck-Rinck, *Die Polen in Offenbach*, 12–17; for an interesting analysis of Frank's dress, see Lenowitz, "The Struggle over Images in the Propaganda of the Frankist Movement," 105–30; cf. also a description of Sabbatai's dress in Leyb ben Ozer's *Beshraibung fun Shabsai Zevi*, quoted in Scholem, *Sabbatai Sevi*, 618–19.

8. "Die immerwährende Maskarade," col. 3.

9. "Der heilige Herr: Ein geheimnissvoller Glaubensfürst," *Gartenlaube* 1865, 535.

10. Schenck-Rinck, *Die Polen in Offenbach*, 14.

11. Dr. L-n., "Die Polen in Offenbach," *Frankfurter Didaskalia* 1868, col. 6; Schumacher, *Geschichte der katolischen Gemeinde in Offenbach am Main*, 10.

12. "Die immerwährende Maskarade," col. 1.

13. Werner, "Die Sekte der 'Frankisten,'" 2:110.

14. See documents quoted in Kraushar, *Frank i frankiści polscy*, 2:162–63.

15. For descriptions of Frank's funeral, see "Nachricht von dem Tode und der Beerdigung des als Haupt der sich in Offenbach niedergelassenden Pohlen Herrn Baron von Frank," 1791, Warsaw, AGAD, Teki Skimborowicza XXI-2/135; cf. Kraushar, *Frank i frankiści polscy*, 2:132–34. According to an anonymous anti-Frankist pamphlet, *Śmierć Frenka*, 600 people came from Poland to take part in the funeral; see *Śmierć Frenka: Przez urodzonego L. A. M.* (Warsaw[?], 1792), 8.

16. "Nachricht von dem Tode,". 2ʳ. Also Prince Wolfgang Ernst noted that "in accordance with the Moldavian custom(?), [the Frankists'] mourning is only white"; see a letter of Prince Wolfgang Ernst to his son, quoted in Kraushar, *Frank i frankiści polscy*, 2:154.

17. See, e.g., P. E., "Die Pohlen in Offenbach," *Main-Zeitung* 14 (1867); Lamm, "Eine eigenartige Ausstellung: Beitrag zur Geschichte Jakob Franks und seinen Anhänger," 34–35; and von Leonhard, "Der Sectenhäuptling Frank in Offenbach."

18. See Emil Pirazzi, "Jacob Frank, der Messias aus Podolien"; Anonymous, "Der Prophet von Offenbach: Eine historische Erinnerung," *Offenbacher Zeitung*, 21 April 1910.

19. Appell, "Dobruschki-Frank, die Polnische Sektehäuptung in Offenbach"; von Sacher-Masoch, "Der Prophet von Offenbach," col. 26.

20. Anklein, "Der Polackenfürst," col. 27.

21. Schenck-Rinck, *Die Polen in Offenbach*, 11. The publication in the *Gartenlaube* of 1865 of an anonymous article, "Der heilige Herr: Ein geheimnissvoller Glaubensfürst," *Die Gartenlaube* 33 and 34 (1865): 521–23 and 534–36, was the earliest account challenging the legend. Abraham Duker attributes this publication to Dominik Zieliński; see Duker, "Polish Frankism's Duration," 293–94. In response to the article of 1865, a number of articles were written in Offenbach's and Frankfurt's newspapers, and a certain A.-G. Schenck-Rinck, whose grandfather had numerous dealings with the Frankist court, wrote a brochure titled "Die Polen in Offenbach am Main." The aim of the brochure is to prove

Eve Frank's royal lineage and at the same time to discredit all claims regarding the Jewish background of Frankism,

22. Anklein, "Der Polackenfürst," col. 28.

23. Anonymous, *Vertraute Briefe über Frankreich: Auf einer Reise im Jahre 1792 geschrieben* (Berlin, 1792), 21–23, quoted in Mandel, *The Militant Messiah*, 172. Mandel attributes this work to Johann Friedrich Reinhardt, the orchestra conductor at the court of Frederick the Great.

24. "Die immerwährende Maskarade," col. 1.

25. Ibid., col. 2.

26. Schenck-Rinck, *Die Polen in Offenbach*, 7.

27. Sacher-Masoch, "Der Prophet von Offenbach," col. 26.

28. Cf. Anonymous, "Der Prophet von Offenbach: Eine historische Erinnerung." *Offenbacher Zeitung*, 1910; see also Reimers, "Die Grafschaft Ysenburg als Freistatt des Glaubens," 102–7.

29. Arnsberg, *Von Podolien nach Offenbach*, 24; and Hoensch, "Der Pollackenfürst von Offenbach," 193.

30. "Die immerwährende Maskarade," col. 2.

31. Trautenbereger, *Chronik der Landeshauptstadt Brünn*, 4:164; and Schenck-Rinck, *Die Polen in Offenbach am Main*, 34.

32. See testimonies from the official investigation conducted by the authorities after Eve's death in 1816. These testimonies have been discovered by Aleksander Kraushar after the publication of his monograph; see Kraushar, "Nowe szczegóły o Frankistach w Offenbachu," in his *Obrazy i wizerunki historyczne*, 261.

33. "Zwei fürstliche Geheimnisse neuerer Zeit," *Gartenlaube*, May 1866, 347.

34. Kraushar, *Frank i frankiści polscy*, 2:221–23. A contemporary etching documenting Alexander's visit is housed at the SAO, M 736/1, "Die anspruschslosen Kossaken in Offenbach."

35. Schenck-Rinck, *Die Polen in Offenbach*, 17; and Kraushar, *Frank i frankiści polscy*, 2:157.

36. The letter is reproduced in ibid., 2:236–37.

37. Ibid., 226–35.

38. Kirchenbuch, 7:724, first mentioned in Emil Pirazzi, "Zur Geschichte Offenbachs," col. 28; also quoted in Werner, "Die Sekte der 'Frankisten,'" 113.

39. Anklein, "Der Polackenfürst," col. 26.

40. In a handwritten note dated Darmstadt, 2 September 1791. The note is reproduced in Wahle, "Aus dem Goethe- und Schillerarchiv," 99–100, first mentioned in Arnsberg, *Von Podolien nach Offenbach*, 9 (Arnsberg's reference is erroneous).

41. Brentano, *Tagebuch: Briefwechsel Goethes mit einem Kinde*, 3:641; first quoted in Pirazzi, *Bilder und Geschichten aus Offenbachs Vergangenheit*, 271; see also Kraushar, *Frank i frankiści polscy*, 2:170–71.

42. P. Beer, *Geschichte, Lehren und Meinungen*, 329.

43. Porges, "Texte de la lettre adressée par les Frankistes aux communautés Juives de Boheme," 285.

44. Wacholder, "Jacob Frank and the Frankists," 272; BT Sanhedrin 97a; Sota 9:15.

45. Zohar 1:235b, 2:48b, 2:141b.

46. Wacholder, "Jacob Frank and the Frankists," 272.

47. Ibid., 272–73.

48. Scholem, "Redemption through Sin," 138.

49. A note from Alex von Szeczesny to Councillor Joseph Szily, dated 25 August 1786, published in *Magyar Zsidó Szemle* 15 (1898): 376–77.

50. Back, "Aufgefundene Aktenstücke zur Geschichte der Frankisten in Offenbach," 191.

51. Gelber, "Zur Geschichte der Frankistenpropaganda im Jahre 1800," 59.

52. Vishnitzer, "Poslanie Frankistow 1800 goda," 1.

53. Paul's letter from 18 March, quoted in ibid., 2.

54. Ibid.

55. Berlin, GStA, I HA Geheimer Rat Rep. 7A Neuostpreußen, 190 Nr. 32 fasc. 2, Acta betreffend die neue jüdische Sekte Edom gennant, 8ᵛ.

56. A copy of Friesek's account was also sent to the Prussian authorities and is preserved (together with a German translation of a Red Letter) in Berlin, GStA, I HA Geheimer Rat Rep. 7A Neuostpreußen, 190 Nr. 32 fasc. 2, Acta betreffend die neue jüdische Sekte Edom genannt und die Aktivitäten und Schriften des Oberhaupts der Sabbatianer Jacob Leyb Frank, 4ᵛ–7ᵛ.

57. Ibid., 5ᵛ⁻ʳ; for the background of the affair, see Gelber, "Zur Geschichte der Frankistenpropaganda," 59.

58. Berlin, GStA, I HA Geheimer Rat Rep. 7A Neuostpreußen, 190 Nr. 32 fasc. 2, Acta betreffend die neue jüdische Sekte Edom gennant, 8ᵛ.

59. Letter of Friedrich Wilhelm to Formey dated 21 April 1800, Berlin, GStA, I. HA. Rep. 81 Frankfurt V B Nr. 23, Die Frankesche Secte zu Offenbach, 1ʳ⁻ᵛ.

60. Berlin, GStA, I. HA. Rep. 81 Frankfurt V B Nr. 23, Über die Familie Franck zu Offenbach, 3ᵛ–6ᵛ.

61. See letters to Formey dated 29 June and 4 July 1800, Berlin, GstA, I. HA. Rep. 81 Frankfurt V B Nr. 23, Wegen der Frankesche Secte zu Offenbach, 7ᵛ and 9ᵛ.

62. Berlin, GStA, I. HA. Rep. 81 Frankfurt V B Nr. 23, Über die Familie Franck zu Offenbach, 3ᵛ.

63. Berlin, GstA, I. HA. Rep. 81 Frankfurt V B Nr. 23, Wegen der Frankesche Secte zu Offenbach, 6ʳ, 8ʳ.

64. Berlin, GStA, I. HA. Rep. 81 Frankfurt V B Nr. 23, Wegen der Frankesche Secte zu Offenbach, 8ʳ.

65. Berlin, GstA, I. HA. Rep. 81 Frankfurt V B Nr. 23, Über die Familie Frank zu Offenbach, 3ᵛ.

66. Berlin, GStA, I HA Geheimer Rat Rep. 7A Neuostpreußen, 190 Nr 32 fasc.2 Acta betreffend die neue jüdische Sekte Edom gennant, 9ᵛ–10ᵛ. Another, shorter, version is quoted in Gelber, "Zur Geschichte der Frankistenpropaganda," 68–69. Gelber's version came from the Archiv des Ministeriums des Innern in Vienna, Polizeiakten ex 1800, no. 106.

67. Katz, "A State within a State," 29–58.

68. Johann Gottlob Fichte, *Beitrag zur Berichtung der Urtheile des Publikums über die Französische Revolution* (Berlin, 1793), quoted in Katz, "A State within a State," 44.

69. Katz, "A State within a State," 47.

70. Kraushar, *Frank i frankiści polscy*, 2:185.

71. Ibid., 211.

72. Ibid., 187–88.

73. Ibid., 208.

74. Ibid., 210.

75. Ibid., 204.

76. Ibid., 209, 211.

77. Ibid., 215.

78. Ibid., 211.

79. Ibid., 196.

80. Ibid., 193.

81. Ibid., 187.

82. Ibid., 196.

83. Ibid., 199.

84. Ibid., 203; cf. 193.

85. Ibid., 189.

86. Ibid., 191.

87. Ibid., 188–89.

88. Ibid., 211.

89. Ibid., 189.

90. Ibid., 192.

91. Ibid., 189.

92. Weber, *The Theory of Social and Economic Organization*, trans. Henderson and Parsons, 363–70.

93. Ibid., 364.

94. Ibid., 367.

95. "The Memoirs of Moses Porges," in: Mandel, *The Militant Messiah*, 163; see also Back, "Aufgefundene Aktenstücke zur Geschichte der Frankisten in Offenbach," 232, 235.

96. Back, "Aufgefundene Aktenstücke," 237.

97. Ibid., 235.

98. Moses Porges himself became disillusioned and escaped, together with two companions.

99. Cf. Bałaban, "Zur Geschichte der Familie Wehle in Prag," 113–15; and Back, "Aufgefundene Aktenstücke," 191–92.

100. "The Memoirs of Moses Porges," in Mandel, *The Militant Messiah*, 153.

101. Ibid., 153.

102. Ibid., 157.

103. Ibid., 161.

104. Ibid., 162.

105. Ibid.

106. Moses Porges mentions that he met in Offenbach "Wolowski, Dembitski, Matushewski, Czerwinski"; see ibid.

107. Werner, "Versuch einer Quantifizierung des Frankschen Gefolges in Offenbach am Main 1788–1818," 153–212.

108. Scholem, "A Frankist Document from Prague," 787–89; Dr. Klein, "Zuschrift an Herrn Moses Mendelson in Hamburg," 526; and Werses., *Haskalah ve-Shabbeta'ut*, 81–94.

109. Žáček, "Zwei Beiträge," 369, gives the names of twelve Sabbatian families from Prague.

110. Dr. Klein, "Zuschrift," 540.

111. The text of the ban is not extant, but it is described in Fleckeles, *Ahavat David*, 23^v.

112. Sid Leiman has argued that the similar principle guided Landau's attitude toward Eibeschütz; see Leiman, "When a Rabbi Is Accused of Heresy: R. Ezekiel Landau's Attitude toward R. Jonathan Eibeschütz in the Emden-Eibeschütz Controversy," 179–94.

113. I did not manage to find a printed copy of the ban of 1800. I follow a photographic reproduction published by Žáček, "Zwei Beiträge," 375.

114. Fleckeles, *Ahavat David*.

115. Ibid., 5^v.

116. Ibid., introduction.

117. Ibid., 26^v.

118. Ibid., introduction, 19^r, 28^v.

119. Ibid., 25^r.

120. Ibid., intoduction, 5^r.

121. Ibid., 17^v.

122. Ibid., introduction.

123. See ibid., 17^r; see also 4^v, 6^{r-v}, 35^v.

124. Ibid., 5^v–6^r.

125. Ibid., 25^v.

126. Ibid., 17^v.

127. Ibid., introduction.

128. Žáček, "Zwei Beiträge," 374–75.

129. Kestenberg-Gladstein, *Neuere Geschichte der Juden in den böhmischen Ländern*, 175; and Žáček, "Zwei Beiträge," 376–77. Also the daughter of the Elisha Shorr, Hayah was known to study the Zohar; for Hayah Shorr, see Rapoport-Albert, "Al ma'amad ha-nashim ba-Shabbeta'ut," in Elior (ed.), *Ha-halom ve-shivro*, 163–65; for the accounts of women studying kabbalah in Prague, see Fleckeles, *Ahavat David*, 25^v, 26^r.

130. The document was first discussed by Žáček, "Zwei Beiträge," 386–90, and then published by Scholem as "A Frankist Document from Prague," in *Salo W. Baron Jubilee Volume* (Jerusalem, 1975), 2:787–812.

131. Scholem, "A Frankist Document," 789; Kestenberg-Gladstein, *Neuere Geschichte*, 183; and Žáček, "Zwei Beiträge," 384.

132. Scholem, "A Frankist Document," 795–99.

133. See, esp., ibid., 809.

134. Ibid., 802–3.

135. The extant manuscript of Hönigsberg's opus consists of a lengthy collection of documents written in German in Hebrew characters with numerous Hebrew and Aramaic interpolations. The manuscript is currently housed in the Jewish National and University Library Jerusalem, JNUL, Ms. Heb 8° 2921, Drushim ve-iggerot mi-hug ha-Frankistim be-Prag. For the authorship, see Scholem, "A Frankist Document," 789. The documents were known since the mid-nineteenth century, when Wolfgang Wessely published excerpts as "Aus den Briefen eines Sabbatianers," *Der Orient* 12 (1851): cols. 534–44, 568–74. Another fragment was published by Scholem as "Iggeret Frankistit al Toledot ha'emunah," in *Mehkere Shabbeta'ut* (Tel Aviv, 1991), 634–51. An excerpt from another manuscript was published by Scholem as "A Frankist Commentary to the Hallel," in Salo W. Baron (ed.), *Yitzhak F. Baer Jubilee Volume on the Occasion of His Seventieth Birthday* (Jerusalem, 1960), 409–30. Scholem's lecture on the manuscripts was scheduled for the opening of the 8th Congress of Jewish Studies in Jerusalem; however, the presentation was canceled because of his poor health. A draft of this paper titled *Frankism and Enlightenment* is preserved in Scholem's archive in Jerusalem, JNUL, Arch. 4/1599, file 156. Ada Rapoport-Albert and Cesar Merchan Hamman published yet another excerpt, together with a commentary and an English translation, as "'Something for the Female Sex': A Call for the Liberation of Women, and the Release of the Female Libido from the 'Shackles of Shame,' in an Anonymous Frankist Manuscript from Prague c. 1800," in Joseph Dan (ed.), *Gershom Scholem (1897–1982), in Memoriam* (Jerusalem, 2007), 77–135. However, the full content of the manuscript remains unanalyzed.

136. For the dating of the manuscript, see Scholem, "Iggeret Frankistit," 636–37.

137. Wessely, "Aus den Briefen eines Sabbatianers," cols. 570–71.

138. Ibid., cols. 538, 570.

139. Jerusalem, JNUL, Ms. Heb 8° 2921, Drushim ve-iggerot mi-hug ha-Frankistim be-Prag, 53[r].

140. Ibid., 93r.

141. Ibid., 64[v], 67[r]; cf. Scholem, "Iggeret Frankistit," 641. AMIRa"H is a Hebrew acronym for "Our Lord and King, His Majesty be exalted"; see Scholem, *Sabbatai Sevi*, 110 n. 25.

142. Ibid., 16[v], 66[r]; cf. Scholem, "Iggeret Frankistit," 641.

143. Ibid., 96[v], 32[r].

144. See, e.g., ibid., 87[v].

145. See "The Memoirs of Moses Porges," in Mandel, *The Militant Messiah*, 163; cf. also Scholem, "Iggeret Frankistit," 643 n. 53.

146. See ibid., 66[v]–68[v]; cf. Scholem, "Iggeret Frankistit," 641–48; and Wessely, "Aus den Briefen eines Sabbatianers," col. 536.

147. Drushim ve-iggerot, 53[r].

148. Ibid., 17[v].

149. Wessely, "Aus den Briefen eines Sabbatianers," col. 538; cf. col. 570.

150. Ibid., col. 568.

151. Drushim ve-iggerot, 81^r–82^v, 97^r.

152. Ibid., 68^v.

153. Ibid., 93^r.

154. Ibid., 67^v.

155. Ibid., 86^v–93^v.

156. Ibid., 94^v.

157. Ibid., 83^v–85^r.

158. Ibid., 87^v; for the change of the status of women in early Sabbatianism, see Scholem, *Sabbatai Sevi*, 403; and Rapoport-Albert, "Al ma'amad ha-nashim."

159. Rapoport-Albert and Hamman, "Something for the Female Sex," 120.

160. Ibid., 121.

161. Ibid, 135.

162. Ibid., 125, 130, 136.

163. This is the description of one of the sources of Hönigsberg's writings in the pamphlet of Baruch Jeitless, *Sihah bein shnat 5560 uvein 5561* (Prague, 1800), 23 quoted in Katz, "Relationship between Sabbatianism, Haskalah, and Reform," 519.

164. Scholem, "A Frankist Document," 810.

165. *Ha-me'assef* 12 (1797): 22–37; see Scholem, "A Frankist Document," 788; and Werses, *Haskalah ve-Shabbeta'ut*, 85–86, 88.

166. "The Memories of Moses Porges,", in Mandel, *The Militant Messiah*, 156.

167. See, e.g., praises of women's and children's wisdom, *ZSP*, nos. 278, 908, 911, 292, passim.

168. See P. Beer, *Geschichte, Lehren und Meinungen*, 341, 343, passim. This perception became a commonplace in literary works inspired by Frankism; see, e.g., Becker, *Des Rabbis Vermächtniss*; and Osiecki, *Zofia Kossakowska*.

169. "The Memoirs of Moses Porges," in Mandel, *The Militant Messiah*, 155–57; and Scholem, "Iggeret Frankistit," 637.

170. Scholem application of the term to the Prague group is based on his identification of Frankism and Sabbatianism; see Introduction to this volume.

171. Scholem claimed that the ms. contains quotations from *The Words of the Lord* in Hebrew. Indeed, there are a few fragments that resemble ideas appearing in *The Words of the Lord*. But there are no exact quotations and—until evidence to the contrary is found—there is no reason to believe that they knew the Frankist dicta.

172. Drushim ve-iggerot, 13^v.

173. Ibid., 28^v.

174. Ibid., 28^v, 119^{v-r}.

175. Guttman, "Lazarus Bendavid," 206; and Gelber, "Zur Geschichte," 292.

176. Kraushar dates Czerniawski's mission for the end of the Brünn period (1785). According to *RA*, no. 101, in 1785 Czerniewski was in Istanbul.

177. *ZSP*, no. 240; see also BT Ta'anit 5b: "Jacob our patriarch is not dead"; Zohar 2:48b.

178. Kraushar, *Frank i frankiści polscy*, 2:258 n. 2.

179. Ibid., 2:155.

180. He is mentioned in Bidermann, *Die Bukowina*, 78.

181. Scholem, "Iggeret Frankistit," 643.

182. Calmanson, *Uwagi nad nineyszym stanem Żydów Polskich*, 20.

183. *Dwór Franka czyli polityka nowochrzczeńców, odkryta przez Neofitę jednego dla poprawy rządu* (Warsaw, 1790), reprinted in Eisenbach and Michalski (eds.), *Materiały do dziejów Sejmu Czteroletniego*, 6:179. The same figure is given by Czacki, *Rozprawa o Żydach i Karaitach*, 41. Julian Brinken estimated the figures for 25,000 in the whole of Poland and for 8,000 in Warsaw; Warsaw, BN, Ms. 1345, Józef Frank. Patriarcha Neofitów, 386.

184. Endelmann, "Jewish Converts in Nineteenth-Century Warsaw," 35; see also the introductory chapter to Garncarska-Kadary, *Helkam shel ha-Yehudim be-hitpathut ha-ta'asiyah shel Varshah be-shanim 1816/20–1914.*

185. Goldberg, "*De non tolerandis Judaeis*," 43, and references therein.

186. Hundert, *The Jews in a Polish Private Town*, 11.

187. For examples, see Tollet, *Historie des Juifs en Pologne du XVI*ᵉ *siècle à nos jours*, 116–17, 119; Horn, *Regesty dokumentów*, registers eighty cases of anti-Jewish cases brought before magistrates in 1764–79 and ninety-two in 1779–94.

188. Goldberg, "*De non tolerandis Judaeis*," 41.

189. Ibid., 40 n. 2; see Schipper, *Dzieje handlu żydowskiego na ziemiach polskich*, 195–210.

190. This was emphasized in the pamphlet *Basałyk pod imieniem Ćwika na jestestwo dawniey nieużyteczne sporzadzony*, 2.

191. Kraszewski, *Polska w czasie trzech rozbiorów 1772–1799*, 2:248.

192. Ibid., 2:248–49.

193. *List przyjaciela polaka . . . do obywatela warszawskiego wyjawiający sekreta neofitów* ([Warsaw], 1790), reprinted in Eisenbach and Michalski (eds.), *Materiały do dziejów Sejmu*, 6:170.

194. Jellinek, "Nachrichten von Frankisten in Warschau," *Das jüdische Literaturblatt* 27 (1882): 107.

195. *List przyjaciela polaka*, 170.

196. *Dwór Franka*, 180; *Zwierciadło polskie dla publiczności. Choć nie kształtne, ale w reprezentacji rzetelne, w którym widzieć można różnych ludzi i wielorakie ich defekta a osobliwie Żydów szczególności i powszechności szkodliwych*, 31; *Katechizm o Żydach i Neofitach*, 2, 4, passim; and *Basałyk pod imieniem Ćwika*, 4–5.

197. Ignatz Bernstein, "Brief an Eduard Jellinek," *Das jüdische Literaturblatt* 27 (1882): 107. Sulima derives *meches* from *machna* and treats it as synonymous with "the Frankist"; see *Historya Franka*, 202 n. 1.

198. *Katechizm o Żydach*, 5.

199. Ibid., 18; and *Dwór Franka*, 177.

200. *Zwierciadło polskie*, 30; *Dwór Franka*, 178; and *Basałyk pod imieniem Ćwika*, 3.

201. *Katechizm o Żydach*, 18; and *Basałyk pod imieniem Ćwika*, 3–4.

202. *Katechizm o Żydach*, 18; *Dwór Franka*, 177; and Kraszewski, *Polska w czasie*, 248.

203. *List przyjaciela Polaka*, 171; *Dwór Franka*, 177; and *Katechizm o Żydach*, 19, *Zwierciadło polskie*, 30.

204. Kraszewski, *Polska w czasie*, 248; Calmanson, *Uwagi nad nineyszym stanem Żydów Polskich*, 29–30; *Śmierć Frenka*, 4, 6. *Katechizm o Żydach*, 22, claims that 4,392,000 złotys was sent to Offenbach every year; *Dwór Franka*, 179, estimates the sum at 438,000 złotys; Władysław Smoleński, *Stan i sprawa Żydów polskich w w. XVIII*, 37, mentions that in 1790 a transport was intercepted on the border and 40,000 złotys was confiscated. Reportedly, this was 1/20 of the total sum that was moved out of the country.

205. *Dwór Franka*, 176.

206. *Śmierć Frenka*, 5, 9; and *Basałyk pod imieniem Ćwika*, 1–3.

207. *Zwierciadło polskie*, 31.

208. Aleksander I, Car Rosji, Król Polski, *Ukaz o Towarzystwie izraelskich chrześcijan i komitecie opiekuństwa dla tego ustanowionym*.

209. [Wincenty Krasiński], *Aperçu sur les Juifs de Pologne*; idem, *Sposób na Żydów, czyli środki niezawodne zrobienia z nich ludzi uczciwych i dobrych obywateli*; see also Gelber, "Ein 'Krimprojekt' im Jahre 1841," in idem, *Zur Vorgeschichte des Zionismus*, 213–20.

210. The Jellinek report was originally published in Czech in *Narodni Listy*, then in German in *Das jüdische Literaturblatt*, and finally in Russian in *Razsviet*; for references, see Shatzky, "Alexander Kraushar and His Road to Total Assimilation," 167 n. 33.

211. Aleksander Świętochowski published an account of Frankism in *Nowiny* 26 (1881); another article appeared in the conservative *Głos* 2, no. 26 (1881); the Jewish weekly *Izraelita* also devoted a series of articles to Frank in 1882.

212. Shatzky, "Alexander Kraushar," 167.

213. Ibid., 168.

214. *Głos* 2, no. 26 (1881), quoted in ibid., 167.

215. See ibid., 168–69.

216. Kraushar, *Frank i frankiści polscy*, 1:31–32.

217. Jeske-Choiński, *Neofici polscy*, 69.

218. Shatzky, "Alexander Kraushar," 170.

219. For a discussion of recent (as of the 1970s) anti-Semitic literature on Frankism, see Duker, "Frankism as a Movement of Polish-Jewish Synthesis," 152–53.

220. For the discussion of these debates, see Duker, "The Mystery of the Jews in Mickiewicz's Towianist Lectures on Slav Literature," 40–66; idem, "Some Cabbalistic and Frankist Elements in Adam Mickiewicz's 'Dziady,'" 213–35; Maurer, "Celina Szymanowska as a Frankist," 335–47; and idem, *"Z Matki Obcej . . .": Szkice o powiązaniach Mickiewicza ze światem Żydów*.

221. Syga and Szenic, *Maria Szymanowska i jej czasy*, 15, 465–67, 479–80; also quoted in Duker, "Frankism as a Movement," 137.

222. Bronikowski (Julian Brinken), "Józef Frank: Patriarcha Neofitów," *Biblioteka Warszawska* 3 (1845): 112; Warsaw, BN, Ms. 1345, 10, 241.

223. For the history of the publication, see Scholem, "Julian von Brinkens Roman-hafte Erzählung über die Frankisten," 479–503. Scholem presumed the manuscript lost.

224. Brinken, *Sekta Judeev-Soharistov v Polsche i Sapadnoj Jevropie.*

225. Kuzmin, *Materyaly k voprosu ob obvinienich Yevreev v ritualnych postupleniach*, first mentioned in Bałaban, "Studien und Quellen," 25.

226. Rzewuski (ed.), *Pamiętniki Bartłomieja Michałowskiego*, 1:77–78.

Bibliography

MANUSCRIPT AND ARCHIVAL SOURCES

Moravský Zemský Archiv, Brno (MZA)

B1 1251/F123, "Franck."
B1 1702/J2 (Jewish tax).
B1 1705/J4 (Jewish census).
B1 1746/J47 (conversions).

Archiv Města Brna, Brno (AMB)

T 44, PhDr Gustav Trautenberger Nachlaß.

Biblioteka Narodowa, Warsaw (BN)

Ms. 1345, Aleksander Bronikowski (Julian Brinken), "Józef Frank: Patriarcha Neofitów." Powieść historyczna z drugiej połowy XVIII wieku (first three chapters were published in *Biblioteka Warszawska* 3 [1845]).

Ms. 3207, Józef Andrzej Załuski, Information touchant les Juifs, leur Talmud et les infanticides par I. Z. E. de Kiovie.

Ms. 3208, Józef Andrzej Załuski, Information touchant les Juifs, leur Talmud et les infanticides par J. Z[ałuski] Ev[êque] de Kiovie à l'occasion de l'infanticide commis récemment dans son Diocèse et de l'objection faite aux Talmudistes de Pologne par les Contre-Talmudistes néophytes en 1759.

Ms. 3209, Józef Andrzej Załuski, Cała Polska za złoty, to jest opisanie Polski trojakie, z historii duchownej, z historii cywilnej, z historii literackiej . . . w areszcie smoleńskim r. 1768.

Ms. 3260, Józef Andrzej Załuski, Korespondencja z roku 1760.

Ms. 3261, Józef Andrzej Załuski, Korespondencja z roku 1761.

Biblioteka Uniwersytecka w Warszawie, Warsaw (BUW)

Ms. 85, Manifestacja żydów kontrtalmudystów w dniu 2 VIII 1756 w sądzie biskupim w Kamieńcu Podoliskim złożona.
Ms. 802, Adryan Krzyżanowski, O dziejowości Talmudu. Dziejowość Antytalmudystów polskich.
Ms. 1069, Antoni Kosakowski, Katarzyna II carowa rosyjska. Oszukaniec. Komedia. Tłum. 7 marca 1786.

Archiwum Główne Akt Dawnych, Warsaw (AGAD)

Archiwum Nuncjatury 006 (pastoral letters of Polish bishops).
Archiwum Masońskie Skimborowicza II-1/I, Hipolit Skimborowicz, Rys historyczny wolnomularstwa polskiego.
Teki Skimborowicza XXI-2/135, Nachricht von dem Tode und der Beerdigung des als Haupt der sich in Offenbach niedergelassenden Pohlen Herrn Baron von Frank.

Biblioteka Czartoryskich, Kraków

Ms. 700, August Moszyński, Mes observations.
Ms. 809, August Moszyński, Réflections sur la science Hermétique présentées au Roi par le Comte Moszyński Stolnik de la Couronne en 1768.

Biblioteka Jagiellońska, Kraków (BJ)

Ms. 6968, Zbiór słów pańskich w Brünnie mówionych.
Ms. 6969, Zbiór słów pańskich w Brünnie mówionych.

Biblioteka Publiczna im. H. Łopacińskiego, Lublin (BPL)

Ms. 2118, Życiorys i nauki Jakuba Franka, założyciela sekty Frankistów.

Archiwum Jasnej Góry, Częstochowa (AJG)

534, Annalium ordinis S. Pauli Primi Eremitae Monachorum sub regula Divi Augustini Deo Famulantium Vol. Tertium Quo.

194, Acta Conventus C[lari] M[ontis] Cz[estochoviensis] Almam Provinciae Poloniam (1731–1815).

748/1, Memorabilia celeberrimi monasteri C[lari] M[ontis] Cz[estochoviensis].

540, Actorum provinciae ordinis s. Pauli primi Eremitae tomus XI (September 1959– September 1780).

Geheimes Staatsarchiv Preußischer Kulturbesitz, Berlin (GStA)

I. HA Geheimer Rat, Rep 7, Neuostpreußen, 190 Nr. 32 Fasz. 1 Acta betreffend die neue jüdische Sekte Edom genannt und die Aktivitäten und Schriften des Oberhaupts der Sabbatianer Jacob Leyb Frank.

I. HA Rep. 81, Frankfurt, V B Nr. 23, Wegen der Frankesche Secte zu Offenbach.

Staatsarchiv Offenbach (SAO)

O 1450/13, Alkies-Zaleski, Z. Barbara Königin von Polen.

O 1450/15/2, Frank, Jakob, und die Frankisten. Zeitungs- und Zeitschriftenaufsätze.

M 736/1, Die anspruchslosen Kosaken in Offenbach.

M 736/5a–5b, Druck: Baron Frank bei der Ausfahrt.

Unitätsarchiv, Herrnhut (UA)

R.16, Judenmission.

R.19.J.1.A, David Kirchoffs Bericht von Lissa 1757.

R.19.B.d.2.a.42, David Kirchoff, Diarium aus Lithauen 1758/59.

R.19.B.d.2.a.42, David Kirchoff, Diarium aus Pohlen 1758.

R.22.53.19, Lebenslauf Benjamin David Kirchoffs.

Archivio Segreto Vaticano (ASV)

ARCHIVIO DELLA NUNZIATURA APOSTOLICA DI VARSAVIA

94 Miscelanee ecclesiastiche. Tomo II. Giudei, Regicidio, Delitti di Stato.

SEGRETERIA DI STATO, POLONIA

270 Di mons[ignore] Nunzio Serra 1757 e 1758. Lett[ere] orig[inale] del nunzio alla Segreteria, 5 January 1757–10 May 1758.

271 Di mons[ignore] Nunzio Serra 1757 e 1758. Lett[ere] orig[inale] del nunzio alla Segreteria, 12 April 1758–25 April 1759.

272 Di mons[ignore] Nunzio Serra 1757 e 1758. Lett[ere] orig[inale] del nunzio alla Segreteria, 2 May 1759–27 July 1760.

289 Minutari di lett[ere] del nunzio a Congregazioni Romane ed a diversi, 13 August 1760–3 March 1773.

CONGREGAZIONE DEL CONCILIO

Relationes Dioecesum 272 Cracovien.

Jewish National and University Library, Jerusalem (JNUL)

Ms. Heb 8° 2921, Drushim ve-iggerot mi-hug ha-Frankistim be-Prag.

Ms. Heb 8° 7507, Ber Birkenthal of Bolechów, *Sefer divre binah.*

Bodleian Library, Oxford (Bod)

· Ms. 2187, [Joseph Prager], Sefer gahale esh.

Ms. 955, 4 Sefer ve-avo ha-yom el ha-ayyin.

Ms. 259, Hoda'at ba'al din.

PRINTED PRIMARY SOURCES

Anonymous pamphlets and articles in contemporary periodicals.

Acta Illustristimi excellentristimi Domini Nicolai Dembowsky. Berdyczów, 1798.

Basałyk pod imieniem Ćwika na jestestwo dawniey nieużyteczne sporządzony. Warsaw, 1790.

"Ein Beitrag zur Geschichtsromantik." *Frankfurter Zeitung.* 1 February 1867.

Błędy talmudowe od samychże Żydów uznane y przez nową sektę Siapwscieciuchów, czyli Contratalmudystów wyiawione. Lwów, 1758.

Die Brüder St. Johannis des Evangelisten aus Asien in Europa oder die einzige wahre und ächte Freimauerei nebst einem Anh. Die Fellersche kritische Geschichte der Freimaurerbrüderschaft und ihre Nichtkeit betreffend von einem hohen Obern. Berlin, 1803.

Documenta Judaeos in Polonia concernentia ad acta metrices Regni suscepta at ex iis fideliter iterum descripta et extradicta. Warsaw, 1763.

Dwór Franka czyli polityka nowochrzczeńców, odkryta przez Neofitę jednego dla poprawy rządu roku 1790. Warsaw, 1790. Reprinted in Artur Eisenbach and Jerzy Michalski (eds.), *Materiały do dziejów Sejmu Czteroletniego.* Warsaw, 1969. 4 vols.

Evreiskiie religioznyie sekty v Rossyi. Saint Petersburg, 1847.

"Die Frankistensecte in Offenbach." *Frankfurter Familienbläter.* January 1868.

"Die immerwährende Maskarade: Aus zwey Schreiben." *Journal des Luxus und der Modern.* Weimar, 1800.

Katechizm o Żydach y neofitach. Czym oni są y co z niemi zrobić należy? Dla poprawy formy rządu do Deputacyi przesłany. Warsaw, [1791].

Krótkie zebranie obrządków żydowskich i ich ku chrześcijanom wieczna nienawiść z okazji nowej sekty kontrtalmudystów. Vilna, 1759.

Kuryer Polski. 1759, 1760.

List przyjaciela Polaka. Warsaw, 1790. Reprinted in Artur Eisenbach and Jerzy Michalski (eds.), *Materiały do dziejów Sejmu Czteroletniego.* Warsaw, 1969. 4 vols

Memorial de los Judíos de Polonia y de otras varias provincias confinantes de la Turquía presentaron al nuevo Arzobispo de Gnesne, primado de aquel Reino, siendo Arzobispo de Léopold, en que le pedían se dignase admitirlos en el gremio de la Santa Iglesia Católica Romana, y de hacerles conferir el Santo Baptismo. Impreso en Madrid, en la imprenta de los Herederos de la Viuda de Juan Gracia Infanzon, y en Original reimpreso en México en la imprenta de la Biblioteca Mexicana Año De. 1759.

Memorial que os Judeos de Polonia, e de outras varias provincias, confinantes da Turquia, apresentaram ao novo Arcebispo de Gnesne, primaz daquelle reyno, sendo Arcebispo de Leopold, em que lhe pediam se dignasse de admittirlos no gremio ds santa Igreja Catholica Romana, mandandolhes conferir o sagrado bautismo. Lisbon, 1759.

Myśli z historii o Contra-Talmudystach wiernie, krótko i zupełnie zebraney z okazyi nastąpionej do zwierzchności i temiż Contra-Talmudystami dyspozycyi na zawstydzenie żydowskiego urągania z przyłączonemi uwagami o stanie teraźniejszym chrześcijan pomieszanych przez pewnego. Zamość, 1761.

"Die Pohlen in Offenbach." *Main-Zeitung* 14 (1867).

Processus judicarius in causa patrati cruenti infanticidii per infidels Judaeos seniores synogae Woyslaviencis. Lublin[?], 1761.

Śmierć Frenka: Przez urodzonego L. A. M. Warsaw[?], 1792.

Supplex Libellus a Judaeis fidem catholicam amplectentibus et baptismum expetentibus Illustrissimo et Reverendissimo DD Łubieński Archiepiscopo Leopolienski.[sic] nunc celsissimo nominato principi primati porrectus. N.p., 1759.

Supplique présentée à monseigneur l'archeveque de Leopold: Au nom de plusieurs milliers de juifs polonois, hongrois, &c. qui désirent embrasser la foi catholique, & reçevoir le s. baptême. N.p., 1759[?].

"Zwei fürstliche Geheimnisse neuerer Zeit." *Gartenlaube* 3 (1866).

Zwierciadło polskie dla publiczności. Choć nie kształtne, ale w reprezentacji rzetelne, w którym widzieć można różnych ludzi i wielorakie ich defekta a osobliwie Żydów szczególności i powrzechności szkodliwych. Dnia 12 października 1789 roku zrobione a teraz dla przeyrzenia się w nim i widzenia wielu ciekawości dnia 10 listopada 1790 roku odkryte. Warsaw, 1790.

OTHER PRINTED PRIMARY SOURCES

Abravanel, Isaac. *Nahalat avot.* Venice, 1545.

Aleksander, I., Car Rosji, Król Polski. *Ukaz o Towarzystwie izraelskich chrześcijan i komitecie opiekuństwa dla tego ustanowionym.* Petersburg, 1817.

Anklein, C. "Der Polackenfürst." *Frankfurter Zeitung.* 1 March 1889.

Anton, Karl. *Kurze Nachricht von dem falschen Messias Sabbathai Zebbi und den neulich seinetwegen in Hamburg und Altona entstandenden Bewegungen zu besseren Beurtheilung derer bisher in den Zeitungen und anderen Schriften davon bekannt gewordenen Erzählungen.* Wolfenbüttel, 1752.

———. *Nachlese zu seiner letzteren Nachricht von Sabbathai Zebbi worin zugleich das Ende dieser Streitigkeit erzählt wird.* Braunschweig, 1753.

Appell, Johann Wilhelm. "Dobruschki-Frank, die Polnische Sektehäuptung in Offenbach." Frankfurter Museum. *Süddeutsche Wochenschrift,* 20 October 1855.

Avraham Hayyim of Zlotshov. *Orah la-hayyim.* Żółkiew, 1817.

Awedyk, Konstanty. *Kazanie po dysputach contra talmudystów w Lwowie, w Kościele Katedralnym Lwowskim przy tym Historia o contra-talmudystach wszystkie dwornieysze okoliczności, nawrócenia ich do Wiary S. y dalszych postępków opisująca imieniem J. W. Jć Pana Ignacego na Wielkim Rozwadowie Rozwadowskiego Kasztelanica Halickiego Starosty Ostrowskiego, Generała Majora Buławy Polney Koronney Zaszczycona.* Lwów, 1760.

———. *Opisanie wszytskich dworniejszych okoliczności nawrócenia do wiary s. Contra-Talmudystów albo historia krótka ich początki i dalsze sposoby przystępowania do wiary s. wyrażająca.* Lwów, 1760.

Bagiński, Wojciech Wincenty. *Rękopism.* Vilna, 1854.

Becker, August. *Des Rabbis Vermächtniss.* Berlin, 1866.

Beer, Yeshashakhar. "Toledot bne Yehonatan." In M[arcus] Bondi, *Mi-kitve sefat kodesh.* Prague, 1856.

Ber Levinsohn, Isaac. *Efes Damim: A Series of Conversations at Jerusalem between a Patriarch of the Greek Church and the Chief Rabbi of the Jews concerning the Malicious Charge against the Jews of Using Christian Blood.* London, 1841.

Bernstein, Ignatz. "Brief an Eduard Jellinek," *Das jüdische Literaturblatt* 27 (1882)

Börner, Christian Friedrich. *Auserlesene Bedanken der theologischen Facultät zu Leipzig.* Leipzig, 1751.

Brentano, Bettina. *Tagebuch: Briefwechsel Goethes mit einem Kinde.* Berlin, 1928. 4 vols.

Brenz, Samuel Friedrich. *Jüdischer abgestreifter Schlangenbalg.* Nuremberg, 1614.

Brinken, Julian. *Sekta Judeev-Soharistov v Polsche i Sapadnoj Jevropie: Josif Frank, evo utschenie i posledovateli.* Saint Petersburg, 1892.

Callenberg, Johann Heinrich. *Bericht an einige christliche Freunde von einem Versuch, das arme jüdische Volck zur Erkäntniss und Annehmung der christlichen Wahrheit anzuleiten.* Halle, 1730. 14 vols.

———. *Sefer Besorah Tovah al pi ha-Mevasher Lukas. Evangelium Lucae ab erudito proselyte*

Henr. Christ. Imman. Frommano Doc. Med. in linguam ebraeam transferri ea explicari curauit editique Io. Henr. Callenberg. Halle, 1737.

Calmanson, Jacob. *Essai sur l'état actuel des Juifs de Pologne et leur perfectibilité.* Warsaw, 1791.

———. *Uwagi nad nineyszym stanem Żydów Polskich y ich wydoskonaleniem.* Warsaw, 1797.

Cardozo, Abraham Miguel. *Selected Writings.* Trans. D. J. Halperin. New York, 2001.

Casanova, Giacomo. *Briefwechsel.* Ed. Aldo Rava and Gustav Gugitz. Vol. 15. Munich, 1913.

———. *Briefwechsel mit J. F. Opiz.* Ed. Frantisek Kohl and Otto Pick. Berlin, 1922.

———. *Patrizi e avventurieri, dame e ballerine.* Milan, 1930.

———. *The History of My Life.* Trans. Willard R. Trask. New York, 1967. 12 vols.

Czacki, Tadeusz. *Rozprawa o Żydach i Karaitach.* Wilno, 1807.

Czartoryski, Kazimierz Florian. *Instructio circa judicia sagarum judicibus eorumque consilia-riis accomodata Romae primum 11657.* Swarzewice, 1669.

da Costa, Uriel. *Exemplar Humanae Vitae.* In Carl Gebhardt (ed.), *Die Schriften des Uriel da Costa.* Amsterdam, 1922.

D[alman], G[ustav]. "Dokumente eines christlichen Geheimbundes unter den Juden im achtzenten Jahrhundert. *Saat und Hoffnung: Zeitschrift für die Mission der Kirche an Israel* 27 (1890).

Diariusze sejmowe z wieku XVIII. Diaria Comitiorum Poloniae Saeculi XVIII. Ed. W. Konopczyński. Warsaw, 1937.

Dienemann, Max. "Als Page bei Eva Frank." *Alt-Offenbach* 7 (1931).

Doktór, Jan (ed.). *Księga słów Pańskich: Ezoteryczne wykłady Jakuba Franka.* Warsaw, 1997.

———. *Rozmaite adnotacje, przypadki, czynności i anekdoty pańskie.* Warsaw, 1996.

Dov Baer ben Samuel. *In Praise of the Baal Shem Tov.* Trans. Dan Ben-Amos and Jerome R. Mintz. Northvale, N.J., 1993.

Dubnow, Simon. *Pinkas va'ad ha-kehillot ha-rashiyyot be-medinat Lita.* Berlin, 1925.

Eck, Johannes. *Ains Judenbüechlins Verlegung: Darin ain Christ gantzer Christenhait zu schmach will es geschehe den Juden vnrecht in bezichtigung der Christen kinder mordt.* Ingolstadt, 1541.

Etheridge, J[ohn] W[esley]. *The Targums of Onkelos and Jonathan Ben Uzziel on the Penta-teuch with the Fragments of the Jerusalem Targum from the Chaldee.* London, 1862,

Eisenmenger, Andreas. *Entdecktes Judenthum.* Heidelberg, 1742. 4 vols.

Emden, Jacob. *Akitsat akrav.* Amsterdam [in fact: Altona], 1752.

———. *Aspaklaria ha-me'ira.* Altona, 1753.

———. *Beit Yehonatan ha-sofer.* Altona, 1762.

———. *Birat migdal oz.* Altona, 1748.

———. *Edut be-Ya'akov.* Altona, 1756.

———. *Kitsur tsitsat novel Tsevi.* Altona, 1757.

———. *Megillat sefer.* Ed. David Kahana. Warsaw, 1897.

———. *Mitpahat sefarim.* Lemberg, 1870.

————. *Petah eyna'im*. Altona, 1757.

————. *Sefer hitabbkut*. Lemberg, 1877.

————. *Sefer shimush*. Amsterdam [Altona], 1760.

————. *Sefer torat ha-kena'ot*. Lemberg, 1870.

————. *She'elat YAVe"Ts*. Altona, 1739–59.

————. *Shevirat luhot ha-even*. Żółkiew, 1756.

Fleckeles, Eleazar. *Ahavat David*. Prague, 1800.

————. *Teshuvah me-ahavah*. Prague, 1809.

Galatino, Pietro. *De Arcanis Catholicæ veritatis: Hoc est, in omnia difficilia loca Veteris Testamenti, ex Talmud, aliq[ue] hebraicis libris, quum ante natum Christum, tum postscriptis, contra obstinatam Iudæorum perfidiam, absolutissimus commentarius*. Basel, 1550.

Gamalski, Serafin. *Przestrogi duchowne sądziom inwestygatorom i instygatorom czarownic*. Poznań, 1742.

Gelber, Nahum M. (ed.). "Di zikhroynes fun Mozes Porges vegn des Frankistn-Hoyf in Ofenbakh." *YIVO Historishe Schriftn* 1 (1929).

Gikatilla, Joseph. *Sha'are orah (Gates of Light)*. Trans. Avi Weinstein. London, 1994.

Goethe, Johann Wolfgang, *Italian Journey*. Trans. Robert R. Heitner. New York, 1989

Hagiz, Moses. *Lehishat saraf*. Hanau, 1726.

————. *Shever poshe'im*. Amsterdam [in fact: London], 1714.

Hannower, Nathan Nata. *Sefer yeven metsulah: Marbeh lesaper gezerot u-milhamot she hayu . . . mi-shenat 408 ad shenat 412*. Warsaw, 1872.

Hayon, Nehemiah. *Oz le-Elohim*. Berlin, 1713.

Hirschfeld, Ephraim Joseph. *Biblisches Organon oder Realübersetzung der Bibel mit mystischen Begleitungen*. Offenbach, 1796.

[Jeiteless, Baruch]. *Sihah bein shenat 5560 u-vein 5561*. Prague, 1800.

Kaidanover, Tsevi Hirsh. *Sefer kav ha-yashar*. Lublin, 1912.

Kiedrzyński, Anastazy. *Mensa Nazarea seu Historia imaginis Divae Claromontanae*. N.p., 1763.

Kirchner, Paul Christian. *Jüdisches Ceremoniel [sic] oder Beschreibung derjenigen Gebräucher, welche die Juden sowol inn—als ausser dem Tempel, bey allen und jeden Fest-Tagen, im Gebet, bey der Beschneidung . . ., in acht zu nehmen pflegen*. Nuremberg, 1734; photo offset, Leipzig, 1999.

Kleczewski, Stanisław. *Dissertacya albo mowa o pismach żydowskich i Talmudzie podczas walnej dysputy Contra-Talmudystów z Talmudystami pod rządem J. W. Jmci Xiedza Szczepana z Mikulicz Mikluskiego Oboyga Prawa Doktora, Archidyakona y Kanonika Archi-Katedralnego, Administratora Generalnego Metropolij Lwowskiey agituiącey się na sessyi czwartey, przez wielebnego w Bogu Jmci Xiędza Stanisława Kleczewskiego, Zakonu S. Franciszka Braci Mnieyszych Reformackiego Kustodii Ruskiey Exkustorza publico ore miana we Lwowie Roku Pańskiego 1759*. Lwów[?], 1759.

Klein, Dr. "Zuschrift an Herrn Moses Mendelson in Hamburg." *Literaturblatt des Orients* 33 (1848): col. 526.

Kleyn, Franciszek Kazimierz. *Coram iudicio recolendae memoriae Nicolai de stemmate Je-*

litarum a Dembowa Góra Dembowski, Dei & Apostolicae Sedis Gratia Episcopi Ca-
menecenis, Postulati Archi-Episcopi Metropolitani Leopoliensis, Praepositi Generalis
Commendatarii Michoviens. Aequitis Aquilae Albae. Pars III: De decisoriis Processus inter
infideles Iudaeos Dioecesis camenecensis, in materia iudaicae eorum perfidiae, aliorumque
muto obiectorum A.D. *1757 expedita ac in executis pendens.* Lwów, 1758.

Kobielski, Franciszek Antoni. *Światło na oświecenie narodu niewiernego, to iest kazania w*
Synagogach Żydowskich miane oraz Reflexye y List odpowiadający na pytania Synagogi
Brodzkiey z Rozkazu Jaśnie wielmożnego Jego Mości Xiędza Franciszka Antoniego Kobiel-
skiego Biskupa Łuckiego y Brzeskiego, Kanclerza Nayiaśniejszey Królowey JeyMci Polskiey
o pozyskanie Dusz zelesem nieustannym pracującego. Lwów, 1746.

Koźmian, Kajetan. *Pamiętniki.* Wrocław, 1972.

[Krasiński, Wincenty]. *Aperçu sur les Juifs de Pologne par un officier general polonais.* [Vilna],
1818.

———. *Sposób na Żydów, czyli środki niezawodne zrobienia z nich ludzi uczciwych i dobrych*
obywateli. Vilna, 1818.

Ha-kronika: Te'udah le-toledot Ya'akov Frank ve-tenu'ato. Ed. Hillel Levine. Jerusalem,
1984.

Kuzmin, I. *Materyaly k voprosu ob obvinienich Yevreev v ritualnych postupleniach.* Saint Petersburg, 1913.

Lamm, Louis. "Eine eigenartige Ausstellung: Beitrag zur Geschichte Jakob Franks und
seinen Anhänger." *Offenbacher Zeitung,* 15 July 1899.

Landau, Ezekiel. *Noda bi-Yehuda.* Prague, 1776.

Lauda sejmikowe wiszeńskie, lwowskie, przemyskie i sanockie 1731–1772. Ed. A. Prochaska.
Lwów, 1928.

Maimon, Salomon. *Geschichte des eigenen Lebens, 1754–1800.* Berlin, 1935.

Mauthner, Fritz. *Lebenserinnerungen.* Munich, 1918.

Megerlin, David Friedrich. *Geheime Zeugnisse vor die Wahrheit der christlichen Religion, aus*
vier und zwanzig neuen und selten jüdischen Amuleten oder Anhang-Zetteln gezogen.
Frankfurt am Main, 1756.

Memoirs of Ber of Bolechów, 1723–1805. Ed. M. Vishnitzer. London, 1922.

Menahem Mendel ben Abraham Krochmal. *She'elot u-teshuvot tsemah tsedek.* Altdorf,
1766.

[Moszyński, August]. *Cagliostro démasqua à Varsovie, ou relation autentique de ses opera-*
tions alchemiques et magiques faites dans cette capitale en 1780, par un témoin oculaire.
Warsaw, 1781.

Pamiętnik Króla Stanisława Augusta. Warsaw, 1915.

"Pamiętnik Thulliego." Ed. S. Schnür-Pepłowski. *Przewodnik Naukowy i Literacki* 23
(1895).

Pamiętniki Bartłomieja Michałowskiego od roku 1786 do 1815. Ed. H. Rzewuski. Warsaw,
1858.

Pikulski, Gaudenty *Złość żydowska przeciwko Bogu i bliźniemu, prawdzie i sumieniu, na ob-*
jaśnienie talmudystów, na dowód ich zaślepienia i religii dalekiej od Prawa Boskiego przez

Mojżesza danego Rozdzielona na trzy części opisana przez X. Gaudentego Pikulskiego Zakonu O.S. Franciszka, Regularney Obserwancji Prowincji Ruskiey z Dozwoleniem Starszych Drugi Raz do druku z ustną Relacją Dysputy Contra Talmudystów z Talmudystami, y przydatkiem innych Osobliwości. Lwów, 1760.

Pinkas Va'ad Arba Aratsot: Acta Congressus Generalis Judaeorum Regni Poloniae, 1580–1764. Ed. Israel Halperin. Jerusalem, 1945.

Pirazzi, Emil. *Bilder und Geschichten aus Offenbachs Vergangenheit.* Offenbach, 1879.

———. "Ein enthülltes Geheimniss aus Offenbachs Vergangenheit." *Offenbacher Zeitung,* 31 December 1894.

———. "Jacob Frank, der Messias aus Podolien." *Frankfurter Zeitung,* 3 October 1895.

———. "Neue Beiträge zu einer alten Geschichte." *Frankfurter Didaskalia* (1868).

———. "Die Polen in Offenbach am Main." *Frankfurter Familienblatt,* 15 January 1867.

———. "Zur Geschichte Offenbachs." *Offenbacher Zeitung,* 10–11 February 1894.

Porges, Nathan. "Texte de la lettre adressée par les Frankistes aux communautés Juives de Boheme." *Revue des études juives* 29 (1894).

Putean, Kazimierz. *Judaismus convictus seu demonstratio evidentissima legem veterem cessasse, promissum Messiam advenisse, eumque esse Jesum Christum invictis argumentis e vaticiniis antique testamenti deducta . . . anno elapso a Judaeis factae publicae data, authore Casimiro Putelano.* Warsaw, 1757.

Quelle, Eginhard (= Arnold Hirsch). "Das Grab eines Propheten in Offenbach." *Illustriertes Familienbuch zur Unterhaltung und Belehrung haeuslicher Kreise* 7, no. 6 (1857).

Radlinski, Jakób Paweł. *Prawda chrzescianska od nieprzyiaciela swego zeznana, to iest Traktat Rabina Samuela Pokazujący błędy żydowskie około zachowania prawa mojżeszowego y przyścia Messyaszowego, którego czekają z Łacińskiego na Polski przetłumaczony Roku Pańskiego 1733 Przez Przewielebnego Jegomości X Jakoba Radlińskiego S. T. I.* Lublin, 1753.

Regulus, Wojciech. *Czarownica powołana abo krótka nauka y przestroga z strony czarownic zebrana zrozmaitych Doktorów tak uprawie Bożym iako y świeckim biegłych dla ochrony y poratowania sumnienia, osobliwie na takie Sądy wysądzonych.* Poznań, 1639.

Reuchlin, Johann. *De Arte Cabalistica: On the Art of the Kabbalah.* Trans. Martin and Sarah Goodman. Lincoln, Nebr., 1993.

Roth, Cecil (ed.). *The Ritual Murder Libel and the Jew: The Report by Cardinal Lorenzo Ganganelli (Pope Clement XIV).* London, 1935.

Sasportas, Jacob. *Tsitsat novel Tsevi.* Ed. Isaiah Tishby. Jerusalem, 1954.

Schenck-Rinck, A. G. *Die Polen in Offenbach am Main.* Frankfurt am Main, 1866.

Schudt, Johannes Jacob. *Jüdische Merckwürdigkeiten, vorstellende was sich curieuses und denckwürdiges in den neuern Zeiten bey einigen Jahrhunderten mit denen in alle IV Theile der Welt, sonderlich durch Teutschland, zerstreuten Juden zugetragen.* Frankfurt, 1714.

Semler, Johann Salomo. *Historischtheologische Abhandlungen: Zweite Sammlung.* Halle, 1762.

Shirot ve-tushbahot shel ha-Shabbeta'im. Ed. M. Attias and G. Scholem. Tel Aviv, 1947.

Sleszkowski, Sebastyan. *Odkrycie zdrad złośliwych żydowskich.* Brunsberg, 1621.

Sołtyk, Kajetan. *Złość żydowska w zamęczeniu dzieci katolickich przez list następujący y dekreta grodzkie wydana.* Lublin, ca. 1761.

————. *Złość żydowska w zamęczeniu dzieci katolickich przez list następujący y dekreta grodzkie wydana.* Lublin, 1774.

Stern, Moritz. *Die Papstlichen Bullen über die Blutbeschuldigung.* Berlin 1899.

Thomas of Monmouth. *The Life and Miracles of Saint William of Norwich.* Cambridge, 1896.

Tishby, Isaiah. *The Wisdom of the Zohar.* Trans. David Goldstein. Oxford, 1985. 3 vols.

[Turski, Feliks Paweł]. *Uwiadomienie Zwierzchności Duchownej co do osoby Józefa Franka i Żydów przechodzących na wiarę chrześcijańską.* [Warsaw], 1760.

Vetera Monumenta Poloniae et Lithuaniae. Ed. Augustinus Theiner. Vol. 4, 1679–1775. Rome, 1864.

Vital, Hayyim. *Sefer ets hayyim.* Jerusalem, 1970.

Vishnitzer, Mark. "Poslanie Frankistov 1800 goda." *Memories de l'academie imperiale des Sciences de St. Petersburg.* 2d series, 12, no. 3 (1914).

Volumina Legum. Przedruk Zbioru Praw staraniem XX Pijarów w Warszawie od roku 1732 do roku 1782 wydanego. Ed. S. Konarski. Petersburg, 1860.

Von Leonhard, K. C. "Der Sectenhäuptling Frank in Offenbach." *Frankfurter Konversationsblatt* 4 (1854).

Von Sacher-Masoch, Leopold. "Der Prophet von Offenbach." *Frankfurter Zeitung,* 24 February 1889.

Wacholder, Ben-Zion. "Jacob Frank and the Frankists: Hebrew Zoharic Letters." *Hebrew Union College Annual* 53 (1982).

Wagenseil, Johann Christian. *Der denen Juden fälschlich beygemessene Gebrauch des Christen-Bluts, das ist Benachrichtigungen wegen einiger die Judenschaft angehenden wichtigen Sachen.* Leipzig, 1705.

————. *Hoffnung der Erlösung Israels.* Nuremberg, 1707.

Wessely, Wolfgang. "Aus den Briefen eines Sabbatianers." *Der Orient* 12 (1851).

Załuski, Józef Andrzej. *Objaśnienie błędami zabobonów zarażonych oraz opisanie niegodziwości, która pochodzi z sądzenia przez próbę pławienia w wodzie niecnych czarownic, jako takowa próba jest omylna . . . aby sędziowie poznali niepewność takiej próby, a spowiednicy wierzących takim próbom z błędu wyprowadzić mogli.* Berdyczów, 1766.

Żuchowski, Stefan. *Process kryminalny o niewinne Dziecie Jerzego Krasnowskiego . . . okrótnie od Żydów zamordowane.* [Sandomierz], 1713 [1720].

Other Works Cited

Abafi, Ludwig. *Geschichte der Freimauererei in Österreich-Ungarn.* Budapest, 1823. 5 vols.

Agnon, Shmuel Joseph. "Ein Wort über Jakob Frank: Nach polemischer Schriften seiner Zeitgenossen." In S. J. Agnon and Ahron Eliasberg, *Das Buch von den polnischen Juden.* Berlin, 1916.

Anderson, George Kumler. *The Legend of the Wandering Jew*. Hanover, N.H., 1991.

Arnsberg, Paul. *Von Podolien nach Offenbach: Die jüdische Heilsarmee des Jakob Frank. Zur Geschichte der frankistischen Bewegung*. Offenbach, 1965.

Askenazy, Szymon. *Die letzte polnische Königswahl*. Göttingen, 1894.

Back, Samuel. "Aufgefundene Aktenstücke zur Geschichte der Frankisten in Offenbach." *MGWJ* 26 (1877).

Baer, Yitzhak. "Gezerat TaTN"U." In M. D. Cassuto (ed.), *Sefer Assaf*. Jerusalem, 1953.

———. *A History of the Jews in Christian Spain*. Philadelphia, 1971. 2 vols.

———. "Ha-reka ha-histori shel Ra'ya Mehemna." *Zion* 5 (1939).

Bałaban, Majer. "Epizody iz istorii ritual'nykh protsessov i antievreiskoi literatury v Polshe." *Evreska Starina* 7 (1912).

———. "Hugo Grotius und die Ritualmordprozesse in Lublin, 1636." In Ismar Elbogen et al. (eds.), *Festschrift zu Simon Dubnows siebzigstem Geburtstag*. Berlin, 1930.

———. "Karaici w Polsce." In idem. *Studia historyczne*. Warsaw, 1927.

———. *Le-toledot ha-tenu'ah ha-Frankit*. Tel Aviv, 1935. 2 vols.

———. "Mistyka i ruchy mesjańskie wśród żydów z dawnej Rzeczypospolitej." In *Żydzi w Polsce Odrodzonej*. Warsaw, 1933.

———. "Sabataizm w Polsce: Ustęp z 'Dziejów mistyki żydowskiej w Polsce.'" In *Księga jubileuszowa ku czci Prof. Mojżesza Schrorra*. Warsaw, 1935.

———. *Studia historyczne*. Warsaw, 1927.

———. "Studien und Quellen zur Geschichte der Frankistischen Bewegung in Polen." In *Livre d'hommage à la memoire du Dr. Samuel Poznański*. Warsaw, 1927.

———. *Z historii Żydów w Polsce. Studia i szkice*. Warsaw, 1920.

———. "Z zagadnień ustrojowych żydostwa polskiego." In Karol Badecki et al. (eds.), *Studia lwowskie*. Lwów, 1932.

———. "Zbytek u Żydów polskich i jego zwalczanie." *Księga pamiątkowa 50–lecia Gimnazjum IV im. Jana Długosza we Lwowie*. Lwów, 1928.

———. "Zur Geschichte der Familie Wehle in Prag." *Zeitschrift für Geschichte der Juden in der Tschechoslowakei* 3 (1932).

———. *Zur Geschichte der Juden in Polen*. Vienna, 1915.

Balbinder, Karel. *Listy z dějin brněnského obchodu*. Brno, 1928.

Baliński, Michał (ed.). *Pielgrzymka do Jasnej Góry w Częstochowie odbyta przez pątnika XIX wieku i wydana z rękopisu*. Warsaw, 1846.

Baranowski, Bogdan. *Procesy czarownic w Polsce w XVII i XVIII w.* Łódź, 1952.

Bartal, Israel. "Politika Yehudit terom-modernit: Va'ade ha-arastot be-mizrah Eyropa." In *Ha-tsiyonut ve-ha-hazarah le-historia: Ha-arakhah me-hadash*. Jerusalem, 1999.

———. "Yehudim Polanim bi-darom-ma'arav Eyropa ba-me'a ha-18." In Shmuel Almog et al. (eds.), *Temurot ba-historia ha-Yehudit ha-hadashah*. Jerusalem, 1987.

Bartoszewicz, Kazimierz. *Antysemityzm w literaturze polskiej XV–XVII wieku*. Warsaw, 1914.

Baumgarten, Jean. "Yiddish Ethical Texts and the Diffusion of the Kabbalah in the Seventeenth and Eighteenth Centuries." *Bulletin du Centre de recherche français de Jérusalem* 18 (2007).

Beer, Peter. *Geschichte, Lehren und Meinungen aller bestandenen und noch heute bestehenden religiösen Sekten der Juden und der Geheimlehre oder Kabbalah*. Brünn, 1922–23. 2 vols.

Benayahu, Meir. "Ha-'havurah ha-kedoshah' shel R' Yehuda Hasid." *Sefunot* 3 (1960).

Bentkowski, Feliks. *Starożytności polskie*. Warsaw, 1857.

Ben-Zvi, Itzhak. *The Exiled and the Redeemed*. Philadelphia, 1957.

———. "Kuntrasim be-kabbalah Shabbeta'it mi-hugo shel Berukhiah." *Sefunot* 3–4 (1960).

Berger, Abraham. "Ayalta: From the Doe in the Field to the Mother of the Messiahs." In Saul Lieberman (ed.), *Salo Wittmayer Baron Jubilee Volume*. Jerusalem, 1974. 2 vols.

Berliner, Abraham. *Gutachten Ganganellis (Clemens XIV) in Angelegenheit der Blutbeschuldigung der Juden*. Berlin, 1888.

———. [A letter of Elyakim Asher ben Zelig], *Otsar Tov*, a Hebrew supplement to the *Magazin für Wissenschaft des Judenthums* 15 (1888).

Bidermann, Hermann-Ignaz. *Die Bukowina unter österreichischer Verwaltung 1775–1875*. Lemberg, 1876.

Birge, John Kingsley. *The Bektashi Order of Dervishes*. London, 1937.

Blau, Joseph Leon. *The Christian Interpretation of the Cabala in the Renaissance*. New York, 1944.

Bloch, Philipp. *Die General-Privilegien der polnischen Judenschaft*. Poznań, 1892.

Bonfil, Robert. *Rabbis and Jewish Communities in Renaissance Italy*. Oxford, 1990.

Brauner, Sigrid. *Fearless Wives and Frightened Shrews: The Construction of the Witch in Early Modern Germany*. Amherst, Mass., 1995.

Brawer, Avraham Ya'akov. *Galitsiah vi-Yehudehah*. Jerusalem, 1956.

Brilling, Bernhard. "Eibenschütziana." *HUCA* 36–38 (1964–66).

———. "Das erste Gedicht auf einen deutschen Rabbiner aus dem Jahre 1752." *Bulletin of the Leo Baeck Institute* 2 (1969).

Brockey, Liam Matthew. *Journey to the East: The Jesuit Mission to China 1579–1724*. Cambridge, Mass., 2007.

Carlebach, Elisheva. "Attributions of Secrecy and Perceptions of Jewry." *Jewish Social Studies* 2 (1996).

———. *Divided Souls: Converts from Judaism in Germany, 1500–1750*. New Haven, Conn., 2001.

———. *The Pursuit of Heresy: Rabbi Moses Hagiz and the Sabbatian Controversy*. New York, 1990.

Carmilly-Weinberger, Moshe. *Censorship and Freedom of Expression*. New York, 1977.

———. "Wolf Jonas Eibeschütz: An 'Enlightened' Sabbatean in Transylvania." *Studia Judaica* 6 (1997).

Caro, Jecheskiel. *Geschichte der Juden in Lemberg von den ältesten Zeiten bis zur Theilung Polens im Jahre 1792*. Kraków, 1894.

Chazan, Robert. *Barcelona and Beyond: The Disputation of 1263 and Its Aftermath*. Berkeley, Calif., 1992.

————. *Daggers of Faith: Thirteenth-Century Christian Missionizing and the Jewish Response.* Berkeley, Calif., 1989.

————. *European Jewry and the First Crusade.* Berkeley, Calif., 1987.

Chomętowski, Ignacy. *Przygody ks. Marcina Lubomirskiego.* Warsaw, 1867.

Clark, Christopher M. *The Politics of Conversion: Missionary Protestantism and the Jews in Prussia, 1728–1941.* Oxford, 1995.

Cohen, Gershon D. "Esau as Symbol in Early Medieval Thought." In Alexander Altmann (ed.), *Jewish Medieval and Renaissance Studies,* 19–48. Cambridge, Mass., 1967.

Cohen, Jeremy (ed.). *Essential Papers on Judaism and Christianity in Conflict.* New York, 1991.

————. *The Friars and the Jews: The Evolution of Medieval Anti-Judaism.* Ithaca, N.Y., 1982.

Cohen, Mortimer J. *Jacob Emden: A Man of Controversy.* Philadelphia, 1937.

Cooper-Oakely, Isabel. *The Comte de St. Germain.* London, 1927.

Czeppe, Maria. "Biskup Kajetan Sołtyk a innowiercy: Argumentacja użyta w wystąpieniach na Sejmie w 1766 r." In Adam Kaźmierczyk et al. (eds.), *Rzeczpospolita wielu wyznań.* Kraków, 2004.

Darowski, Adam (ed.). *Pamiętniki Józefa Kossakowskiego, biskupa Inflanckiego.* Warsaw, 1891.

Davidowicz, Samuel Klaus. *Jakob Frank, der Messias aus dem Ghetto.* Frankfurt am Main, 1988.

De Francesco, Grete. *The Power of the Charlatan.* New Haven, Conn., 1939.

De Le Roi, Johann F. A. "Aus der früheren Geschichte der Brüdergemeine." *Dibre Emeth oder Stimmen der Wahrheit* 36 (1880).

————. *Die evangelische Christenheit und die Juden unter dem Gesichtspunkte der Mission geschichtlich betrachtet.* Karlsruhe, 1884. 3 vols.

Dengel Ignaz Philipp. *Nuntius Josef Garampi in preussich Schlesien und in Sachsen im Jahre 1776.* Rome, 1903.

Doktór, Jan. "Frankistowscy maruderzy." In Michał Galas (ed.), *Duchowość żydowska w Polsce: Materiały z międzynarodowej konferencji Dedykowanej pamięci Chone Shmeruka.* Kraków, 2000.

————. *Jakub Frank i jego nauka na tle kryzysu religijnej tradycji osiemnastowiecznego żydostwa polskiego.* Warsaw, 1991.

————. "The Non-Christian Frankists." *Polin: Studies in Polish Jewry* 15 (2002).

————. "Saloniki—Częstochowa—Offenbach: Stacje mesjańskiej drogi Jakuba Franka." In idem, *Rozmaite adnotacje, przypadki, czynności i anektody pańskie.* Warsaw, 1996.

————. *Śladami mesjasza-apostaty: Żydowskie ruchy mesjańskie w XVII i XVIII wieku a problem konwersji.* Wrocław, 1998.

————. *W poszukiwaniu żydowskich kryptochrześcijan: Dzienniki ewangelickich misjonarzy z ich wędrówek po Rzeczypospolitej w latach 1730–1747.* Warsaw, 1999.

Dubnow, Simon. *History of the Jews in Russia and Poland: From the Earliest Times until the Present Day.* Trans. I . Friedlander. Philadelphia, 1946.

————. "Istoriya Frankizma po novootkrytym istochnikam." *Voskhod* 17 (1896).

————. "Yakov Frank i ego sekta khrictianstvuyushchikh." *Voskhod* 3–10 (1883).

Duker, Abraham. "Frankism as a Movement of Polish-Jewish Synthesis." In Bela Kiraly (ed.), *Tolerance and Movements of Religious Dissent in Eastern Europe*. Boulder, Colo., 1975.

————. "The Mystery of the Jews in Mickiewicz's Towianist Lectures on Slav Literature." *Polish Review* 7 (1962).

————. "Polish Frankism's Duration: From Cabbalistic Judaism to Roman Catholicism and from Jewishness to Polishness." *Jewish Social Studies* 25 (1963).

————. "Some Cabbalistic and Frankist Elements in Adam Mickiewicz's 'Dziady.'" In D. Wandycz (ed.), *Selected Papers Delivered at the First Congress of Scholars and Scientists Convened by the Polish Institute of Arts and Sciences in America, November 1966*. New York, 1971.

Dunham, Samuel Astley. *The History of Poland*. London, 1840.

Dworkin, A. *Woman Hating*. New York, 1974.

Elior, Rachel (ed.). *Ha-halom ve-shivro. Ha-tenu'ah ha-Shabbta'it u-sheluhoteha: meshihiyut, Shabbeta'ut u-Frankizm*. Jerusalem, 2000. 2vols.

Ellemunter, Anton. *Antonio Eugenio Visconti und die Anfänge des Josephinismus: Eine Untersuchung über das theresianische Staatskirchentum unter besonderer Berücksichtigung der Nuntiaturberichte, 1767–1774*. Graz, 1963.

Elqayam, Avraham. "Leidato ha-sheniyah shel ha-mashi'ah: Giluyyim hadashim le-Rabbi Ber Perlhafter." *Kabbalah* 1 (1997).

Encyklopedia kościelna. Warsaw, 1874. 21 vols.

Endelman, Todd M. (ed.). *Jewish Apostasy in the Modern World*. New York, 1987.

————. "Jewish Converts in Nineteenth-Century Warsaw: A Quantitative Analysis." *Jewish Social Studies* 1, no. 4 (1997).

Ettinger, Shmuel. "Va'ad arba aratsot." In idem, *Ben Polin le-Rusya*. Jerusalem, 1994.

Evans, Robert. "Moravia and the Culture of Enlightenment in the Habsburg Monarchy." In Grete Klingenstein and Franz Szabo (eds.), *Staatskanzler Wenzel Anton von Kaunitz-Rietberg, 1711–1794*. Graz, 1996.

Fahn, Ruven. *Legenden der Karaiten*. Vienna, 1921.

Falk, H. "Rabbi Jacob Emden's Views on Christianity." *Journal of Ecumenical Studies* 19, no. 1 (1982).

Fasman O. "An Epistle on Tolerance by a 'Rabbinic Zealot.'" In Leo Jung (ed.), *Judaism in a Changing World*. Oxford, 1939.

Fijałek, Jan (ed.). *Zbiór dokumentów zakonu oo. Paulinów w Polsce*. Kraków, 1938.

Fischer-Colbrie, A. *Michael Denis: Im schwerigen Tale des Mondes*. Graz, 1958.

Fishman, David S. *Russia's First Modern Jews: The Jews of Shklov*. New York, 1995.

Forster, Georg. *Sammtliche Schriften*. Ed. G. G. Gervinus. Leipzig, 1843. 7 vols.

Fram, Edward. "Perception and Reception of Repentant Apostates in Medieval Ashkenaz and Premodern Poland." *AJS Review* 21, no. 2 (1996).

Frankel, Jonathan. *The Damascus Affair: "Ritual Murder," Politics and the Jews in 1840*. Cambridge, 1997.

Freiman, Aharon. *Inyane Shabbatai Tsevi: Sammelband kleiner Schriften über Sabbatai Zebi und dessen Anhänger*. Berlin, 1912.

Friedenthal, Max. "Michael Chasid und die Sabbatianer." *MGWJ* 40 (1932).

Galant, I. "Ritual'nyi protsess v Dunaigorod v 1748 g." *Evreska Starina* 4 (1911).

———. "Zhertvy ritual'nogo obvineniia v Zaslavii v 1747 g." *Evreska Starina* 5 (1912).

Galante, Abraham. *Nouveaux documents sur Sabbetai Sevi:⬚ Organisation et us et coutumes de ses adeptes*. Istanbul, 1935.

Galas, Michał. "Nieznane XVII-wieczne źródła polskie do historii sabataizmu." In Krzysztof Pilarczyk (ed.), *Żydzi i judaizm we współczesnych badaniach polskich. Materiały z konferencji, Kraków 21–23 December 1995*. Kraków, 1997. 2 vols.

Garncarska-Kadary, Bina. *Helkam shel ha-Yehudim be-hitpathut ha-ta'asiyah shel Varshah be-shanim 1816/20–1914*. Tel Aviv, 1985.

Gelber, Nahum M. *Aus zwei Jahrhunderten: Beiträge zur neueren Geschichte der Juden*. Leipzig, 1924.

———. "Die Taufenbewegung unter den polnischen Juden in XVIII. Jahrhundert." *MGJW* 68 (1926).

———. "Zur Geschichte der Frankistenpropaganda im Jahre 1800." In idem, *Aus zwei Jahrhunderten: Beiträge zur neueren Geschichte der Juden*. Leipzig, 1924.

———. *Zur Vorgeschichte des Zionismus*. Vienna, 1927.

Goldberg, Jakub. "*De non tolerandis Judaeis*: On the Introduction of the Anti-Jewish Laws into Polish Towns and the Struggle against Them." In Sh. Yeivin (ed.), *Studies in Jewish History Presented to Professor Raphael Mahler on His Seventy-Fifth Birthday*. Tel Aviv, 1974.

———. "Leipziger Theologen gegen die Ritualmordprozesse: Das Gutachten vom Jahre 1714." *Herbergen der Christenheit: Jahrbuch für deutsche Kirchengeschichte* 23 (1999).

———. *Ha-mumarim be-mamlekhet Polin-Lita*. Jerusalem, 1985.

———. "Żydowscy konwertyci w społeczeństwie staropolskim." In A. Izydorczyk (ed.), *Społeczeństwo staropolskie*, vol. 4. Warsaw, 1986.

Goldish, Matt. *The Sabbatean Prophets*. Cambridge, Mass., 2004.

Gomulicki, Juliusz. "Athos i królewska ptaszarnia." In idem, *Zygzakiem*. Warsaw, 1981.

Gordon, Joseph. "Georg Foster und die Juden." *Jahrbuch des Instituts für deutsche Geschichte* 8 (1978).

Graetz, Heinrich. "Ezechiel Landau's Gesuch an Maria Theresia gegen Jonathan Eibeschütz: Ein Aktenstück." *MGJW* 26 (1877).

———. *Frank und die Frankisten: Eine Sekten-Geschichte aus dem letzten Hälfte des vorigen Jahrhunderts*. Breslau, 1868.

———. *Geschichte der Juden von den ältersten Zeiten bis auf die Gegenwart*. Leipzig, 1882. 11 vols.

———. *History of the Jews*. Trans. Bella Loewy. London, 1901. 5 vols.

Graus, Frantsisek. *Pest, Geissler, Judenmorde: Das 14. Jahrhundert als Krisenzeit*. Göttingen, 1977.

Green, Arthur. "Shekhinah, the Virgin Mary, and the Song of Songs." *AJS Review* 26, no. 1 (2002).

Greenberg, Blu. "Rabbi Jacob Emden: The Views of an Enlightened Traditionalist on Christianity." *Judaism* 27, no. 3 (1978).

Grunwald, Matthias. *Hamburgs deutsche Juden bis zur Auflösung der Dreigemeinden 1811.* Hamburg, 1904.

Guldon, Zenon, and Jacek Wijaczka. *Procesy o mordy rytualne w Polsce w XVI–XVIII wieku.* Kielce, 1995.

Guttmann, Julius. "Lazarus Bendavid: Seine Stellung zum Judentum und seine literarische Wirksamkeit; Anhang III: Jacob Frank und seine Angehörigen." *MGWJ* 25 (1917).

Hadas-Lebel, Mireille. "Les études hebraiques en France au XVIIIe siècle et la creation de la première chaire d'Écriture Sainte en Sorbonne." *Revue des études juives* 144, nos. 1–3 (1985).

Halbronn, Jacques. *Le monde Juif et l'astrologie.* Milan, 1985.

Halperin, David. "The Snake and the Ayalta: A Sabbatian Reworking of the Zoharic Myth." Unpublished paper delivered at the AJS conference in December 2008.

Hames, Hayyim. "'And on This Rock I Will Build My Community': Jewish Use of the Gospel in Fifteenth-Century Spain." Unpublished ms.

Hammermayer, Ludwig. *Der Wilhelmsbader Freimaurer-Konvent von 1782.* Heidelberg, 1980.

Hass, Ludwig. "Żydzi i 'kwestia żydowska' w dawnym wolnomularstwie polskim." *Biuletyn Żydowskiego Instytutu Historycznego* 4, no. 104 (1977).

Heymann, Fritz. *Die Chevalier von Geldern: Eine Chronik vom Abenteuer der Juden.* Amsterdam, 1937.

Hilburg, Erwin. "Jacob Frank, die Frankisten und ihre Nachkommen." *Emuna-Israel Forum* 1–2 (1977).

Hoensch, Jörg. "Der Pollackenfürst von Offenbach." In Richard Schneider (ed.), *Juden in Deutschland: Lebenswelten und Einzelschicksale.* Saint Ingbert, 1994.

Horn, Maurycy. *Regesty dokumentów i ekscerpty z Metryki Koronnej do historii Żydów w Polsce, 1697–1795.* Wrocław, 1984.

Hundert, Gershon David. *The Jews in a Polish Private Town: The Case of Opatów in the Eighteenth Century.* Baltimore, 1992.

———. *Jews in Poland-Lithuania in the Eighteenth Century: A Genealogy of Modernity.* Berkeley, Calif., 2004.

———. *Security and Dependence: Perspectives on Seventeenth-Century Polish-Jewish Society Gained through a Study of Jewish Merchants in Little Poland.* New York, 1978.

Hutton, J[ames] E. *A History of Moravian Missions.* London, 1922.

Idel, Moshe. *Ascensions on High in Jewish Mysticism: Pillars, Lines, Ladders.* Budapest and New York, 2005.

———. "Le-toledot ha-issur lilmod kabbalah lifne gil arba'im." *AJS Review* 5 (1980).

———. "Perceptions of Kabbalah in the Second Half of the Eighteenth Century." *Journal of Jewish Thought and Philosophy* 1 (1991).

———. "Saturn and Sabbatai Tsevi: A New Approach to the Study of Sabbatianism." In Peter Schäfer and Mark Cohen (eds.), *Toward the Millennium: Messianic Expectations from the Bible to Waco.* Leiden, 1998.

Jacobs, Louis. *Theology in Responsa.* London, 1975.

———. *A Tree of Life: Diversity, Flexibility, and Creativity in Jewish Law.* Oxford, 1984.

Jałbrzykowska, Anna, and Jerzy Zathey. *Inwentarz rękopisów Biblioteki Jagiellońskiej, Cz. II, Nr 6501–7000.* Kraków, 1963.

Janecki, Marcelli. *Erhielten die Juden in Polen durch die Taufe den Adelstand?* Berlin, 1888.

Janocki, Jan Daniel. *Józef Andrzej Hrabia na Załuskach Załuski.* Trans. K. Kantak. Warsaw, 1928.

Javary, G. "A propos du thème de la Šekina: Variations sur le nom de Dieu," in *Kabbalistes Chrétiens.* Paris, 1979.

Jellinek, Eduard. "Nachrichten von Frankisten in Warschau." *Das jüdische Literaturblatt,* 27 (1882).

Jeske-Choiński, Teodor. *Neofici polscy.* Warsaw, 1904.

Jost, Marcus. *Allgemeine Geschichte des Israeliten Volkes.* Leipzig, 1828. 3 vols.

———. *Geschichte der Israeliten seit der Tage der Maccabaeer bis auf unsere Tage.* Berlin, 1827. 10 vols.

Kahana, David. *Toledot ha-mekkubbalim, ha-Shabbeta'im, ve-ha-Hassidim.* Tel Aviv, 1941. 2 vols.

Kahana, Maoz. "Mi-Prag le-Prossnitz: Ktiva hilkhatit ve-olam mishtaneh me-ha-Noda bi-Yehuda le-Hatam Sofer." Ph.D. diss., Hebrew University of Jerusalem, 2009.

Kaplan, Yosef. *From Christianity to Judaism: The Story of Isaac Orobio de Castro.* Oxford, 1989.

———. "'Karaites' in Early Eighteenth-Century Amsterdam." In *An Alternative Path to Modernity: The Sephardi Diaspora in Western Europe.* Leiden, 2000.

Karniel, Josef. "Joseph von Sonnenfels: Das Welt- und Gesellschaftsbild eines Kämpfers um ein 'glückliches' Österreich." *Jahrbuch des Instituts für Deutsche Geschichte* 7 (1978).

———. "Jüdischer Pseudomessianismus und deutsche Kultur: Der Weg der frankistischen Familie Dobruschka-Schönfeld im Zeitalter der Aufklärung." *Jahrbuch des Instituts für Deutsche Geschichte* 4 (1982).

———. *Die Toleranzpolitik Kaiser Josefs II.* [Gerlingen], 1986.

Kassner, Salomon. *Die Juden in der Bukowina.* Vienna, 1917.

Katz, Jacob. *Divine Law in Human Hands: Case Studies in Halakhic Flexibility.* Jerusalem, 1988.

———. *Exclusiveness and Tolerance: Studies in Jewish-Gentile Relations in Medieval and Modern Times.* London, 1961.

———. *Jewish Emancipation and Self-Emancipation.* Philadelphia, 1986.

———. *Jews and Freemasons in Europe, 1723–1939.* Cambridge, 1970.

———. "Kavim le-biografia shel Hatam Sofer." In *Halakhah ve-kabbalah.* Jerusalem, 1984.

———. "Moses Mendelsson und E. Hirschfeld." *Bulletin of the Leo Baeck Institute* 7 (1962).

———. *Out of the Ghetto: The Social Background of Jewish Emancipation, 1770–1870.* New York, 1978.

————. "Ha-pulmus ha-rishon al kabbalat Yehudim be-kerev ha-bonim ha-hofshim." *Zion* 30, nos. 3–4 (1965).

————. "A State within a State: The History of an Anti-Semitic Slogan." *Israel Academy of Sciences and Humanities Proceedings* 4 (1969–70).

————. *Tradition and Crisis: Jewish Society at the End of the Middle Ages.* Trans. Bernard Cooperman. New York, 1993.

Kaźmierczyk, Adam. "Converted Jews in Kraków, 1650–1763." *Gal-Ed* 21 (2007).

Kedar, Benjamin Z. "Canon Law and the Burning of the Talmud." *Bulletin of Medieval Canon Law* 9 (1979).

Kęder, Wojciech. "Jasna Góra wobec przemian politycznych w Rzeczypospolitej w latach 1661–1813." *Studia Claromontana* 13 (1993).

————. *Stolica Apostolska wobec Rzeczypospolitej w okresie Konfederacji Barskiej.* Opole, 2006.

Kestenberg-Gladstein, Ruth. *Neuere Geschichte der Juden in den böhmischen Ländern.* Tübingen, 1969.

Kieval, Hillel J. *Languages of Community: The Jewish Experience in the Czech Lands.* Berkeley, Calif., 2000.

Kisch, Egon Erwin. "Dantons Tod und Poppers Neffen." In *Prager Pitaval / Späte Reportagen.* Berlin, 1969.

Klemperer, Gutmann. *Rabbi Jonathan Eibeschütz: Eine biographische Skizze.* Prague, 1858.

Kołodziejczyk, Dariusz. *Podole pod panowaniem tureckim: Ejalet Kamieniecki 1672–1699.* Warsaw, 1994.

Konopczyński, Władysław. *Fryderyk Wielki a Polska.* Poznań, 1947.

————. *Konfederacja barska.* Warsaw, 1936–38.

————. *Konfederacja barska: Wybór tekstów.* Wrocław, 2004.

Kot, Stanisław. *Hugo Grotius a Polska: W trzydziestolecie dzieła 'O prawie wojny i pokoju.'* Kraków, 1926.

Kraszewski, Józef Ignacy. *Polska w czasie trzech rozbiorów, 1772–1799.* Poznań, 1874. 3 vols.

Kraushar, Aleksander. *Frank i frankiści polscy, 1726–1816: Monografia historyczna osnuta na źródłach archiwalnych i rękopiśmiennych.* Kraków, 1895. 2 vols.

————. *Frank ve-Adato.* Warsaw, 1895.

————. *Książę Repnin a Polska.* Warsaw, 1900. 2 vols.

————. "Nowe szczegóły o Frankistach w Offenbachu." In idem, *Obrazy i wizerunki historyczne.* Warsaw, 1906.

Krauss, Samuel. *Joachim Edler von Popper: Ein Zeit- und Lebensbild aus der Geschichte der Juden in Böhmen.* Vienna, 1928.

————. "Die Palästinasiedlung der polnischen Hasidim und die Wiener Kreise im Jahre 1700." In *Abhandlungen zur Erinnerung an Hirsch Perez Chajes.* Vienna, 1933.

————. "Schöndl Dobruschka." In *Festschrift Armand Kaminka zum 70. Geburtstag.* Vienna, 1937.

Krętosz, Józef. *Organizacja Archidiecezji Lwowskiej obrządku łacińskiego od XV wieku do 1772 roku.* Lublin, 1986.

Kriegseisen, Wojciech. *Ewangelicy polscy i litewscy w epoce saskiej (1696–1763)*. Warsaw, 1996.

Kroupa, Jiří. *Alchymie štěstí: Pozdní osvícenství a moravská společnost*. Kroměříž, 1987.

———. "Die Mährische Gesellschaft und die Französische Revolution." In Helmut Reinalter (ed.), *Aufklärung, Vormärz, Revolution: Jahrbuch der Internationalen Forschungsstelle Demokratische Bewegungen in Mitteleuropa von 1770–1850*. Frankfurt am Main, 1996/97.

Krzyżanowski, Adryan. *Dawna Polska*. Warsaw, 1857.

Kwasnik-Rabinowicz, Oskar. "Wolf Eibeschütz." *Zeitschrift für die Geschichte der Juden in der Tschechoslovakei* 1 (1930).

Lasker, Daniel. *Jewish Philosophical Polemics against Christianity in the Middle Ages*. New York, 1977.

——— (ed.). *The Refutation of the Christian Principles by Hasdai Crescas*. Albany, N.Y., 1992.

Leiman, Sid. "Rabbi Jonathan Eibeschütz's Attitude toward the Frankists." *Polin* 15 (2002).

———. "When a Rabbi Is Accused of Heresy: R. Ezekiel Landau's Attitude toward R. Jonathan Eibeschütz in the Emden-Eibeschütz Controversy." In Nahum M. Sarna (ed.), *From Ancient Israel to Modern Judaism: Essays in Honor of Marvin Fox*. Atlanta, 1989. 3 vols.

———. "When a Rabbi Is Accused of Heresy: The Stance of Rabbi Jacob Joshua Falk in the Emden-Eibeschütz Controversy." In Daniel Frank and Matt Goldish, *Rabbinic Culture and Its Critics*. Detroit, 2008.

Lenowitz, Harris. "The Charlatan at the Gottes Haus in Offenbach." In R. H. Popkin et al. (eds.), *Millenarianism and Messianism in Early Modern European Culture: Jewish Messianism in Early Modern World*. Amsterdam, 2001.

———. "Fifty Sayings of the Lord Jacob Frank." *Alcheringa, Ethnopoetics* 2 (1977).

———. "An Introduction to the Sayings of Jacob Frank." In *Proceedings of the Eighth World Congress of Jewish Studies*. Jerusalem, 1982.

———. *The Jewish Messiahs: From the Galilee to Crown Heights*. New York, 1998.

———. "The Struggle over Images in the Propaganda of the Frankist Movement." *Polin: Studies in Polish Jewry* 15 (2002).

———. "The Threefold Tales of Jacob Frank." *Proceedings of the Ninth World Congress of Jewish Studies*. Jerusalem, 1986.

Lewin, Isaac. "Ein Bannfluch." In *Festschrift zum 70. Geburtstage D. Hoffmans*. Berlin, 1914.

Lewin, Izak. *Klątwa żydowska na Litwie w XVI i XVII wieku*. Lwów, 1932.

Lewinsky, A. "Zur Geschichte der Juden in Polen und Russland während des 18. Jahrhunderts." *Hakedem* 1–2 (1907).

Lieben, S. H. "Rabbi Eleasar Fleckeles." *Jahrbuch der Jüdisch-Literarischen Gesellschaft* 10 (1912).

Liebes, Yehuda. "Hibbur bi-lashon ha-Zohar le-Rabbi Wolf ben Rabbi Yehonatan Aybeshits al havurato ve-al sod ha-ge'ulah." In idem, *Sod ha'emunah ha-Shabbeta'it.* Jerusalem, 1995.

———. "Ketavim hadashim be-kabbalah Shabbeta'it mi-hugo shel R' Yehonatan Aybeshits." In idem, *Sod ha'emunah ha-Shabbeta'it.* Jerusalem, 1995.

———. "Perakim be-milon Sefer ha-Zohar." Ph.D. diss., Hebrew University of Jerusalem, 1976.

———. "Shabbeta'ut ve-gevulot ha-dat." In Rachel Elior (ed.), *Ha-halom ve-shivro: Hatenu'ah ha-Shabbta'it u-sheluhoteha: meshihiyut, Shabbeta'ut u-Frankizm,* vol. 1. Jerusalem, 2000.

———. *Sod ha-emunah ha-Shabbeta'it.* Jerusalem, 1995.

———. *Studies in Jewish Myth and Jewish Messianism.* New York, 1993.

———. *Studies in the Zohar.* New York, 1993.

———. "Tren urzilin de-Ayalta: Drashato ha-sodit shel ha-AR"I lifne mitato." *Jerusalem Studies in Jewish Thought* (1992).

Loeb, Israel. "Un mémoir de Laurent Ganganelli sur la Calomnie du Meurtre Rituel." *Revue des Etudes Juives* 18 (1889).

Löw, Leopold. "Zur Geschichte der ungarischen Sabbathäer." In *Gesammelte Schriften.* Szegedein, 1890. 3 vols.

Loret, Maciej. *Polacy w Rzymie w 18 wieku.* Rome, 1930.

Łubieńska, Cecylia. *Sprawa dysydencka, 1764–1766.* Warsaw, 1911.

Luccichenti, Furio. "Casanova e gli ebrei." *L'Intermédiare des Casanovistes* 18 (2001).

——— (ed.). *Vita di Giacomo Casanova dopo le sue memorie, 1774–1798.* Rome, 1997.

Maccoby, Hyam. *Judaism on Trial: Jewish-Christian Disputations in the Middle Ages.* London, 1981.

Macfarlane, Alan. *Witchcraft in Tudor and Stuart England.* London, 1970.

Maciejewski, Janusz. (ed.). *Literatura konfederacji barskiej.* Warsaw, 2008.

Maciejko, Paweł. "Baruch me-Erets Yavan and the Frankists: Intercession in the Age of Upheaval." *Yearbook of the Simon Dubnow Institute for Jewish History* 4 (2005).

———. "Christian Accusations of Jewish Human Sacrifice in Early Modern Poland: The Case of Jan Serafinowicz." *Gal-Ed* 22. (2010).

———. "Christian Elements in the Frankist Doctrine." *Gal-Ed* 20 (2005).

———. "A Jewish-Christian Sect with a Sabbatian Background Revisited." *Kabbalah* 14 (2006).

———. "The Jews' Entry into the Public Sphere: The Emden-Eibeschütz Controversy Reconsidered." *Yearbook of the Simon Dubnow Institute for Jewish History* 6 (2007).

———. "The Literary Character and Doctrine of Jacob Frank's *The Words of the Lord*," *Kabbalah* 9 (2003).

Mahler, Raphael. "Statistik fun Yidn in der Lubliner Voyevodstve." *Yunger Historiker / Młody Historyk* 2 (1929).

———. *Yidn in amolikn Poyln in likht fun tsifern.* Warsaw, 1958. 2 vols.

Mandel, Arthur. "He'arot-shulayim al aharit toledotehah shel ha-tenu'ah ha-Frankistit." *Zion* 43, nos. 1–2 (1978).

———. *The Militant Messiah or the Flight from the Ghetto*. New York, 1979.

Mann, Jacob. *Texts and Studies in Jewish History and Literature*. Cincinnati, 1931. 2 vols.

Mannheim, Karl. *Ideology and Utopia: An Introduction to the Sociology of Knowledge*. London, 1952.

Manuel, Frank E. *The Broken Staff: Judaism through Christian Eyes*. Cambridge, 1992.

Maurer, Jadwiga. "Celina Szymanowska as a Frankist." *Polish Review* 34 (1989).

———. *"Z Matki Obcej . . .": Szkice o powiązaniach Mickiewicza ze światem Żydów*. London, 1990.

McCagg, William O. *A History of Habsburg Jews, 1670–1918*. Bloomington, Ind., 1989.

McIntosh, Christopher. *The Rose Cross and the Age of Reason: Eighteenth-Century Rosicrucianism in Central Europe and Its Relationship to Enlightenment*. Leiden, 1992.

Mieses, Mateusz. *Polacy - chrześcijanie pochodzenia żydowskiego*. Warsaw, 1938.

Michalski, Jerzy. *Schyłek Konfederacji Barskiej*. Wrocław, 1970.

Molkho, Yitshak, and Rivka Shatz-Uffenheimer. "Perush lekh lekha." *Sefunot* 3–4 (1960).

Mopsik, Charles. *La Cabale*. Paris, 1988.

Müller, Willibald. *Urkundliche Beiträge zur Geschichte der Mähr[ischen] Judenschaft im 17. und 18. Jahrhundert*. N.p., 1903.

Neubauer, Adolf. *Aus der Petersburger Bibliothek: Beiträge und Documente zur Geschichte Karäerthums*. Leipzig, 1866.

———. "Der Wahnwitz und die Schwindelein der Sabbatianer, nach ungedruckten Quellen." *MGJW* 36 (1887).

Nowicki, Andrzej. "Pięć fragmentów z dzieła 'De non existentia dei' Kazimierza Łyszczyńskiego (według rękopisu Biblioteki Kórnickiej no. 443)." *Euhemer* 1 (1957).

Oron, Michal. *Mi-Ba'al shem le-ba'al shed: Shemu'el Falk, ha-Ba'al Shem mi-London*. Jerusalem, 2002.

Osiecki, Józef. *Zofia Kossakowska*. Vienna, 1863.

Patai, Raphael. *The Jewish Alchemists: A History and Source Book*. Princeton, N.J., 1994.

———. *Sex and Family in the Bible and the Middle East*. New York, 1959.

Perlmuter, Moshe Aryeh. *Rabbi Yehonatan Aybeshits ve-yahaso el ha-Shabbeta'ut*. Jerusalem, 1947.

Po-Hsia, Ronnie. *The Myth of Ritual Murder: Jews and Magic in Reformation Germany*. New Haven, Conn., 1988.

Polišenský, Josef V. *Casanova a jeho svet*. Prague, 1997.

———. "Casanova v Čechach." *Sborník Národního Muzea v Praze*, series C, 4, no. 22 (1977).

Pollak, Michael. *Mandarins, Jews, and Missionaries: The Jewish Experience in the Chinese Empire*. Philadelphia, 1980.

Pomian, Krzysztof. *Collectionneurs, amateurs et curieux Paris, Venise: XVIe–XVIIIe siècle*. Paris, 1987.

Popkin, Richard H. "Christian Interests and Concerns about Sabbatai Zevi." In Matt

Goldish and Richard H. Popkin (eds.), *Jewish Messianism in the Early Modern World*. Dordrecht, 2001.

———. "The Lost Tribes, the Caraites and the English Millenarians." *Journal of Jewish Studies* 37, no. 2 (1986).

Pribram, A. F. *Urkunden und Akten zur Geschichte der Juden in Wien*. Vienna, 1918.

Rabinowicz, Oskar K. "Jacob Frank in Brno." *Jewish Quarterly Review*, seventy-fifth anniversary vol. (1967).

Rapoport-Albert, Ada. "Al ma'amad ha-nashim ba-Shabbeta'ut." In Rachel Elior (ed.), *Ha-halom ve-shivro. Ha-tenu'ah ha-Shabbta'it u-sheluhoteha: Meshihiyut, Shabbeta'ut u-Frankizm*, vol. 2. Jerusalem, 2000.

———, and Cesar Merchan Hamman. "'Something for the Female Sex': A Call for the Liberation of Women, and the Release of the Female Libido from the 'Shackles of Shame.' In an Anonymous Frankist Manuscript from Prague c. 1800." In Joseph Dan (ed.), *Gershom Scholem, 1897–1982, in Memoriam*. Jerusalem, 2007.

Reck, J. S. *Geschichte der gräfischen und fürstlichen Häuser Isenburg, Runkel, Wied, verbunden mit der Geschichte des Reinthals zwischen Koblenz und Andernach*. Weimar, 1825.

Reeves, Marjorie. *The Influence of Prophecy in the Later Middle Ages: A Study in Joachimism*. Notre Dame, Ind., 1993.

Reimers, Dagmar. "Die Grafschaft Ysenburg als Freistatt des Glaubens." In Irene Fürstin von Isenburg-Birstein et al. (eds.), *Isenburg-Ysenburg, 963–1963: Zur tausendjährigen Geschichte des Geschlechtes*. Hanau, 1964.

Roberts, J. M. *The Mythology of the Secret Societies*. New York, 1972.

Röder, Julius. "Judentaufen in Mähren Schlessen während der letzten Regierungsjahre Maria Thersias." *Sudetendeutsche Familienforschung* 8 (1935).

Roper, Lyndal. *Oedipus and the Devil: Witchcraft, Sexuality and Religion in Early Modern Europe*. London, 1994.

Rosenberg, Shalom. "Emunat hakhamim." In Isadore Twersky and Bernard Septimus (eds.), *Jewish Thought in the Seventeenth Century*. Cambridge, Mass., 1987.

Rosman, Moshe. "The Role of Non-Jewish Authorities in Resolving Conflicts within Jewish Communities in the Early Modern Period." *Jewish Political Studies Review* 12, nos. 3–4 (2000).

Rowlands, Alison. *Witchcraft Narratives in Germany: Rothenburg, 1561–1652*. Manchester, 2003.

Rudnicki, Kazimierz. *Biskup Kajetan Sołtyk*. Kraków, 1906.

Rudolph, Kurt. *Die Gnosis: Wesen und Geschichte einer spätantiken Religion*. Leipzig, 1977.

Ruether, Rosemary Radford. *Faith and Fratricide: The Christian Theological Roots of Anti-Semitism*. New York, 1974.

Ruzička, Leon. "Die österreichischen Dichter jüdischer Abstammung Moses Dobruschka = Franz Thomas von Schönfeld und David Dobruschka = Emanuel von Schönfeld." *Jüdische Familienforschung* 2 (1930).

Rymatzki, Christoph. *Hallischer Pietismus und Judenmission: Johann Heinrich Callenbergs Institutum Judaicum und dessen Freundkreis, 1728–1736*. Tübingen, 2004.

Saperstein, Marc (ed.). *Essential Papers on Messianic Movements and Personalities in Jewish History*. New York, 1992.

Schacter, J. J. "Rabbi Jacob Emden: Life and Major Works." Ph.D. diss., Harvard University, 1988.

Schipper, Ignacy. *Dzieje handlu żydowskiego na ziemiach polskich*. Warsaw, 1937.

Schnee, Heinrich. *Die Hoffinanz und der moderne Staat: Geschichte und System der Hoffaktoren an deutschen Fürstenhöfen im Zeitalter des Absolutismus. Nach archivalischen Quellen*. Berlin, 1953. 3 vols.

Scholem, Gershom. "The Beginnings of the Christian Kabbalah." In Joseph Dan (ed.), *The Christian Kabbalah: Jewish Mystical Books and Their Christian Interpreters*. Cambridge, Mass., 1997.

———. "Berukhiah: Rosh ha-Shabbeta'im be-Saloniki." In idem, *Mehkare Shabbeta'ut*. Tel Aviv, 1991.

———. "The Crypto-Jewish Sect of the Dönmeh." In idem, *The Messianic Idea in Judaism and Other Essays on Jewish Spirituality*. New York, 1995.

———. *Du frankisme au jacobinisme: La vie de Moses Dobruska alias Franz Thomas von Schonfeld alias Junius Frey*. Paris, 1981.

———. "A Frankist Document from Prague." In *Salo W. Baron Jubilee Volume*, vol. 2. Jerusalem, 1975.

———. "Ein Frankist: Moses Dobruschka und seine Metamorphosen." In Hugo Gold (ed.), *Max Brod: Ein Gedenkbuch*. Tel Aviv, 1969.

———. *Halomotav shel ha-Shabbatai R' Mordechai Ashkenazi: al devar pinkas ha-halomot shel R' Mordechai Ashkenazi talmido shel R' Avraham Rovigo*. Jerusalem, 1938.

———. "Iggeret Frankistit al toledot ha-emunah." In idem, *Mehkare Shabbeta'ut*. Tel Aviv, 1991.

———. "Julian von Brinkens Romanhafte Erzählung über die Frankisten." In Gerhard Nahon et al. (eds.), *Hommage a Georges Vajda: Etudes d'historie et de pensée juives*. Louvain, 1980.

———. *Kabbalah*. New York, 1978.

———. *Major Trends in Jewish Mysticism*. New York, 1961.

———. *Mehkare Shabbeta'ut*. Tel Aviv, 1991.

———. *Mehkarim u-mekorot le-toledot ha-Shabbeta'ut ve-gilgulehah*. Jerusalem, 1974.

———. *The Messianic Idea in Judaism and Other Essays on Jewish Spirituality*. New York, 1995.

———. "Die Metamorphose des häretischen Messianismus der Sabbatianer in religiösen Nihilismus im 18. Jahrhundert." In idem, *Judaica 3*. Frankfurt am Main, 1987.

———. "Le mouvement sabbataïste en Pologne." *Revue de l'histoire des religions* 43–44 (1953).

———. "Der Nihilismus als Religiöses Phänomen." In idem, *Judaica 4*. Frankfurt am Main, 1988.

———. "Perush mizmore tehillim mi-hugo shel Shabbata'i Tsevi mi-Adrianopol." In idem, *Mehkare Shabbeta'ut*. Tel Aviv, 1991.

————."Redemption through Sin." Trans. Hillel Halkin. In idem, *The Messianic Idea in Judaism and Other Essays on Jewish Spirituality.* New York, 1995.

————. *Sabbatai Sevi: The Mystical Messiah, 1626–1676.* Trans. R. J. Z. Werblowski. London, 1973.

————. "*Shekhinah*: The Feminine Element in Divinity." In idem, *On the Mystical Shape of the Godhead.* New York, 1991.

————. "Ha-tenu'ah ha-Shabbeta'it be-Polin." In idem, *Mehkarim u-mekorot le-toledot ha-Shabbeta'it ve-gilguleha.* Jerusalem, 1974.

————. "Ein verschollener jüdischer Mystiker der Aufklärungszeit: E. J. Hirschfeld." *Leo Baeck Institute Year Book* 6 (1962).

———— (ed.). *Be-ikvot mashi'ah.* Jerusalem, 1944.

Schreiner, Stefan. "'Der Messiah kommt zuerst nach Polen': Jakob Franks Idee von Polen als gelobtem Land und ihre Vorgeschichte." *Judaica* 4, no. 27 (2001).

Schuchard, Marsha Keith. "Yeats and the 'Unknown Superiors': Swedenborg, Falk, and Cagliostro." In Marie Mulvey Roberts and Hugh Ormsby-Lennon (eds.), *Secret Texts: The Literature of Secret Societies.* New York, 1995.

Schumacher, Nicolas. *Geschichte der katolischen Gemeinde in Offenbach am Main.* Offenbach, 1954.

Selingman, Cäsar. "Eine Wallfahrt nach Offenbach." *Frankfurter israelitisches Gemeindeblatt* (1932).

Semkowicz, Władysław. *Przewodnik po Zbiorze Rękopisów Wilanowskich.* Warsaw, 1961.

Shai, Eli. *Mashi'ah shel gilui arayot: Historia hadasha u-vilti metsunzeret shel ha-yesod ha-mini ba-mistika ha-meshihit ha-Yehudit.* Tel Aviv, 2002.

————. "Netiot antinomiot be-etika shel hayye ha-ishut be-kat ha-Donmeh." Ph.D. diss., Hebrew University of Jerusalem, 2003.

Shatzky, Jacob. "Alexander Kraushar and His Road to Total Assimilation." *YIVO Annual of Jewish Social Science* 7 (1952).

————. *Geshikhte fun jidn in Varshe.* New York, 1947. 3 vols.

Shatzmiller, Joseph. "Ha-kefirah ha-albigenzit be-eyne ha-Yehudim bne ha-zeman." In Menahem Ben-Sasson et al. (eds.), *Culture and Society in Medieval Jewry: Studies Dedicated to the Memory of Haim Hillel Ben-Sasson.* Jerusalem, 1989.

Shatz-Uffenheimer, Rivka. *Ha-ra'ayon ha-meshihi me-az girush Sefarad.* Jerusalem, 2005.

Shmeruk, Chone. "'Księga Słów Pana' Jakuba Franka: Nowe spojrzenie." *Teksty Drugie* 36 (1995).

Skimborowicz, Hipolit. *Żywot, skon i nauka Jakóba Józefa Franka ze spółczesnych i dawnych źródeł oraz z 2 rękopisów.* Warsaw, 1866.

Słowaczyński, Jędrzej. *Polska w kształcie dykcjonarza historyczno-statystyczno-jeograficznego.* Paris, 1833–38.

Stampfer, Shaul. "What Actually Happened to the Jews of Ukraine in 1648." *Jewish History* 17 (2003).

Stein, Leopold. "Mittheilung über die Frankistensekte." *Achawa Jahrbüch* (1868).

Steinschneider, Moritz. *Polemische und apologetische Literatur in arabischer Sprache: Zwischen Muslimen, Christen und Juden, nebst Anhängen verwandten Inhalts.* Leipzig, 1877.

Strack, Hermann L. *Das Blut im Glauben und Aberglauben der Menschheit: Mit besonderer Berücksichtigung der "Volksmedizin" und des "jüdischen Blutritus."* Munich, 1900.

Sulima, Zygmunt Lucyan [Walery Przyborowski]. *Historya Franka i frankistów.* Kraków, 1893.

Świderska, Hanna. "Three Polish Pamphlets on Pseudo-Messiah Sabbatai Tsevi." *British Library Journal* 2, no. 15 (1989).

Syga, Teofil, and Stanisław Szenic. *Maria Szymanowska i jej czasy.* Warsaw, 1960.

Szafraniec, Stanisław. "Opis przeniesienia obrazu Matki Boskiej Częstochowskiej z Jerozolimy na Jasną Górę." *Archiwa Biblioteki i Muzea Kościelne* 1, no. 2 (1959/60).

Szwarcówna, Zofia. *Katalog rękopisów Biblioteki Publicznej im. H. Łopacińskiego w Lublinie.* Vol. 4. Lublin, 1980.

Tazbir, Janusz. "Anti-Jewish Trials in Old Poland." In Adam Teller (ed.), *Studies in the History of the Jews in Old Poland in Honor of Jacob Goldberg.* Jerusalem, 1988.

Tchernowitz, Hayyim. *Toledot ha-poskim.* New York, 1947.

Teter, Magda. *Jews and Heretics in Catholic Poland: A Beleaguered Church in the Post-Reformation Era.* New York, 2006.

Tishby, Isaiah. *Netive emunah u-minut.* Jerusalem, 1982.

Tollet, Daniel. *Historie des Juifs en Pologne du XVIe siecle a nos jours.* Paris, 1992.

———. "La littérature antisémite polonaise de 1588 à 1668." *Revue française d'histoire du livre* 16 (1977).

Trautenberger, Gustav. *Chronik der Landeshauptstadt Brünn von der ältesten Zeit bis zum Jahre 1848.* Brünn, 1897. 4 vols.

Trevor-Roper, Hugh. *The European Witch-Craze of the Sixteenth and the Seventeenth Centuries.* London, 1990 [1969].

Turowski, Stanisław. "Polska rajem dla Żydów." *Kwartalnik poświęcony badaniu przeszłości Żydów w Polsce* 3 (1913).

Uhlíř, Dušan. "Brněnská židovská obec v 18. století a sekta Jakuba Franka." *Forum Brunense* (1993).

———. "Juden in Mähren und das Mährische Zentrum des Frankismus im ausgehenden 18. Jahrhundert." In Helmut Reinalter (ed.), *Aufklärung—Vormärz—Revolution: Jahrbuch der Internationalen Forschungsstelle Demokratische Bewegungen in Mitteleuropa von 1770–1850.* Frankfurt am Main, 1996–97.

Van den Berg, J. "Proto-Protestants? The Image of the Karaites as a Mirror of the Catholic-Protestant Controversy in the Seventeenth Century." In J. Van den Berg and Ernestine G. E. van der Wall (eds.), *Jewish Christian Relations in the Seventeenth Century.* Dordrecht, 1988.

Wahle, Julius. "Aus dem Goethe- und Schillerarchiv." *Jahrbuch der Goethe-Gesellschaft* 14 (1928).

Waliszewski, Kazimierz. *The Story of a Throne: Catherine II of Russia.* London, 1895.

Weber, Max. *The Theory of Social and Economic Organization.* Trans. A. R. Henderson and Talcott Parsons. London, 1947.

Węgrzynek, Hanna. *"Czarna legenda" Żydów: Procesy o rzekome mordy rytualne w dawnej Polsce*. Warsaw, 1995.

Weinryb, Bernard D. *The Jews of Poland: A Social and Economic History of the Jewish Community in Poland from 1100 to Recent Times*. Philadelphia, 1973.

Wellnow, E. "Der 'heilige Herr' zu Offenbach." *Offenbacher Zeitung*, 25 March 1896.

Werner, Klaus. "Ein neues 'Frankisten'-Dokument." *Frankfurter judaistische Beiträge* 18 (1988).

———. "Die Sekte der 'Frankisten.'" In *Zur Geschichte der Juden in Offenbach am Main*. Offenbach, 1990. 3 vols.

———. "Versuch einer Quantifizierung des Frankschen Gefolges in Offenbach am Main 1788–1818." *Frankfurter judaistische Beiträge* 16 (1986).

Werses, Shmuel, *Haskalah ve-Shabbeta'ut*. Jerusalem, 1988.

Wilhelm, Kurt. "An English Echo of the Frankist Movement." *Journal of Jewish Studies* 16 (1967).

Willi, Thomas. "Das Christentum im Lichte der Tora—Jakob Emdens Sendschreiben: Theologische und philologische Beobachtungen zu einem unbekannten hebräischen Dokument der Lessinzeit." In C. Bultmann et al. (eds.), *Vergegenwärtigung des Alten Testaments: Beiträge zur biblischen Hermeneutik*. Göttingen, 2002.

Wirszubski, Chaim. "Ha-mekkubbal ha-Shabbeta'i Moshe David mi-Podhayyts." In idem, *Ben ha-shittin*. Jerusalem, 1990.

———. *Pico della Mirandola's Encounter with Jewish Mysticism*. Cambridge, Mass., 1989.

Wölfle-Fischer, Susanne. *Junius Frey, 1753–1794: Jude, Aristokrat, Revolutionär*. Frankfurt am Main, 1997.

Wolf, Gerson. *Judentaufen in Österreich*. Vienna, 1863.

Wolf, Lucien (ed.). *Menasseh ben Israel Mission to Oliver Cromwell*. London, 1901.

Wolfson, Elliot R. *Circle in the Square: Studies in the Use of Gender in Kabbalistic Symbolism*. Albany, N.Y., 1995.

Wurm, Dawid. *Z dziejów żydowstwa brodzkiego za czasow danej Rzeczypospolitej*. Brody, 1935.

Wyporska, Wanda. "Male Witches in the Polish-Lithuanian Commonwealth." Ph.D. diss., Hertford College, University of Oxford, 2006.

Ya'ari, Abraham. "Le-toldot milhamtam shel hakhame Polin bi-tenu'at Frank." *Sinai* 35 (1954).

———. "Srefat ha-Talmud be-Kamnits Podolsk." *Sinai* 42 (1958).

———. *Toledot hag Simhat Torah*. Jerusalem, 1964.

Yerushalmi, Yosef Hayim. *From Spanish Court to Italian Ghetto*. Seattle, 1981.

Yuval, Israel. *Two Nations in Your Womb: Perceptions of Jews and Christians in Late Antiquity and the Middle Ages*. Trans. Barbara Harshav and Jonathan Chipman. Berkeley, Calif., 2006.

Žáček, Václav. "Zwei Beiträge zur Geschichte des Frankismus in den böhmischen Ländern." *Jahrbuch für Geschichte der Juden in der Tschechoslowakei* 9 (1938).

Zafran, Eric. "Saturn and the Jews." *Journal of the Warburg and Courtauld Institutes* 42 (1979).

Zajączkowski, Ananiasz. "Na marginesie studjum Bałabana 'Karaici w Polsce.'" *Myśl Kara-imska* 4–5 (1928).

———. "Przywileje nadane Karaimom przez Królów polskich." *Myśl Karaimska* 1 (1924).

Załęski, Stanisław. *Jezuici w Polsce.* Lwów, 1821.

Zarzycki, Wacław. *Książe Marcin Lubomirski 1738–1811.* Warsaw, 1998.

Zitron, Samuel Leib. *Meshumodim: Tipn un siluetn funm noentn over.* Warsaw, 1923.

Zweig, Stefan. *Casanova: A Study in Self-Portraiture.* London, 1998.

Index

Acknowledgments

I am immensely grateful for the help and advice of many people without whose assistance this book could never have been written. My adventure with Frankism began at Oxford; Professor R. J. W. Evans of the Modern History Faculty and Oriel College was extremely generous with his help and advice. During my brief tenure as a Whiting Fellow at the University of Chicago, I learned a lot from discussions with Paul Mendes-Flohr. Most of this book was written in Jerusalem; my friends and colleagues Israel Bartal, Maoz Kahana, Jonatan Meir, Elchanan Reiner, Michael Silber, and Israel Yuval offered many valuable comments. I would also like to extend my gratitude to Gershon Hundert, Adam Kaźmierczyk, Harris Lenowitz, and Ada Rapoport-Albert, whose suggestions regarding specific points or particular sections of *The Mixed Multitude* greatly helped me refine my argument. Special thanks are due to David Ruderman, whose help and support greatly contributed to the publication of this book.

Many institutions and other bodies have provided invaluable support. Hertford College, Oxford, sponsored my initial research in the U.K. I am most grateful to the Simon Dubnow Institute in Leipzig for extending me its hospitality during my visits to Germany. My home university, the Hebrew University of Jerusalem, has provided financial assistance for my trips to Poland, the Czech Republic, and the Vatican. My special gratitude goes to Scholion – Interdisciplinary Center for Jewish Studies at the Hebrew University and the Mandel Foundation, whose generosity allowed me to write this book in the most vivid and stimulating intellectual environment.

I would also like to thank the staff of the many libraries and archives in which I worked—in particular, the staff of the Bodleian Library and Taylor Institution Library, Oxford; the Jewish National and University Library, Jerusalem; the Vatican Secret Archives; and Tomasz Makowski from the National Library in Warsaw and Hans-Georg Ruppel from the Staatsarchiv Offenbach.

For the shortcomings, I alone am responsible.